As Peter Horrobin weaves the strands of th
has experienced over the years, a fascinatin
emerges. His own personal stories are told alongside the incredible
miracles he has witnessed in the birthing of a ministry that has touched
thousands of lives. God's sovereignty can be clearly seen in this journey of
faith and discovery. I encourage all who are called to serve in ministry of
any kind to read this book!

Peter Tsukahira

Co-founder, Carmel Congregation, Haifa (Israel)

Having just completed a run through Peter Horrobin's *Strands of Destiny*,
I am sitting here at my desk weeping. The stories of God's leading and
provision are extraordinary in themselves, but what moves me so deeply is
the fresh reminder of the extent of God's redemptive grace.

For many years, my own calling in pursuit of transforming revival
has sensitized me to the vital importance of hope. And this book exudes
hope from cover to cover. It is a stirring reminder that those who plant
themselves at the feet of Jesus in humility and desperation will arise to a
glorious future.

Take an hour or two to curl up with this book. It will change your life!

George Otis, Jr.

President, The Sentinel Group (USA)
Producer of the Transformations Video Series

Shortly after I became a Christian, I read a book entitled *A Man Called
Peter* that described the life and ministry of Peter Marshall – a Scottish
preacher who eventually became Chaplain to the U.S. Senate. This book
had a profound effect upon my life as a young Christian since it so
explained the faithfulness of God amidst impossible situations. *Strands
Of Destiny* describes the life of another man called Peter, that has
thrilled and inspired me to keep pressing on towards the goal that Paul
the Apostle refers to in Philippians 3:13-14. This book is a remarkable

combination of vision, obedience, and faith on the part of a man who responded to God's call in a manner that has yielded an incalculable harvest for the Kingdom of God.

This is the story of Peter Horrobin's obedience to a vision that continues to expand globally, bearing extraordinary fruit in spite of obstacles and challenges and disappointments that could easily cause most people simply to give up. Peter's transparency, honesty, and integrity mixed with tenacity and perseverance, are a testimony to the manner in which the Kingdom of God is advanced through ordinary people who choose to believe in the God of the extraordinary, Who makes possible what is impossible with men. (Luke 18:27).

I strongly recommend *Strands of Destiny* as a book that will thoroughly inspire and equip you for these challenging days in the 21st Century. Anyone who is serious about their life in Christ needs to read through these pages carefully and prayerfully since, as you do so, you will meet with the Lord who is able to do immeasurably more than all we can ask or imagine, according to His power that is at work within us. (Ephesians 3:20)

Rev. Dr. Alistair P. Petrie

Executive Director, Partnership Ministries (Canada)

It is a privilege for me to recommend *Strands of Eternity*. Peter has made himself vulnerable in sharing the amazing way that the Lord has worked through his life, so that the younger generations may understand that in all things God is working out His best for us and, as in Peter's case, used him to bring untold numbers to a place of freedom and new life in the Lord. One of the wonderful things of reaching the later decades of life is to be able to look back and marvel at the amazing way God works through all the situations in our lives to form us – not only in the things we would call "good", but in ALL things, including in the most painful and difficult, or even when we think we are only "marking time" as Peter calls it. In fact, some of these experiences prove to be "critical life-directional moments".

I am most grateful that he has taken the time to write *Strands of Destiny* and highly recommend it.

Ruth Ruibal
Julio C. Ruibal Ministries (Colombia)

"Strands of Destiny" tells the wonderful and extraordinary story of the development of Ellel Ministries. Those of us in Australia who were privileged to be present on the night when Lynda was healed, as told in Chapter 20, have never been the same. Many of us involved in health care had our eyes opened to the depths of ministry God desires to do in so many of the people that we see. For this and much else we are extremely thankful to Peter Horrobin and the Ellel team and for the subsequent development of Ellel Ministries in our and many other nations. *"Strands of Destiny"* is a truly inspiring story of God's faithfulness and wondrous ways, as He weaves His Kingdom purposes into being in the lives of His servants. I commend this book to all.

Ken and Roslyn Curry
Directors, Health Care in Christ (Australia)

What I so value about Peter Horrobin and Ellel Ministries is what he so deftly captures in his personal story: the pursuit of God and His miraculous work, in a way that is integral to the Scriptures. *Strands of Destiny* is not just Peter's spiritual journey – and the story of the flowering of Ellel worldwide – but a roadmap for anyone who wants all that God has in the purest way possible. This book is a spiritual plumb-line, not just a memoir – and will envision all who read it that they, too, can rise to their full destiny in God and their full privileges as His children.

Steven Fry
Founder and President, the Messenger Fellowship (USA)

So many Christians find the resurrection power of Christ----yet, like Lazarus, remain bound in the grave clothes of their past. They need someone to say: "Unbind him and let him go." I'm so grateful for my friend, Peter Horrobin, who felt called by God many years ago to offer freedom and deliverance to Christians. His passion led him to form a vital work that has trained thousands of believers in all aspects of the healing ministry.

As I travel around the world, I see the huge need for the work of Ellel Ministries. Peter has challenged me to learn how to set captives free: from abuse, trauma, addiction, fear and shame. His spiritual journey will not only inspire you; it will equip you to be a vessel of Christ's healing.

J. Lee Grady

*Former editor, **Charisma** magazine*

Director, The Mordecai Project (USA)

I have read many stirring accounts of people of faith proclaiming the gospel across the world. For me, this account of God's amazing work through Ellel Ministries stands alongside the most thrilling I have read. It is contemporary. It is full of faith, lessons learnt, fierce demonic opposition, brokenness, discipleship, team building, healings, deliverance and miraculous financial provision. Beginning in 1986, God has not only restored thousands of broken lives through the ministry, but He has established healing and training centres in a rapidly increasing number of countries across the world. What God has done in 30 years is utterly astonishing. I have just loved reading this book. Praise God that in our time the wonder of Christ's full salvation is being restored through His Church.

Bishop Graham Dow

Formerly Bishop of Carlisle (UK)

STRANDS
of
DESTINY

"Strands of Destiny
are woven together by Him
to create a rope of opportunity
and a tapestry of grace."

(from Chapter 24)

STRANDS
of
DESTINY

Peter Horrobin

Founder and International Director
of Ellel Ministries

Sovereign World

Published by
Sovereign World Ltd

PO Box 784
Ellel
Lancaster
LA1 9DA
United Kingdom

www.sovereignworld.com

Twitter: @sovereignworld
Facebook: www.facebook.com/sovereignworld

Published November 2017
Copyright © 2017 Peter Horrobin

ISBN 978-1-852408-35-0

British Library Cataloguing-in-Publication Data
A catalogue record for this book is available from the British Library.

Front cover image by Paul Stanier (PfCO, CAA drone licensed)

DEDICATION

In thanksgiving to all those
whose lives have touched mine
and through whom I have
learned so much.

To my parents especially,
and all those down the years of my family
history who have walked in the ways of God
and inspired the succeeding generations.

To every single member of the Ellel Teams
with whom it has been my privilege to walk
since the work of Ellel Ministries
was founded in 1986.
This story is their story also.

Thanks be to God.

To him
who is able to keep you from stumbling
and to present you before his glorious presence
without fault and with great joy.
To the only God our Saviour
be glory, majesty, power and authority,
through Jesus Christ our Lord, before all ages,
now and forevermore! Amen.
(Jude 24, 25)

CONTENTS

FOREWORD
BY JIM GRAHAM

This is the story of a man who was willing to risk everything for the Kingdom of God and the triumphant, liberating cause of Jesus Christ. The man – Peter Horrobin – was gripped by a vision and founded a ministry focused on freedom and hope; with trust in a God who is magnificently alive in the midst of His Creation.

In these pages, Peter becomes very vulnerable as he discovers it would be easier to serve God without a vision and easier to work for God without a call – for then you are not bothered by what God requires! Walking that road would have ensured that common sense, logic, and acceptability became his road map for life. But having met and heard God in a garage, been inspired by the example and challenges of his ancestors, been divinely led through the pages of Scripture and the unmistakable promptings of the Holy Spirit, he was never able to walk that road – especially when confronted by the needs of a broken and bleeding world.

The vision of God's purposes for him, and the harnessing of his life to that vision, meant that forever he was pursued by the mercy and the majesty of God. In all of this his perception of the significance of ordinary events, his sense of destiny in his own life and in the lives of others, and of the part friendships and relationships play, make it a compelling and challenging read. As I have read of Peter's journey I was reminded of a poem I read years ago, attributed to Corrie ten Boom:

My life is but a weaving between my God and me,
I do not choose the colour, He worketh steadily.
Oft-times He weaveth sorrow, and I in foolish pride,
Forget He sees the upper, and I the underside.
Not till the loom is silent, and the shuttles cease to fly
Will God unroll the canvas and explain the reason why
The dark threads are as needful in the skilful Weaver's hand
As the threads of gold and silver in the pattern He has planned.

The ministry – Ellel Ministries – is based on the warmth of the welcoming heart of Jesus. It is unquestionably Bible-based and rigorously demands theological integrity. No circumstance is too complicated; no shame too humiliating; no darkness too impenetrable; no wound too deep; no prison too dark; no failure too severe; no habit too enslaving; no life too messed up to deny the open arms of Jesus, expressed in love through the lives of ordinary men and women.

This could sound like feckless sentimentality, but in that climate of acceptance, the Good News of the Kingdom of God is clearly taught and communicated so that the lost will be found; the broken will be mended; the sick will be healed; the captive will be set free; the believers will be equipped; the poor will be cared for; the disadvantaged will be restored; the voiceless will be heard; the lonely will be enfolded in community; and God will get the credit for it.

It is a ministry for wholeness, not only taught but practiced in the power of the Holy Spirit, according to biblical principles. It is a ministry to proclaim and practice 'shalom' in its original meaning! The fact that, to date, over 30 Centres have already been established throughout the world is an eloquent testimony to the nature, the need, and the relevance of this ministry.

God – clearly understood as the God and Father of our Lord Jesus Christ as revealed in the Scriptures of the Old and New Testaments – is realistically here. '*Strands of Destiny*' begs the questions; "Have we lowered the revelation of Scripture to the level of our experience?" "Is it possible to have a correct theology of God without fully understanding who He really is and what He really wants to do in the complicated and compelling circumstances of life?" "Does God always come to us with the offer of a future and a hope?" "Are there depths of His grace that we have not yet fully explored?".

Here, surely, is a God who pierces our darkness with His light; challenges our despair with His hope; transforms our weakness with His strength; confronts our tragedies with His triumph; cleanses our shame with His holiness; confronts our failure with His forgiveness; touches our sickness with His healing; replaces our error with His truth; removes our confusion with His stability; releases our captivity with His freedom; invades our humanity with His divinity; and envelopes our history in His eternity.

Of course, these pages are about a man and a ministry, but overshadowing every page is the reality of a God whose knowledge, presence, and power know no bounds. You could meet Him here and discover a future and a hope. The last sentence of '*Strands of Destiny*' is:

"To God be all the glory, great things He has done – this is His story – not mine!"

Rev. Jim Graham,
Pastor Emeritus,
Gold Hill Baptist Church,
Buckinghamshire.

Note: This Foreword was written by Jim Graham before he knew the medical diagnosis of the condition from which he subsequently died on the 5th July 2016.

AUTHOR'S PREFACE

"Let this be written for a future generation, that a people not yet created may praise the Lord" (Psalms 102:18)

This is a story of God's overriding grace and faithfulness in the midst of human weakness and fallibility. It is not an autobiography in the traditional sense of the word – far too much has been omitted from the story for it to be called as such. But it is unashamedly autobiographical in that it draws heavily on my own personal life experiences.

My life, like a football match, has been a life of two halves. Firstly the years of upbringing, academic and business life, which preceded the purchase of Ellel Grange in 1986. And, secondly, the 30–year adventure of faith which embraces the subsequent story of Ellel Ministries. The objective of the book, however, is not just to tell either my own story or the story of Ellel Ministries, although key elements of these are inevitably central to the narrative, but to use those personal experiences to illustrate the ways of God in leading men and women in the fulfilment of His purposes for their lives.

It was particularly exciting for me, as the contents of the book unfolded, to see how the experiences of my early life were critical training for the work God had called me to do. And that, without the extraordinary blessing of godly parents, and a generational history that was rich in what I call strands of destiny, none of what I have been privileged to experience could ever have happened! To see and record the hand of God at work down the generation lines has been a very humbling experience.

The effect on me, personally, of writing this book has been much the same as the effect on the Anglican clergyman, who had the embarrassing experience of being converted through listening to his own preaching! By this I mean that I have been very deeply convicted by the extreme graciousness of God and been filled with thanksgiving to Him for His hand on my life. And I have been challenged afresh not to look on the present season of my life as an opportunity for self-indulgence in years of retirement, but as a season in which to strategically press on towards the goal, with all the energy and determination that God and circumstances allow.

While the chapters containing the essence of the Ellel story, naturally focus on my own experiences and perspective, there are several thousand people world-wide who have contributed sacrificially to the work across the years. Without these, none of what I have described in this book could ever have happened – and I am deeply grateful to every single one of them who has shared in the journey. Their loyalty and commitment to the vision have been a continuing inspiration to keep on pressing on, especially when the going has been tough. It hasn't, however, been the tough who have kept going in such circumstances, but the faithful who, with the daily inspiration of God's Holy Spirit, have persevered!

I wish to make it very clear, therefore, that this story is ultimately God's story, describing God's work that has been carried out by God's people for His purposes. What God has done is truly beyond my wildest dreams (as the chapter on Asia and China has been called). It is not written as a record of what I have done, but a record of what God has done, in spite of severe weaknesses in the vessel He chose for the task.

At stages in the story the names of certain individuals are mentioned, when they were key to the developing theme of the book. But there are hundreds of other people whose names could have been mentioned and I would not want anyone whose name doesn't appear to feel they have been overlooked. Or, anyone whose name has been mentioned, to feel they have been given preferential treatment! All are important and all matter.

In due course, fuller accounts of the stories behind the different sections of Ellel Ministries will provide the opportunity to correct any apparent imbalance. Great effort has been made to check out all the details of the stories referred to, but if any errors have crept into the text unawares, I am sorry. I take full responsibility for anything that has been said wrongly and ask anyone who thinks they have reason to be offended to accept my heartfelt apology and forgive me.

I am deeply grateful also to Jim Graham for writing the Foreword to the book shortly before he died in July 2016 – but I am indebted to Jim for much more than his precious words. Not only was he a much-loved and faithful Pastor of Gold Hill Baptist Church for twenty-seven years, but for the next twenty years his wider national and international ministry impacted and blessed many different places and organisations, especially the work of Ellel Ministries.

Jim was one of my closest friends and mentors for twenty-five years. His input into my life was a constant thread of encouragement, support, correction and direction for which I will be eternally grateful. While Jim was a regular visiting teacher to many of our Centres, he was much more than a visitor. As a companion on the journey of faith, there was nothing that I could not share with him. He knew the inside track on both my own life and every major aspect of the work and was well-placed, therefore, to write the Foreword. I will be ever thankful to the Lord for the impact of his life and ministry.

Throughout the writing of the book I have been deeply grateful to the small team of people who have read each chapter for me and given me their feedback. Their comments have been a huge help in shaping the text and building the story – thank you. As has Paul Stanier of Zaccmedia, whose professional skill in converting the manuscript and all the photos into a good-looking book was very much appreciated.

Finally, and most importantly, I would like to put on record my grateful thanks to my wife, Fiona, without whom this book could never have been written and many of the events recorded in the latter part of the story could not have happened. God called us together for a purpose and as the years have gone by, that purpose has become more and more evident. Also, her input to the writing, and her memory for some of the details, have added colour to some of the pages that my more pragmatic masculine sense might have overlooked!

Fiona's constant support, inspiration, prayers and love have provided that supernatural thread of encouragement throughout our marriage which has enabled so much of what God has done through Ellel Ministries to have been fulfilled. Words are an inadequate means of conveying my thanks and appreciation for everything she means to me, and has come to mean to so many other people also, who have been blessed through her life and ministry. Some of the stories of how God brought healing to very hurting and broken people, which make the pages live with the reality of what God has done, would never have happened, were it not for her loving perseverance in faith, sometimes against all odds, until victory came.

Ultimately, of course, all thanks and praise go to the Lord for what He has done. It is my prayer that as you read the pages you, too, will be freshly impacted by the love, mercy and grace of God.

PROLOGUE

From Restoring a Broken Car
to Healing Broken Lives

Thursday 18th June, 1970

It was the day of the General Election in the United Kingdom. The pre-election polls had been moving backwards and forwards, showing typical swings of voting intentions. It was going to be a very close and exciting contest. The following day, the leader of the party with an overall majority in the House of Commons, would be invited by the Queen to form the next government and become the Prime Minister.

I always enjoyed listening to the election results coming through on the radio or television, and so I decided that this would be the day (and the night!) when I would start the work of rebuilding the remains of my 1933 *Alvis Speed 20,* completely strip the chassis of all its components and begin the process of restoring the car. I was looking forward to working through the night and listening to the election excitement on the radio as the results came in.

While an *Alvis Speed 20* had become the car of my dreams, the vehicle I am talking about could hardly have been described as a

1

car – it was a total wreck! It had first been stolen, and then crashed, before being vandalised and set on fire. Finally, the remains of the vehicle had been pushed into the River Mersey in an attempt to destroy the evidence! News of the car's fate had reached my friend Harold Lord who, not wanting to see a classic Alvis car disappear from history in the mud of the Mersey, spent £50 on rescuing the remains from the river.

The *Alvis Speed 20* was one of the greatest British sports cars of the early nineteen thirties. I'd read all the books and there was little I didn't know about these amazing machines, and the company that made them. I was passionate about having one. But even in 1970, a good Speed 20, especially an open touring version would have cost me much more than I could ever afford. I had accepted as fact that the idea of owning and running one would have to remain one of life's unfulfilled ambitions!

Until, that is, Harold gave me a call and asked if I was still interested in having a *Speed 20*. He didn't wait for my answer before offering me a 1933 *Speed 20* tourer, with bodywork built by Cross and Ellis, my favourite version of the car, for the absolute bargain basement price of just £50! I could afford that and, unhesitatingly, said YES! This was the chance of a lifetime and I wasn't going to miss it. I agreed the deal even before he told me what was wrong with it!

In spite of its condition, I grabbed the opportunity with both hands and was soon the proud owner of a total wreck! On sight of the vehicle, any normal person would have given it a decent burial and got on with his life! But this was a *Speed 20* . . . the car of my dreams! This was my opportunity, probably my only opportunity ever, to fulfil a long-held dream. The extent of the damage held no fears for me – the massive obstacles I would face when starting the restoration job, were simply hurdles to be jumped, one fence at a time. Nothing could be allowed to stand in the way of the dream of completely rebuilding the car and restoring it to its former glory. I was twenty-six years old, and with the vision and energy of youth, I overcame every rational objection to taking on such a massive project.

And so it was that I chose June 18th 1970 to start the restoration work. Every single part of the car had to be dismantled and removed from the chassis, the simple steel framework on which the whole car was built, and carefully stored away. Little by little I removed all the parts that were still attached to the chassis and put them on one side. The election polls closed at 9.00pm and it would be several hours before the first results would start coming through. The radio provided non-stop comment on the progress of the election and as the hours slipped by I was totally engrossed in getting to know all the parts of my *Alvis Speed 20*. When the real results finally started to come through, it was becoming clear that the Conservatives, with Ted Heath as their leader, might just take the lead and unseat the governing Labour Party.

Politically it was proving to be a fascinating night and nothing could have persuaded me to go to bed and wait till the morning to get the results. Besides, working on the car was so utterly fascinating and exciting, that I was really glad of the excuse to keep on working through the night, stripping the car down to the bare chassis.

It was four o'clock in the morning when the chassis was finally stripped bare. I was covered in dirt and grease from head to foot, but that didn't stop me using my imagination to envision what the car would be like when every single part had been lovingly restored and the whole car rebuilt. Already, in my mind, I was driving this beautiful machine, hearing the roar of the six cylinder engine and feeling the wind blowing through my hair as, with the hood down, the car ate up the miles that lay before it on the open road!

For a moment I thrilled to the exhilaration of the vision that would surely be fulfilled. But then I noticed something I hadn't seen before and, suddenly, the bottom fell out of my dreams as I stared hard at a particular part of the frame that was lying before me. The chassis was bent! The crash had done more than superficial damage to the car. One of the 15ft long steel chassis members had clearly taken an enormous hit and been bent out of shape by the impact. A car with a bent chassis is an un-driveable liability. It's impossible to steer such a car properly and when you put your foot on the brakes, it won't stop in a straight line. To put it simply – the car would be too dangerous to drive. It was a write-off.

Tears began to flow down my grease covered cheeks! The dream was over. The election results, that were still blaring out over the radio had become an irrelevancy. I was totally consumed by the pain of the bent chassis and the massive disappointment of thinking it would now be impossible to restore my *Alvis Speed 20* and to drive my dream! I was heart-broken.

And then it happened! Suddenly, I became very conscious of God speaking to me through my emotion and pain as I stared mindlessly at the broken car lying before me. It was an experience unlike anything I had ever known before. The car, the election and, indeed, everything else melted into insignificance. It was as if God was standing alongside me looking down the length of the bent chassis of my beloved *Speed 20*. And He was speaking to me.

I will never know whether or not what I heard could have been heard by anyone else, had they been with me in the garage – I doubt it. But what God said through that broken car was loud and clear to me, was spoken deep into my spirit and became indelibly printed on my mind. It was a moment I would never forget.

"You could restore this broken car, but I can restore broken lives." And then God asked me a very simple question, *"Which is more important – a broken car or a broken life?"* The correct answer to the question was obvious, but in my humanity I would love to have said, the broken car! But I knew that God wasn't just

speaking to me about the car, he was speaking to me about the rest of my life. This was my destiny moment when the seventeen-year cry of my heart to know what God wanted me to do with my life was being answered.

As I looked at the remains of the broken car, I realised that the world is full of hurting and broken people, and the embryonic vision for what would become my life's work was birthed in my spirit.

The election results were still coming through on the radio in the garage, but my world had just changed shape. Fascinating though the results of the 1970 election were, they were now of minimal importance. My personal encounter with God in the garage became the focus of my attention and I tried to come to terms with what had just happened. The experience was now hidden in my heart. I turned the lights and radio off, got myself as clean as it was sensible to do at that time of night, and dropped into bed like a stone in a pond.

I can never forget what God did in my heart at four o'clock in the early morning of the 19th June 1970! At the time I had no idea what the experience would eventually mean, but I knew that my life's work had now begun. It was the beginning of a lifelong pilgrimage, which sixteen years later would take me first to Ellel Grange and then to every continent in the world through Ellel Ministries.

Thanks to the Alvis Company, who were able to supply me with a blueprint of what the car's chassis should have been like, I was able to get the chassis of the Speed 20 straightened by Rubery Owen Engineering. They put it back together exactly as the maker originally intended. And that in itself provided me with a wonderful vision of what God meant when He spoke about the restoration of broken lives – people need to be restored according to the original intentions of God their maker!

And what now of the car? Over forty-five years later it is still a work in progress! All the mechanics of the vehicle are now in good order, but the work of restoring the car's bodywork is still awaiting completion. Meanwhile, the real work of restoring broken lives continues unabated through Ellel Ministries Centres all over the world!

Chapter 1

ORIGINS

From Lancashire Lad
to the Dreaming Spires

I don't remember the actual day or the date in 1952, but I know for certain what happened in that year when I knelt at my bedside with my father and invited Jesus into my heart to be my Saviour and the Lord of my life. An eternal transaction took place which changed two things – first, my eternal destination was now Heaven and secondly, even though I was still of a tender age, deep inside I knew that God had a work for me to do. I didn't know the word 'destiny' at the time, but what I experienced was an awareness that God had a destiny for me. I know, now, how important it was for me to have made a commitment to Jesus as a child. My own life experience has taught me never to undervalue the power of the Holy Spirit to transform the life of a child and, in so doing, to transform the future life of a man or a woman.

My own Dad gave his life to the Lord through a children's mission in 1920, led by the CSSM *(Children's Special Service Mission)* Children's Evangelist, Hudson Pope. He was ten years old. I still have the letter he wrote to Hudson Pope saying that he would like to

7

become a Christian – and Hudson Pope's reply. Dad never went back on his childhood commitment to the Lord and all his life thanked God for what Hudson Pope did for him. Throughout his days he sought to put God first in everything he and the family did. Family prayer was normal and an ever-present awareness of God's love and His care for His children became the spiritual air we breathed. I knew that, as believers, we were loved by a God who speaks to us when we listen, and wants to lead and direct His people. This deeply impacted every area of my life.

In 1937 the young lady who was to become my mother was visiting London from South Africa, for the Coronation of King Edward the Eighth. But Edward abdicated, so he could marry the divorcee Mrs Simpson, and on Coronation Day, 12th May 1937, it was his younger brother who was crowned King George the Sixth instead. My Mum and her sister were in a special stand at the gates of Buckingham Palace watching all the processions go by, as the visiting royals and Prime Ministers paraded past on their way to and from Westminster Abbey for the Coronation service. They were there as special guests.

Mum's Dad, my Oupa (Grandpa in Afrikaans), went to South Africa in 1900 to fight for Britain in the Boer War. He loved South Africa so much that after the war was over he stayed there and became a founder member of the Union of South Africa police corps and worked with General Smuts in building the new country. He married Elizabeth de Villiers, a Huguenot descendant, whose ancestor Jacob de Villiers had fled the terrible persecutions in France, when hundreds of thousands were massacred for their faith as Bible believing Protestants. Mum had a solid Christian ancestry going right back to 1689 when the three de Villiers brothers, Abraham, Jacob and Pierre sailed for South Africa from Holland on the good ship *Zion*. Ouma was truly of pioneering stock, her own mother having been born on an ox cart on one of the great treks from Cape Town to the Transvaal.

Mum was born in 1913, the year before Oupa volunteered again for the army, serving throughout the first world war. One of Mum's earliest memories was being carried, aged five, on the shoulders of her father through the streets of Dundee (Natal) in a victory parade, on the day the war was declared to be over. Her mother pleaded with Oupa not to take her because of the huge crowds. But his argument won the day – *"she'll never get another chance to see anything like this."* Little did he know that just twenty-one years later he would again be in uniform for the Second World War, becoming one of the very, very few serving soldiers with medals from the Boer War, the First and the Second World Wars.

There was one other episode from Mum's childhood that merits mention in my story, for it had a significant bearing on an event that was to be highly strategic in my life over fifty years later. While Mum was playing in the garden of their home in the early nineteen-twenties, she watched a puff-adder slither beneath the floor of their house. Mum ran in to tell Oupa what she had seen. The bite of a puff-adder is lethally dangerous, so Oupa and the house-boy set about finding and killing the snake. The house boy had to slither beneath the floor boards and a little while later he came out holding up the dead snake in one hand and dragging a sack in the other.

On examination, the sack was found to be absolutely full of used postage stamps torn from envelopes. All the stamps were from the very earliest days of the postal services in the provinces of Cape of Good Hope, Orange Free State and Natal, long before the Union of South Africa was established in 1910. Oupa borrowed a stamp catalogue and it wasn't very long before they realised that many of the stamps were of significant value, including examples of some of the well-known errors. Because they now knew the stamps to be valuable, Oupa took the sack to the local Police Station where it was recorded as lost property. But three months later, no-one had claimed the sack and it was returned to Oupa and the stamps now legally belonged to him.

Oupa then took my Mum with him on the train to Johannesburg, where Stanley Gibbons, the world's largest stamp dealer from The Strand, in London, had an office and offered the stamps for sale. They spent the whole day in the Stanley Gibbons Offices and at the end of the day they walked away with cash totalling more than a year's pay of a senior Army Officer – a relatively huge sum! Mum didn't need any more lessons in the value of collecting stamps and it was no surprise, therefore, that when still a young boy, she encouraged me to take an interest in stamps and start a collection. More than fifty years later I would repeat her experience on a never to be forgotten visit to Stanley Gibbons, this time in London!

Oupa was a senior member of the police between the wars and in 1925 was responsible for coordinating the tour of South Africa by the Prince of Wales, the future King Edward the Eighth. Oupa and Ouma later received invitations to London for the Coronation, but they declined to accept the invitations for themselves and passed the invitation tickets on to their two daughters for the experience of a lifetime.

The two girls sailed together from Cape Town to Southampton on the *Dunottar Castle*, but before the Coronation, they visited Europe and as part of their tour stayed in a hotel on the shores of Lake Lucerne. Also staying in the same hotel was a Christian holiday party led by Sir Kynaston Studd, the Lord Mayor of London. My Dad was in the party and saw a notice that Sir Kynaston had put on the hotel notice board, about a prayer meeting that would take place in the hotel lounge at 7.00am the following morning. My Mum also saw the notice – and so it was, that as Fred Horrobin and Betty Lane entered the lounge for the prayer meeting, their eyes met and the rest, as they say, is history! Whenever I'm speaking in Switzerland I enjoy telling the people that this was where Ellel Ministries had its beginnings!

After the Coronation Mum sailed back to South Africa. A few weeks later my Dad's written proposal of marriage was responded to in the affirmative and an engagement ring was sent from England by registered mail. Dad sailed for South Africa on Christmas Day, 1937 to marry his bride on the 26th January 1938 in Pretoria. They honeymooned on board ship, as Dad brought his bride home to Bolton, in Lancashire. At that time Dad was a teacher, with his foot on the bottom rung of a career in building education, a career which he subsequently followed with considerable distinction.

The Second World War was a month old when my brother, David, was born in October 1939. I put in an appearance during the bombing of Berlin in November 1943. Some of my earliest life experiences included being hastily gathered up in a blanket in my mother's arms, whenever the air raid siren went off. She would carry me down into the shelter that Dad had dug and built at the bottom of the garden, where many of the neighbours also gathered, grateful for Dad's expertise in building the shelter!

When the war was over Dad was appointed Head of the Building Department at Blackburn Technical College and for the next seven years Blackburn became our home. We lived at Lammack in a new-build house, in a relatively new community on the outskirts of the town. They were wonderfully enjoyable and very happy years. As a family we became ardent supporters of the local football team, Blackburn Rovers – a passion which has continued even today, through my son and my grandsons all of whom went with me to Ewood Park to watch Blackburn Rovers beat Leeds United 2-1, in the middle of writing this book!

There was no church at Lammack, but there were a lot of young boys in the area who just hung around the streets playing together, but with very little to do. Dad tackled the problem with his usual enthusiasm by sending round a letter to the parents of all the boys, saying that he was going to start a Sunday evening Boys Class in the lounge of 24 Montreal Road. The room itself wasn't very big, so every Sunday all the big heavy furniture had to be moved out and very utilitarian wooden benches, that Dad used his carpentry skills to knock together, were moved in from the garage. The room was full on the first night and before very long he needed to have two meetings – an early one for the younger boys and a later one for the older ones.

During each preceeding week Dad would make models and large illustrations to make his talks to the boys come alive. At the meetings Mum would play lively choruses on the piano to accompany the often raucous singing of enthusiastic boys! Many of whom gave their lives to the Lord and remained faithful friends of the family, throughout my parent's lifetime. Dad would let me 'help' make the models and pictures he used and he would always tell me the story being illustrated as we worked together. In so doing I learnt a huge amount of Biblical truth without even knowing I was being taught! God used those times to teach me how important it is to capture the interest of your hearers – for if you don't the opportunity will be lost.

Before long the Methodist Church in Blackburn heard what Dad was doing and out of that weekly boys class grew a church, which first met in the changing rooms of the rugby club behind the local pub. Today Lammack Methodist Church is one of the liveliest Methodist Churches in the area and the work of evangelism there still goes on nearly seventy years later.

Having moved to Blackburn and left Dad's parents and wider family behind in Bolton, there was a regular need to make the journey back to Dad's hometown to visit Granny and Grandpa, as we called our English grandparents. Bolton had been home to the Horrobins for generations, at least since the eighteenth century when one family moved from Derbyshire to seek employment. As hand lace-makers, the big new industrial machines had robbed them of their trade and Bolton was a booming community, built on cotton spinning. In those days the skyline was dominated by literally hundreds of mill chimneys which continuously spewed out polluting smoke. No-one thought very much about the environmental consequences to the workers' health! The great steam engines that powered the cotton industry had to be kept going at all costs. They provided the energy to keep a whole town employed.

Granny and Grandpa were not in the best of health. Granny's back had been injured during the birth of her son, Fred, my father. For the rest of her life she was a semi-invalid, whose only way of getting about was in her wheelchair, which had to be pushed. Dad was the only male member of the family able to do the pushing – hence the very regular fifteen mile journey on the *Ribble* bus, which went backwards and forwards between Bolton and Blackburn.

As a boy, Grandpa had been an apprentice decorator, but it wasn't long before he joined the thousands of men for whom work in the mill was the sum total of life, with the only icing on the cake being the home football matches of Bolton Wanderers at Burnden Park. But the working environment took its toll on Grandpa's health and for many years since his retirement he had been a sick man, and in the early nineteen-fifties it was obvious his days on earth were limited.

On our last visit to Bolton before he died, in January 1953, my brother and I were ushered into the back room of their mill-workers terraced house, where a bed had been made up for Grandpa beside the open coal fire on which Granny had done all the cooking for close on fifty years. The blackened range was the only source of heating in the house and in winter it was a common sight to see all the members of the family huddled round the fire.

Granny and Grandpa were very godly people – in their poverty they never complained but simply exuded the love of Jesus to all who visited their home. David and I knew that Grandpa was dying and we were brought close to his bedside to say goodbye. He then did two things, neither of which I have ever forgotten. He slowly put out his right hand and laid it gently on David's head, prayed for him and blessed him. Then he did the same for me. Finally he picked up a leather purse that was lying on the bed, in readiness for our visit. He carefully sorted through the coins it contained and picked out two two-shilling pieces, known as florins, (10p in today's coinage, but equivalent in value to about £3 in 2016). This was a huge amount of money to a child in those far off days. It was the most money either David or myself had ever been given. Grandpa was wanting us to have a personal gift from himself, so we could buy something to remember him by. But neither David nor I could ever bring ourselves to spend those two-shilling pieces! They became Grandpa's inheritance gift and I still have mine to this day!

When in Bolton we would also usually visit Grandpa's brother, Will, my great Uncle. Uncle Will was an amazing man. He had trodden the boards of the cotton spinning mill, which stood six stories high, right next door to his house at 50 Homer Street, all his days. He had given his life to Jesus as a boy and his greatest joy in life was to tell people about His Lord. He also had a passion for missions and in 1894, as a young man, he was deeply impacted by the news coming out of China of the work of Hudson Taylor and the China Inland Mission (CIM). He started the first CIM prayer meeting in the town – a monthly meeting that never failed to meet between then and 1960! Many missionaries went out to China through the instigation of those monthly prayer meetings in his home. His back room was filled with little artefacts of China that had been brought back for him by missionaries returning home on furlough for a well-earned rest.

I often sat as a child at his feet and played with some of those precious items – such as a pair of the tiny shoes, which could only be worn by women whose feet had been cruelly bound as children so they would never grow. What bondage these people were in –

these shoes were a daily prayer reminder to Uncle Will to pray for the Chinese people who were in such spiritual bondage also. I was deeply influenced as a child by my experience of being in 'little China' for a short time whenever we visited Uncle Will. The whole family became deeply committed to mission work in China, something that was still impacting me two generations later when the work of Ellel Ministries began to touch the Chinese peoples. We will return to this in Chapter 26 when we see some of the fruit of Uncle Will's prayers in China itself.

Our regular visits from Blackburn to Bolton were soon to come to an end, however. Dad's career was developing and in order to make progress he had to move – and this time Granny came too, complete with wheelchair, and lived with us at Cheam, in Surrey, until she died at the grand old age of 90 in 1967. Dad had been appointed Head of the Building Department of a new Technical College that was being built at Ewell (now the North East Surrey College of Technology). It was a huge step for him to move from Lancashire to Surrey and start the work of building up a new School of Building from scratch, but we all benefitted from the move, especially David and I in respect of our schooling and education.

In Bolton, Dad and Mum had been members of a wonderful evangelical Anglican Church, St. Peter's, Halliwell. In Blackburn our church involvement took on a Scottish flavour as we became members of St. George's Presbyterian Church on Preston New Road. But in Cheam neither the Anglican nor the Presbyterian Churches were sufficiently evangelical for Dad's evangelistic heart, so we joined the Baptists and were richly blessed by many years of wonderful preaching and teaching from the ministry of Arthur J Matthews at Cheam Baptist Church.

These were important years for me. Many lifelong friendships were established through the *Young People's Fellowship*. Especially Chris Mungeam, who features later on in this story, and also followed a career in publishing – we're still close friends today. It was at Cheam Baptist that my own personal faith in Jesus was confirmed and reinforced when I put myself forward for believer's baptism by immersion. I had of course been baptised as a baby at St.Peter's, Halliwell, but this was now me, as a young person, making my own personal choice to follow Jesus into adulthood.

In 1954 I came face to face with raw American evangelism in the face of Billy Graham. For those who were present at London's Harringay arena in 1954, this was a presentation of Gospel truth in a manner that was unprecedented in twentieth century post-war Britain. The nation was on its knees, recovering from the vast cost of winning the Second World War – nothing like this had been seen since the nineteenth century when D.L.Moody's preaching, alongside the captivating singing of Ira D.Sankey, gripped the nation. Events such as these have the capacity to change the lives of thousands of people and, even, to impact the destiny of a nation.

In 1886, Sir Kynaston Studd, the leader of the Christian holiday in Switzerland when my Mum met my Dad, had been converted, as a young man, through the preaching of D.L.Moody. His brother, C.T.Studd, was one of the most successful and famous members of the England cricket team, and it caused a sensation when he gave up his sporting career to become a missionary in China, then India and finally Africa. If it wasn't for the visit of Moody and Sankey, the Studd family would have remained in spiritual darkness. Sir Kynaston Studd would never have taken a group of young people to Switzerland for a Christian House Party. My parents would never have met and I wouldn't even exist or know the Lord! Many great missionaries and Christian leaders began their life of faith in Moody and Sankey meetings.

In a similar way, the impact of the Billy Graham meetings on post-war London was nothing short of sensational. The meetings in the Harringay Arena went on and on and tens of thousands of people gave their lives to the Lord as they went to the front of Billy Graham's meetings and prayed the sinner's prayer. Jill Southern-Jones, the first Director of Ellel Pierrepont was one of them. I will never forget going with my Dad to Harringay and sharing in what was, for me, a totally unforgettable and influential experience. Years later I was to relive that experience as one of the organisers of Billy Graham's meetings in the North-West of England, which were part of the 1984 *Mission England*.

Throughout his life, Dad used every opportunity that would come his way to share the Gospel. He became a leader of the Ewell Boys Crusader Class, which started to meet in the hall of the new Ewell Technical College. He was Padre on many Crusaders Camps, through which many hundreds of boys (and girls) gave their lives to the Lord. In the college people loved and respected him – even though he was occasionally called '*Hallelujah Horrobin*' behind his back!

Ann, one of the 'girls' working in the college office was one of many young people, both men and women, who owe their response to the Gospel to this rather unusual college Head who was never shy of sharing the most important message the world has ever known, with anyone who was willing to listen. Ann eventually married Malcolm Colmer, a young Christian trainee Doctor, and it was Malcolm who, many years later, by then a Consultant Surgeon, was to become Chairman of the Trustees of the Charity that became responsible for the work of Ellel Ministries!

My primary hobby as a boy was collecting stamps. During the post-war years of severe austerity a weekly parcel would arrive from Ouma and Oupa in South Africa. Most things that mattered in the UK were severely rationed and Ouma made sure that her English grandchildren had precious extra supplies from what was then, relatively, a land of plenty. Each parcel was carefully wrapped in tea-towels, or cloth from which Mum could make clothes and on the outside were many of the stamps of South Africa. These were carefully soaked off and preserved. They formed the basis of both my brother's and my original stamp collections.

I became so interested in stamps that In 1956 I started saving up my weekly pocket money to buy a specialist album for the stamps of the British Commonwealth of the reign of King George the Sixth. Thirty seven and six (one pound, seventeen shillings and sixpence) was a huge price in those days to pay for an empty stamp album, but I've never regretted beginning a life-time fun journey filling in those spaces in the collection.

But God was doing something more than giving me a fascinating hobby, he was opening my eyes through collecting stamps to the whole of His world. I studied the stamp catalogues, pored over the stamps I had managed to collect and in my mind I visited all the places, whose amazing names graced the pages of my album. God was doing something in me, that I didn't understand at the time, as I became very familiar with the world that one day Ellel Ministries would be serving. Papua New Guinea, Australia, Singapore, Canada, North Borneo (now Sabah) and many other places were not strange to me – even though I had never been to any of the exotic countries whose stamps I loved to look at and where, today, there are either Ellel Centres or people working there, who have been trained through the ministry!

Collecting stamps also introduced me to the world of business! There was a stamp shop near my school in Wimbledon which I would often visit on my way home. I liked to buy a small collection or 'job lot' of stamps that the dealer had lumped together for a quick sale. On the train or bus home. I would quickly sort through what I had bought, extract the ones I wanted for my own collection and then take the remainder to another dealer in Sutton – and sell them, usually for more than I had paid for the whole lot in Wimbledon – and all before I'd reached home! I don't think my Mum and Dad ever knew why sometimes I was home from school rather later than

I should have been, or how it was that my collection was steadily growing! Thirty years later I would own a stamp shop of my own and the day would come when God used my philatelic knowledge and experience to make a £125,000 contribution to the funds of Ellel Ministries, but more of that later!

In my teenage years it seemed as though people were always asking what was, to me, an embarrassing question, *"What are you going to do when you grow up?"* Knowing that there was a real call of God on my life I would usually answer that I was going to be a minister or a pastor, without having any real idea of what that would mean. In my growing years, the Christian Union at King's College School provided wonderful opportunities to serve the Lord in the school environment. They were important and challenging days.

Notwithstanding all the usual school-related hoops that children have to jump through, I enjoyed every aspect of school days – except having to serve in the Army Section of the Combined Cadet Force – a post-war pre-military training that was still in place in the event of there being another war. My brother, David, born in 1939, was the first generation of children to escape compulsory National Service.

By the time I was wondering what I would do when I left school, David was well into the first stages of his medical career, studying physiology at Balliol College, Oxford. He had swept into Oxford, winning all the top scholarships that were available to him and I think everyone, especially me, was rather surprised when I also managed to get a place at Christ Church, Oxford, to study chemistry – my best subject in my recent 'A' Level exams.

I loved my days at Oxford. The way the courses are organised leaves you plenty of time to indulge in a huge range of extra-curricular activities. For the politically motivated there was the Oxford Union, where vast amounts of time and energy were devoted to debating interesting irrelevancies. I chose to play a lot of sport – especially rugby, hockey, squash and cross-country running. I joined the college Christian Union and was soon involved in regular Christian meetings in the rooms of other college members. I made many friends along the way.

During my first year at Christ Church the Christian Union organised a college mission under the leadership of a young Anglican minister called David Watson. As I chatted with David in my college room, before one of the meetings, I didn't realise I was talking with the man who would become one of the leading figures of the renewal movement that would sweep through the churches in the late sixties and seventies. The next time we would meet was when I shared with him the vision God had given me for the work that would become known as Ellel Ministries!

Just across the road from Christ Church is St.Aldates, the largest and most influential of the Oxford churches which has, for centuries, specialised in serving the student population. St.Aldates was close enough to my rooms in Christ Church be able to roll out of bed at 10.25am, pull a track suit over my pyjamas and stroll nonchalantly into church dead on time! The Rector of St.Aldates, Keith de Berry, specialised in preparing a wonderful sequence of guest speakers to preach at these Sunday morning services and then provided an opportunity, for those who were interested, to meet with the speakers later in the day, in the rectory rooms. I rarely missed one of these services and met some very distinguished people in the process. Over the years thousands of undergraduates either found their faith in Jesus, or had their faith well anchored in Him, at St. Aldates during these very influential series of meetings. Going back there to preach, many years later, when Charlie Cleverly was the rector was a very moving occasion in my life.

In 1956 my South African grandparents, Ouma and Oupa, sailed from South Africa to see us all in our new home in Cheam. It was to be the last time Mum would see her parents. Oupa died in Cape

Town at the end of the voyage home and Ouma later died at home in Benoni, where my cousins, the daughters of my Mother's only sister are still living today. Ouma had left each of her grandchildren a small amount in her will and I calculated that it was just enough to pay for a round Africa ticket on one of the ships of the famed *Union Castle Line*. Mum completed eight and a half round trips between England and South Africa in her life time – the half-trip being Mum and Dad's honeymoon voyage which was, for her, a one-way ticket.

The sailing dates were such that I could just squeeze in the complete voyage, together with an extended stay in South Africa itself, during my first long vacation with the help of special permission from Christ Church to return to college a couple of days late. I wanted to see for myself the land where my mother was born and brought up, spend time with her wider family and enjoy the adventure of a lifetime. It was a totally brilliant experience calling in at Madeira, Cape Town, Durban, Beira, Tanga, Dar es Salaam, Zanzibar, Aden, Port Said (for Cairo), Naples and Gibraltar.

Every one of these places holds different memories for me. It was great to spend an extended period of time staying with Uncle Bob, Aunty Isobel and my cousins Jinny and Elaine. They gave me a wonderful time, including an amazing visit to the Kruger game reserve. But perhaps the most spiritually significant time was spent in the tiny land-locked Kingdom of Swaziland. The stamps of Swaziland in my collection had really caught my attention and I wanted to go there, so I hitch-hiked down to Swaziland from Johannesburg and met up in Mbabane, the capital of the country, with a Canadian missionary family who were working with the South African General Mission. They kindly gave me a home-base for a couple of weeks during which I worked on the buildings at the Mbuluzi mission station. It was there that I preached my first "missionary sermon". I was overjoyed when four Swazi girls gave their lives to the Lord after the meeting.

But I also wanted to experience first-hand what it was like living with a Swazi family out in the country. I walked up and down the various stalls in Mbabane market where people were selling their produce. At last I plucked up the courage to explain to a man who was selling pineapples, and looked as though he could be trusted, what I wanted to do. He generously invited me to come with him and stay with his family in their native village, but it would take a couple of hours to walk there over the surrounding hills – there was no other way to go. I went back to the mission house and told the missionaries what I was going to do and, somewhat nervously they said goodbye with a cheery *"see you tomorrow"* and, I think some intense praying for my safety!

I followed the man from the market out of town and was soon climbing steeply, then dropping down to the next valley and up more hills before reaching the place where he lived inside a native kraal made of mud and grass. After a few words of explanation his wife welcomed me into their home and I will never forget the experience of sharing their food round the fire as the Swazi sun sank over the mountain ridge horizon. Sleeping on the only chair they owned was a new experience. It was pitch black and I became aware of things crawling over and up my legs, but not knowing what they were I daren't move, just in case they were poisonous or would sting me if I tried to brush them off in the dark. I will never know what creatures had used me as a climbing frame during the night, but I survived the experience, shared an African breakfast with the whole family and returned with my new friend to the market the same way we had come.

It was in experiences like this that God touched my heart for the African peoples. Seeds were sown deep inside, as God opened my eyes to their spiritual needs. They were seeds that would grow and bear enormous fruit in the years to come as God opened many African doors to the developing work of Ellel Ministries International. In

1963 it felt as though I had left something of my heart in South Africa. I had no idea how long it would be before I would be able to reconnect with the land of my maternal ancestors – but one day, I knew it would happen, and it did. Back at college I had to get my head down and catch up on all the work I was supposed to have done during the summer vacation!

While at Christ Church, I was very aware that my college had also been attended by both John and Charles Wesley, a couple of centuries previously. I loved the hymns of Charles Wesley and John Wesley became one of my personal heroes as I studied the life of this extraordinary pioneer of eighteenth century revival. I learnt much about persevering in God through the many experiences recorded in his journals. He pressed on irrespective of the opposition and problems that he encountered on the way. In years to come I would draw heavily on Wesley's example – both as a powerful illustration to use in my teaching, and, more personally, as a huge encouragement to keep going in the face of opposition and when not everyone seemed to appreciate the message you brought and what you were doing!

Oxford Cathedral, the church within the walls of Christ Church, the college, also doubled as our college chapel. It was in this very place that both the Wesley brothers, John (1728) and Charles (1735), had been ordained! The fact that at chapel services I could have been sitting in the same place where John and Charles Wesley had sat, was thrilling to me.

While at Christ Church I was the typical hard-up student and I learned that I could earn some extra money by becoming a part-time librarian. This meant that for a couple of hours, twice a week, I became custodian of one of the most amazing and wonderful libraries in the world. I just loved the library and used every moment I could to soak up the atmosphere – especially in the magnificent upstairs galleries, where there was the most extraordinary library of ancient antiquarian books – as well as a wonderful collection of drawings by Leonardo da Vinci and other famous artists. I drew especial inspiration from just looking close-up at those incredible original examples of da Vinci's work. It's hard to believe now that the college actually paid me to enjoy this amazing privilege – and I was the only 'security guard' protecting them!

I also drew inspiration from the original models, stored in the library, that had been made of the characters from Alice in Wonderland, a story which had been written in Christ Church for the children of the Dean by the Rev Charles Lutwidge Dodgson (otherwise known as Lewis Carroll) towards the end of the nineteenth century. Those few hours every week in the library gave me a life-long love of books and the arts which I have benefitted from on many occasions. Eventually, at one stage of my later business career, I established an antiquarian and second-hand bookshop of my own which, though no longer in my ownership, is still one of the largest such enterprises in the north of England!

By some miracle I completed my chemistry course and eventually emerged from the dreaming spires just about qualified as a chemist , as well as having absorbed a vast amount of other experience which, in the long run, has proved more important and valuable to me than my knowledge of chemistry and science. But I had no idea what I wanted to do with my degree.

Such was the demand for chemists in the burgeoning industrial world of those days, that I was offered a well-paid research job with *Formica*, developing new artificial surface materials, even before I was qualified. But the thought of being locked in a laboratory for the rest of my life, playing around with complicated and very smelly chemicals, was more than I could stand and I turned down the opportunity.

During my third and fourth years at College we had been required to find living accommodation outside of Christ Church and I chose to live within the confines of an Anglican theological college, *Wycliffe Hall*. So, even though I was actually studying chemistry, this gave me the chance to join in with the college pastoralia teams, which went out every week to conduct services in hospitals and prisons, or to lead youth evenings at the local approved institution for young offenders. These were precious experiences which God used to put me in touch with a lot of hurting people. I didn't realise it at the time, but I was already learning, on the job, about the need for healing, long before God gave me the vision that would eventually lead to the establishment of Ellel Ministries.

It was also about this time that I bought my first car, a 1949 MG, a car which I dearly loved until, that is, I was seduced by an even greater love for Alvis cars! An Alvis TA14 Tourer became the first of several Alvis cars I would own. I began to read everything I could get hold of about these amazing cars. Unwittingly, I was laying the foundation for that God-moment which would so radically change the rest of my life. It was as if God was setting a divine trap for me!

Chapter 2

RUNNING HARD – BUT MARKING TIME

From Oxford's Dreams to Vision of Destiny

I remember well, but not with a great deal of pleasure, those sessions on the parade ground in the Combined Cadet Force (CCF) when we had to practice marching up and down for, seemingly, hours on end and for no real purpose. It was hard work, especially on a hot summer's day when only the drill Sergeant-Major seemed to get any pleasure out of putting us through our paces! One of the exercises was marching 'on the spot', with everyone keeping in time with each other, but going nowhere. We were working hard, but only 'marking time'!

In many ways, although during the next season of my life I was running very hard, it felt as though I was only marking time. They were years full of creative activity and hard work, but I didn't seem to be getting any nearer to fulfilling my childhood calling into Christian ministry. But these were, nevertheless, very busy, important and influential years, waiting to discover what it was that God had called me to do when I was only nine years old! I was constantly on the look-out for that unmistakeable *'neon light in the sky'* moment of guidance from God. But it just wasn't there. So I continued to pursue every opportunity that life offered, trusting that God would lead me through the jungle of available options and eventually show me what it was He really wanted me to do.

In the fourth year of the Oxford chemistry course all students are required to conduct their own research programme on some aspect of chemistry. I opted to spend this research year working on a biochemical problem in the Microbiology Department and wrote a short thesis on *"Cyanocobalamin and the regulation of methionine synthesis in Escherichia Coli."* This was as far away from pure chemistry as my tutors would allow me to go! When I look at that thesis today I can't really believe that I ever did such a thing!

My first day in the microbiology lab proved to be eventful and life-changing, for it was there that I met a young laboratory technician. She was the same age as me and we began to go out with each other. It wasn't long before we began to wonder if one day we would get married. But it wasn't a totally smooth relationship as we both wrestled with issues associated with making the big decision about a future together.

We talked with older Christian friends who tried to help us in our journey but, as with all such matters, the ultimate decision has to be your own. Eventually I invited her to marry me, she accepted and we took the leap of faith together. We became officially engaged and we got married in December 1967. Like most young couples, we were full of ambitious dreams for our future.

Prior to our wedding, during my year of biochemical research in the Microbiology Department, I was finding that old cars were great fun, but maintaining them cost time and money. My hands began to take on a permanent look of having just been inside an engine and I needed to earn some extra cash! Notwithstanding my disillusion with chemistry as a research subject, I offered myself as a part-time teacher to the Head of the Chemistry Department, at the local College of Technology, at Headington, but there were no available jobs.

However, the Head of Chemistry directed me along the corridor to the Department of Building. Apparently Philip Goddard, the head of the department, needed someone urgently to teach Maths and Building Science to part-time day release builders, who spent one day a week at college getting their qualifications. Because of my father's life-long involvement with building education I was very familiar with the set up and knew that I would feel at home working in the department, even though I had no relevant qualifications or experience!

When I walked into Philip Goddard's office, the first thing I noticed was the Crusader Badge in his lapel. Having also been a Crusader, we immediately began to share our Christian experiences – we had much in common and became friends, long before we started talking about the possibility of a job! I was beginning to learn the ways of the Lord.

My meeting with Philip Goddard, late on a Friday afternoon, proved to be one of those critical life-directional moments when God points you along the way in which He wants you to go. Philip needed someone to start teaching Maths and Science for Builders at 8.30am on the following Monday morning and, if I could do that, this one day a week job was mine for the taking! It seemed strange that after four years of training in Chemistry, I was accepting a job in the building department of a technical college! I didn't realise it at the time, but this was a vital step on life's road towards the destiny moment that would change my life forever.

I was clearly an answer to Philip Goddard's prayer and he was an answer to mine! He gave me a copy of the syllabus for the course and said he would look forward to introducing me to the class on Monday morning. I left the college delighted that I had solved my need for extra income – even though I had never taught anything before and was totally unqualified for the job! I raced down to Blackwell's Bookshop in the centre of Oxford to buy the Building Science textbook that I would need and spent the weekend getting familiar with the first few lessons of the course, so that I could keep just a few pages ahead of the students I would be teaching.

In the end, I so enjoyed teaching Building Science and Maths to these very down-to-earth building students, that when I was invited by Philip Goddard to apply for a new, full-time Lectureship in Building Science at Oxford Polytechnic, I jumped at the chance. Somewhat miraculously, I got the job and went from researching in microbiology to my first permanent job – teaching builders how to use maths and science in their work. This meant that I had enough income to apply for a mortgage and we could start buying a small house.

I loved the opportunity to try and make the course really interesting for people who were not naturally, academically minded – they were practical people, who just wanted to get a qualification, so they could get on with the real work of putting up buildings. Because they weren't really interested in learning, this was quite a challenge. But those two years gave me absolutely priceless experience in learning how to communicate with people in a way that they would listen and not forget the lessons. I remembered how Dad had communicated so well with the boys who came Sunday by Sunday to our house in Blackburn and put those lessons to good use. I would draw heavily on this experience in years to come. Even though I felt as though I was marking time, they were priceless years in God's school of life.

There was no text book for the maths part of the course, just a syllabus, so I had to make up the course material as we went. But just across the road from the college was the headquarters of *Pergamon Press*, the scientific publishing house established by the famous, and later infamous, Robert Maxwell. I decided to go and talk to someone at Pergamon about the possibility of using the course material I was writing as a book on *Constructional Mathematics*. Amazingly, my time with the appropriate editor was interrupted by a few minutes of personal pleasantries with the great man himself. The size of Robert Maxwell's cigar complemented his physical stature and after shaking hands with him, brushing off the ash which had burnt my hand and waving aside the clouds of blue smoke that surrounded him, I signed a contract to write my first, (and last!) maths text book. *Constructional Mathematics* was eventually published by Pergamon in 1970. Writing this book, however, taught me a lot about the whole publishing process and later I was to discover how God used this valuable experience as a critical part of my preparation for what lay ahead.

Various motoring adventures, too numerous to record here, had given me a fairly advanced knowledge of the inner workings of the motor car and, in my enthusiasm, I offered to use my experience in running a new sort of Crusader holiday for boys. The result was the first ever Crusaders *Motor Enthusiast's Course*. I bought four old Morris Minors, recruited four mechanically skilled friends to help and, in ten hectic days, twenty-eight boys, divided into four groups, rebuilt the engines and mechanics of all four cars!

It was a major achievement to have all four cars restored and running well on the final day – even if the leader of one group had to work right through the final night to get the engine back in! At the end I sold all the rebuilt cars for more than I'd paid for them, all the costs of the course were met and we finished up with a small profit! Those boys left the course having learnt so much – not just about cars, but about God as well. Some came to personal faith while they were there and one, many years, later, was to become one of the leaders in the work God eventually called me to do!

After teaching at Oxford College of Technology for nearly two years, I began to feel the need to move on – not because I wasn't enjoying the job, but because I realised that if this was the beginning of a career in building science education, then, at the very least,

I would need to get some relevant educational experience and qualification. So I applied to the University of Manchester Institute of Science and Technology (UMIST) to do a PhD. This would then equip me for getting a university post and begin an academic career. There were many new educational facilities opening up in the country at the time and a PhD would be the key to getting my foot in the university door.

Giving up my job and going back to being a student would be a tough walk for us financially, but we reckoned that the eventual pay-back would be well worth the sacrifice of a three year struggle. We would have to depend on getting additional grants and whatever extra work we could both find to supplement our income. It was a considerable act of faith to resign what was a very well paid lectureship at the college and to start all over again. We would be sad to say good-bye to Oxford, but it seemed clear enough that this was the way God was leading us. My father, however, was shocked! How could I possibly give up, after only two years, the sort of job he had worked so hard to obtain. He was not impressed with my decision!

Our house was already on the market and we were preparing to move, when I got an unexpected telephone call from Denis Harper, the Professor of Building at UMIST. He wanted me to go and see him as soon as possible. I had no idea what was on his mind as I was not expecting to join the department as a student for another eight weeks. When I entered his office I was met by an extremely affable professor who, obviously, had something he wanted to talk about.

We talked for a while about cricket, the weather and various other small-talk topics before he turned to the real reason he had asked me to visit him in Manchester. He hesitated, coughed, and then came out with his proposal. *"Peter,"* he said, *"would you be willing to consider postponing your PhD?"* I had no idea where this conversation was going.

"I have a problem," he said. *"My lecturer in Architectural and Building Science has just resigned at very short notice and I have absolutely no-one to teach the undergraduates who will be starting their degree course in just a few weeks time. You already have two years experience teaching Building Science at College level and I am sure that with your chemistry degree you could quickly step up to teaching at degree level."*

I sat there, totally dumb-founded and in a state of shock. Here I was, once again, completely unqualified in any aspect of building science or technology, now being offered the sort of job that I thought I might get, once I had my PhD! The professor was staring hard at me, waiting for my answer, perhaps not understanding the depth of emotional trauma that I was now experiencing! I have no idea what words actually came out of my mouth – but I knew deep inside that 'this was God at work' and I had to say *"Yes."*

The professor was profoundly relieved and I was profoundly shocked, but at the same time I found it hard to contain how thrilled, excited and amazed I actually was. I couldn't wait to call my father to tell him that instead of going back to living on a student grant, I had now been offered a university lectureship, without having to get the PhD! I still didn't realise what was really happening, but God had got me on a fast-track learning experience and He was pulling the strings. Once again He was taking me right out of my comfort zone, but I was enjoying the ride.

The Professor warned me that I would still have to come for a formal interview with the University Appointments Committee, but there were no other candidates for the job! As it happened the interview came right in the middle of the *Motor Enthusiasts Course* I was running for Crusaders, which meant a major de-grease and clean-up of every area of exposed skin, and a rapid drive from Oxford to Manchester and back. But in spite of my almost total pre-occupation with re-building four Morris Minors, I was formally offered the job and returned to the course an official Manchester University Lecturer in Building Science!

With an appointment letter in my hand, we were then able to buy a new house in Bramhall and I quickly settled into the routine of being a university lecturer. This was October 1968. By this time, my brother David's medical career had taken off in a big way. He had applied for, and got, the job of being the first Professor of Medical Physiology at the University of Nairobi when he was still under thirty. He had become a Fellow of Magdalen College, Oxford at a very early age and had already written some major medical text books, which had been published by Arnold.

But there was a lot more he wanted to write about and I was already planning to write books for the courses I was running at Manchester. So we began to talk together about starting our own publishing company! On the face of it, the company had little chance of ever being commercially successful. It was born through the agency of many letters and international phone calls, long before the age of convenience which was ushered in with the internet, emails and Skype!

In his college days David had led an Expedition to Nepal, collecting blood samples as preparation for the establishment of a Nepalese blood transfusion service. The administrator of the trip was a young Oxford lawyer, the son of the Bishop of Carlisle, David Bloomer. David was then working for the Roche Drug Company and my brother knew how competent he was and invited him to become the third Director of our new company, which we grandly named the *Medical and Technical Publishing Company Ltd,* or MTP for short. My brother was the 'medic', I was the 'technic' and David Bloomer was going to run the business from a small office near his home in Aylesbury. Miraculously the company took off. David Bloomer was an extremely good image builder and Managing Director for the company, enabling my brother and I to simultaneously pursue our respective academic careers.

My brother's first book to be published by MTP was so good that David Bloomer managed to get it serialised in the *Sunday Times*, providing a wonderful launch for the new company. I started to produce a series of books on building technology and architecture, recruiting staff members from UMIST to act as compilers and contributors. And we laid plans for the launch of an extremely ambitious project, a many volume series of biennial publications called the *MTP International Review of Science*. For this I drew on the relationships I had had with my chemistry professors at Oxford and my brother coordinated the series of medical volumes. We eventually sold the rights to this series to Butterworth's, a much bigger scientific publisher, in a deal which both saved MTP from oblivion and provided the foundation for the company's later success.

For daily transport at this time, my MG had been replaced by my first Alvis – a 1949 open-touring, Alvis TA14. This was my first introduction to the world of Alvis cars. On my way to the science labs at Oxford, a similar vehicle was always parked by the roadside, most days. I would stop and admire it and I made a mental note to look out for one. Before long I had exchanged the MG for what then became the car of my dreams.

I loved this car and even today, nearly fifty years later, in different ownership, OVW 152 is regularly seen at Alvis club events. But life moves on, and even though I didn't want to say goodbye to the TA14, we were looking forward to the possibility of having a family, and a two-door, open touring car was not a realistic option for family motoring. We now needed a much newer saloon car, which would be safe for a young family and also be suitable for making quick trips up and down the country to see editors and authors about the books MTP would be producing. By then I was thoroughly converted to the joys of Alvis motoring and the next car had, of course, to be another Alvis. And so it was we said goodbye to OVW 152 and acquired 1501 VF, a magnificent, shining silver, 1960 Alvis TD21 saloon.

Whilst these two Alvis cars were wonderful vehicles, both of which I had loved to drive, my affections were now also beginning to embrace one of the greatest Alvis cars of all time. In the early thirties many great motor manufacturers went bankrupt in the severely challenging recession that prevailed between the wars. They were tough times to do business, especially in the up-market end of the motor industry. The Alvis cars of the twenties had been extremely reliable machines, but the thirties was a new era – long, low and very fast cars were becoming the order of the day and the Alvis company would have joined the long list of motoring business failures, were it not for Charles Follett, the London sales agent who knew what the market wanted and told the company what to produce.

In just fourteen weeks Alvis turned their whole factory upside down to produce the totally amazing, 90 miles per hour, *Alvis Speed 20*. This car changed the fortunes of the company, saving it from bankruptcy and extinction. I drooled over the pictures of Speed 20s in the books, but I knew that I could never afford to own a specimen of this amazing car. I was content, or so I thought, with my beautiful, silver, modern 3-litre Alvis TD21.

The Alvis parked outside our house attracted the attention of other car-loving neighbours, one of whom, Harold Lord, also proved to be an Alvis enthusiast. Harold was also a member of the Alvis Owner Club and we enjoyed many a natter about our mutual interests. Harold knew of my love for the Speed 20 and casually said, *"I'll look out for one for you."* In my heart I hoped he wouldn't actually find one, for I didn't really want to tell him that I couldn't afford it. To come so close to the ownership of my ultimate dream, but not actually be able to complete the deal would be too painful!

And then it was that I received what would prove to be that life-changing, destiny fulfilling, 'neon light in the sky', phone call.

"Peter, I've got a Speed 20 for you," was quickly followed by my inquisitive, *"How much?"* Harold's reply of £50 totally took my breath away. The car was a wreck, but it was a bargain and a couple of weeks later all that remained of DG 8625 was delivered to my house on a trailer and, as recounted in the *Prologue*, the journey of a lifetime was about to begin!

Chapter 3

NORTHWARD
BOUND – AGAIN

From Academia to the Business World

L ife in Manchester was moving into the fast lane, very quickly.
I was seriously committed at the University with developing
new courses in the School of Building. I was regularly teaching
building science to architects in the Victoria University of Manchester.
And MTP was going through its company birthing process and, like
any new-born, was demanding a lot of attention.

I had also started work, with Dave Culshaw another member
of the Alvis Owner Club, on the compilation of *The Complete
Catalogue of British Cars* – a book which would become a standard
encyclopaedic reference volume, giving the known specification of
every model of every make of British car that had ever been made
and sold between the years of 1895 and 1974! Converting my vision
for the book into the finished work was, in itself, a monumental
task, demanding a considerable amount of time and attention. It
was eventually published by Macmillan in 1974.

Add to all the above the normal activities of life, our involvement in local church and my occasional preaching appointments in Baptist churches around South Manchester and it's not hard to see that life was getting busier than could easily be handled within the confines of a normal working day!

Then the day came when we were able to share the exciting news that our first child was on the way. We had to empty our spare bedroom of lots of accumulated stuff and prepare and decorate it appropriately for the expected new arrival. We were totally thrilled when Anne Elizabeth was safely delivered at Wythenshawe Hospital on the 27th April 1970.

Anne was welcomed into the family at almost the same time as the wreck of the *Alvis Speed 20* was delivered to our home! It was just seven weeks later, on election day, that I began to work on the restoration of the Speed 20, and had that most dramatic of experiences in the garage that would change my life forever. And the more I thought about it, the more it grew into a vision for healing and restoration. While I had no idea what the vision would eventually produce, I knew there was something being conceived in my spirit which was not of me, but God.

It was that experience which eventually helped me make sense of the whole of my life's pilgrimage. But had I known that another sixteen years would pass, before the vision for healing broken lives would become a practical reality, I might have been tempted to not even begin the necessary journey of faith! But I was already praying into the vision on a daily basis – something I was constrained to do every single day from then until the work began in 1986. Of course I wondered how it could be fulfilled and what it might look like when it became operational, but faith doesn't dwell on the unknowns and the impossibilities of a situation, only on the completion of the task!

On the home front everything was now being stretched to the limit and something had to give. It was becoming clear that the embryonic publishing house was, indeed, a very demanding baby. I would have to decide whether to give up any involvement in the development of MTP and remain a University Lecturer or, once again, resign a well-paid lectureship, and also give up the academic objective of adding a PhD to my name.

I had, by then, been a lecturer in building for five years. I had learnt a huge amount in the process and had loved the whole experience. I had made many friends and had many contacts throughout the world of building education. The books on building construction that I had organised and edited were looking good and there were many more possible titles waiting to be published. But it seemed as though the desire to remain in the secure bubble of the academic world, albeit in a very practical subject, was waning. The time had come to move on and risk sailing on the open, and often very rough, seas of the business world in the tiny vessel that was MTP.

The two Davids and I began to look around at where it would be good to establish MTP in a permanent home. We were all northerners by origin, so we drew a line across the country north of Birmingham and started the search. We wanted to be in a university town, but in one that was close enough to the countryside for it to be a pleasant working environment for us and everyone who would work in the company. One by one the big northern universities were eliminated until finally we chose Lancaster, where there was a brand new and vibrant university campus being built on the south side of the city. Lancaster was also close to the Lake District, an area of the country which we all knew and loved.

In the summer of 1971, therefore, I handed in my notice to the university and began the search for suitable offices for MTP in and around Lancaster. Lancaster City Council were encouraging new companies to come and establish themselves in the town and were offering very generous rental terms for start-up businesses. We finished up with two whole floors of St.Leonard's House, right in the centre of the city and with a large car park adjacent. The offices were huge, but that meant there was plenty of room to expand and also to warehouse our stock and dispatch it all over the world to our customers from the same address. St.Leonard's House was ideal for our purposes.

We found a lovely old stone house for our new home in the village of Silverdale, about twelve miles to the north-west of Lancaster. David and Paula Bloomer found a house in the same village and this proved to be a wonderful and safe village environment for bringing up a family. But in time it became much more than that – for living in Silverdale was to be very significant and strategic in the growth and development of the vision for healing broken lives, which still burned brightly in my daily thinking. I couldn't forget what had happened to me in the garage! I was completely at peace that joining MTP and moving to Lancaster was God's plan and part of the journey of faith I was on, but I had no idea how He was going to orchestrate future events.

About this time, we were totally thrilled that on the 16th September 1972 God blessed us with the gift of a son, Peter Mark, a younger brother for Anne The family was growing in all sorts of ways and we soon added Sam, an adorable black Labrador, to the family complement as well.

There were only two churches actually in the centre of Silverdale village, the Anglican Parish Church and the Methodist Church, part of the circuit of Lancaster Methodist Churches. Just outside the village in the former Hazelwood Hall, there was a terminal care hospice being run under the auspices of the Sisters of Our Lady of Apostles. The Hall had been bequeathed to the Roman Catholic Church and the Chapel that was built in the grounds had become the place of worship for the surrounding Catholic community.

Shortly after arriving in Silverdale I invited all the Christian leaders in the village to meet and talk together about putting on a combined programme of meetings during the *Week of Prayer for Christian Unity*. In time this developed into the Silverdale Inter-Church Fellowship (SICF) which, for many years, was a focus for different corporate Christian activities in the village. The head of the hospice, Sister John, became the Catholic representative on the SICF Committee, and when she retired she was replaced by an extraordinary lady, Sister Aine, who earned the respect and love of believers of every denomination. Before coming to Silverdale she had been a missionary nurse in Nigeria and had personally delivered over 10,000 babies during her years of service in West Africa. Sister Aine was to become a very close friend and supporter of the work of Ellel Ministries.

During this season, I became very conscious of the way God was using my business experiences with MTP to teach me some very profound lessons. I discovered that God was a very good businessman and that His ideas were always good ones! For example, as a college lecturer I had thoroughly researched the available resources of quality information for my students. One hugely important resource I discovered was the series of illustrated Digests that were put out by the Building Research Establishment and published by HMSO (Her Majesty's Stationery Office). They were generally known as the BRE Digests, ranging from four to sixteen pages in length and each one was a mine of important information. Our file copies in the staff room at Oxford College of Technology were constantly being borrowed by various lecturers and the one you urgently needed always seemed to be missing.

One day I found myself thinking about possible new publishing projects for the company and the idea dropped into my head that I should go to the Building Research Establishment and talk with whoever was in charge of the BRE Digests about the possibility of re-publishing them in book form. How much easier it would be if this wonderful resource could be bound together in separate subject related volumes, and always be available for whoever wanted to use them.

With this, and other 'ideas', I was beginning to realise how important some of my childhood influences had been. I've already explained how it was through Great Uncle Will, my grandfather's brother, that the seed of mission to China was sown into my young life. But this wasn't the only way he had exercised a very godly spiritual influence on the whole family. He already seemed to me to be an old man, when I first got to know him in my early growing years. Just before he retired, he took me on a tour of the cotton spinning mill next door to his home, where he had spent the whole of his working life. The incredible noise of the massive steam engines that drove the spinning machinery, and the row upon row of men and women who operated those machines from dawn to dusk, was etched on my memory for ever. Uncle Will had worked in the same mill all his life, but everyone knew that his real work was to be available for the Lord in whatever form of service God led him to – a work from which he never retired!

One day when Uncle Will was sitting in his special chair in the corner, by the fireplace, he was talking about all sorts of things, including, of course, his beloved *China Inland Mission*. One thing I well remember him saying was *"Never sit on a spiritual urge!"* By which he meant, and even as a young boy I totally understood what he was saying, *"if you know God has spoken to you, then don't question what He has said, just get on and do it!"*

Starting the first CIM prayer meeting for China in Bolton was just one of his spiritual urges! As a result, Uncle Will was full of amazing stories, told to him by missionaries who had gone out from Bolton to China – stories of God's intervention in their lives and of wonderful answers to prayer. There were even the genuinely miraculous things that God had done in response to the faith and actions of missionaries in service. I can recall some of those stories today and Uncle Will's words to me *never sit on a spiritual urge* became a strategic maxim for me throughout my life. I wouldn't have had the courage to have left two secure and well-paid teaching jobs, in faith that God was leading me, without Uncle Will's words having become part of my spiritual DNA at a very early age.

So, when I sensed God telling me to contact the Building Research Establishment about the BRE Digests, I didn't waste even one day thinking about it. Even though this was for my business, it was very definitely a spiritual urge and I wasn't going to sit on it! The following morning I telephoned the BRE, explained what I was calling about to the receptionist, and was put through to the Director of Information, Keith Alsop. He was very hesitant when I explained what I wanted to see him about, for he wasn't aware that either the BRE or the HMSO had ever agreed to anything like that before – licensing a non-government organisation to publish their material. But, having let me know this *caveat*, he kindly agreed to see me at the BRE.

I made the 200 mile journey on the first day that Keith was available, and between my call and the visit I prepared a comprehensive analysis of all the BRE digests, divided them into four different grouped topics and set out the contents of what would become four different volumes. The work looked very convincing and would also, I believed, have the potential to earn quite a bit of royalty income for the Building Research Establishment.

As I walked into Keith Alsop's office, he smiled and shook my hands, but I was already staring at his lapel! This was proving to be a re-run of the day that I walked into Philip Goddard's office at Oxford College of Technology, when God used that seemingly chance meeting to point me in the right direction for the next season of my life. I couldn't believe what I was now seeing as I stared at the same Crusader Badge that had also been in Philip's lapel!

Our conversation was long and pleasant as we shared Crusader experiences and stories about people we both knew, and talked about the Lord and our faith in Him. Eventually we turned to the reason I had come to see him. I showed him my presentations and it seemed as though all the possible difficulties and objections there might have been to the idea, from the BRE's point of view, had melted away in the fellowship we had been enjoying together.

But Keith didn't give me any false encouragement. He made it very clear that, even though he would be happy to recommend the project to HMSO, the ultimate decision wasn't his to make and rested solely within the HMSO, who owned the copyright of the BRE Digests. It was from the London office that I would have to gain permission to negotiate a contract and Keith had no personal influence over the decision maker at the HMSO.

My next appointment, therefore, was with the HMSO Directorate in London. The man I was seeing was not wearing a Crusader badge, and on the face of it this was not going to be an easy interview. In the nineteen seventies HMSO had never done anything like this before and to give us a contract for such a series of books would be breaking very new ground – not an easy thing to do for a government organisation that had been set in its ways for generations!

Our conversation began with the usual pleasantries of a new business contact. He asked me where I had come from that morning and what I had come to see him about. But as soon as he heard the word 'Lancaster', his eyes lit up and he began to tell me of the adventures he had had in the army, training engineers how to throw Bailey Bridges across Lancaster's River Lune. It had obviously been a thoroughly enjoyable experience for him and his stories were long! But I was getting worried, for by the time he had finished telling me the whole story, my half hour appointment time was already up and I feared that I wouldn't even get the chance to talk about my BRE Digests project.

Suddenly he also realised that our allotted time in his diary had gone and said, *"Now, tell, me what did you want to see me about?"* As quickly as I could I told him that I wanted a government contract to publish the BRE Digests in book form. *"Sounds like a good idea to me,"* he quickly said. *"I'll see you have a contract in the post by the end of next week."* There was no time or need for any more discussion as he hurried me out of his office, and turned to his next appointment, who was waiting on the chair outside. I literally danced down the streets of London, knowing that I had been offered the equivalent of a pot of gold in publishing terms!

Those books were printed and reprinted in various editions time and time again. They proved to be the bedrock of our construction publishing operation, selling many thousands of copies to people who, like me in my Oxford teaching days, needed to know that the BRE Digest they wanted would always be available in the office, in a bound volume, whenever anyone wanted or needed them. I have no doubt that the idea to contact the BRE and talk to them about the BRE Digests was a God-implanted idea – but that idea needed me not to sit on what was clearly a *'spiritual urge'*. I had to play my part and act accordingly and then God worked the miracle.

I'm so glad Uncle Will had taught me well. I was now learning vital lessons in the business arena that would be critical for me in the years that were to come, for there would be many times in the history of Ellel Ministries when it became necessary to act urgently in faith in response to the prompting of God's Holy Spirit. Indeed, without having learned that lesson when I was young I doubt if the work of Ellel Ministries would ever have got off the ground. I am often reminded of the words from Proverbs 22:6, *"Train up a child in the way that he should go, and when he is old he will not turn from it."*

MTP was growing as a company. But as with any new and growing company, it was not without its problems and many different hurdles had to be crossed – not the least of which, with my brother still in

Kenya and then for a season working in Canada, was maintaining good communications between the three Directors. Both the medical and the technical sides of the company were independently doing well, but there were internal pressures caused by the demands of a medical publishing company conflicting with the demands of the technical side of the company, which was specialising in books for the construction industry and the architectural professions. They had very different needs – especially in the area of marketing.

By 1974 it was becoming difficult to maintain the company in its present form and an agreement was reached between the three founding directors to separate out the two sides of the operation. I would have no further share in the medical side and I would re-establish the construction company as a separate operation under the name *The Construction Press*. While the separation was entirely amicable and mutually beneficial, I was now entirely on my own in the business world and couldn't depend any longer on the expertise and support of either David Bloomer, who had masterminded the business development of the MTP operation, or my brother. Looking back now, however, I realise how absolutely critical that was, so that I would, in time, be free to move forward, without restriction, into the vision for a ministry of healing and restoration, that I was still nurturing in prayer on a day-by-day basis.

I was, however, by this time, really wondering what God was doing with my vision! Surely, if it really was from Him, it was time for the work to begin – I felt as though I was getting old, after all I was thirty years of age! I was walking a spiritual tight rope of wanting to be obedient to the Lord on a daily basis in the business world and looking for the place and time when I would jump off another spiritual cliff into the work that I knew God was calling me to do, the vision for which would not go away. So, even though I was still in the publishing business, it was around this time that I tried to take things into my own hands and make things happen my way – I know now that that is not a good idea! But I was desperate to see some action in the right direction, so I started applying for ordination, thinking that if I became a 'reverend' it might be a help when, finally things got going with the vision.

First, I tried the Methodists and went through some of the pre-ordination hoops at Cliff College, the most well-known of the Methodist Colleges. In his youth my Dad had shared in evangelistic missions with the Cliff College trekkers, and Cliff was certainly a great place. But I soon discovered it wasn't for me at that stage of my life. I also tried the Baptists where, theologically I had felt most at home, but I soon hit a brick wall here as well.

And finally I thought I'd try the Anglicans. I went through the preliminary hoops with the Diocesan Director of Ordination and then applied to St. John's College Durham. The principal called me up to Durham for an interview which was to take place at 9.00am in the morning, so I would need to come the day before and stay in the college overnight. I was deeply asleep in one of the college bedrooms, when I was suddenly wide awake and having an Elijah moment! By which I mean God was saying just the same thing to me as he had said to Elijah thousands of years ago, *"What are you doing here?!"* (1 Kings 19:13).

I knew this was not a moment for discussion with God, I was clearly in the wrong place and God was telling me to get out before I committed myself to a direction in life that was not of Him. This was an unmistakeable spiritual urge! I didn't hesitate. I jumped out of bed, got dressed, wrote a hurried apologetic note to the Principal which I pinned on his door and tried to escape from the college. But all the doors were locked and without triggering the alarm systems I could find no way out. But there was an open window along one of the corridors, so I threw my bag out of the window, scrambled down the wall, fled to my car and escaped!

I looked at the clock in the car. It was 2.00am in the morning, my heart was pounding and all the way home I kept on telling God how sorry I was for trying to make things happen my way. I was deeply repentant and returned home somewhat chastened, but grateful for my own personal Elijah experience. I know now that if I had been ordained in any one of the Church denominations, the work God was raising up would have been labelled by that denomination – and that is what God did not want to happen. This was going to be a Kingdom ministry, designed by God to be a blessing to believers of every denomination – and none. And I very nearly wrecked what God had in mind. I returned to work determined that I would get on with running the business in the best possible way and wait God's timing.

As a separate company The Construction Press was doing fairly well. We had found a new base for the company in the former offices of the now disbanded Lunesdale Rural District Council – a building which was, in reality, also the former Workhouse for the Lune valley where people would come to live and work until they were too ill to live, and there they died. I even inherited a working mortuary, including two huge slate slabs on which the dead bodies would have been laid out, together with a wooden body-bearer for carrying the corpses from the living accommodation to the mortuary and then to the graveyard!

God was certainly leading me and the company in some quite unusual and supernatural ways. One week The *Sunday Times* newspaper announced it was going to produce a strip cartoon version of a *Do-it-Yourself* home manual, in weekly instalments. I thought their first issue was really well done and I surmised that the whole series could form the basis of another excellent project for The Construction Press. But as a totally unknown person, from a totally unknown company, I had no personal influence with the Sunday Times switchboard and was unable to talk with the Editor.

So I wasted no more time, travelled to London, and presented myself at the Sunday Times offices saying that I needed to see the Editor, Harold Evans, urgently about an important business project associated with this week's issue of the Colour Supplement! My boldness was rewarded and even though I had to wait a while, for the few minutes I had been granted with the great man, I got my opportunity!

I had the Colour Supplement in my hand, quickly congratulated him on the first instalment of the DIY cartoons and offered to publish the whole series as *The Sunday Times Book of Do-it-Yourself*! And would he be willing to give me a publishing contract so I could work on producing the book week by week! His response amazed me, *"Oh, we've only planned six instalments initially as an experiment. If it isn't popular we'll kill it!"* I was convinced it was going to be popular and decided instantly to take a risk. I knew that if I didn't get in first, one of the big boys of the publishing world would quickly snap up the rights.

"Well," I said, *"I'm willing to risk that happening. If I give you a cheque for £500, as a non-returnable advance royalty on the book, will you give me a contract?"* I knew that £500 was a nothing sum to a paper as big as *The Sunday Times*, but it was the most that I dared risk of the little money we had. I don't think it was the £500 cheque that influenced the Editor, although it was a declaration of intent, but I walked out of his office having shaken hands on the deal and even though we were a tiny, unknown company, Harold Evans honoured the agreement and *The Sunday Times Book of Do-it-Yourself!* became my first and biggest best-seller. This, together with the ongoing series of BRE Digests volumes became the financial foundation of the company. Both were unquestionably God-ideas

These two projects, where God had so clearly gone ahead and not only provided me with the business idea, but also provided me with the contacts who could make them happen, gave me enormous confidence in God's business acumen! But, as with all successful exploits there is also a hidden danger, for I was also becoming confident in my own abilities and when the next potential money-earning project came along I fell into an enemy trap, which I didn't recognise until it was too late. It very nearly cost me my life and my business, from which I would likely have emerged either dead or bankrupt, or both!

One day I received a letter from a man who wanted to write a comprehensive dossier on all the buildings that were failing catastrophically around the country, some of them even causing serious loss of life. His idea for a book on *Building Disasters and Failures* seemed to be well-founded and, I saw the huge media potential there could be for such a book. I contacted the author and arranged to visit him. I drove over two hundred miles to his home, parked my car, walked up his drive and put out my hand to ring his doorbell. But before I could touch the push-button, God spoke to me so clearly that I was physically startled by His intervention. The words were simple and direct, *"Have nothing to do with this man."*

I pulled my hand back and started to question in my mind whether or not that really could be what God was saying. Surely it would be best if, at least, I were to see him and so I over-rode the voice of God in my heart and pushed the door-bell anyway. I didn't like the man, his language was of a type that I wasn't used to and I felt very uncomfortable. But his wife was, in contrast, surprisingly nice and made me some sandwiches as well. Before I left their home, two hours later, I had given the man a contract for the book.

My journey home that day was one of the most miserable of my life. On the one hand I really did know that I had done wrong, but at the same time, I was trying to make excuses for myself and before long, I had convinced myself that, as with the previous projects, I could make a success of this one as well. By the time I got home, I had decided that God had got this one wrong, and I decided to press on with it! It was the worst decision I had ever made.

To cut a long story short, in spite of the fact that I did manage to produce the book and then get it front page billing in the *Sunday Times Colour Supplement*, there was something inherently bad about the author. The process of converting his very badly written material into a publishable volume, totally pre-occupied me for months. The rest of the company began to go down-hill through lack of attention and the finances were in a mess. The very existence of the company was in danger – we were too small to withstand such pressure.

Then, as soon as the book was published, he began to try and blackmail me for more money, even though the book had not yet earned the royalties he was demanding. Over the next few months he sent me the most rude, vulgar and threatening letters you could ever imagine and then on one Sunday night I received seven telegrams over the space of a few hours, every one of them increasingly threatening and the final one contained an implied murder threat, saying *"neither you nor your company will exist in ten days time."*

I took the telegram to the police who calmly told me that he hadn't yet committed a crime, but if he did they would investigate it. It was little comfort! Time and again I had gone over and over that moment when God spoke to me on his doorstep. How I wish I'd listened and obeyed God, instead of trusting in my belief in my own abilities to succeed, when even God had warned me off! Pride had led me to the brink of disaster. I was now sitting on a knife edge, with bankruptcy on one side and murder on the other. Repentance at this point was, as they say, a no-brainer. I was deeply sorry and deeply repentant. I had learned a huge lesson – namely that pride can blind one's judgement and make you turn away from what God had clearly spoken into your life.

I shared the situation with a number of close Christian friends who were committed to praying for me. I was now trusting God more than ever before, even though I was having to live with the consequences of my own mistakes and as a result was on a downhill slide to disaster. My prayer life intensified during those ten days following the receipt of that fateful final telegram. I was totally desperate. I continued to receive more abusive and threatening letters from him. My lawyer then advised me not to speak to him any more if he telephoned, for I might be tempted to say something that would go against me in any subsequent legal case. On the ninth day there was an eerie silence. I had no idea where the man was or what he was doing. It was with a great deal of wariness that I went to the office on the tenth day and tried get on with my work.

Half way through the morning my secretary's telephone rang and she spoke to me on the intercom. *"It's his wife on the phone, will you speak with her?"* It was time for another quick prayer – but I sensed no spiritual resistance from the Lord, so I took the call and was utterly shocked by what I was about to hear. *"Mr Horrobin?"* she asked. *"Yes,"* I replied. *"I think you ought to be the first person to hear that my husband has just dropped dead."* His wife clearly knew what had been going on and wanted me to be the first to know what had happened. On the tenth day of his ultimate threat against me, as far as he was concerned, I did not exist. We were now in very different places and I no longer had anything to fear from him.

A huge burden was instantly lifted – and yet I was already in my heart feeling guilty! For, yes, I was rejoicing that God had answered my prayers, but I was even then asking the question, should I be rejoicing at the death of a sinner? I desperately needed to know that this was God's action and not just an extraordinary coincidence. Only then could I be at peace about how this man entered his eternal destiny. On the way home that night I called to see Reg Smith, an elderly man who had been committed to praying for me through the crisis. I wanted to give him the news and thank him for praying.

As he opened his front door I couldn't stop myself from blurting out, *"Reg, it's all over!"* His response amazed me: *"Yes, I know!"* I was trying to work out how it was that he had already got the news from the office. But he hadn't, for Reg continued, *"As I was praying for you this morning, I was reading my Bible and came across Isaiah 14:4 in which the prophet says 'The oppressor has now ceased.' As I read those words I knew that God had answered our prayers for you and that there was no need to pray for you anymore."*

For the second time that day I was in a state of shock. It really had been God who had intervened and delivered me from my oppressor. The oppressor in Isaiah 14 was the King of Babylon who had been opposing the people of God. This was direct confirmation that God had acted and delivered me from my own personal oppressor.

But what lessons I had learned from this whole episode! I realised how the enemy of souls will do everything he can to deceive us into disobeying God. I saw how pride, Satan's own original sin, can become the ultimate weapon that Satan uses against us when trying to lead us astray and to follow our own understanding instead of God's (*see* Proverbs 3:5-6). No wonder the Scripture warns us that sometimes *"Satan, himself, masquerades as an angel of light"* (2 Corinthians 11:14) to try and make us obey his temptations instead of the voice of God.

I have no doubt that this is what I had experienced. Satan used my pride to do everything he could to take me off course. But equally, I have no doubt, that God heard the cry of my repentant heart and intervened to save me from the consequences of having been deceived. It was a huge and unforgettable lesson. And finally, God showed me that it was indeed Him who, following my repentance and owning my sin, delivered me from my own personal 'King of Babylon'!

I was learning through my business experiences, not only how God can bless us through his direct leading, but how, also, there can be serious consequences of not listening to what God is saying and doing what He has said. I didn't realise it at the time, but God was teaching me lessons that would be absolutely priceless for all the years that lay ahead.

Chapter 4

BUSINESS ADVENTURES!

From Publishing New Books
to Selling Old Ones

A mazingly, the publishing business quickly recovered from the huge crisis we had just been through. I was learning that, when we repent, God forgives us for what we did wrong, and also that, when we put things back into godly order, God's covenant blessings can be quickly restored.

But in spite of all the concentration on business developments, the *'bent chassis vision'* wouldn't go away! I was constantly aware of the fact that somewhere down the line I would have to leave whatever it was I would be doing at the time and step into that destiny calling. I just had to trust that, as and when that happened, God would look after all the details. But I was getting very frustrated with the waiting process – it was only much later that I realised that this wasn't just a waiting process, but it was a unique training school that God had got me on, and I couldn't speed up the lessons he wanted me to learn! Nothing was going to be wasted.

One night I had a very clear and vivid dream. In this dream I was buying a property in which to start a bookshop in the small town of Carnforth – home of Steamtown, the north-west of England's only railway museum – and the place where the station platform scenes from that most famous of films, *Brief Encounter*, were shot. I quite often had dreams, but this one was different – it wasn't just an inconsequential dream, I knew that God was showing me something he wanted me to do. If you ask me how I knew that this dream was God, I couldn't give you a logical answer that would make sense. It was, well, different! It was like receiving a letter and going to the foot of the letter to look at the signature. If the signature was genuine, then the letter was genuine. Well, the dream had God's signature on it and what God was saying was definitely in the category of one of Uncle Will's spiritual urges!

I had to pass through Carnforth every day, on the way from Silverdale to my offices in the Old Workhouse. The next morning, as I passed through the town, I noticed a huge *For Sale* sign prominently positioned on the wall of one of the shops. It got my attention. I remembered the name of the agent and gave him a call as soon as I got to the office. I was surprised to hear that the sign I had just seen wasn't new at all, but that it had been there for several months! It was just that on the morning after the dream, I actually noticed it for the first time. On the face of it a bookshop in Carnforth would be a complete non-starter as a business proposal. The town wasn't big enough to support a bookshop. I knew the dynamics and economics of the bookselling industry quite well – but if God thought it was a good idea, who was I to question his business acumen or what he was doing?! I did not want to make another big mistake!

So, in faith that God knew what He was doing, I made an offer for the property that very day which was accepted by the vendor. I then arranged the finance to purchase the shop and within a few weeks was the owner of an empty three storey property – 38 Market Street, Carnforth! By now I had many contacts in the book trade and very quickly managed to get the ground floor space decorated and carpeted, then equipped with book shelves and racks for greetings cards and stationery. I employed a young Christian, who was looking for a career, to run the shop for me and opened *The Carnforth Bookshop* for business. I had no idea what God's plan was, but I was completely at peace that this was of Him!

I used to call in at the shop every morning and evening on the way to and from the office to see how things were doing. There was a flurry of interest in the shop when it first opened, but the early sales figures were not impressive. The shop had only been open for a few weeks when, one day, on my daily morning visit, the telephone rang and as I was standing by the phone, I answered it. At that time we had done very little advertising, we were not in the telephone directory and, as far as I knew, no-one even had our phone number!

A lady on the other end of the phone began to tell me that she had heard we were buying second-hand books and she had some to sell. Would we come and buy them! I started to explain that the shop had only just opened and that we were a new book shop and that we didn't buy second-hand books. The lady was about to hang up when that unmistakeable sense that this was, again, God at work, stopped me in my tracks. I managed to keep her on the line and I found myself asking for her address and said that I would be very pleased to come and look at her books!

A few hours later I arrived back at the shop with about ten large boxes of books. I had no idea what they were really worth, but I had offered her what seemed to me a reasonable price and she seemed pleased. So I loaded the books in the back of my car and brought them back to Carnforth. I carried them upstairs into the semi-derelict first floor area and dumped them on the floor. And this process kept on happening! Over the next few months we accumulated so many boxes of books that the whole of the first floor was covered with boxes, several feet deep. The staff were wondering what I was doing as I bought yet more second-hand books and dumped them on the premises. They knew I loved books – but this was getting ridiculous. But if God was telling me to buy books who was I to say 'No'?

In reality, I didn't really know what I was doing, except that this was the most unusual business I had ever been involved in! It had begun with a dream, and now we were storing thousands of books in boxes that no-one could see and no-one was buying. But also about this time I had begun to pray with our church organist. Bruce was the son of Methodist minister, a classics scholar, a brilliant musician and had played the organ in Methodist churches all his life. He became the classics master at a well-known school, but in mid-life he suffered a nervous break-down, was hospitalised, had to take early retirement and chose to live in Silverdale. Everything was fine until he had a recurrence of his symptoms and was hospitalised once again.

The vision for healing was still burning strongly within me and I sensed that God wanted me to spend time praying for Bruce and, at the same time, start learning about the needs of hurting people. I visited him in hospital and after he returned home, and started playing the organ again, he started to come round every Sunday evening after church and we would just talk – about him, his life and his problems and pray together for his healing. Bruce was a man of great integrity and it soon transpired that one of his fundamental problems was that he knew all about God, was adept at understanding every possible angle of Christian theology, but he didn't actually know God for himself. I was experiencing first-hand exactly what Jesus experienced with Nicodemus in John Chapter 3. Nicodemus was a well-versed theologian, but he wasn't born-again. He knew all about God but he couldn't really understand what Jesus was saying because his spiritual eyes were closed to the reality of having a personal relationship with God.

This was exactly Bruce's situation and he needed help to step through the hoop of faith, lay aside his intellectual concerns and come, as Jesus recommended, like a little child! It wasn't long before he took that giant step, laid aside all his intellectual arguments and simply received Jesus into his heart by faith. It was as if a massive transforming light had been switched on inside. He wasn't instantly healed of all his problems, but God was now able to move in his life in a way that hadn't been possible before. This was a simple, but at the same time, massive lesson for me in understanding that whatever the healing vision that God had given would look like in practice, it couldn't be separated from evangelism. Being born again is like being raised from the dead and that is, indeed, the most profound healing that anyone can ever receive.

We kept on talking and praying together regularly and I began to realise that an important part of Bruce's healing would be the restoration of his self-worth and value through recreation, or preferably, meaningful work. But what could he do? He couldn't now go back into teaching and I began to enquire as to what sort of things he loved doing and was really interested in. His answer suddenly made sense of what had been happening at Carnforth Bookshop! For Bruce's life-long love was hunting in second-hand bookshops for books to add to his collection – especially of books related to Iona and the early development of Christianity through the influence of St.Columba.

I started thinking very quickly and began to tell Bruce all about the shop at Carnforth and that there were now thousands of books upstairs in the shop that needed sorting – how would he like, as part of his healing journey, to help me by unpacking the boxes, finding out what was there and sorting the books. He was thrilled at the prospect and the next day Bruce and I started together unpacking some of the boxes. He was totally in his element and it wasn't very long before Bruce joined the staff as the first manager of the Carnforth Bookshop, second-hand department, on the first floor of the premises. As soon as the second-hand department opened it was constantly full of visitors – it became a hub of the town.

God had not only provided a vital key to Bruce's ongoing healing journey – but at the same time He had provided me with the absolutely ideal person to launch what would eventually become the largest second-hand bookshop in the north of England – a mine of pleasure for book-lovers. All the knowledge and love of books which I had imbibed when working in Christ Church Library, all those years ago, was now being put to good use!

Two years later the next door premises became available and we expanded the business by connecting the two buildings together. And another two years later we repeated the process. The one original shop was now three and the second-hand books had spread so that every room on all three floors of the building was packed with books – and still is to this day. I also added a stamp shop to the business and most of the large collection of stamps I had accumulated over the years was put into the shop which was now run by another friend who was also a keen stamp collector. I no longer own the business but the rent which came in from the property helped fund us in the ministry for almost forty years – God certainly knew what he was doing when He gave me that dream!

But none of that was obvious on the day I took the phone call in the shop. Only God knew what lay ahead and learning to walk in obedience to His leading was proving to be an exciting ride. With the benefit of hindsight, it's now easy to see that all these business experiences were simply God's training school for what He had in mind!

My experience with Bruce served to focus my attention on that time when God spoke so clearly to me in the garage. Six years had now passed and I was beginning to think what would happen if it suddenly became clear that God had fired the starting gun and the work was getting under way. In the UK, when people give to a

Charity, the Charity can benefit by claiming back all the tax that has been paid by the donor on the donation from the government. But, without a legally established charity in place this isn't possible.

So, as an act of faith I decided to get ready by establishing a Charity that would be used as the legally registered vehicle for the work when it actually began. I made the application for a charity that would have general Christian purposes, but first I would have to choose a name. I went round and round many different fancy names but I kept on coming back to the simplest name of all – *The Christian Trust*. But this title was so general that my lawyer said you would be very unlikely to be granted approval for it by the Charity Commissioners, even if it was available. But as it seemed to be the name that would fit the unknown future of a Christian charity best, I asked the lawyer to put the name forward anyway and see what happened. I felt confident that we would get it.

The lawyer was extremely surprised when a few weeks later he received back the registration certificate for *The Christian Trust*! Amazingly, in the whole history of charities in the United Kingdom no-one had ever before tried to register a charity with this simplest of names before and yes, it was, therefore, available. The Charity Commissioners raised no objections to its generality, and so it was that *The Christian Trust* was registered in faith in 1976 – a name which would cover every possible eventuality that might transpire when developing the work God had put into my heart. God was preparing the way by having me put the legal foundations for the work in place, but more than that He was also preparing the way for the first major donation to the ministry – a donation through which God would put his totally supernatural imprint on the way He was going to fund the ministry. This was going to be His work!

One Sunday evening I was planned to preach at the local Methodist Church. There was only a small congregation as I poured my heart out, sharing the message God had given me. I always liked to illustrate some point in the sermon with a story from personal experience and for the first, and I believe only time, I chose to mention my hobby of stamp collecting in the sermon. After the service, a man spoke to me on the way out saying he had some stamps in the attic and asked if I would like to see them. I was always pleased to look at someone else's collection, even though most of the time such collections were not of a great deal of interest to a keen philatelist. But you never know!

During the week he brought an old stamp album round, together with a brown envelope containing portions of some small sheets of stamps. He left everything for me to look at. I quickly looked in the envelope and saw they were all stamps of Libya, not a country whose stamps were known to be of any significant interest or value, so I put them on one side, for the time being, and devoted my time to looking through the old album. It was certainly an interesting old-time collection.

I then turned to the Libyan stamps and got out my catalogue to check their value. Apart from the possible value of the stamps themselves, however, the collection of mint stamps was interesting for another reason. The man who owned the collection had been in charge of postal services for the British Army in Montgomery's North African Campaign during the second world war. He was with the troops that marched into Tripoli in January 1943. He was then delegated to take over the Post Office and part of his brief over the next few weeks was to remove all evidence of the Italian Occupation of Libya from the Post Office and turn it into a British Military Post Office.

Before destroying all the stamps that were in the safe he decided to tear some samples off from each different sheet as a souvenir of this historic North African campaign. He put them in a large envelope, between a couple of Army issue writing boards – and nearly forty years later handed me that self-same envelope to have a look at. It was the first time anyone had opened the envelope since the end of the war! It was an amazing story, but I had no expectation of finding anything there of great value. At some time during the war he had actually torn one stamp out of the corner of each block of stamps and stuck it onto a separate piece of paper – not with collector's stamp hinges, but with the stamp's own gum!

There is only one exceedingly rare Libyan stamp in the whole of Libyan postal history. There are two variants of the lowest five cent value in a particular set – one of which is worth a few pence and the other is so rare that the cataloguer had declined to put a value on it! The difference between the two designs is so small that a non-philatelist probably wouldn't even notice the difference.

I looked at each of the stamps that were stuck on that piece of army paper and was not surprised to see that the five cent value was the common one – although I did look carefully, just in case! I then took the blocks of mint stamps out of the envelopes. They were all in good condition and the higher values in the set were reasonably valuable. There was a missing stamp from each block where one specimen had been taken out and stuck on the paper. I was fascinated by the story of how these stamps had been carried from the theatre of war and I was now looking at them on my desk.

And then I had the most extraordinary moment in the whole of my philatelic career. I began to shake at what I was seeing, for when I examined the block of five cent stamps more carefully I saw that this was not a block of the common variety, but the rare one. I was staring at probably the rarest block of Libyan stamps that had ever been discovered – but more than that I was looking at a physical impossibility. There was absolutely no way that the stamp which had been torn from the block could be of a different design from the stamps in the block from which it had come! I was looking at a philatelic miracle!

In order to realise the value of stamps as rare as this, it's first necessary to get an expert certificate of genuineness. I took the stamps to London and they were pronounced genuine. I then took them to Stanley Gibbons, the world's foremost philatelic dealer, in what was a repeat episode of what my mother had done with her father, back in the early twenties in Johannesburg, when they found a sack of stamps under the floorboards of their home.

Stanley Gibbons had never seen such a block of these stamps before. Their expert valued them for purchase and they offered me £7000 (over £50,000 in 2017's money) – a massive amount of money for what, in reality, were just a few pieces of printed paper! As a stamp dealer, I knew that if Stanley Gibbons could make a profit after buying them at this price, so could I. But how could I personally make a profit from what was clearly a God-ordained miracle which had come to light through me preaching the Gospel? That definitely wouldn't be right.

On returning home I shared with the man the sequence of events and he was as amazed and shocked as I was at the whole story. I told him the story of the bent Alvis chassis and of the vision God had given me for a work, through which God would bring healing to hurting people and broken lives, and I decided to ask if he would be willing for the newly formed charity, *The Christian Trust,* to buy the stamps, instead of Stanley Gibbons, so that I could use my philatelic expertise to sell them and put any profit into the newly formed Charity. He gladly agreed and I then had to borrow the money from my publishing business and loan it to The Christian Trust, so that the Charity could buy the stamps.

Over the next twelve months I was able to sell the stamps for The Christian Trust and I decided to invest the profits in a small house so that the Charity could benefit from what were then appreciating property values. I was able to provide a small home for two elderly Christian ladies who were thrilled at the opportunity of having a bungalow in Silverdale. In time they both died, and by this time the work of Ellel Ministries was well established, but desperately in need of significant funding for the development of the work. Properties had shot up in value in the late seventies, eighties and nineties and when the house was eventually sold it brought in a donation of £125,000 for the ministry at a critical time for the work.

I will never know or understand how God miraculously changed a block of common stamps into the much rarer variety – but the common variety stuck on the separate piece of paper was proof that this is what had actually happened. When I look back now at that extraordinary sequence of events I marvel at the totally supernatural way God arranged for the very first financial contribution to the work of The Christian Trust to be received.

At almost exactly the same time as I was conceived in England, early in 1943, God was at work in Libya making supernatural provision for the work of Ellel Ministries! Even today when I think about this, I stand amazed at the miracle I discovered in that brown army envelope! It's a constant reminder that God is able to do over and above anything we can ever dream of.

While all these things were happening, back in The Construction Press another big change lay ahead. It is never easy to fund the capital needs of a developing publishing company at the same time as paying the overheads, book production costs, staff salaries and, as well, supporting one's family with a personal salary taken out of the business. Every month there were serious financial pressures and although there were many times that God answered our cries for help, in what were sometimes quite remarkable ways, finding the money to pay all the bills was a constant pressure. There was also a niggling concern, deep down in my spirit, that the demands of the publishing business were such that one day they might conflict with the healing vision that kept on coming to the forefront of my mind. It would be very difficult to run a new ministry and a busy publishing company at the same time. And surely, it can't be long now, I would say to myself, on many occasions, as I prayed on my daily drive to and from work.

Then, right out of the blue, an answer to my increasing concern came through a surprising phone call. I was approached by the Longman Group, one of the most distinguished and respected educational publishers in the world, to ask if I might be interested in selling The Construction Press and working for Longman's. They were looking to expand the Architecture and Construction side of their publishing list and they saw The Construction Press as a natural fit with their company.

Although Longman's were based in Harlow, in the south of the country, they were happy to give me a five year salaried contract to continue running the company in the north where I lived. This suited me well, for the arrangement provided The Construction Press with the working capital to develop the business and me with a secure salary. But my contract did tie me in to running the company for another five years – which pushed the time when God might open the doors for the vision to become reality to at least 1983! More frustration – and more patience needed! I would be forty years old by then – could God possibly use me to start something new when I was so old? I took comfort from the fact that Moses was eighty when his destiny fulfilment came – but I did pray that I wouldn't have to wait that long!

At the end of my contract, Longmans made it clear that they wanted me to stay as Managing Director of The Construction Press, but the time had come to move the whole operation to Harlow. The Construction Press was moving south, but I definitely wasn't! I knew that God had so clearly led us to the Lancaster area and if Longmans wanted the company in Harlow then they would have to find someone else to run it. For the third time in my short career I resigned a secure and very well paid job in favour of trusting God with an unknown future.

I organised the transfer of the company to Harlow for Longmans and said goodbye to what had been a very significant part of my life. My educational and publishing adventure into the world of architecture and building had come to an end. I packed up my office at the Old Workhouse, put the property on the market and got myself deeply involved in the other business that I really loved – the growing second-hand and antiquarian bookshop, that was now so well known it was being written about in up-market magazines and even the BBC featured it in one of their most popular radio programmes!

Chapter 5

THE VISION IN SIGHT

Encountering the Holy Spirit

1979 proved to be a significant watershed. When I said goodbye to Longmans and watched as all the property of *The Construction Press* headed south down the motorway, it was as if God was liberating me from any external responsibilities and commitments. I sensed He wanted me to be free. Surely, I thought, this must now be the time when God intends the work of restoring broken lives to begin!

The Carnforth Bookshop was under good management and was providing us with some income. The children were growing rapidly and loving village life. We had moved to a larger house, right next door to our original home in Silverdale, and added one of Sam's puppies, Job, to the family menagerie – which also included an ancient tortoise, given to me at the age of nine by a neighbour, when we moved to Cheam. Originally there were two tortoises, Oswald and Mr Jinks, but only Mr Jinks survives today – he's somewhere about 117 years old and I've looked after him for well over 60 of those years!

But no matter how hard I looked, I couldn't see where or how the work, which was now coming to fruition in my spirit, could begin. So I settled down to another season of active waiting – more marking time as I started another cycle of trusting God to show me what He wanted me to do when He was ready. I was learning at each stage of the journey, that it was only when I was resting patiently in Him that He could show me the next step.

Following the sale of my company, this was the first time in my life that I had any spare money and my thoughts turned once again to the Speed 20, which was still languishing in the garage. In order to get the steel frame of the chassis repaired I had had to get a copy of the blueprint from the Alvis company, so that the engineers could heat treat the steel and bend it back into exactly the right dimensions. Looking at a huge pile of bits and pieces which made up the rest of the car was a bit daunting to me as an amateur engineer without something to copy and I needed another driveable example of the car that I could use like the picture of a jigsaw, to help me put the bits back together as they should be. The example I found had been built only a few months apart from my own precious wreck and I thrilled once again to the vision of seeing it back on the road as I drove FG 8989 home. What I didn't know at the time was that I had bought the very car which, unbeknown to me, had been critical to the restoration of the bent chassis!

On the night of the 15th November 1940 the German Luftwaffe targeted Coventry. For ten hours relays of enemy aircraft dropped bombs indiscriminately on the city. One of the many buildings hit included the 14th century cathedral, which was all but destroyed. Hundreds of other buildings and companies were obliterated in a night which demolished 4330 homes and three-quarters of the city's factories – including Alvis. The Alvis factory took a direct hit and all the company's precious records went up in flames.

The work of rebuilding the factory began the very next day and the company was soon back in production making vital aircraft engines and armoured cars till the war was over. But when peace returned and cars were again the focus of the company's production, the technical department began the work of replacing all the vital engineering drawings which had been destroyed, so that they could continue to service and restore classic Alvis cars of the pre-war period, including the Speed 20. The company bought an example of the Speed 20, totally dismantled it and using the chassis frame as their model reconstructed a set of blue-prints. Incredibly the Speed 20 they had used for this pain-staking operation was FG 8989, the very car that thirty years later I was to buy and use as a model for putting DG 8625 back together!

Apart from doing some work on the Alvis, it was during this season that I spent more time with the books and stamps in Carnforth Bookshop, something that I really enjoyed doing. I loved, especially, the adventure of finding rare books among the collections we bought. On one occasion I was shown a huge quantity of books stacked in tea chests in a rather smelly stable. You could hardly call it a collection or a library, it was just an accumulation that had been dumped in a rather unsavoury place – at least for books! The chests were open to the air and the books at the top of each chest were liberally sprinkled with straw laced with significant quantities of manure. I was not very hopeful of finding anything interesting. Slowly I cleared away the mess and tried to assess what the books might be worth. Then I had one of those unforgettable 'Eureka' moments!

Allegedly, Archimedes, around 1200 years ago in ancient Greece, had shouted "Eureka!" when sudden revelation hit him as he climbed into his bath. He had been wrestling with the scientific problem of how to measure the volume of an irregular object when he realised that the volume of bath water he displaced must be equivalent to the volume of his own body that was beneath the water. Ever since, the weight of ships has been measured by their displacement of water and the scientific world has remembered the discovery of Archimedes Principle, celebrated by his naked run through the town shouting *'Eureka'!*

For the times in which he lived, about 250 BC, this was an extraordinary revelation and the Greek word *'Eureka'* says it all – meaning *a cry of joy or satisfaction on making a significant discovery.* As I pulled a first edition of Lewis Carroll's *Alice in Wonderland* out of a tea chest, followed by a lot of other interesting and valuable nineteenth century books from which I needed to blow or brush off the straw and manure, the smile on my face grew wider and wider. There were many *'Eureka'* moments, as I sat there on a pile of straw bales reeking of manure, examining the treasures I had discovered.

Finding that almost pristine copy of a first edition of *Alice in Wonderland* took me straight back to my Christ Church library days, when I had been custodian of all the Lewis Carroll items stored there, from the time when this uniquely creative mathematics don and clergyman lived and would tell his fanciful stories to the children of the Dean. I never tired of the adventure of discovery, when looking at collections of books and stamps and for a period of time I was content to lose myself in the adventure. After all, I had to do something while waiting for whatever it was that God had for me round the next corner.

I still have the very first real book discovery I ever made – it was, in fact, the very first second-hand book that I ever bought at the age of twelve. I was on one of my stamp-selling exploits on the way home from School. There was on old book dealer in Sutton who put racks of bargain books on a shelf outside his shop. I'd walked past his store on many occasions, but for a reason that, with the benefit of hindsight I can only construe was God-inspired, I decided on this occasion to stop and have a look. I picked up a really old book – the outside boards were a bit battered and falling off, but all the pages were there and it was dated 1644. I'd never touched anything so old before.

I didn't understand its significance at the time – to me it was just a very, very old book and I thought it deserved a better home than a sixpenny bargain rack! The book was one of the very early English editions of probably the most important theological book of the Reformation – Martin Luther's commentary on Galatians – the book which alerted a generation to the corruption and deception which had become endemic in the church of his day. I knew who Martin Luther was and thought it would be fun to own such an old book by such a famous person. I didn't know that the book was of priceless significance, being the first book printed in England to set out so clearly the heart of the Gospel message as expounded by Paul in his letter to the Galatians. After the Bible it was probably one of the most important Christian books to have been published in the last five hundred years! What a title God chose with which to begin my personal book collection!

I picked it up, marched into the shop, put my sixpence down on the counter and walked out clutching a treasure! I still have the book on my shelves, exactly as it was on the day I took it home. Rebound, the book could be worth up to a thousand pounds in today's money – but it's not for sale! That book was instrumental in giving me a love for old books and, many years later, was a source of encouragement and inspiration when I realised how, so early in my life, God had been using that unlikely purchase, to prepare me for the later stages of my Christian journey.

One day, I was sitting at the desk in the shop, mulling over the frustration of being the custodian of a vision that was going nowhere, when I suddenly found myself entertaining yet another crazy idea – although by now I had ceased to call God's ideas crazy, even though, from man's point of view, they sometimes are! Who would have disagreed with Joshua if, when he was writing his autobiography (the book of Joshua!), he hadn't been tempted to say that *"suddenly I had a crazy idea, let's put the music group at the head of the army and march seven times round the walls of Jericho, blowing our trumpets, and see what happens!"* On the face of it, it was madness personified – except it was God! And how about that day when the young boy David went to do battle against Goliath with a leather sling and five small stones. The people thought he was mad, and before long they would have been expecting to have to bury what was left of him, but it was God! And then there was the day when Jesus looked at the five barley loaves and two small fish He'd been given, and told twelve big men to take a bit each and go and feed five thousand men, together with their families. Doesn't sound like a good idea to me! Except it was Jesus who told them to do it!

As I sat at my desk staring at thousands of second-hand books, with many piles of incoming stock littering the floor, I sensed God telling me to start a prayer meeting – right here, in the shop! But, Lord, why here? There are lots of good church buildings nearby, or even private homes around. Why can't we meet there? God was silent. And *"OK, Lord,"* became the equally silent response in my heart. *"But are you sure, Lord, that's really what you want me to do?"* I daren't say *"No!"*

I picked up a piece of paper and began to write. In my mind I saw all the Christian leaders, ordained and lay leaders of the churches in the area, all of them working independently on their own little moat-surrounded Christian island. I set out the purpose of the letter – to invite them to a prayer meeting – in a second-hand bookshop! *"Who would come to that,"* I was thinking. I explained that if as Christian Leaders we were wanting God to move by His Spirit in our area and start touching people with the Gospel, then spiritual principles and Christian history tell us that we needed to be praying together in unity of heart and purpose.

The message was simple, straightforward and without any gloss. I simply set out the need for us to be praying together for our area and offered the bookshop as a denominationally neutral venue, right at the centre of our community. I got out a map of Carnforth and district, drew an elongated ring around the town centre, taking in all the places that saw Carnforth as their nearest small town. I mailed the letter to every church minister, and everyone else I either knew, or had heard of in the area, who was involved in some form of Christian work, without consideration for denomination or whether or not I agreed with their theology or they with mine!

I had no idea what to expect when the day for the meeting came. The time of the meeting, close of business at 5.30pm, was not the usual time for Christian meetings – surely God could only bless mid-week meetings that began at 7.30pm, I might have thought! Whether it was the unusual location, sheer curiosity or people were genuinely being moved by the Spirit of God, the second-hand department of Carnforth Bookshop overflowed with people. There had never been so many people in the shop at the same time and for a moment I began to worry about whether the ancient timbers that supported the floors could take the strain!

It was a remarkable collection of people, most of whom had never met each other before, who were hovering uneasily among the piles of books. Leaders from all denominations and none were there – from Baptists to Catholics and Anglicans to Pentecostals – all drawn by the simple invitation to start praying together for their area, in a venue which wasn't labelled by any of their traditions. It was the most unusual prayer meeting I'd ever been to – and two of the people who came were to have a huge influence on the direction of my own life. I shared with everyone why I had invited them all to come and people really prayed together in unity for the district. I didn't know it at the time, but that prayer meeting was to prove one of the most strategic of personal steps towards the fulfilment of the vision. I couldn't fight back all the tears as I surveyed the scene and realised how stupid I'd been for thinking it was a mad idea!

People who would never normally be relating together were fervently praying for God to move by His Spirit in the area. Everyone (or at least everyone who said anything!) wanted to repeat the experience. The group began to meet every couple of months or so and that meeting proved to be the starting point for a whole series of Kingdom initiatives in the area. Only in eternity will we fully comprehend the extent of the work God was doing in bringing that unique group of people together to pray regularly in a second-hand bookshop for the area in which they were serving the Lord. The two people who were later to have such a significant influence on my own journey were Sister Aine – the Catholic nun who was now running the terminal care hospice in Silverdale and Edgar Pye, the Managing Director of one of the largest Christian businesses in the area, W & J Pye Ltd, and a highly respected Christian leader.

All my background Christian experience had been in evangelical churches whose brand of theology was very conservative. This usually meant that they were resistant to any expression of the work of the Spirit in the present day, and any mention of both the baptism of the Holy Spirit and the practise of the gifts of the Spirit in today's church was systematically resisted. But I knew in my heart that there was something missing – both from church life in general and my own personal experience of the Lord in particular. I was looking for more and was beginning to realise that unless I discovered 'the more' – whatever that was, the work that was still bubbling away in vision, in my heart, could never begin. I was in a cleft stick – I was desperate to move on with the vision, but I was bereft of a vital missing ingredient. I was like a car trying to go somewhere with no fuel in the tank!

As I began to hear stories of what God was doing in various parts of the world to bring renewal into some churches, I began to be more and more aware of the fact that I was singularly ignorant of the work of the Holy Spirit. There was something seriously missing in my life and I began to be desperate as I looked to the Lord for answers to my growing problem. The first step towards an answer came in a rather unusual way.

Various boxes of second-hand books were waiting to be sorted and I was working through these one at a time. There were a lot to do, but the next box stopped me in my tracks and I don't think anything else got done that day! They were all books that had been published around the turn of the twentieth century. They were up to a hundred years old and the pages had clearly not been turned for a very long time. Every book in that particular box was about the work of the Holy Spirit and hailed from the beginnings of the Pentecostal churches in America in about 1906 or even earlier. None of them were well known titles, most had been published privately by people who were determined to get an important message out.

I not only browsed through the books, I began to read them avidly, almost oblivious to who was coming and going in the shop. Here was a box of books that were not going to get put on the open shelves for sale. They had already been sold – to me! I had no idea where the box of books came from – they were just there. One in particular was called *Signs and Wonders* and was all about the things *God Wrought in the Ministry for Forty Years* by someone I'd never heard of before, Mrs M.B. Woodworth-Etter, Evangelist. It was published in London in 1918 at a cost of two shillings and six-pence, an expensive book for those days. But this was a condensed version of the original much larger book published in America.

Any caution I might have had about its contents was swept away by what Stanley Smith had written about Mrs Etter and her book in the opening pages. Stanley Smith was one of the Cambridge Seven who had been called with C.T.Studd (of cricketing fame), through the ministry of D.L.Moody to leave everything behind and go to China and serve with Hudson Taylor in the *China Inland Mission*. It was through C.T.'s brother, Sir Kynaston Studd, that my Mum and Dad had met, and G.B.Studd, the other Studd brother, was quoted as saying, *"I know Mrs Etter and her work first-hand. She was at our Los Angeles meetings last year and there were many wonderful healings. She is sound of faith and mightily used of God, and has been so for years. I have known many other reliable saints who have known her work for years."*

Stanley Smith said of her book, *"I value this next to my Bible . . . it is a present day record of 'The Acts' multiplied. Mrs Etter has had a ministry of healing since 1885, her call as an evangelist being some years previous to this. I venture to think that this ministry is unparalleled in the history of the church for which I give all the glory to the Lord Jesus Christ . . . this ministry should be made known, for the glory of the Triune God and the good of believers."*

As I read these words and dipped into the book God certainly got my attention. If Mrs Etter's ministry came with such strong commendations, from people I knew could be respected and trusted, I couldn't understand why I'd never heard of her before. I devoured her book, and the many others that I found in that treasure chest of material that God had put before me in a box of old books, but there was a problem! Every book I read made me even more desperate for the same reality that I was reading about in the books. I now knew, for certain, that there would be no way I could ever enter a ministry of healing without being baptised in the Holy Spirit. This wasn't an optional extra for a strange band of people called Pentecostals, but a present-day necessity for anyone who wanted to live and move in the presence and power of the Holy Spirit. God was on my case – yet again!

But nothing seemed to happen. I was ready, but where was God?

One Sunday evening I sat in Silverdale Methodist Church waiting for the service to begin. I was privately praying and crying out to God for an answer to my present dilemma. Bruce was quietly praying on the organ and I was sitting right up against the pitch-pine wooden panels at the right-hand side of the church. Suddenly I was aware of God speaking to me – it was like an audible voice speaking right into my ear out of the wooden panel! There could be no-one else there between me and the wall – it had to be God. And the message was simple, *"Go home and read your Bible."* That was it. Nothing else.

Initially I was a little angry with God, if that was all He had to say! I'd been reading a portion of the Bible every day since I was a small boy. I was already more familiar with the Bible than any other book I'd ever owned or read. What did God mean by telling me to go home and read it some more? Wasn't He satisfied with what I was already doing? Of course, I never spoke out these things, but the thoughts were certainly in my heart. By the time the service was over I'd repented of my initial attitude and when I got home I settled down to read the Bible just like I would read any other book, from beginning to end. Excepting that I did decide that as my problem was definitely a New Testament issue, I'd start with the Gospel of Matthew instead of the book of Genesis!

I read through the whole of Matthew, the whole of Mark and I was just preparing to start on the Gospel of Luke when I was arrested by the last few verses of Mark's Gospel and I could go no further. I had found what God was wanting me to discover *"These signs will accompany those who believe . . . they will cast out demons . . . they will lay their hands on sick people who will be healed."* (from Mark 16:17-18).

I looked at my hands – I knew they were just ordinary hands, but I knew, too, God was saying that under the anointing of His Holy Spirit signs will follow those who believe. I was frightened of getting involved in anything that wasn't of God – but desperate for everything that was of Him. I read on through Luke and John's Gospels and into the Acts of the Apostles when, once again, I was arrested by the Lord at Acts 1:8, *"You will receive power when the Holy Spirit comes upon you."* These words, spoken originally to the apostles were clearly meant to be a general provision for the whole of the Body of Christ, as was very soon to be made clear on the Day of Pentecost, when over 3000 were baptised in the Holy Spirit. I knew that this was what I needed – and desperately.

Over the next few days I kept on thinking about all the books I had just read and did everything I could to get baptised in the Holy Spirit – my way! I took our dogs out in the fields and tried to force my way into an experience of speaking with tongues, in a place where no-one could hear me! And even if they did, they would just think I was training the dogs! But all that came out of my mouth were forced noises of no consequence. Nothing was happening.

I knew there was a promised land of the vision that wouldn't go away, somewhere out there. But there was still a gulf separating me from its reality. I desperately didn't want anything artificial – I only wanted, as the Coca-Cola adverts sometimes called their drink, *"the real thing!"* I was spiritually exhausted as I reached the end of myself. I had tried everything I knew to get hold of what God's Word said and it seemed as though God was either on strike or gone away on holiday. It wasn't fair! Or was it, perhaps, that God was equally desperately trying to teach me an even more important lesson?

I had to get to the end of myself and stop trying to do God's work my way! Deep down I said something like this, *"OK, Lord. I know what I want, but seeing as You don't seem to be giving it to me, I'm giving up. I can't do Your work without Your Spirit and I'm through with trying to tap into the pipes of Heaven and get a private supply through the back door! I only want what's real.*

Maybe all those people who've tried to put me off believing for the vision were right and it's all going nowhere – but Lord, I do love You and I will always want to serve You – just let me know anytime you need me. I'll be ready. And if you really do want to baptise me in your Holy Spirit, I'm here, waiting!" And with that I gave up trying, was at the end of myself and, strangely, was also at peace. It was now up to God and I didn't have to wait long. I was learning that when we do God's work God's way, He comes running to pour out His blessing.

It was only a few nights later that I was in bed earlier than usual and quickly fell into a very deep sleep. Suddenly I was instantly out of my sleep and totally alert. Everything around me was hot and burning. All my alarm buttons were instantly pressed – it was so hot I thought the house must be on fire. Instinctively I put out my hand to grab the phone and call the fire brigade. I was about to dial 999 (911 in the USA) when I began to think a bit more rationally. There was no noise, no smoke and no smell of burning, so it couldn't be a fire. I sank back onto my pillow and tried to sort out what was happening. I was already praying and beginning to ask the Lord what it all meant.

His reply, as usual in very non-religious language, was just whispered into my spirit, *"It's OK, it's only Me!"* God used words that He knew would mean something special to me. When I was a child my Mum would sometimes go out shopping, leaving me alone in the house. Whenever she returned home, and opened the door, she would call out to me, saying, *"It's OK, it's only me."* And immediately I heard those words I knew that it was the owner of the house who had come in and I was safe. In using those words when He baptised me with His Holy Spirit, God was assuring me that it was the owner of the House who was in residence and I was safe in Him.

I was so overwhelmed by the Lord's presence as he baptised me in His Holy Spirit that I felt, almost literally, as if I was on fire! And God was doing a deep cleansing work in me, as the flames of Holy Spirit fire burned within. I knew that I would never be the same again after this experience. A few nights later I discovered that I was able to speak in tongues without the effort of trying to make it happen, as I worshipped God in a new language. My spiritual world had suddenly gone from black and white to 3D and technicolour!

I was about to discover a whole new world of spiritual reality. It wasn't that I didn't previously know the Lord, or had never heard His voice speaking to me, for I had, on many occasions, but I was beginning to discover the reality of what it meant to be using the gifts of the Spirit In normal everyday life. I felt like a learner driver who had just got behind the wheel of a new car and was on his own for the first time! I wondered what this might mean for me on this unpredictable journey of faith.

Through the committee meetings of the Silverdale Inter-Church Fellowship, I was getting to know the Catholic representative, Sister Aine, quite well. The Irish sparkle in her eye, her unrelenting commitment to her work in caring for the patients in the hospice, but above all her love for Jesus and her desire to serve Him, endeared her to everyone who knew her. She had that extraordinary ability to bridge the gaps to all the denominations and even those who, from their reformed theological position, might want to question some of the doctrines of the Catholic Church, could never question her personal relationship with the Lord and the powerful evidence of the Holy Spirit moving freely in and through her life.

Up until this time I had kept the vision I was nurturing very much to myself. I'd learnt the hard way that it wasn't easy for others to relate to what was burning within me. On several occasions I had been really hurt by the dismissive way in which some people had reacted, when I tried to share with them the core of what I believed God was preparing me for. But there were some who listened with their spirit to what I was trying to say and, notwithstanding the seeming impossibility of God using an ex-University Lecturer businessman to start a healing ministry, they encouraged me to press on in faith, no matter how impossible it may seem.

One of those who encouraged me was Chris Mungeam, my life-long friend from days in the Young People's Fellowship at Cheam Baptist. This was a really tough time in his life as he was coming to terms with discovering that his wife was in another relationship and his marriage had fallen apart as a result. Those in need never have a problem with the ministry of healing – they are desperate for the Lord's intervention in their lives and Chris was no exception. Although I was so inexperienced, the time we spent talking and praying together was precious, and standing together with Chris deepened and strengthened our friendship.

But some of the rebuffs I received from others were very challenging and threw me firmly back on the Lord, to test with Him once again whether or not I really had heard from Him about this vision. I needed a very clear word from Him that I hadn't been believing all these years for a fruitless dream, instead of a God-given vision. If it was the former then it would never come to pass and I could spend the rest of my life in permanent frustration. At this time, another man of my own age committed himself to praying with me on a regular basis. His life was coming to a crossroads as well and so we decided to meet and pray together every Saturday morning at 6.00am until we had come to a place of peace about our respective callings.

Those were precious meetings as we shared with each other what we sensed God had been saying to us during the previous week. I will never forget the Saturday morning when, with the usual cup of coffee in his hand, he began our conversation by lifting his head, looking me in the eyes and saying, *"Your vision, Peter, I know now that it really is from God. You mustn't give it up."* We had shared deeply over the months and during that week God had spoken clearly to him. His words came like a blanket of love and comfort from the Lord – I wasn't mad after all!

Another person who helped me greatly at that time was Alan Redpath, one of the most well-loved Senior Pastors in the Body of Christ who was then living quite close to me at Capernwray Bible School. His ministry had included being Pastor of one of the most well-known Baptist Churches in England, Duke Street, Richmond, and a ten year spell at the Moody Church in Chicago. He was kind enough to offer to help and he invited me to pray with him on a regular basis. We would carve out a couple of hours once a month from our diaries and just fellowship together. Maybe it was because he himself had gone through some bouts of severe depression in his own life, that he was far more sympathetic to the healing ministry than most other evangelical leaders might have been in that season of church history.

I was in my late thirties when, at one of our meetings, he said that in his experience most of the people he had known whom God had called into a specific ministry, were at least forty before their work began. They needed all those years of preparation for God to get them ready for what would lie ahead. I took great encouragement from Alan's wisdom, which helped moderate the constant frustration I felt at having to spend so many years marking time! I wasn't quite forty yet, so perhaps I hadn't missed what God had planned after all!

From time to time Sister Aine would invite me to lead a Bible Study for some of the Sisters who were the nursing staff at the hospital. After the meetings we would share a cup of tea in the convent kitchen and I decided to risk telling her of my vision and hoped and prayed she wouldn't reject me as a friend as a result. I told her all about the vision I had been nurturing for so long. It was such a relief when she said that she had no doubts whatsoever that the vision was from God. It sometimes takes a person who has already risked all for God, to understand the heart of someone else who was daring to do the same.

One day Sister Aine called me on the phone. She had someone coming to the convent for prayer who was very depressed and in need of help. She didn't know how to pray for the lady and she wondered if I could come and pray with her as well. We spent quite a long time listening to her problems. She told us all about the symptoms she was experiencing. Her life truly was in a mess.

But as I listened to her story, and watched as Sister Aine talked with her, it felt as though the Lord was showing me something else, which kept on coming to the front of my mind and the more I tried to dismiss it the more strongly the thought would return. I was experiencing my first ever word of knowledge in a ministry situation. How could I possibly share what the Lord was saying to me, especially in front of a nun!

I knew that the things she was already talking about were not the real issue – the real root of her problems lay somewhere else, in a place that she either wasn't willing to go to or she was too afraid to talk about, which is often the case when dealing with abuse victims, who can often be under a threat of secrecy. But the Lord kept on prompting me *to tell her that you know what her problem really is*. It took a lot of courage for me to eventually broach the subject and ask her if there had been someone close to her who had been sexually abusing her.

Today sexual abuse and its consequences is talked about almost on a daily basis in the media. Hardly a day seems to go by when some fresh revelation hits the headlines about yet another famous person who has used their position of trust to violate a young girl or boy. But that was not the case in those days and up to that moment I don't think I had personally ever mentioned the words 'sexual abuse' to anyone else – and certainly not in front of a nun! I was terribly shy, very nervous, but had learned the hard way not to ignore a spiritual urge when it comes, and this was definitely a spiritual urge to use the word of knowledge God had given me!

Up to that moment the lady had been gently sobbing in her seeming hopelessness, but as I spoke out those words she suddenly stopped crying, looked up at me as if she had been shot, her jaw dropped wide open and in a state of trembling fear and shock she said, *"How did you know?"* Her first thought was that someone must have told me, for the abuse was a terrible secret which she didn't want anyone to know about – she was trying to get help through having prayer for her symptoms, without coming into the open about what she was really going through, probably through fear of her abuser.

This was a new experience for me. Never before had the Lord given me a direct word of knowledge like that, for someone else, as a means of getting to the root of the real problem. This was my first experience of how God can use the gifts of the Spirit to unlock problems in other people's lives. For this lady, it was the first and most critical step on her journey to healing. When I simply told her that no person had told me about the abuse, but that God had spoken it into my heart, it was a huge encouragement to her. Probably for the first time in her Christian walk she really knew that God loved her enough to care about what was happening in her life. She took the biggest possible step towards her healing that night, as she forgave her abuser. Sister Aine and I kept on looking at each other in amazement as we watched what God was doing to bring healing into this lady's life.

The time over a cup of tea that night, in the convent kitchen, was rather longer than on previous occasions. It felt as though the Lord had removed all barriers in my heart to sharing everything that He had given me so far about the vision. I found I was sharing things that I hadn't even thought through myself before but, as I shared them, it felt as though I'd known about them all my life. I told

Sister Aine how I felt God wanted me to be running a special centre where people in need could come for personal prayer away from the often damaging environment they were living in. We bounced ideas off each other and I forget how many cups of tea we drank, but as I climbed into my car that night I was absolutely thrilled and overjoyed at what God had done – it seemed as though God had fired a starting gun in Heaven which had been heard on Earth and that the race of my life had, at last, begun.

What happened next electrified my spirit and has been motivating me ever since. I could take you to the very spot on my short journey home from the hospice where, once again, I heard the unmistakeable voice of God. There were many occasions when the Lord had spoken directly into my life. My various business experiences had been an excellent training ground for learning to recognise God's voice. But on this occasion it filled the car and I had to pull over to the side of the road. I was overwhelmed by God's presence, as I tried to take in what God was saying. I knew I'd never forget that moment, but I was desperate to write down what God had said, just in case!

The words were simple, straightforward, non-religious but very specific, *"I want you to spend the rest of your life bringing healing to those in need and teaching others how to do it."* The first part of the word was to be expected, especially in view of having just seen God bring deep and profound healing into one lady's life. But the second part was new – and it was this part of the word that made sense of those five years that God had me learning the craft of teaching. I don't remember the rest of the journey home, but the words *'rest of my life'* were resonating through my spirit. This wasn't a calling from which I could ever retire!

I don't think I slept much that night as adrenaline surged through my body and kept me thinking about all the ramifications of running a centre of healing. But spiritual adrenaline was also charging through my spirit, as the excitement of realising that God had now spoken so clearly made me think, again wrongly, that the work must be just about to start. What was actually about to start was yet another intensive personal training school that would give me many opportunities to learn from God about leadership and to build relationships with other Christian leaders all over the country, many of whom would play strategic roles in helping bring the vision to its fulfilment.

Fred and Bertha Horrobin's wedding. My English Grandparents.

Grandpa Horrobin with Wiliam (Uncle) Grundy, CIM Missionary.

Uncle Grundy home from China with the Horrobin brothers and family.

Dad, aged 3, with Granny and Grandpa Horrobin.

Your friend,

R.Hudson Pope.

Children's evangelist, R.Hudson Pope – my 'spiritual grand-father'.

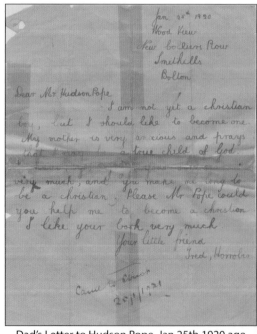

Dad's Letter to Hudson Pope, Jan 25th 1920 age almost 10, telling the evangelist that he wanted to become a Christian. Annotated by Hudson Pope: "Came to Christ 26/1/1921."

Dad, aged 13, wth his home-made radio receiver with which he was the first in Bolton
to hear that Bolton Wanderers had won the 1923 FA Cup Final at Wembley.

Fred and Bertha Horrobin with son Fred age about 23.

Dad, age 24, teaching carpentry and joinery to an
eager group of apprentice boys.

The South African family, 1935. Oupa and Ouma (grandparents) with their
two daughters Isobel and Betty (Mum).

Oupa in his dress police uniform, as worn for
the Royal Visit of the Prince of Wales – 1925.

Mum – on the day she met Dad in
Switzerland.

Mum and Dad's wedding – Pretoria, 26th January 1938.

Peter, with Mum, aged about two.

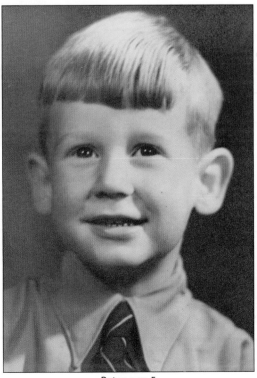

Peter, age 5.

Three generations of Horrobins, Morecambe beach, 1947.

Age 7, with Uncle Will and family.

With both sets of Grandparents – Bolton 1950.

Peter, the enthusiastic young
cricketer, age 7.

Age 11 at St Dunstan's Primary
School, Cheam.

A Cricketing family – Peter, Dad and brother David.

Granny Horrobin – age 90.

Oxford Graduation Day.

Christ Church, Oxford during the big freeze of 1962-63.

The Horrobin family – on the day of brother David's wedding.

Oxford College room at Christ Church.

Alvis Speed 20 – the picture that sparked the vision!

The remains of my Alvis Speed 20 – as bought for £50 in 1970.

A stage in the journey of restoration.

Alvis Speed 20 – some of the wrecked
bits and pieces.

Alvis Speed 20

Alvis Speed 20 engine restored ...

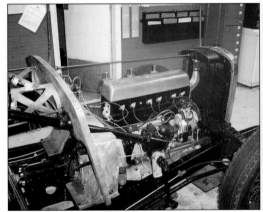

... and installed on the chassis.

Starting the work of rebuilding the body.

The young publisher – checking proofs at the printers (1974).

Carnforth Bookshop – the original premises.

Sorting mountains of books at Carnforth.

With George Verwer at the opening of the Lancaster Christan Bookshop 1982.

Mission England Leaders Conference 1982.
With Selwyn Hughes (CWR), Gavin Reid (National Director) and
Bishop Bill Flagg (Chairman of Mission England, North West).

MIssion England Praise.
The song book for Mission England.

Mission England – with the Liverpool team and Billy Graham, 1984.

Mission England meeting at Anfield, Liverpool Football Stadium.

A Centre for
Christian Healing, Counselling and Training

Ellel Grange
THE CHRISTIAN TRUST

A PERSONAL WORD FROM THE DIRECTOR

It is my privilege to introduce you to the work of Ellel Grange. Specialising in Christian Counselling and Healing it will be a place of training for these important ministries and a place where personal help will always be available to those in need.

People today are not only in need of physical healing. There are also those who are suffering the consequences of broken homes, child abuse, drug addiction, pornography and the occult — to quote but a few of today's damaging influences. Their effect can be beyond comprehension to those who are not affected — but for those who are, we believe that the Christian healing ministry is the only long-lasting answer. That is why the establishment and work of Ellel Grange is of such vital importance at the present time.

We are thankful to God for the vision He has given for this work and for the provision of an ideal building in an outstandingly convenient location. For the ministry to become established, however, it will require the determined commitment and generous giving of many people. Will you join those who are already committed to its fulfilment by giving careful consideration to the contents of this brochure?

Peter Horrobin

Peter Horrobin

The whole cost of producing this brochure has been met by an anonymous donation.

THE VISION

The vision for a healing and training centre in the North West of England originated about ten years ago. Since then a small group of Christians in the region have been praying and working towards its fulfilment. Now, with wide support from within the region, encouragement from national Christian leaders and with a suitable building in prospect, the vision can be realised.

The healing and counselling ministry that will be conducted at Ellel Grange will be interdenominational in foundation and practice. It will be firmly based on the love of God, the saving and healing power of Jesus Christ, the work of the Holy Spirit and the teaching of Scripture.

The ministry will be conducted by a resident team of people who are experienced in the counselling and healing ministries. They will be assisted by individuals from right across the region who will help to provide the 24-hour ministry cover on a rota basis, and a large team of Associate Counsellors who will share in the ministry from time to time as occasion demands.

The whole ministry will be conducted under the guidance of the Advisory Board and with the encouragement and support of the Council of Reference. The work is administered by The Christian Trust (Registered Charity No. 273927).

* HEALING AND COUNSELLING
* TRAINING COURSES
* RETREATS * CONFERENCES

Ellel Grange – the first publicity brochure.

Ellel Grange front.

Ellel Grange from the air.

The Front Tower of Ellel Grange restored by John Allen as a prayer room.

Ellel Grange – the chapel in the grounds.

Ellel Grange rear.

Centre for Christian Healing, Counselling and Training

THE CHRISTIAN TRUST
Ellel Grange

NEWSLETTER 31st October 1986 **Number 4**

REJOICE! `Our God Reigns´

Completion on Schedule

Today, Friday the 31st October 1986, purchase contracts for the acquisition of Ellel Grange, the contents and the Chapel were completed on schedule on the agreed date. We rejoice and give thanks to God for His faithfulness.

The past few weeks have been very thrilling as the gap between the cash in hand and what was still needed steadily closed. Just nine days ago we needed a minimum of £56,000, plus pledges to support the repayments on an additional £35,000 of mortgage borrowing so as to bring the loan potential up to our agreed maximum of £175,000.

By last Saturday (one week to go) the cash gap had closed to £27,633 and just 48 hours ago it was £15,500. THE FINAL HURDLE WAS CLEARED LESS THAN TWELVE HOURS BEFORE THE DEADLINE. After taking into account the tax that will be recovered on covenants, enough pledges had also been received to cover repayments on the full £175,000 loan mortgage that is available to us. It was with a tremendous sense of relief and thankfulness, both to the Lord and all who have given, that we handed over cheques to our solicitors covering the full amount due.

At the last meeting of the Prayer Support Group a vision was shared that as the 31st October approached the trickle of money being received would become a stream which would then turn into a flood and finally a torrent. That vision has been fulfilled!

Daily Thanksgiving

We have been overwhelmed by the love and support that we have received from God´s people, both from within the North West region and also from the far flung corners of Great Britain. Throughout this period of seeing the vision for a regional centre become reality at Ellel Grange, the letters and gifts (many of which have clearly been very sacrificial) have been a tremendous encouragement to us.

Each day as the post has arrived, and telephone calls have come in, we have been able to say with the Psalmist:

"The steadfast love of the Lord never fails, His mercy is forever sure, it is new every morning. Great is your faithfulness O Lord."

It has been a privilege and a very humbling experience to be on the receiving end of so much love and encouragement. To all of you who have prayed, shared, worked, given or had any part whatsoever in the work of the past six months, we would say in the words of Scripture:

"We want you to know what God´s grace has accomplished. You gave as much as you could, and even more than you could.....It was more than we could have hoped for. You gave yourselves to the Lord; and then by God´s will, you gave yourselves to us as well.....And with all His abundant wealth through Christ Jesus, our God shall supply all your needs.....Indeed, you will receive a full measure, a generous helping, poured into your hands, all that you can hold."

198 Days

Contracts were signed on April 16th when deposits were handed over. Since that date 90,000 brochures (all paid for with an anonymous donation), 20,000 mini-leaflets, and 20,000 Newsletters have been distributed throughout the North West Region and beyond. Thousands of letters have been personally typed and many thousands more printed or

Ellel Grange purchased. The Rejoice Newsletter – 31 October 1986.

Peter, at the time of purchasing Ellel Grange.

My brother David – at the time of his ground-breaking donation.

Ellel Grange – Main entrance.

Mum and Dad sharing in the joy at the doors of Ellel Grange.

Chapter 6

MISSION ENGLAND

A Vital Diversion

Edgar Pye was both a very successful Lancaster business man and a very well-respected Christian leader. Our paths had crossed at various Christian meetings and he was an enthusiastic supporter of the Carnforth Book Shop prayer meetings. He saw them as a strategic development for the promotion of evangelism within the area.

It was shortly after the start of the Carnforth meetings that Edgar asked if he could come round and have a chat with me. He'd never done this before, so I knew there must be an item on his agenda! The agenda item turned out to be *Mission England*, which I hadn't yet heard of. I learnt from Edgar that for some time a small group of national leaders had been preparing the ground for another visit to England by Billy Graham in 1984, exactly thirty years after the 1954 Harringay meetings.

Billy Graham at Harringay had majorly impacted the nation. Since then there had been a series of subsequent missions across the years, in various parts of the UK such as Manchester, Glasgow, and London. Each one had been very successful as a one-off mission, but what was being planned for 1984 was much bigger. For the first time there would be a national campaign with six week-long events being planned in six major football stadia covering the whole country. The north-west of England meetings would be at Anfield, the home of Liverpool Football Club. Gavin Reid had been appointed the National Director of Mission England and Bishop Bill Flagg, the Assistant Bishop of Liverpool, had been appointed as the North-West Mission England Chairman.

I was certainly interested in all that Edgar was telling me, but where was the conversation heading? Edgar went on to explain that for Mission England each of the national regions had also been divided into areas, each one of which would be under the Chairmanship of a local leader. Carnforth fell in the North Lancashire and Cumbria region, which took in the whole of the Lake District. The bottom-line question that Edgar was asking was, *"Would you, Peter, be willing to consider becoming Chairman of the North Lancashire and Cumbria area of Mission England?"*

I had no idea what that would entail, but my mind slipped into overdrive as Edgar outlined all that could be involved in three years of prayer, planning and preparation for the main event at Anfield. Edgar had already seen how God had given me a vision for the area through the Carnforth Bookshop prayer meetings and was aware that I no longer had the publishing company and that I could, therefore, have available time. But he knew nothing of the vision for a ministry of healing that had been motivating me for over ten years. I had some praying to do. It was just the sort of work that I would enjoy doing – but was it what God wanted me to do? Was it a diversion from the vision – or was this the next stage of preparation for the vision? For me, these were very big questions.

I didn't give Edgar an immediate answer, but as I prayed I couldn't think of any good reason why I shouldn't take it on. God was not putting anything else forward for me to do and the only place of peace I could come to was to call Edgar, and say, *"Yes"*, even though it would mean another three years of marking time. But God had used every cycle of my Christian and business walk so far to widen my experience and perhaps this would be a God-ordained way of laying down further necessary foundations for the ministry that lay ahead. I particularly noted that Bishop Bill Flagg, whom I hadn't yet met, had also been appointed by Liverpool's Bishop David Shepherd to carry the diocesan responsibility for the healing ministry – I made a mental note to get to know him!

Each Area Chairman of Mission England had the freedom to organise their own programme of events in the years that preceded the main Mission Meetings at Anfield. Having begun to express my evangelistic concerns for the Carnforth area by setting up a series of prayer meetings at the shop, I felt strongly led by the Lord to do something similar right across my Mission England Area, which included the whole of the Lake District. The first of a series of what I called *Praise and Prayer Nights* for Mission England was held in Zion Baptist Church, Morecambe.

The plan was to share the vision for Mission England, then intersperse times of group prayer with songs of praise and worship, and finally bring the meeting to a close with an inspirational word. A good crowd attended that first event, but the worship times fell rather flat. We were limited to choosing items from the contents of the rather old Baptist Hymn Book, whereas most of the songs that people were singing, during those early years of what became known as the charismatic renewal, were missing. In my car on the way home, I was thanking God for the way the first meeting had gone, but was also mulling over the problem we had with the selection of songs for the times of praise and worship.

I was driving through Bolton-le-Sands, just north of Morecambe, when I had a sudden and complete revelation of what was needed, not just for our local area or the North-West region, but for the whole of the UK! I still had my 1954 Harringay Crusade Song Book. The hymns and songs between its pages became national favourites and it was not unusual in those extraordinary days in the fifties, for spontaneous choirs to strike up on the London Underground, singing hymns like *To God be the Glory* and *Blessed Assurance*! In 1954, people only became familiar with the songbook when they went to the Billy Graham meetings. But what if, I thought, we could have a national hymn and song book available two years ahead of the main events. It could become an inspirational and unifying agent for Christians from every sector of the Church, with items in the selection from all strands and traditions of the Body of Christ, so that everyone would feel at home with the music and be more welcoming to the whole concept and strategy for Mission England.

The whole idea seemed so obvious and straightforward that by the time I reached home the vision for the new book, which I'd already called *Mission England Praise*, was well formed in my thinking. The book would combine, in alphabetical sequence, hymns, choruses and the new generation of worship songs from all the different traditions and, at least in my mind, the whole concept was a done deal! This was a very big spiritual urge, the ramifications of which would spread far beyond anything I could ever have thought or dreamt of.

The next Praise and Prayer event had been planned for Barrow-in-Furness and I had already booked Gavin Reid, the National Director of Mission England to be the speaker. This was my opportunity to tell him about the vision for *Mission England Praise* in the hour-long car journey round the top of Morecambe Bay to Barrow. He said very little by way of response on the way to Barrow, as he was thinking about his message for the meeting. But we weren't long into our return journey when he said, *"I think that's a very good idea, Peter."* And before we had reached home, where he was staying the night with us, the work of compiling and publishing *Mission England Praise* as the national hymn and song book for Mission England had been added to my job brief!

If the vision was going to work the book had to be available very soon. I hadn't anticipated that all my publishing experience was so quickly going to be brought out of retirement and put back into service. I recruited the help of two local musicians and worship leaders, both of whom brought unique and different contributions to the pioneering team. Roland Fudge was a classical violinist who had ministered so very deeply to me personally on occasions when I had visited St.Thomas's, the local charismatic Anglican Church in Lancaster. Cyril Ashton, the Vicar of St.Thomas's had been a great help to me during my crisis of threatened bankruptcy and murder a few years earlier, and I had been really blessed by Roland's music ministry.

Roland was an obvious choice to represent the more Anglican end of the Christian community. Greg Leavers was a brilliant, spontaneous pianist/guitar player who also had an amazing music leadership gift – but his experience was largely in the so-called free churches and he brought a huge amount of knowledge and experience of that sector of the Church. My own background bridged a wide spectrum of Christian musical experience and I would be the publisher, who would bring the whole project together and arrange for the book's production.

For the next twelve weeks I was absent from the bookshop as we lived and breathed everything to do with *Mission England Praise* until the work was finished. It was a massive job for the three of us to research all the available new and old material and make a definitive selection for Mission England. The list of 282 items first passed the scrutiny of Cliff Barrows, who had been Billy Graham's worship leader since the very beginning of their campaigns together. And then the national Mission England committee gave it their approval and the book was ready to go to press in record time. But who was going to publish it?

The book needed maximum exposure in the Christian book world. The book in itself would be a huge means of publicising Mission England across the churches and, indeed, put a significant amount of money into the mission's funds. Marshall Pickering were one of the oldest publishers of both Christian books and music and at that time my old friend Chris Mungeam was a key player in the Marshall's team. He was hugely excited about *Mission England Praise* and Marshall's did everything they possibly could to get the book out quickly. They came up with a great design for the book cover and Chris ordered 100,000 copies of the words-only edition, content that it would sell many more than that and before long would need reprinting.

Chris's Managing Director feared that such a huge printing might bankrupt the company if they didn't sell and before long Chris found himself out of a job, but with a lump of redundancy money in his pocket. In the end Chris's faith in the project was entirely justified. It didn't bankrupt the company but had the totally opposite effect on the company's finances and just as Chris had expected, so many copies of the book were sold that it went into many reprints!

Chris, however, had to think carefully about what to do with his redundancy money – it had to be the seed corn for his financial future. After much thought and prayer he decided to launch his own publishing company and he registered the name *Sovereign World* and set about rebuilding his career – courtesy of *Mission England Praise*! That massive step of faith for Chris was, in the future, going to have enormous ramifications for the work that would eventually become known as Ellel Ministries as is explained more fully in Chapter 28. Once again, God was at work on His divine tapestry, weaving together many different threads in order to create an extraordinary picture.

In 1983 Cliff Barrows came over to the UK for a few weeks for the launch meetings of *Mission England Praise*. I gathered a touring music group to go with him under the leadership of Graham Kendrick, who was by then the most well-known of the up and coming song-writers, and we set out to launch meetings in each of the six Mission England areas. With Bishop Bill Flagg's help, Liverpool Cathedral became the venue for the North-West's event. It's now well over thirty years since those Mission England Meetings and the book, now called, more simply, *Mission Praise* contains 1385 items and, amazingly, the *Foreword* to the 30th Anniversary Edition was written by Cliff Barrows, shortly before his passing in 2016.

The various editions of Mission Praise have sold hundreds of thousands of copies, have gone all over the world, been used in every major denomination from the Falklands Islands to Hong Kong and whenever I see them being used in unusual places I think back to that Praise and Prayer night at Morecambe and shake my head with utter amazement at what God has done with the vision He downloaded into my spirit as I drove through Bolton-le-Sands!

Mission England gave me the opportunity to meet and get to know Christian leaders all over the country, many of whom, in years to come, would become personal friends. God was certainly in the decision to say "*Yes*" to Edgar's invitation. In the year or so prior to the main Mission England meetings, we had the opportunity to conduct local missions in the areas which were furthest away from the main event at Liverpool. Eric Delve, another wonderfully unconventional and anointed evangelist, was the main speaker at these, and even today I am in touch with people who look back to Eric's meetings in Barrow, Penrith and Workington when God invaded their lives and they came to know Jesus as their Lord and Saviour.

Another strategic initiative which flowed out of our Mission England area was a series of inspirational Leaders Conferences held under the Mission England banner at Lancaster University. I had long understood that unless leaders were personally alive in God they would have little capacity to lead others into a season of renewal in the power of the Holy Spirit. Many years earlier I had written a book on the theme but never dared publish it! But Mission England was an opportunity to plan a series of Conferences to give leaders the opportunity to receive for themselves, away from the glare of their own people. With speakers such as Alan Redpath, Bishop Richard Hare, the totally unconventional, ground-breaking, charismatic bishop; Clive Calver, the General Secretary of the Evangelical Alliance; Selwyn Hughes, the writer of the hugely popular *Every Day with Jesus Devotional;* and Gavin Reid, it's no surprise that these conferences were so very well attended that they impacted people across the whole of the North-West region.

As the days of the Anfield Meetings drew near, there was a massive groundswell of interest. There had been a huge response to Billy Graham's preaching at the meetings in the other stadia around the country. But now it was Liverpool's turn. Chris Woods was the Area Chairman for the St.Helens area of the North West. He and his wife Kathy had become close friends and because of his interest in the healing ministry Chris was to become one of the members of our Advisory Group for the future ministry. But at Anfield we were delegated to work together as Counselling Advisors behind the scenes.

We were on the pitch at the end of each meeting watching all the proceedings and ready to intervene at any moment if anything seemed to be getting out of hand. One of the unpublicised moments of the mission was when Chris was called in to help a counsellor because the person he was praying with was manifesting behaviour which looked suspiciously like that of demons – though neither Chris nor I really understood what that meant in those days! How we both finished up in the players changing rooms, attempting to minister healing and deliverance to the young man in question, I will never know. But it served as a strong reminder that there were many people 'out there' whose needs were truly desperate and that I mustn't forget the vision and that God was still preparing me for its fulfilment.

Those three years, when I was almost totally committed to working for Mission England, were a precious and priceless opportunity to learn so much about the ways of the Lord in drawing men and women to Himself, organising Christian events and in the dos and don'ts of Christian leadership. I will always be grateful for people like Gavin Reid, soon to become a Bishop himself following Mission England, and many other wonderful people, who taught me so much and who have proved to be such good and loyal friends across the years since.

As Mission England began to draw to a close my thoughts and my heart turned once more to the vision, that had been largely on hold for another three years. Surely, Lord, the time must be getting close? Don't you know how old I am – as my fortieth birthday clicked by on the milometer of life?! It seemed as though many things were coming to a head in what would prove to be a critical, but heart-breaking next step of the journey.

Chapter 7

HEARTBREAK HOUSE

From Expectation to Devastation

M ission England had been a wonderful experience, but the vision that had begun with a bent chassis was now burning deeper into my spirit than ever before. By the time the mission was over, I had been praying every single day into the vision for over fourteen years. I'd not only had to learn the lesson of patience, but I was beginning to understand some of the Scriptures which talk about endurance and perseverance as well.

While God had blessed my family and businesses down the years, in many amazing ways, there was a continuing ache in my heart because of our increasingly strained and fragile marital relationship. I was not only, therefore, wrestling with the uncertainty of a vision that kept on being pushed into the future. I am sure that my wife, also, was struggling with the pain of our situation as we both made every effort to try and keep the family as close together as possible. I was continually hoping that things would change, but our relationship was going through a very difficult time and deep down

I feared that stormy waters lay ahead. This was truly the season of my own long dark night of the soul.

The phrase *"dark night of the soul"* comes from a poem by St. John of the Cross (1542-1591). According to the poet, the *"dark night of the soul"* is a picture of what it can sometimes be like when travelling on the "narrow way" that Jesus spoke of in Matthew 7:13-14. It is a time of testing and sometimes agony of heart accompanied by confusion, fear, uncertainty and even doubts about God—but on the other side of that dark night is Christ's peace and a deep sense of knowing Christ's glorious presence. It was certainly a very confusing time for me and yes, I did fear – fear that maybe after all these years of praying and believing for God to do it, the vision may never be fulfilled and I would have to look back on a wasted life and realise that I had been dreaming for nothing!

There was one particular day when my personal dark night of the soul culminated in the most horrendous of spiritual experiences. This experience left me with absolutely no doubt about the reality of Satan and all the powers of darkness. From that time onwards I knew with total certainty that all the Scriptural stories about people being healed through deliverance were true. They weren't just a first century way of interpreting what they saw without the benefit of modern day medical understandings!

During the previous week I had been going through a particularly challenging set of circumstances. I was tired and getting desperate. I was in bed, and already deeply asleep when out of absolutely nowhere I began to be attacked in a very menacing dream. At least it felt as though it must be a dream, but I was now wide awake and the 'dream' was still going on. This was no dream! This was for real.

The attack turned into a one-to-one fight, but I had no idea what or who it was I was fighting! I couldn't see it, but it was very physically there. It didn't have a body, but the wrestling was as real as if it did. I had no idea what was going on and wanted to cry out to someone for help, but the only cries I could make were silent and desperate ones from within, that I was trying to make to God. But, somehow, the cry wasn't getting through. Where was God when I needed Him?!

The battle must have been going on for at least two hours, I was covered in sweat and was getting exhausted and weak. It felt as though whoever it was, was gaining the upper hand. All I knew was that I was wrestling with the most evil thing I had ever encountered. If this wasn't Satan himself it must have been a spiritual being of significant rank in the hierarchy of Satan's Kingdom. I certainly wasn't going to give up, but I was weakening and wondering how the battle was going to end. Even as the battle ensued, I was reminded of the fight Christian had with Apollyon in Bunyan's *Pilgrim's Progress*. I was trying to get through to Jesus, but he seemed a very long way away.

Suddenly, I became aware of what the battle was all about. Satan only had one objective – to make me give up the vision. Instinctively I knew that Satan was using a time when I was at my weakest to challenge my commitment to my calling. I knew that if I simply said, *"I'll give up the vision"* that the battle would be instantly over – and I would have lost, but at least I wouldn't have to fight any more. I was offered peace, but I knew it would be a false peace. It felt as though I was in the middle of a supernatural gambling arena where the stakes were very, very high and Satan had thrown everything at me that God would allow.

When I finally understood what the battle was all about and what Satan was trying to do, strength began to rise from the deepest depths of my spirit. If Satan was so desperate for me to give up the vision, then God must have purposes for the vision that go far beyond anything I had ever thought of. I determined that whatever it cost I wasn't going to give up.

Then the battle entered a new phase. In a series of pictures, the enemy I was fighting showed me all the things I would lose if I kept going with the vision. I was forced to work through them one by one. What about this, what about that, as Satan reminded me of all the things in my life that were precious to me – and which he said I would lose if I carried on with my obedience to the call of God. Then he showed me the other side of the coin – all the things that he would do for me if I would but give up this ridiculous vision. But through all this I knew, also, that Satan was a liar from the beginning and that I didn't need to go into fear about his threats or take a second look at what he was offering me, attractive though all the trappings of materialism might seem to be, when in such a desperate situation!

Now the battle was reaching a climax – more new strength was coming into my spirit from somewhere unknown and I was finally able to rise up and shout out in my spirit to Satan, *"NO – I will not give up the vision. This is my calling under God and YOU are not going to rob me or God of everything that the Lord has purposed for my life."* Suddenly, Jesus was there. The battle was over and Satan, or whichever spiritual being it was that I had been fighting with, had gone. I was totally exhausted, bathed in sweat from head to foot, but I had come through to the other side of the long dark night of my soul and I was experiencing the ministering love of the Lord Jesus, bathed in His peace and enjoying His glorious presence.

As I looked back on that very traumatic experience, the Lord showed me what had been happening. Satan was indeed challenging the vision. He had not been able to stop me pressing on with it through any of the circumstances I had experienced, or the opposition from people who would question whether the vision really was from God. At the same time this was something that God had allowed for He was testing my heart to see if, without His obvious presence and help, I would still make the same decision as if He had been there. Would I still want to love and serve Him if I couldn't either see Him or know His presence? It was a severe test and as I wiped the sweat off my body and climbed back into bed, I knew that not only was the long dark night of the soul over, but that I would not have to wait long before the work would begin.

Shortly after this experience I read in the Christian press that John Wimber was coming from the USA to Sheffield for a conference on healing. John Wimber, the founder of the Vineyard group of churches, was a significant name in the early eighties on both sides of the Atlantic so I decided to go and spend four days concentrating on whatever the Lord had to say to me through the teaching and ministry. I found that I was in complete agreement with all that John Wimber picked out from the Scriptures about both healing and deliverance. My heart was beating in rhythm with what he was teaching from the Word of God.

At times during that amazing conference I felt as though I was the only person there. I was aware of crowds of people in one sense, but at the same time I was oblivious to their presence. God had got my attention. In my previous frightening spiritual experience I had been wrestling with the enemy, but this was different. It felt as though now it was God's turn! I knew there were still deep issues to be tackled in my own life, and was struggling with my own sense of rejection. Even though I had been praying into the vision for such a long time, I was in my heart beginning to question whether I was the reason that the vision hadn't yet come to fruition!

The inner wrestling was going deep into the inner recesses of my soul – touching depths that I didn't even know were there, and facing challenges in the spirit that I knew one day I would have to face in the flesh. I felt so inadequate, unsuited and unprepared but at the same time I was straining at the leash desperate to get going. But God was showing me that if He had let the leash go too soon, I would have gone out like a greyhound on a track, to try and build God's Kingdom in my way instead of His!

There is a breaking that leads to wholeness and destiny. And deep inside me there was a breaking of my own will taking place as one by one I placed every area of my life into God's hands, decided to trust Him unconditionally with the consequences and agreed to follow Him wherever the journey would take me.

On the last night of the conference I was extraordinarily aware of the presence of God during the worship. I felt as though I was being pinned to that back wall of Sheffield City Hall by the presence, the power and the overwhelming love of God. It was as if a series of three huge waves came rolling in to cover me and across the top of the first wave was written, in huge letters, the word ACCEPTED.

At that moment I didn't just know God's forgiveness as a theological proposition, it was pervading my whole being. And realising that there was nothing that God hadn't forgiven, meant that I could unconditionally believe that He really loved me – every single bit of me. The acceptance I felt at that moment was totally life transforming.

I was just recovering from this wonderful experience when I sensed a second wave coming in. Across the tops of the wave were spread the letters of the word RESTORED. It seemed as though in all the areas of my life where I had known God's acceptance and forgiveness, He was now healing and restoring me. New strength came into my being as I realised that the restoration of God was equipping me for whatever lay ahead.

I had no idea what would happen next. I was relaxing once again in the presence of God – the joy of His love was filling my spirit and my soul – when the third wave came rolling in and to my enormous surprise, written across the top of the wave, was written the word COMMISSIONED. Deep down I knew exactly what this word meant. It was as if in a moment of time, years of preparation were coming to a head and that whatever it was that God was calling me to do, was about to happen.

A commissioning marks the beginning of something new. On the day a new ship for the Royal Navy is commissioned, the years of building and preparation are over, and it enters service. I had no idea what commissioning would mean for me, but as the impact of those three waves subsided, I knew that a new phase of my life was beginning and that I was entering service. It was as if, at that conference, God had said that the time had come. I knew that I would never forget those days in Sheffield. I came home from the conference knowing that fulfilment of the vision was just around the corner.

Even though I had no idea where the ministry would be operating from, I had by now formulated in my mind all the details of a structure for the running of the ministry. I even prepared hand-written brochures, describing what would happen at the centre when it opened. Ever since God had spoken to me about not only ministering to people in need of healing, but also teaching others about how to do it, these two arms of the work had become clearly established in my thinking and praying.

The ministry of healing would be conducted on Healing Retreats, and these would be spread over two nights and three days. We would invite people who needed help to come on a retreat, which would be totally free of charge, and teach them about healing as well as pray for them – only there was one thing there in my planning which I'd got seriously wrong – the idea that we would teach people on the retreats about healing!

I wanted to prepare myself for teaching on the retreats, so one evening I sat down with my Bible and started looking for the teaching Jesus gave about healing. I was in for a shock. There wasn't any. So what would we teach on the retreats? I turned back to the beginning of the Gospel of Matthew and started reading the New Testament one more time. Each time I had done this in the past the Lord had shown me something new, so I was ready for another lesson. I didn't know what I was looking for, but I knew the Lord was telling me to look for it all the same! I read the whole of Matthew and then the whole of Mark. All great stuff, of course, but I hadn't yet found the crock of gold which I was sure was lying at the end of my Healing Retreat rainbow!

Several cups of coffee accompanied my search as I ploughed on through Mark's Gospel and into Luke's. Then, suddenly, there it was, in a verse I must have read dozens of times, but had never seen the extraordinary truth it contained. I realised why I hadn't noticed Luke 9:11 before – verses 10 and 11 were just the introductory verses prefacing the amazing scenes that were being described by Luke in verses 12 to 17. This is where the focus was – in the feeding of the five thousand. No wonder I'd missed what was in those really important preceding two verses.

When I got to verse 11 this time, however, it was as if my reading had suddenly been stopped by a set of red traffic lights! STOP – don't go any further, this is it. You've found the treasure – now read it – again and again and again. *"Jesus welcomed the people, he spoke to them about the Kingdom of God and healed those in need of healing."* I had never seen the logical significance before of how the careful Dr. Luke had described what Jesus was doing.

First, he said, *"Jesus welcomed the people."* That word welcome embraces a whole heap of meaning. But in essence a welcome is a practical expression of love. If people are loved and welcomed, they are a hundred times more likely to listen to what you have to say, than if they get the message from how you speak, and what you do, that they're not wanted. Jesus didn't just want us to teach words, He wanted people to learn by receiving love. I made a mental note that the Healing Retreats had to be really warm and welcoming – and that didn't just mean giving people a hug when they came through the door, it meant everything from good food to comfy beds and everything else in between which spells out in practical terms what the word love really means.

I realised also that we would need to recruit a ministry team of welcoming, loving people – people who would be able to convey the heart of Jesus to everyone in need who walked through the door. This would be God's strategy for Kingdom unity – the ministry team would be recruited from people of every denomination – but whatever denomination people were from would be irrelevant in the Kingdom ministry that God was establishing. There could be no disunity or denominational legalism at the heart of such a ministry, otherwise it wouldn't be a ministry of healing. And there could be no argument about the essential doctrinal foundations, that would unite the team in the practice of their faith.

I read on, *"Jesus spoke to them about the Kingdom of God."* This was the ultimate key I was looking for in asking the question, *"What would we teach on Healing Retreats?"* When I saw it, it was so obvious I was spiritually kicking myself for having previously been so blind! God didn't want us to teach about healing, but to show them love and tell them about the Kingdom of God and what it really means to live one's life according to Kingdom principles.

John the Baptist had said *"Repent for the Kingdom of God is at hand."* I was seeing that what He meant, in a free translation, was *"Get your life into godly order for the King is coming!"* And that didn't mean any old king, it meant the King of the Universe, the very Son of God, the King of Kings! I thought back to some of the people I'd tried to help through prayer for healing. I realised that many of them were living very unordered lives, which were a long way from what God intended for His children – it's no surprise that their lives were in a mess and they needed healing. I made a mental note to really study all the Kingdom principles that are there in the Scriptures. I instinctively knew that in these I would find the keys to healing for many people.

Finally I came to the last part of the verse, *"and Jesus healed those in need of healing."* There was a definite sequence here – show love, teach about the Kingdom and help them get their lives in order and then pray with them for healing. The pattern for the Healing Retreats was emerging and I was really excited. I knew, too, that Luke 9:11 had to become the foundational Scripture for the whole of the ministry. It was as if God had spoken with an audible and contemporary voice out of the pages of Scripture. At last I knew the direction we would need to be going in.

Next, I had to start preparing the actual Kingdom teachings for each session of a Healing Retreat. The first would certainly need to include teaching about making Jesus Lord of your life – for without that how can anyone get their lives into godly order? And after that there was the need to be both forgiven and to forgive others. The teaching was coming together – but I needed to practise. Who shall I practise on? I decided to practice on sheep! I used to exercise the dogs on a flat piece of grassy shore-land. Here there were always lots of sheep and I used them to represent the very first people who would receive the Kingdom teaching on a Healing Retreat. After all, Jesus had talked about people as if they were sheep, so it didn't seem too far off track to be looking at sheep as if they were people!

I laughed at myself as I spoke out the teaching into the air. I looked at the faces of the sheep – they were all different – and extraordinarily God began to show me the very different faces of dozens of different people, who would come on future retreats. He was giving me understanding of the hurts and pain that so often lie behind the facial signals people give out. I had to grow in discernment and understand more about what God sees when He looks into our faces and into our hearts. If we could learn to see as He sees, then the work would be so much easier! At the end of John Chapter 2 it says that Jesus *"did not need man's testimony about man, for he knew what was in man."* No wonder Jesus's healing ministry was always so effective – He knew exactly what the problem was as He looked into their faces and into their hearts. His prayers were spot on every single time!

During this long season of preparing myself for whatever lay ahead, there were two occasions when Ruth Hawkey was the preacher at Silverdale Methodist Church, when she spoke a vital and encouraging word into my life through her preaching. The first was from the story of Abraham in Hebrews 11:8 when the writer says that Abraham went out in obedience *"even though he did not know where he was going."* That's exactly how I had felt for many years – I was trying to be obedient to the vision that burned within me, but I had no idea where it was going to lead. I learned that ignorance of the destination was not a reason for not starting the journey!

Then there came an unforgettable Sunday when Ruth Hawkey was again the preacher. There weren't many people in the evening service, but I knew that Ruth always brought a good word. This time she preached from the story of the wedding at Cana in Galilee in John 2:5, *"Do whatever He tells you to do."* Her sermon wasn't just a good word, it was a word straight from the heart of God to me. I knew that God was saying it was time for action and I mustn't hesitate in my obedience. As I went out of the church that night and shook hands with Ruth at the door we exchanged a few words as I thanked her for the message. She was unhesitant in her response, confirming that God had given her that word for me. Much later she wrote, *"I knew in my spirit it was for you – although I must admit I didn't know what He would be telling you to do or where it would lead you, or that a few years later Joe and I would be involved as well."*

Clearly the process of getting ready for the work to start was speeding up. God was certainly on the move. Now that we had the pattern for the Healing Retreats, God reminded me of those vital meetings that had taken place in the second-hand department of Carnforth Bookshop. Those prayers opened the doors for what God did next. It was time to start a special prayer meeting for the vision to come into being! I now had to involve others in the work – this wasn't going to be a one-man ministry, it had to involve the wider

Body of Christ. My dark night of the soul experience had taught me that Satan really hated what God was doing and that we needed each other, so we could stand together.

But this was now getting scary! Up till then I had learned the hard way that it was best to keep quiet about what was burning in your heart, but now it seemed different. But how could something be birthed for believers in the area, if people in the area were not gathering to pray it into being? So, I took the plunge, told people in a letter about the vision for a healing centre and invited them to our home for a time of sharing hearts, vision and, of course, prayer.

I sent it to all those I'd invited to the Bookshop prayer meeting – as well as many others I'd got to know during the Mission England years. I had absolutely no idea whether anyone would come, but come they did and our large lounge was filled to overflowing with about fifty people, most of whom were genuinely excited about the possibility of a healing centre in their local area, serving the people of North-West England. Sister Aine was there of course – her eyes twinkling with enthusiasm as she sensed that the bare-bones of the work that had been talked about in the convent kitchen were beginning to get some flesh on them!

Some of those who came to the first meeting were missing the second time round, but there were new faces of people who had since heard about the vision. God was shaking out the people for whom this was not their primary interest or calling, and shaking in those who He was calling to be the intercessors, who would press on until the work was established. There were people there from as far away as Chester, Preston, Kendal and East Lancashire – representatives from all over the North-West of England. The horizons were spreading.

Then Sister Aine came to see me with some really exciting news, but unbeknown to either of us at the time, this news was the edge of what would become a dark and challenging cloud. She told me the news, hot off the press, that a new and much bigger hospice was going to be built at Lancaster, in a place that was much more convenient for both patients and their visitors. This meant that the St.John of God hospice in Silverdale would be closing.

As she shared with me the news, my mind was already racing ahead. For the former Hazelwood Hall, that had become the hospice, was a wonderful property, and having had a chapel added to the facilities, it seemed the obvious place for the work to begin. It was so obviously the right place, for a whole lot of reasons, that we began to plan how the buildings could be best adapted for their new role as a healing centre for the North-West of England! In our minds it was, as they say, a done deal! There was of course a small matter of the money that would be needed to pay for the property but, if this was going to be the place where sixteen years of praying would reach their conclusion, then surely the money wouldn't be a problem to God!

At the next meeting of the Prayer Support Group (PSG) Sister Aine shared the exciting news with everyone present. A buzz of excitement, expectancy and thanksgiving went round the room as people turned to intercession to start praying for the release of the funds to buy the property. No-one even questioned whether or not the Sisters would be willing to sell the property to us or whether this was the right place. It just seemed so obvious that this was what God was doing.

One of the great pioneers of the healing ministry in the UK was Morris Maddocks, the former Bishop of Selby. Morris, with his wife Anne, was one of the most gracious and generous hearted people you could ever wish to meet. When news that the St .John of God Hospital was about to become the home of a new healing ministry in the North-West of England, he was quick to be in touch and come over and meet me. He wanted to see the place. We struck up a very warm and long-lasting friendship and he was tremendously encouraging and excited about it all.

We were anxiously waiting to hear how much the Sisters would be asking for the property. We knew that it would have to be at a fair market price, but we were not expecting to have to be in competition with others for the property. But then came the news that the Sisters, who were Trustees of the Charity that owned the property, wouldn't be allowed to sell it to us privately, it had to be offered on the open market. This was a huge blow, but we weren't unduly concerned for this was God's house and He would make sure we would get it, wouldn't He?

It wasn't easy for the agents to describe the property in the sale details. Hazelwood Hall had so many different possible uses, but there couldn't be many potential purchasers who would want a chapel in the grounds! So we were quite relaxed about going through the process, even when the agents announced that the sale would be concluded by all those who were interested in buying the property being asked to submit their sealed bids by a certain time on a certain day.

We had to start preparing material for the season of fund-raising that lay ahead. I was so certain that Hazelwood Hall was God's chosen place that I produced a four page brochure about the vision for the ministry and the place where the work was going to begin. I invited people to send in their donations or make promises of gifts, which they would send in at the time they were needed.

And the very first leaflet I mailed out, was sent to my brother, David. Having well established the Department of Medical Physiology at Nairobi University, he had then moved to Canada to lead a research programme in Montreal. He had made some very significant discoveries and was planning to launch a new company to develop commercially viable products based on his research findings, and was now living at Hindhead, in Surrey. We had always kept closely in touch with each other and I knew he would be interested in seeing the first leaflet about the new work.

A couple of days later we were sitting together in a restaurant having dinner. He was telling me all about his research and I shared with him where we had got to in respect of developing a centre for healing. Whilst he was primarily a research scientist, our respective objectives were in fact remarkably similar – we were both concerned to help those who were in need. We had enjoyed our main course and after the waiter had taken the order for our puddings, my brother put his hand in his pocket and pulled out the brochure I'd sent him about the St. John of God property we were wanting to buy.

He passed it to me across the table, with the gift promise section already filled in. I could not have been more shocked or thrilled at what I saw when I opened it out. David had pledged to give £50,000 towards the purchase. I was totally and utterly gob-smacked, as they say! I couldn't really believe what I was seeing – this was the very first leaflet I'd sent out and the very first pledged donation we received. £50,000 was an unbelievable sum, well over a £150,000 in 2017 money. I was so choked that I could hardly speak and not a few tears were added to my pudding when it came! David respected what I wanted to do and was totally committed to supporting us in whatever way he could.

I returned home even more convinced that God had now put his seal on the finances for the project and this wonderful donation would be the first of many – we would soon have whatever funds were necessary! With regard to our offer price for the property, we took advice from an experienced agent, put our offer into a sealed envelope and delivered it to the selling agent in good time and waited for the news that our bid for Hazelwood Hall had been accepted. And when the news came that our offer was indeed the highest offer, but that there were other offers close to ours as well, the Sisters told the agent that they would not be in a position to accept any offer until they had first gone away and prayed. So the Trustees took time out in Ireland and laid all the offers they had received before the Lord. At the end of this time away, each of the Sisters who were Trustees had to share what they sensed the Lord was saying.

When she got back to St John of God, Sister Aine immediately came to see me, but I could tell by her face that she didn't want to share the news she was bringing. All the Trustees had said the same thing, they believed God wanted them to accept the lower price and sell it to a Catholic lady who would be converting it into an Old People's Home. Sister Aine could hardly look at me. She felt as though she was betraying me and betraying the vision, in spite of the fact that she knew God had clearly spoken through the Trustees.

Both of us were totally and utterly devastated. I just sat in stunned silence as sixteen years of praying faded into insignificance and I began to cry. All the emotion and pain of the years came flooding out, with not a little anger also. *"God, this isn't fair. You've taken me to the edge of fulfilment of the vision and now, not just at the last minute, but at the last second, you've snatched the prize out of my hands."* I was totally undone.

Chapter 8

ALMOST THERE!

From Heartbreak House
to Ellel Grange

I t took more than a few days to recover from the emotional shock of losing the St John of God property. I escaped from the pain by once again burying myself in piles of second-hand books at the shop. To say I was devastated would have been a gross understatement.

Slowly, as I sorted through box after box, a measure of common sense and spiritual reality returned. When the eyes had dried and I could see more clearly, I realised that God had not said that the vision was wrong – just that the place we had chosen wasn't the place He had chosen. My brother confirmed that his opening pledge of £50,000 was still good for whatever property we eventually bought – so that extraordinary sign of God's supernatural provision still held good. Even though I had gone through an experience of total devastation, the light of the vision was still burning within my spirit – it hadn't been blown out by the wind of change. And in the midst of it all I began to experience the ongoing reality that God was the *"God of all comfort"* (2 Corinthians 1:3). If He was still on board with the vision – then so was I!

I picked up the phone and called Malcolm Brownsword. Malcolm was a property agent who had helped me on a number of occasions. He knew all about the work I was believing for and what had happened over the St John of God property. *"Malcolm,"* I said, *"you know we've just had the disappointment of our offer for St John of God being turned down. Do you know of anywhere else in the area that might be suitable for us?"*

His response was immediate. *"Well,"* he said, *"there is a place that would suit you really well, but it isn't actually for sale. I suggest you still go and have a look at it. It would give you an idea of what other buildings there are in the area that could come up for sale."* I wasn't terribly excited about a place that wasn't for sale, but if this was God giving me a lead as to the next stopping place on a divine mystery tour, I was up for it. *"Where is it, Malcolm?"*

"Just by Exit 33 of the M6. It's called Ellel Grange – you can't miss the driveway, it's only a hundred yards from the junction."

I left the books behind, headed down the motorway and came off at Exit 33. I turned up the Ellel Grange drive, over the old canal bridge, round a long curve in the road and finally into a car park at the front of the building. It all looked vaguely familiar and suddenly I remembered – I'd been there before.

Six years previously there had been a massive auction sale of all the contents of the house when Miss Sandeman, the last surviving member of the Sandeman Port family, decided she could no longer live in this massive house by herself. She was moving into the former Home Farm and everything was up for sale – including the books. There were many rare and valuable books in the library and specialist collectors and dealers had come from all over the country for the auction – all of which meant that everything was being sold for prices far too high for me to consider for the shop. But the contents of the bookshelves in the snooker room were being sold as a job lot and I was delighted when they were knocked down to me by the auctioneer – Malcolm Brownsword! At least I had bought something in the sale and hadn't wasted the day!

But that was a long time ago. After the sale, the house had been sold and under new ownership had been converted into an up-market health farm. The snooker room was now a swimming pool; all the rooms that were affected by wet or dry rot had been treated and restored; most of the bedrooms had been fitted with en-suite bath or shower rooms and were beautifully decorated. Deep plush carpets were everywhere. Beautiful chandeliers graced the ceilings. It was a very different place from when I had first walked through the building, filled with the decaying artefacts of a previous century and decoration that displayed the shabbiness of time-worn hangovers from earlier generations. Then, the building would have been a huge and expensive challenge to anyone – but on the day I entered the building for the second time, it was very different. The challenge had been met and it was now a warm and welcoming place.

I wasn't ready for what happened when I pushed open the huge front door of Ellel Grange, and started to cross the large entrance lobby which led to a magnificent flowing staircase, the centre piece of the entrance hall. Once again I was being arrested by that unmistakeable voice of God. *"This is the place, claim it for Me!"*

The message could not have been simpler or clearer – even before I had seen the inside of the building, God was telling me that this was it! I was in the middle of a spiritual urge of unprecedented proportions and, as Uncle Will once said, I mustn't sit on such things! But, Lord, this is a bit big – it far exceeded anything I had ever thought might be suitable for the ministry. It was in a very different league altogether.

But if that was really what God had said, then I had no choice! I explained to the girl behind the reception desk why I was there, and said that I would like to be shown round the building. I asked if I could speak with the owner. I was ushered into the former library, now a lounge, sat in one of the large armchairs and waited. Presently a young lady came and very politely told me that Ellel Grange wasn't for sale, but she would still be very happy to show me round. I gladly accepted her invitation. And yes, she was the owner.

As I took in everything she showed me, my mind was once again working overtime, but this time there was something different from when I went through a similar process over St John of God Hospital. On that occasion I'd made up my own mind that St John of God was the place, and I had been trying to make it work, but this time God had clearly spoken and I didn't need to try and make it work, I just had to follow in His footsteps. Even though the lady had said that Ellel Grange wasn't for sale, I still left her with a piece of paper on which I'd hastily scribbled my phone number.

At the next meeting of the Prayer Support Group (PSG), we all had to work through the disappointment of not getting St John of God, but I also shared with them my experience at Ellel Grange. That wasn't easy, for there was, understandably, an air of scepticism about jumping from one place to another, in spite of what I believed God had said to me. *"But the place isn't for sale, so why are we even thinking about it?"* was the unspoken sense of the meeting. We all prayed and agreed to meet again in a couple of months time in January 1986.

Shortly before that next meeting, I was sitting at my desk when the phone rang. I didn't recognise the lady's voice on the other end, but when I heard the words Ellel Grange I immediately jumped to attention. I hadn't forgotten my visit and had certainly been continuing to claim it for the Lord. But when the call came I remember, very well, trembling with excitement wondering what she was going to say.

"Are you still interested in buying Ellel Grange?"

I didn't actually drop the phone, but came pretty close to it, as I heard myself saying, *"Yes,"* knowing very well that we had no money, other than my brother's £50,000 promise. I explained our situation, that The Christian Trust was a charity and we would have to share the need with our supporters, but I was confident that we would be able to find the money – thus spoke the voice of trembling faith! Did I really say that, especially knowing that the value of Ellel Grange was considerably more than that of St John of God? It was a magnificent building, designed by the same architect who had built Osborne House on the Isle of Wight for Queen Victoria. It had originally been built for the Mayor of Liverpool as his country home.

She replied, *"Well, we have quite a lot of bookings for the health farm over the next six months, which we would want to honour, so, if we can agree a price, then we could give you those six months to raise the money."* We had a deal, even though I still had no idea just how much the price of the deal would be. That eventually turned out to be £457,251, a price that would include the Grange itself, all the carpets (which we understood had cost about £50,000 alone), all the furnishings and the derelict Chapel that still stood in the grounds. (More than £1.5 million in 2017 currency value.)

The next meeting of the PSG was very different. When people heard the news they were really excited and it seemed as though everyone was on board. But wisely, after the previous experience with St John of God, people also wanted to have some clear confirmation from the Lord that this really was the place that He had chosen and that it wasn't just another good, but not God, idea. When I told Sister Aine about Ellel Grange, and where it was located, just by Exit 33 of the M6, she smiled and looked up at me with those twinkling Irish eyes and said, *"That sounds about right, that's what Jesus did, he exited at 33 as well!"*

I arranged for a small group of the PSG to visit Ellel Grange so they could make their own assessment of the property and its suitability. By this time Bishop Bill Flagg, the Diocesan Officer for the Healing Ministry in Liverpool who I had met through Mission England, had become part of our pioneering team. He was a keen supporter of the proposed ministry and he wanted to come and see Ellel Grange for himself. I was watching carefully all their reactions as they walked round the various rooms. People were amazed at the potential of the place. It was a thousand times more suitable than the place I had grieved over so much.

At the end of our tour we finished up in the lounge, waiting for some coffee to be brought to us, when the Bishop looked at us all and said, *"This place has been used for pampering bodies, won't it be wonderful to see it being used to pamper souls!"* We all laughed, but in our hearts there was a real spirit of unity confirming that this was the place that God wanted us to have for the ministry, the place where He would transform broken lives. The vision I had seen as I stared at the bent chassis of the *Alvis Speed 20,* sixteen years previously, was about to be fulfilled. I was weeping now for a different reason!

Since that time I have thought a thousand times about the events of the previous few months – especially that, possibly the greatest miracle of the Ellel story was the fact that those wonderful Irish sisters had listened to God and turned down the best offer they had received for their property, to their own financial detriment. If they hadn't been obedient to God, we would have finished up with a property that was too small and in the wrong place. It would have been a very expensive mistake.

I reported back to everyone who had been at the PSG. We were definitely now in *'go mode'*! All hands now had to be on deck – there was work to do, a lot of work to do! First, enough money had to be collected for the deposit, which would be due at the beginning of April, and that meant there was a real rush on to produce leaflets about the work and get them distributed to everyone we all knew who might be interested in supporting the new ministry at Ellel

Grange. We then received an anonymous donation which was given solely to underwrite the cost of all the publicity that would be needed, so that 100% of everyone else's donations would contribute to the purchase. Eventually 90,000 brochures were sent out, another 20,000 leaflets and 20,000 Newsletters as well as thousands of personal and thank you letters.

The next six months were going to be six of the most challenging, exciting and, even, nerve-wracking months of any of our lives! But we were all confident that God was in it! And God wasn't slow to add several more significant confirmations by way of encouragement to the team as they pressed on with the work.

By now the story was breaking news, and the local newspapers made a lot of the announcement of the new use for Ellel Grange. This prompted an out-of-the-blue phone call from Alec Sayer, the farmer whose land was adjacent to Ellel Grange. He was also a leader of a local church and had just seen the article in the paper. He wanted to know more about what we intended to do there. He listened carefully as I explained, in the best way I knew how, what we believed the Lord had in mind for the property.

When I'd finished he said, *"Can I tell you my side of the story?"* I was eager to hear. *"When the building was put up for sale six years ago I went and stood on the lawns which slope down from the Grange towards my farm. I prayed that the property would be sold to Christians for a Christian work. As I prayed I saw, in vision, a golden mist descending from Heaven and covering the building and then rolling down the lawns and covering my farm as well. I knew it was the blessing of God and that's what I started praying for, but it didn't happen. When the Grange was sold and it wasn't being bought for a Christian use, I thought I must have got it wrong and had mis-heard what the Lord was saying. But now I can see that over the years the present owners have had the building, they have been getting it ready for its new use and it's now ready for the*

*purpose God had in mind all the way along. Now I know that God
did hear and answer my prayer."*

I was speechless as I heard how God had raised Alec up as a
spiritual intercessor and warrior, to stand guard over the property
all this time and watch, as it was being restored by its new owners
for a purpose which they knew nothing about! This story, being such
strong confirmation that God was in our purchase of Ellel Grange,
was a huge encouragement to bring to the next meeting of the PSG.

With the early donations that came flooding in we had enough
money for the deposit and were able to sign the purchase contract
for Ellel Grange on the last day of the final Leaders Conference that I
organised after Mission England, at Lancaster University. Bill Flagg,
alongside Clive Claver and Charles Price, were the main speakers.
There was spontaneous applause as I announced this milestone had
been reached. The property was now legally secure provided, that is,
we managed to find the other £420,000 by the end of August! And
that was quite a challenge. It's one thing for an organisation with
a known track record, headed up by names that were well-known,
to invite people to support a new work, But it's quite another to
be starting from scratch with an unknown ministry and a largely
unknown team. Who would want to risk their money on such an
uncertain cause – excepting that God was in it!

I opened one envelope from Jerusalem. It contained a cheque for
three thousand pounds in which the Rector of Christ Church said
they were standing with us for the establishment of the ministry.
Two decades later I would be privileged to stand in that very Church
and preach on healing! That donation was a spiritual anchor point
for us as, down the years, the Lord drew the ministry in to working
with Messianic believers in the land of Israel.

Another cheque came from a retired Bishop of Coventry who said
that in his youth he had played tennis on the Ellel Grange lawns
with Miss Sandeman and he was sending a donation in memory of

the enjoyable times he had spent there. There were small donations, large donations and letters from people saying I'm praying for you. Every one mattered.

A lady drove up to my house one night and dumped a suitcase full of silver tankards on our doorstep! She'd found them in the attic and decided to give them to the appeal. They sold for several thousand pounds at auction. Another man gave me a collector's wallet full of pristine gold sovereigns. Little by little the money in the bank was growing – but not fast enough. One night, as I prayed, I sensed the Lord wanted me to ask our bank to help. But we had already been told that the bank would not be able to lend us any money by way of a business loan or a mortgage, as we had no guaranteed income with which to support the repayments, and nobody would lend you money without a proven income record.

I continued to think and pray about the bank prompting and woke up one morning with a wild idea in my head. If we could ask people to sign a four year bankers order for £10 a month, thus giving the bank a guaranteed income, would they be willing to lend us £500 for each four year pledge we were given? I asked the bank. They were sympathetic but said it had never been done before. So it had to be referred upwards – and up and up it went till it got to the Board of NatWest Bank. Amazingly, the Board agreed the proposal and down came the decision. Something that had never been done before eventually contributed over £175,000 to the fund.

It was the night of the church prayer meeting for a couple in East Lancashire. The husband went to the prayer meeting while his wife stayed at home with the children. After the meeting he returned home very excited. For the first time in his life the Lord had given him a vision – it was of a place where God was going to establish a healing ministry in the region. It was so clear he started to make a drawing of what he'd seen – but before he could get it down on paper his wife said, *"While you've been away I've been praying and the Lord's given me a vision too of a place where He's going to start a healing ministry!"* So, she got a piece of paper as well and together they drew the pictures of the buildings they had seen in their visions.

Now they were very confused, for the buildings they had drawn looked totally different. But the following morning they received my letter in the post, with the brochure about Ellel Grange and pictures of the building from various angles. As they looked at their pictures and then at the brochure, they realised that one of them had drawn the front of the building and the other had drawn the rear. And between them they were a double witness that what was happening at Ellel Grange was of God.

A lady in Yorkshire had heard about Ellel Grange, and when she was praying the Lord showed her a very tall chimney of complicated design, belching out black smoke. *"The smoke,"* she said, *"was a picture of all the dirt and filth that God was going to release from people's lives through the ministry at Ellel Grange."* She was so impacted by the vision that she drove all the way to Ellel Grange, just to have a look at the chimneys – they looked exactly like the picture she had drawn! These sort of things kept on happening throughout that long summer of 1986. God used these incidents to keep us encouraged and believing that He was going to do it, His way.

Having got to know Selwyn Hughes through the 1984 Leaders Conference at Lancaster University, I wanted to ask if he would be willing to come to Ellel Grange, so we could film a few minutes of him commending the new work to interested people. Normally this would have been something he would have been very reluctant to do, especially for a new and untried ministry. He really needed to know that God wanted him to do this. I made an appointment to see him when he was visiting Blackpool for the Christian Booksellers Convention. But just before he was due to see me, he also saw three other men who were seeking his advice.

That morning Selwyn's personal devotions were based on the

Scripture from Acts 10:20, when the Spirit of God said to Simon Peter, *"Three men are looking for you. So get up and go downstairs. Do not hesitate to go with them, for I have sent them."* As Selwyn read these words he knew the Lord was telling him that he must listen to what these three men had to say, for it was the Lord who had sent them. What they shared was their vision for opening a healing centre in the North of England and they wanted Selwyn's advice as to how to go about it. Selwyn knew that I was waiting outside and what I had come for, and so he called me in and introduced me to the three, who became deeply committed supporters of the work, one of whom is still an Adviser to the ministry to this day. Selwyn needed no more convincing that God had spoken to him through this divine set of coincidences and he was delighted then to come over to the Grange and do the filming!

Part way through the summer we were asked to lead a healing weekend in Scarborough for a Yorkshire church. During the teaching the Spirit of God came down on the meeting and a lady who was sitting there with a sling and bandages protecting her arm, following an accident in which her shoulder had been badly dislocated, was dramatically healed without anyone praying for her. We were probably more shocked than she was. Even though we had so very little experience, that didn't seem to bother God. He was confirming the ministry with signs and wonders following.

The legal side of purchasing Ellel Grange was complicated and as August approached it was clear that the lawyers would struggle to get everything together in time for the end of month. But in reality we, also, were behind with raising all the necessary funds to complete the purchase of the property. We sent out regular newsletters keeping people up to date with the situation but there was still quite a long way to go. I explained the situation to our solicitor and said we were still hoping to be able to complete on time, but he wisely advised us to ask for an extension to take some of the pressure off that he could see we were under. He reported back that the maximum extension the vendors would allow would be the end of October.

With one week to go we were still £27,633 short. Everyone was praying, knowing that God was going to do it – but none of us knew how. But in those final few days there was an amazing increase in the giving, including a large donation from one Vicar, whose Church Council had agreed to donate the money out of their Church funds. On the night of the 30th October, I sat in my office working through all the different sources of funds that would have to be gathered together the following morning in the Solicitor's bank account. It was something like 1.00am when I finally added up the column of figures and discovered that our available funds were now £457,257! We had just £6 too much! I climbed into bed that night both exhausted and elated. God had done it!

Chapter 9

CROSSING THE THRESHOLD

Starting the Work of Building a Ministry

At 4.00pm on the afternoon of Friday October 31st 1986 a group of excited but nervous members of the Prayer Support Group gathered round the doorway of Ellel Grange. Inside, the owners of the Health Farm were preparing to leave. A telephone call to their lawyer confirmed that the full money had been handed over and as they came out, we went in. We shook hands at the door and suddenly The Christian Trust was the legal owner of Ellel Grange and we were responsible for every square metre of this awesome property.

For me it was one of those totally unforgettable moments, when everything I had been looking for since the age of nine, and had been praying for and dreaming about for the previous sixteen years, came to fulfilment. With a single step we crossed the threshold and began an adventure of faith along an unknown road! It felt like crossing from one world into another!

We stood in the enormous hall, beneath the huge chandeliers, and prayed – giving thanks to God for His miraculous provision of this amazing place and dedicating it to God for His service. Sister Aine described what happened next, in a letter she wrote for our tenth Anniversary in 1996. *"No time was lost you'll remember, Peter, in claiming the building for the Lord and in the power of the Spirit your small band of supporters moved from place to place, and room to room, routing the enemy and installing Jesus as Lord and King. We had divided into two groups. You and your group in the direction of the swimming pool and I with the other group up to the tower. Later we all met on the stairs and we sang and praised and thanked the Lord for his mercies."*

We sent out a Newsletter to everyone on our mailing list. It was headed simply, in huge red capital letters, **REJOICE!** – with the words *Our God Reigns* alongside. We were living through a miracle and we wanted everyone to know what God had done – emails didn't yet exist. We also announced in the Newsletter that Ellel Grange would be an *Open House* on November 15th, the date of the next meeting of the PSG – everyone was welcome to come and see, celebrate, give thanks and pray for the ongoing development of the work.

From the very first day of ownership there were people knocking on the door asking for help! The message about Ellel Grange had not only reached those who wanted to help with establishing the ministry, it had also reached those who were in need. But what totally overwhelmed us was not the fact that people were looking for help – it was the depth of the problems they were struggling with and the horrendous nature of some of the things that had happened to them. We quickly realised how little we knew about the depths of pain that so many people had to live through. We very quickly went beyond the limits of our previous experience and were learning to swim in the deep end of God's swimming pool!

Up to this point the sum total of the pioneering team's experience was, almost exclusively, in the realm of inner healing. Most of the books on healing, that were available in the nineteen seventies and eighties, focussed on this aspect of healing. We did not come into the work with any experience of deliverance ministry, or even desire to get involved with it as such, but it wasn't very long before we were dramatically alerted to the possibility and the need! Apart from my eye-opening experience at Liverpool Football Club, during Mission England, I think I may have accidentally cast one evil spirit out prior to this. A lady, whose father had been heavily involved in freemasonry, was supernaturally thrown across the room as she forgave her father and I started praying for healing. But that was it!

We soon discovered that the depth of problems we were facing would, in time, require a significant knowledge of deliverance ministry. Our false expectations that God would lead us slowly and gently, and allow us to gain experience with a lot of what I call "tea and tissues" ministry, before letting us encounter the more difficult cases, were quickly dashed! Yes, we did make many cups of tea and we did need a lot of tissues, but we were also faced with very real and deep issues in people's lives that had not been resolved through any amount of gentle inner-healing ministry. And many of these people had already received much healing prayer in their local church, before venturing up the Ellel Grange drive, still looking for answers.

Martin, for example, was a young man with a huge problem. His Pastor had been trying to help him for a very long time, but at regular intervals he would lose control and try to resolve a domestic problem by beating his wife! He had no difficulty in recognising that this was wrong, very wrong and sinful. He was deeply repentant every time, but it kept on happening. Martin sat with his Pastor in the lounge at Ellel Grange and told us about his problem. After listening for quite a while, I sensed the Lord was urging me to pray the simplest of prayers, *"Lord, expose any darkness in this man's life."*

The Pastor seemed encouraged by my desire to pray and wrongly surmised that I knew what I was doing – the fact is, I'd never ever prayed such a prayer before and had no idea what to expect! I was soon to be glad, however, that by this time, I had broken my childhood discipline of always closing my eyes when I prayed. I had learned to pray with my eyes open, and watch what God was doing in response to our prayers.

The prayer was very simple and full of faith and the effect was very dramatic! Within seconds, Martin's hands began to stiffen, his fingers went rigid and his whole body slid off the chair and wriggled across the floor like a snake. This was my first direct encounter with a demonic manifestation. No-one could have doubted the reality of what was happening – nor of what subsequently happened when he started to become violent and we ordered the demon to leave in Jesus' name. Suddenly the demon was gone and Martin was left lying on the floor like a limp rag, a changed man.

Encounters such as these made us realise the extent of healing need there is in people's lives – even in the Church, especially where demonic power has been welcomed in through many and varied ungodly practices. Martin, for example, had learnt to use occult power to perform feats of supernatural strength – we had a lot to learn!

When the 15th November came round, we were inundated with supporters who had come from all over the region – over 700 people came to see Ellel Grange for themselves and experience first-hand God's answer to their prayers. Many more donations and promises of help came in on the day. There was much joy as we prepared for the meeting of the Prayer Support Group that evening. But there was a shadow over the day that got progressively darker as the day wore on. One of our black Labradors, Job by name, was missing.

Job had been prone to run off when given the opportunity, but he would always, eventually, be found or come back home. Ellel

Grange, however, was unknown territory for him, so when he ran off earlier in the day, we had no idea where he might have gone, and we didn't know whether he would be able to find his way back to the Grange. While it was wonderful showing all those people round the centre during the day, and enjoying the celebrations of thanksgiving, the longer the day went on, and there was no sign of Job, the more a sense of anxiety and apprehension hung over the proceedings. On several occasions during the day I drove round the country lanes nearby, but there was no sign of Job and nobody appeared to have seen him.

From 7.00pm onwards many more were coming through the doors in readiness for the thanksgiving celebration which was due to begin at 7.30. At 7.25 Alec Sayer, the Christian farmer who many years previously had seen the vision of God's blessing being poured down on the Grange, came through the door and I could tell from his face that he wasn't bearing good news. He had just heard that a neighbouring farmer had seen a black Labrador in one of his fields, where there were sheep, and had shot the dog dead.

One of the hardest things I have ever done was to walk into that packed meeting room at Ellel Grange, five minutes later, and say nothing as I led the people in praise and thanksgiving to God for all He had done. The burden of pain I was carrying, without being able to say a word to anyone, was almost unbearable. I did not want anything to be a distraction from the great joy and spontaneous prayers of thanksgiving to the Lord which interspersed the evening of praise and worship. I had no intention of allowing anything to disrupt the precious meeting that took place that night.

Later, after the meeting was over, however, and most people had left, I had to go and tell my family what had happened to Job. There was anger and tears. For the children this was an impossibly hard blow to take – Job was their dog, the family pet, the 'son' of our first black Labrador, Sam. It was particularly hard for Mark, then aged 14, who had been very close to Job. This cruel and unnecessary act significantly affected how they viewed the work their Dad was involved in. It was a direct attack of the enemy. The timing of what happened could not have been more precise or more devastating.

The following day I went to the farm where Job had been shot, recovered his body, took it home and buried him in the garden. Those were really tough days and this event made us very much aware that in seeking to bring hope and healing to those whose lives had been devastated, we were involved at the sharp end of spiritual warfare and we should not be surprised if there was a backlash from the enemy.

It was about this time that someone drew our attention to the date on which the completion of the purchase of Ellel Grange had taken place, October 31st. This is the date on which Halloween is celebrated extensively, and increasingly, in the west – especially in the UK and North America. Halloween night is a highpoint of satanic festivals. The date for completion of the purchase may have been fixed for logistical reasons by the lawyers representing both sides of the transaction, but we do not believe it was an accidental coincidence. It was as if God had chosen Halloween night to raise up a ministry that would be strategic in pulling down the strongholds of the enemy in the lives of His people. It's no wonder that we were sensing spiritual attack and needed to be on our guard. Paul knew what he was doing when he advised believers to *"put on the full armour of God, so that you can take your stand against the devil's schemes"* (Ephesians 6:11).

The first residential guests stayed at the Grange during our very first week of ownership. To each of the major John Wimber Conferences that took place in the UK during the early eighties, there came a large supporting team from America. After the main conference was over, these teams would divide and conduct follow-up events at locations all over the country. Lancaster University, just a couple of miles from Ellel Grange, had been selected for one of these, and we agreed that the visiting team could use Ellel Grange for their accommodation.

They were a real blessing and encouragement to us during those very early days of the ministry, and one couple wrote their name, address and phone number in our new visitors book. Weeks later, when we were struggling with how to help people, we started telephoning Otto and Sharon Bixler in California and asked them to pray. On occasions God would answer their prayers with precise words of knowledge that proved to be critical in bringing healing to some of the people we were praying with. But not only were they of enormous help at that time, God was using these experiences to call Otto and Sharon into the ministry full time and before too many years had passed they were pioneering the establishment of Ellel Ministries in Eastern Europe and Russia – but how that happened will have to wait till a later Chapter.

Just before Christmas, Mary Munro, a young lady who had been working with YWAM in Glasgow, joined the team for six months to learn about the healing ministry. Thirty years later she is still on the Ellel Grange team and has been the ministry manager for most of those years! A young girl called Karen had just left school and came in the summer of 1987 to help with the washing up for six weeks, but God so impacted her life that she is still a key part of the Ellel Grange team and has been the main worship leader for most of those years! Steadily God was drawing key people into the team to be part of what He was doing.

The first Healing Retreat took place in January 1987. The pattern for each retreat had been established in prayer and vision long before I had ever heard of Ellel Grange, when the Lord gave me Luke 9:11 as the foundational Scripture for the ministry, embodying those vital principles of *Welcome, Teach and Heal*. I had taught each of the five sessions of a retreat to the sheep on many occasions, but this was the first time that real people would sit in front of me in the lounge of Ellel Grange. Fifteen of the brave souls who had called or written in, asking for help, had been invited to come for the retreat, but none of them could have known how nervous we were, as we welcomed them to the Grange. But what God did over that weekend was totally extraordinary and totally unrelated to the experience or ability of the team who were praying and ministering. It was all of God. His grace and mercy were present in abundance as He did the work in people's lives.

One thing we discovered on that very first retreat was that a good proportion of those who had come knew about God, but they didn't know God for themselves. So the retreat became not only a healing experience but it was also primary evangelism, introducing people to the Saviour and helping them to make Jesus Lord of their lives. On many, many of the three thousand or so Healing Retreats that have been conducted since then around the world, people have been born again of the Spirit of God and entered into a living and dynamic relationship with Him for the first time. For thousands of people this has been the irreplaceable gateway to their personal healing journey. Salvation is, literally, being raised from the deadness of life outside of God into the living reality of being alive in Him. Two people in particular on that first retreat would probably not be alive today, were it not for what God did for them at Ellel Grange in January 1987.

For Pete, that first Healing Retreat was his last hope. Either God had to do something or he would commit suicide. His emotions were totally locked away in the pain of a very damaged childhood. He couldn't remember the last time he had cried. Physically, his legs were in constant pain and he tried to cover his inner turmoil by smoking sixty cigarettes, or more, a day. As two of the team persevered in prayer, that God would heal his broken heart and restore his lost emotions, there came a moment when a single tear squeezed out of the corner of his eye and ran down his cheek, followed by another and another. God was healing the inner pain.

Pete's life was so radically turned round that he gave up all thoughts of suicide, the pains in his legs were no more and the craving for cigarettes disappeared. Additionally his sense of smell, which had been absent for years was completely restored. But the most important healing he received was the deep inner knowledge that God loved him. Instead of committing suicide, he met his wife whilst teaching her how to drive and shortly after emigrated to the USA to Seattle, where, he says, *"we have lived ever since and just celebrated 19 years of the happiest marriage that one could possibly wish for with our 17 year old twin boys Zachary and Harrison."*

Val was a chronic anorexic. For the previous fourteen years she hadn't eaten any solid food – her diet was liquids only. Her condition was so bad that her husband could not tolerate the relationship any longer. He was ready to throw her out and divorce was imminent. She was desperate and also, like Pete, suicidal. For Val, there was no point in living any more. Life for her was hell on earth. She had come to the end of herself and went into a local church and did a deal with God – telling Him that unless He did something soon, she was going to take her own life.

On her way out of the church she noticed a leaflet about a new ministry that was opening up at Ellel Grange. She noted the phone number and telephoned for help. She tells me now that the receptionist put her through to me and, apparently, I invited her on the first Healing Retreat and on hearing that she was very suicidal, I said, *"Well, why don't you wait till after the retreat before doing it!"* Not exactly the best counselling advice, but I was in faith that God would so impact her life on the retreat that afterwards she wouldn't want to commit suicide! And that's exactly what happened.

On the first night of the retreat she realised that she needed Jesus to be her Saviour and she invited Him into her life. On the next day she faced the issues which had led to her being anorexic, experienced God's healing and was delivered of the demonic powers that were driving her to suicide. Her anorexia was already beginning to be a thing of the past. On the final day of the retreat fifteen inches of snow fell and she couldn't get home. She had to call the husband who didn't want her back and ask him to come and get her. She told him she was now different. Reluctantly he came, but his car got stuck in the thick snow in the Ellel Grange drive and he had to walk in to the building and telephone for the Automobile Association to come and tow him out! It took four hours for them to come.

In those four hours we fed both him and Val. He watched in total shock and amazement as he saw this lady who, for fourteen years, had only ever drunk liquids, consume a full plate of fish and chips! She was so radically changed and healed that he came back on a retreat for himself a few weeks later. He was born again also and then together they went off to Bible College. For the next twenty years Val was a Salvation Army evangelist and Pastor. Today, in her retirement from pastoral work, she is part of the ministry team at Ellel Grange, praying that God will do for others what He did for her on that very first retreat.

Barry and Jan Jay were the first people to be appointed to the Ellel Grange staff in January 1987. Six months previously they had been given a personal vision of themselves welcoming people into a large house, and when they saw the first Newsletters about the developing work at Ellel Grange, they realised that our advertisement for a couple to be at the heart of the ministry, welcoming people to the Grange, exactly fitted the vision they had been given.

Barry and Jan were a true gift of God to the ministry. They were instrumental in establishing the loving welcome as an integral part of the work of healing and were totally servant-hearted. Barry had formerly worked for the Ministry of Defence, Jan was an accountant and together they had also run a hotel in the Lake District. Their maturity and experience was exactly what the work needed in those very early days. Subsequently they became pioneers at Glyndley Manor, and established Prayer Support Groups for the ministry all over the country and remain associated with the work to this day.

As the work developed, the need for more staff became critical. The number of young people on the team was growing and Barry and Jan desperately needed the help of another mature couple to act as Team Pastors and House Managers. One couple, Phil and Pauline, who responded to our advertisement, seemed ideal for the job. They had been married for eleven years and had no children. They had been through all the stages of medical fertility treatment at King's College, Hospital, London, but to no avail, and had come to the conclusion that God was preparing them for service in the Body of Christ in a location where it might be difficult to raise a family. They had become reconciled to their childlessness and the Ellel Grange job suited them well – and they suited us. They had excellent gifts and abilities – and they came with very good recommendations.

They came to stay at the Grange for a couple of days and as we spent time with them it was obvious they would be ideal for the job. We were already talking with them about when they could start. But the night before they were due to return home, I had a disturbed night's sleep and sensed a gentle rebuke from the Lord as He reminded me of how He had ordained marriage as a family institution. I suddenly realised that we were taking advantage of their inability to have children and had to repent of my attitude. As I went downstairs to have breakfast with them I sensed that God's greatest concern for Phil and Pauline at that time was not the job we needed to be filled, but their healing!

I sat with them at breakfast, and as I looked at Pauline the Lord began to show me that there was a curse on her generation line that needed to be broken. I knew those strange words in the ten commandments which talked about the sins of the fathers being visited on the children until the third and the fourth generations (Exodus 20:5), but I had never thought about their practical relevance to today's believers. This was new territory for me to tread on. I was about to have another lesson in the healing ministry!

Over breakfast I shared with Phil and Pauline my overnight experience and asked if they would like to be prayed for. They explained that they had received prayer for healing on many occasions and it was because God hadn't answered their prayers they had reached the conclusion that God didn't want them to have children! All I could say was what God had said to me overnight, that if God had called them to be married, then it was His desire that they would have children. They couldn't disagree with this scriptural truth and said they would be happy to be prayed for one more time.

I will never forget the intense nervousness, as well as the excitement of faith, as I looked at Pauline across the breakfast table and asked her if she would be willing to forgive anyone on her generation line who had done anything that was affecting her ability to conceive. She had no problem in doing this and I then spoke out the words God was putting into my mouth. *"In the name of Jesus I break every curse upon you that has caused you to not be able to conceive and order any evil spirit that has been given authority over you to leave immediately."*

Neither Phil nor I were ready for what happened next. Pauline dropped the piece of toast that had been in her hand and within seconds she had fled from the breakfast table holding her stomach, with Phil running after her to the bathroom in their bedroom. There Pauline was violently sick for some minutes. Until the moment I had prayed that prayer, she felt fine, but as soon as I had prayed to set her free from whatever had come down to her from her ancestors, she knew she had to get to a toilet as quickly as she possibly could. Whatever it was, was coming out – and fast!

When it was all over, she lay on her bed and almost instantly fell into a very deep, supernatural sleep. A lady member of our team, sitting by Pauline at the bedside, was intensely aware that God was ministering to her directly and bringing deep healing to her on the inside. The sleep lasted for just ten minutes, after which she felt fine, got up, went back downstairs and finished her breakfast!

We offered Phil and Pauline the job and were anxiously waiting to hear whether or not they would accept it and be joining the Ellel Grange team. Ten days after their visit I took a phone call from Pauline who first told me that they wouldn't be coming to Ellel Grange after all. I tried hard to disguise the disappointment in my voice – but then she told me the reason why, *"I'm pregnant!"* she said. My instant response was, *"You can't be – it's too soon!"*

"That's what we thought," Pauline replied, *"but we've done two pregnancy tests and both were positive."* And so it was that nine months later Lucy Anne was born – the first of many babies born to previously childless couples following prayer for healing and, often, deliverance as well. Phil and Pauline went on to have two more children and today Lucy Anne is a beautiful young woman with a beautiful voice who loves worshipping the Lord. At university she took on the leadership of the Christian Union and saw it grow from 20 to over 70 members.

God was taking us through some dramatic and unforgettable learning experiences in those early days of the ministry. The lesson we learned with Phil and Pauline has been used to minister to many, many couples around the world who were struggling to conceive, a large percentage of whom have subsequently been blessed with children – including the first Directors of the work in Sabah, Malaysia.

Chapter 10

MY WAYS ARE NOT YOUR WAYS!

Surprising Lessons in the Ways of God

"*For my thoughts are not your thoughts, neither are your ways my ways, declares the Lord. As the heavens are higher than the earth, so are my ways higher than your ways.*" Isaiah 55:8-9
Through watching the ways of God in the lives of my Mum and Dad, I had learned how, when we are available to Him, that He will clearly direct our steps, often in quite supernatural ways – ways that are beyond the strategy of man.

Many years ago my brother bought a house on the west coast of the Isle of Harris in Scotland. Salmon fishing rights came with the house! My Dad was a keen fisherman and in his retirement Mum and Dad spent many weeks, even months, up there during the summer. One day, Dad noticed a man and his son sitting on the bank of the loch watching him fish. Dad always looked for opportunities like this to talk to people about the Lord, especially if there was an opportunity to share the Gospel with a young boy. He never forgot the impact on his own life of Hudson Pope's determination to spend time with him as a ten year-old.

So Dad stopped fishing to have a chat with the man, and, in the ensuing conversation discovered that the boy was mad keen on fishing but had had little opportunity to fish. So Dad welcomed them on to the loch and let the boy fish in the private water. And so began a friendship with Peter Lever and his family – a friendship which was to prove not only precious, but miraculously critical!

Roll the clock forward ten years and Mum and Dad are having a week's holiday at a hotel in Lytham St Anne's, near Blackpool. On the Friday evening of their stay I drove over from Ellel Grange to have dinner with them at their hotel. We had a wonderful evening chatting, reminiscing and enjoying each other's company. It was a very memorable occasion. About 9.45pm I got up to leave and they walked with me to where my car was parked on the road outside. As I was about to drive off, I wound down the driver's window, Dad put his head inside, gave me a big hug and a kiss and I said, *"You're looking so well tonight, Dad."* Dad said his goodbyes and I drove away with wonderful memories of a thoroughly enjoyable evening.

The lights of my car were not even out of sight before my Dad had left this world behind and was in the immediate presence of the Lord. As he watched me drive away he had a massive heart attack, collapsed on the ground, and was lying dead on the pavement by the gate of a private house next door to the hotel. Mum got down on her hands and knees and was bending over her husband's body when a man came down the drive of the house, opened the gate and almost tripped over my mother as she knelt on the ground. Mum looked up into the face of Peter Lever. *"Betty!"* he exclaimed and got down beside her on the pavement and provided all the help and immediate comfort that my Mum needed at that critical moment.

In her moment of direst need the Lord so arranged it that she wasn't alone – and that the very first person who stooped to help her was someone who knew and loved her well. Peter Lever didn't live in that house – he had just decided to visit a friend of his on that particular night, whose house it was that he was leaving, at the very moment my Dad had died. This was no coincidence, it was God doing things His way!

I never cease to be amazed at the ways of the Lord as He does things that are beyond anything we could ever have planned or dreamt of! God spared me the trauma, but also made provision for my Mum as my Dad was entering the gates of Heaven and meeting with the saints in glory. It was nearly two hours before, having heard the news, that I was able to get back to Lytham St Anne's – what a comfort it was, both to me and my mother, that Peter Lever had been there at that critical moment and Mum wasn't alone when she most needed help. It was experiences like this that taught me to be constantly aware that God may surprise us at any moment with His ways, and to always be ready to lay down my own plans and follow His. When God intervenes, there is a reason.

The weekend we chose for the selection of our first Associate Counsellors was an outstanding example of the ways of God trumping the ways of man! Even before Ellel Grange had opened, the Lord showed me that for the work to be truly non-denominational in practice, we would need to have a team of volunteer Associate Counsellors, drawn from as many different mainstream churches and denominations as possible. The work was to be Kingdom and Scripture focussed and not have any particular denominational emphasis. A lot of people had expressed interest in helping with the ministry and we decided, therefore, to invite all of them to come for a weekend of introductory training at Ellel Grange. We knew what we wanted and we had a plan! And on paper it looked a good and sensible plan, which everyone was happy with.

I put together four teaching sessions to be spread over the weekend. Our core team was divided into interviewing pairs, so that over the course of the weekend everyone who came would be seen and talked to personally. After the weekend we planned to compare notes and make a preliminary selection of those who seemed suitable to be part of our prayer and ministry team.

We were all looking forward to the weekend and meeting the people who wanted to join the team. On the preceding Tuesday I started to read the three chapters of the book of Nahum as part of my personal Bible reading. It was not a book I was familiar with, but as I read what the prophet had written, I was gripped with excitement about this amazing treatise on spiritual warfare and victory. It's full of wonderful Scriptures such as *"The Lord is good, a refuge in times of trouble, he cares for those who trust in him . . . he will pursue his foes into darkness . . . Look, there on the mountains, the feet of one who brings good news, who proclaims peace "* (from Chapter 2).

But the words which gripped me more than any others were from chapter one and verse three, where the prophet says (in the Good News version I was reading at the time), *"Where the Lord walks, storms arise."* We had already experienced some of those storms and it was comforting and encouraging to realise that what we might see as severe problems can, in fact, be the reaction of the enemy to the presence of God. Prior to that time, I had never taken much note of this allegedly "minor prophet", but now God had used Nahum to really get my attention. However, it seemed, God's timing wasn't very good, an important weekend was coming up and I would have to put my study of Nahum on one side until after the weekend was over.

Friday night came and everyone was gathered for the first session of worship and teaching. On the Saturday we began our series of interviews, sandwiched between a morning and evening teaching session. Everything was going fine, the core team were gathering their notes and we were looking forward to debriefing with each other when all our guests had gone home. Sunday morning came and I was on my way down the main staircase of Ellel Grange at 9.25am, ready for the Sunday morning worship time and teaching at 9.30.

Suddenly, God surprised me with one of the clearest words I have ever heard him speak into my spirit, *"It's Nahum this morning!"* I instantly knew what God meant – I had to change my teaching and speak from the book of Nahum. But as I continued down the stairs, I started arguing with God and told Him that this final teaching session was very important and the people all had the notes in their hands. But my arguments were just empty words, I knew what God was saying, and what He wanted me to do, and by the time I reached the bottom step, Nahum it would be!

The problem was that I had never before spoken from the book of Nahum, and I desperately needed time to go and do some study and prepare myself. But there was no time. There couldn't be any study. It was trust God or nothing! I asked people to put down the notes they had been given as, instead, we were going to look together at the book of Nahum. The team looked very surprised and it was obvious from the time it took for people to find Nahum in their Bibles, that I wasn't the only person in the room who was unfamiliar with this little book!

I explained how the Lord had shown me earlier in the week that Nahum contained some important principles of spiritual warfare which, as a ministry, we would need to understand. Without any notes or time for preparation, all I could do was read through the Book and let the Holy Spirit fill my mouth with a running commentary, as we read the three chapters together. Even though I was totally unprepared, the teaching just flowed from start to finish. At the end there was a holy quietness in the room which lasted all of two minutes and then 'holy mayhem' broke out. Within minutes the meeting room at Ellel Grange resembled a battlefield!

Several were sobbing in repentance, heads between their knees as they did business with God. Others were flat on the floor being filled with the Holy Spirit. Some went into spontaneous deliverance as they dealt with the issues that God was speaking to them about. Some were even screaming as they wrestled with dark forces. I had never before seen such chaos in a Christian meeting. Members of the team were doing their best to minister to the people, but fundamentally this was a time which was totally God-initiated and He was doing His work, His way. As I stood at the front and surveyed the scene, Nahum 1:3 kept on going through my mind, *"Where the Lord walks storms arise!"* The Lord was indeed walking through the room and all sorts of storms were arising.

That morning meeting began at 9.30am and continued until exhaustion took over at 1.00am the following morning. The anointing of God was so heavy upon the place that wherever people were in the building, they were being confronted by the presence and the power of God. For two or three days when people who had not been present on the Sunday morning came into the building, they were impacted by the almost tangible anointing there was in Ellel Grange.

While all this was happening I was desperately trying to remember the many lessons that God was teaching us in such a short space of time, one of the most important of which was that the Holy Spirit is a HOLY Spirit. And that wherever and whenever He manifests His presence, ungodliness in the lives of God's people will be confronted. The clearest evidence that what is happening is of God will always be the exposure of sin and consequential repentance.

It was clear that a deep, deep work was taking place in the lives of many. I made a mental note to study the genuine revivals of history and look specifically at this point, and take a closer look at Isaiah's experience recorded in Isaiah chapter six, where he describes an extraordinary experience of being carried into the holy presence of God. Isaiah's reaction was to see himself in a totally new light, as he realised just how unclean he personally was, and how unclean the people were to whom God had sent him to proclaim truth as a prophet.

We never got to the final session of interviewing potential members of the team – and the team never even got to discussing who might be suitable. God didn't seem to be interested in what we thought of the different individuals who had come for the weekend, for what He was doing was testing their hearts, to see if they recognised and welcomed His presence. For those were the ones God wanted on His team!

Sadly, there were quite a number of people who sat around in stunned amazement, wondering what on earth they were doing in such a place as Ellel Grange. One by one they left and many of them we never saw again. They had deselected themselves from further consideration. This was not how they envisaged the healing ministry should be!

But the ones who remained, the ones who recognised the work of the Holy Spirit in their lives and who were broken and blessed by the Lord's presence, remained. They did not want to miss even one moment of that extraordinary time of living in the reality of God's presence – whatever the cost. They wanted God at any price – nothing was going to stand in the way of God's best for them. Somewhere about 4.00pm in the afternoon a group of the team gathered to pray for everyone who was ministering to others. But the Spirit of God came down on that prayer meeting so heavily that none of them could pray, they couldn't even stand up! God wanted them out there helping those who were going through their personal spiritual crisis, as He first knocked down the walls of resistance to Him and then built people up again in Him.

These were the people God was choosing to be part of the team – those who had His heart and who were willing to let Him bring His order into their lives. And these were the ones who stood the test of loyalty and perseverance as the testing times came. God knew exactly what He was doing when He changed the programme and sent the Holy Spirit in such a powerful manifestation of His presence. Much deliverance took place on that day and I, and many others, were changed forever by what God did at Ellel Grange on the 8th February 1987.

It wasn't that we never planned anything else ever again – we did. But we were now much more aware of how God wanted to manifest His presence in the hearts of His people and transform their lives. God had shown us that this was His work, and He was concerned that we should do it His way. Nobody would have thought that a Bible study on the book of Nahum was the right way to prepare a body of people to be Associate Counsellors of the ministry. But through this, God was showing us that He wasn't so much concerned about whether or not a person was a gifted counsellor, He was far more concerned about whether or not they recognised and welcomed His presence. These were the ones that God could use.

As the work developed there would be scores of times when God took charge and did things His way – especially with regard to His direction when leading us to a particular Centre for the establishment of the ministry, in country after country. Time and again we have had to stand back and shake our heads in amazement and keep on appreciating Isaiah's words that God's ways are higher than our ways!

Chapter 11

INTO THE UNKNOWN!

Plumbing the Depths of Personal Need

If I were God I wouldn't have chosen me for founding the work of Ellel Ministries! And if I were God I wouldn't have dropped the leaders and supporters of this new work into such deep water – right from the beginning! But I'm not God and I'm grateful that His ways are not my ways and that He knows best. But there truly are many times when I have wondered why He chose me and times when I have thought that a gentle learning curve would have been much more kind than sky-diving into the deepest of deep, unknown waters!

When God gave me the vision for the work He did not place any limitations on the conditions that He could or could not heal – He simply drew my attention to the bent and vandalised chassis of my *Alvis Speed 20* and said that while I could restore that broken car, He could restore broken lives – and that was it! I realised that restoring that particular car was going to be a mountain of Herculean proportions to climb, so I suppose it was to be expected that people who had suffered the very worst of life's experiences, and the enemy's assault on their lives, would be among the first to find their way to the doors of Ellel Grange.

While there have been many wonderful stories of what God has done in bringing healing to thousands of people, there have also been people we have struggled to help, with varying degrees of success. Along the journey, however, I have never lost faith in the God who is able and willing to heal and kept on looking to Him for His answers for all who came. And little by little more of those answers have come.

What a person experiences is their own reality – even though their perception of what they are going through may not be a true reflection of the real issues involved, or of how their problem started. They cannot just walk away from their symptoms – they have to live with them. And if those symptoms are causing a serious disruption to the normalities of life, then the sufferer has to find ways of coping with the limitations imposed by their symptoms, in order to get through everyday life as best they can.

These coping mechanisms can often be of a very complex nature, ranging from the obvious addictions to alcohol or non-prescribed drugs to the complex behavioural patterns that are given psychological or psychiatric labels, such as self-harming, OCD (obsessive compulsive disorder), various phobias and eating disorders, many of which are often treated with varying types of therapy and medication. Only in very exceptional circumstances do these symptoms go away of their own accord. More usually they become accepted as part of the identity of the person who is struggling to cope with the pressures of life, as well as their symptomatic conditions. Prescribed medication and therapy can then become a long-term need and dependency.

So, how has the Lord led us to minister to people, whatever the condition or situation that they may be struggling with? The fundamental definition of healing that God gave us at the beginning of the ministry was simply *the restoration of God's order in a person's life*, with the Bible as the source of God's truth about both Himself and what His order for mankind actually is. While, to some, this may sound simplistic, it does accurately parallel the medical profession. My daughter is a doctor, and as part of her training she had to dissect a dead body, so that she would have a detailed, first-hand knowledge of what the natural physical order for the human body actually is. Knowing what it should be like is a helpful starting place for identifying what might be wrong when someone's sick.

In a similar way, having an understanding of how God created man, and of how He desires and intends us to relate with Him, provides a solid foundation for understanding God's natural order for humanity. Any deviation from God's natural order for human beings in their relationship with God, their Creator, can then be seen as a potential source of dis-ease in a person's spirit and soul. And when this dis-ease is fully out-worked, it may, also, present as dis-ease or, more accurately, disease in the body, or in the bodies of succeeding generations. This is very closely related to the medical analysis of physical conditions, and then to the study of generational (genetic) disorders. Inherited proneness to a particular disease is an increasingly significant realm of medical research, especially with regard to cancers and other life-threatening conditions.

The Scriptures make it clear, in many places, that there can be a very close relationship between spiritual and physical health. For example, Proverbs 3:5-8, expresses the truth that when people choose to live according to the ways of God, then it will bring health to the body and nourishment to the bones. So, when praying for people in need of healing, irrespective of the depths of their problem, the Lord led us to find out if there is any obvious way in which their life is being lived out of order with God for, if so, that is a helpful place to start praying, on their journey of healing. God's Word is intended to be a plumb-line, against which we can measure whether or not life is out of order with God's truth and His way for mankind. It is also the source of great riches and it is only as we press into God's Word that the most precious keys (the gold!) to His healing ways are discovered.

When looking at the need for restoration of God's order in the life of a human being, God showed us not to depend on whatever medical knowledge a person may already have of their body, as the sole indicator of what to pray for. The human body is very wonderful, but it is, in reality, only a transient machine, a temporary home in which we live throughout our life on earth and on which we depend for fulfilling our day to day activities. In addition to having a body, each human being is a living soul and it is our God-given spirit which gives life to the body and soul together. So, when praying with people, we are looking for God to heal disorder in the spirit, the soul or the body.

Paul got it absolutely right when he prayed that the Thessalonian believers he was writing to would be whole in spirit, soul and body (1 Thessalonians 5:23). And over and above those three primary areas of potential concern, we also have to be aware that the person we are praying for may have been affected by the presence of an evil spirit and need deliverance. Much of the healing ministry of Jesus involved setting people free from evil spirits through deliverance, and when He sent His disciples out to pray for people He gave them His delegated power and authority to cast out demons also (Luke 9:1-2). We should not expect, therefore, the healing ministry to be any different today.

It was in those years of preparation for teaching Healing Retreats, long before Ellel Grange was opened, that God showed me how important it is that we should be praying for the right thing and that can mean having some understanding of why a person is sick, and what may be preventing them from receiving God's healing. An important verse in John's Gospel (2:25) tells us that Jesus did not need people to tell him about themselves, for He knew what was in man. He was without sin and had perfect understanding of the heart of everyone who stood before Him. It's vital when ministering to people that we should look to Him for how to pray, so that we will be praying for the right thing. Here's a couple of examples of what I mean.

Karen was eighteen years old, but dying of kidney failure. Her kidneys were swollen, she was in a lot of pain and she had difficulty bending as a result. The medics had diagnosed a viral condition on both kidneys for which there was no known cure. Excepting for the remote possibility of a double kidney transplant, her doctors had given her less than twelve months to live.

Karen came forward for prayer at the monthly healing service at Ellel Grange and it would have been easy to simply lay hands on her, anoint her with oil and pray for her healing in a general way. But as she told me her story, my heart was filled with compassion for her and as I looked to God for His understanding of what to pray for, the answer I sensed God giving me was *"Ask her about her mother!"* Initially this gave me a bit of a problem, because it was her kidneys that were the issue, not her mother! But the Lord seemed insistent and so I asked Karen the rather bizarre question.

"Oh," she replied, *"I have no idea who my mother is. All I know is that my mother fell pregnant as a teenager and had me when she was 16. I was then given up for adoption and I have absolutely no idea as to who my natural mother and father are."* As Karen told me her story, the Lord was showing me that, in her case, Karen needed to forgive her parents for their sexual sin and that she should give thanks to God that her mother didn't have an abortion. Karen had no problem doing either of those things and I then asked her to lay her own hands on her tummy, where she had been joined to her

mother, and anointed the back of her hands with oil and prayed a simple prayer, cutting Karen free from every generational curse of infirmity or death that had been given access through the sexual sin of her parents. At this point there was no prayer for the kidneys.

Immediately Karen began to feel something stirring in her stomach, going round and round in circles. I spoke firmly to what was now obviously an evil spirit and ordered it to leave. The spirit came up through her chest and out through her mouth. I then asked a female member of our young people's team to lay her hands on the kidneys and pray for healing while I prayed for someone else. When I came back to her, twenty minutes later, the swelling and the pain had gone and a very excited Karen was able to bend over and touch her toes!

Six weeks later she wrote to say she'd been back to the hospital and the doctors had re-run all the tests. There was now no evidence whatsoever of there being any virus present. They told her to go away and live a normal life and forget everything they had said to her previously! The key to Karen's healing was dealing with the consequences of her parent's sin and then receiving deliverance prior to prayer for physical healing. Godly order had been restored and the prayer for healing of her body was then effective.

Another example of significant physical healing took place on one of our early Healing Retreats. Pat's spine was 'crumbling' and the doctors had advised her that she would probably be in a wheelchair within twelve months. She wore a thick plastic tube, encasing her back, to prevent it from further damage and she came on the retreat looking for prayer for physical healing. But in the first session of the retreat I taught on the need to forgive those who have hurt us, reminding people of what Jesus said in the Lord's prayer and then, in Matthew 6:15, when He told us that if we don't forgive others then God will not be able to forgive us. At the end of the meeting Pat was very angry with me for what I had said and stormed off home saying *"What right has Peter Horrobin to tell me to forgive – I've been bitter for thirty years and I'm not going to waste one of them!"*

But that night she couldn't sleep and as she lay there, wide awake, God began to speak to her about what I had said at the meeting. This time she decided to do what I had suggested, and prayed through her life. One by one she forgave all the many people who had really hurt her. She then fell into a deep sleep, only to be woken the following morning by the ticking of her clock – which, for her, was a miracle. For she had taken both her hearing aids out before climbing into bed and without them she wouldn't normally be able to hear a thing!

The following day she was back at the Grange to tell us what had happened, how she had forgiven everyone and God had restored her hearing. *"Now,"* she said, *"will you pray for my back?"* When we did so there was an extraordinary anointing of the Spirit upon her as she fell to the floor and for a period of twenty minutes or so she experienced what she said felt like hot electric light bulbs, going up and down her spine as God healed her back. She then went outside and did a cartwheel on the grass to demonstrate her healing!

We could have prayed for the healing of Pat's spine on the first evening of the retreat, but it was only when she had dealt with her bitterness and got her heart in right order before God and she had forgiven all those who had hurt her, that she could receive God's forgiveness for herself and be healed. When her life was brought into line with God's intended order, healing flowed into her body.

Experiences such as this strongly reinforced the principle that God had shown me in advance, by faith, as I "taught" the sheep, while out walking my dog! Many of those walks were deeply spiritual occasions as God used them to prepare me for the ministry that lay ahead, in the deep end of God's swimming pool! Here we had to either sink or swim – and having waited so long for the vision to open up, and trusting that God was in charge, I was determined that we would swim – although there were times when it seemed as though we might drown under the pressure of need which landed on the doorsteps of Ellel Grange.

One day I took a call from David, the elder of a Brethren Assembly, not a church that is known for its charismatic credentials. Normally of a very conservative nature, David began to explain how this lady had started attending their church, there was some rather strange behaviour and her immediate problem was a fear of spiders. For David, with his very conservative theological background, the idea that it was possible for a believer to have a demon, represented a massive change in his theological foundations. But he also recognised that in the church they had done everything they knew to help Carol without any success. And he recognised, also, that, at times, her behaviour seemed to be controlled by something that took her over. She really loved the Lord and was desperate for help.

When David brought her to Ellel Grange, I first spent a little while getting to know both the elder and Carol and explained to them both, as gently as I possibly could, that we can be sick in our spirit, our soul – which includes our mind, emotions and will – and our body, and that sometimes it's possible for a person to need deliverance in the same way that some of the people who came to Jesus needed deliverance. Carol had no problem in understanding what I was saying, for that's exactly what it felt like for her as she struggled to overcome both her immediate fears and the other physical and spiritual problems that she said regularly overtook her.

On that first day of ministry to Carol, God was so very gracious, for she was powerfully delivered of a spirit of fear and later, when she went for a shower, there was a big spider sitting in the corner of the shower cubicle. Previously she would have screamed and run away, but now it was so different – she realised it was just a spider and it held no fear for her. Here was powerful evidence for both

David and Carol that God had, indeed, set her free from that spirit of fear.

What we didn't know on that first day of prayer ministry, however, was that we were just scraping the surface of much deeper issues in Carol's life and that it would take us several years to understand how to bring God's healing to the inner damage that had been caused by the cruel things she, and others we were ministering to at the time, had been forced to experience in their childhood. But the keys we learned along the way have been strategic in bringing healing and freedom to thousands of others in the succeeding years.

From the first day of entering the doors of Ellel Grange, we had experienced contention of every type. For example, I discovered, the hard way, that the container which I thought contained the liquid chemicals for treating the swimming pool, contained diesel oil instead! It took us days to properly clean the swimming bath! In the early days, some spiritually sensitive people would pick up and respond to an atmosphere of loneliness and death in the buildings. Some would sense unseen spiritual powers and others would be drawn to the derelict chapel in the grounds. We found some broken people were particularly vulnerable to a spiritually unclean environment. In the chapel we found satanic worship symbols and signs were being daubed on the building. We found people lying on the ground in an attempt to suck up the powers of darkness! God had us on a dramatic and very steep learning curve about the ways and the powers of the enemy to hold people into the bondage of his deceptions. This was all new to us!

On top of all the above we were trying to help people who had deeply complex stories and backgrounds, the like of which we had never previously heard of. One man and his wife, for example, were referred to us by an Anglican Vicar. The man turned out to be an alcoholic, a drug addict, and a registered psychopath who had served time in prison for committing grievous bodily harm. The vicar had referred him to us because he and his wife were having marriage problems! I wasn't surprised when I discovered the truth about the man's past life. It seemed as though every day we were being driven to our knees in desperate intercession. At times I wished I'd been trained in psychology or psychiatry, but in retrospect I'm not sure that would have helped. The subjects we were being forced to understand were a long way outside the syllabus of a normal college training programme!

For the first few years of the ministry it was necessary for me to spend much time resident at the Grange. They were very sensitive pioneering years, during which God was bringing spiritual strength, keys and reality into the team. And we were learning how to cleanse our land and buildings from the spiritual consequences of all that must have happened there in the past, to give the powers of darkness such access to the place. We were learning first hand why it was that in the wonderful promise of 2 Chronicles 7:14, God said: *"If my people, who are called by my name, will humble themselves and pray and seek my face and turn from their wicked ways, then will I hear from Heaven and will forgive their sin **and will heal their land**."* We were seeing the reality of how land (and buildings) could become poisoned through sin and that it, too, needed healing!

The fact is, we were all being stretched beyond any possible imagination, taken completely out of our natural comfort zone and forced into hanging on to God, through the most testing circumstances I had ever experienced in my entire life. But in the midst of those early ministries, which we took on in faith, in spite of our ignorance and naivety, we were seeing God magnificently at work. He was teaching us, training us – which included learning by our mistakes – and equipping us for the wider work which lay ahead. Sometimes, it almost seemed that the more the mess, the more God showed us He was in it! He was teaching us to let Him show us what His answers are for human need.

The journey of understanding was not for the fainthearted and it was in this crucible of fire that some felt they could no longer continue with the pilgrimage we were on. But God provided a core group of volunteer ministry team, who steadfastly stood alongside us and we were privileged to be able to watch the Holy Spirit at work through them, bringing God's wholeness to these very damaged people, one life at a time. I will never cease to thank God for those precious saints, many of whom have now gone home to glory who formed the backbone of support in every aspect of the ministry. They were totally brilliant. Even today we are awestruck at how God forged the work into being, as we ministered to really hurting people who, in their desperation, were willing to trust their lives to God, and receive help at Ellel Grange.

There was a time during this season, however, when some of the tensions of intensive ministry to individuals spilled over onto the team. Some felt that I was spending too much time in seeking to bring freedom to the one, when there were the many who could be ministered to more efficiently on courses, church visits and conferences. They argued, quite sensibly on the face of it, that by concentrating on trying to get one person free, the rest of the work was suffering. It felt as though I was being pulled in at least two directions. Deep down I knew something would have to give at some point and dreaded the outcome.

In Jeremiah 12:6 we read how Jeremiah experienced something similar, when those who were his brethren were pulling in a different direction to the road he was on. God warned him not to trust what they were saying even *though they speak well of you.* This verse was given to me by someone who knew absolutely nothing of what I was going through at the time. It did seem as though some of the team were wanting to pull me away from what I knew God was calling me to do. I desperately needed a fresh word from the Lord as to how to respond.

The answer came in my private reading of the Scriptures when I came to Jesus's story in the Gospels of a shepherd who had a hundred sheep, but one had wandered off and was lost (Luke 15:3-7). In the story, the shepherd leaves the ninety-nine and goes after the one sheep that was lost, and when he finds it, he joyfully puts it across his shoulders and carries it home. He then calls his friends and neighbours and says *"Rejoice with me. I have found my lost sheep."*

The story goes on to tell of the rejoicing there is in heaven over one 'lost sheep' that is found and brought home – meaning the lost sinner who repents and comes back to God. As I read that story I knew that I, and the ever-faithful ministry team must keep going on the road we were on – *for the sake of the one that was lost*, and also because, as is expressed so profoundly in Matthew 25, it was ministering to the Lord Himself. I simply could not ignore their cries for help and forsake what God had so deeply put within me.

I often tell that story, for the simple reason that it was in ministering to the ones, as God had asked us to do, that eventually the greatest blessings came. For, in persevering with ministry to the ones, we not only saw God bring freedom and healing, but the lessons we learned along the way by ministering to this one and that one *"who was lost"*, have been used to bring hope and healing to the *"ninety and nine"* – or, more accurately, the tens of thousands of people who have benefited from the keys of the Kingdom that God gave us at that time.

To give you but one example – it was through ministering to the ones that we learned the priceless keys of how to bring healing to those who are still suffering the physical, emotional and spiritual consequences of accidents and traumas – even things that had happened many years previously. God has used those keys to bring major physical healing to people in every country Ellel teams have visited – from Rwanda to Australia and from Canada to Hong Kong.

Indeed, those keys have opened up whole nations for this precious life-transforming, Kingdom teaching.

It was during this season, also, that I was experiencing a much deeper heartache than the strain caused by tensions in the team. For it was becoming obvious to everyone who knew me well that the tension in my marriage was increasing. The strain that had been evident for many years, long before the work of Ellel Ministries had started, was coming to a head. Our relationship had reached a complete breaking point. The final breakdown was not sudden, but an outworking of years of struggle, and endeavouring to find and receive help from others on a number of occasions, but to no avail. I longed that things could have been very different and I prayed constantly towards that end throughout this difficult season.

I am so thankful to God, also, that even though I wasn't able to be the Dad I wanted to be during the teenage years of my children, their loving relationships with both Mum and Dad have stood the test of time.

Both Anne and Mark know and love the Lord and Mark, with his lovely wife Kate, is bringing up his four children to know and love the Lord also. What a wonderful generational blessing this is. God has been faithful and answered prayers for them all in an amazing way. And even as the finishing touches were being added to this book, our daughter Anne married Warren, the man of her dreams and God's choice for her, at Ellel Pierrepont.

Many people spoke out about the situation as they saw it and I am aware of many hasty judgements that were made, largely by people who knew nothing about the personal realities of what I was going through and made no attempt to find out. This was a very, very lonely season in my life, especially when one close friend, who I loved and respected greatly, came to see me, putting the case for laying the whole ministry down and leaving my calling behind.

This visit, however, helped me to crystallise my thinking. I could not allow the existing situation to continue. I either had to give up the vision or own the fact that my marriage had irretrievably broken down and continue with the work God had unquestionably called me to do. There was no middle ground. I am incredibly grateful and thankful to the many, many people who stood faithful to the vision, not looking to me but to the One who had brought it into being, and in doing so have remained faithful friends to this day.

In the midst of the joys, that there undoubtedly were at this time in the ministry, there were also times of utter despair. As I wrestled with the pressures, there were definitely times when the temptation to walk away from the vision and the work and to bury myself back in the world of business, seemed very attractive. I had sold my antiquarian book business, but the world of 'old books' was still a constant temptation. On many occasions I walked towards the door of a second-hand bookshop, but found the entrance barred to me spiritually. It felt as though there was a warrior angel guarding the door, preventing me from gaining access to what would have been, for me, a world of temptation. Over fifteen years were to pass before the Lord allowed me once again to enjoy the pleasures of browsing in a second-hand bookshop, without there being any temptation to go back into some aspect of the business world! And it was only a few weeks before starting to write this book that I put a foot down once again in the bookshop I had founded almost forty years previously – twenty-five years had passed since I was last in the shop!

I thank God for those who were interceding for me during what was a long and very dark valley. In the midst of all the different voices I was hearing at that time, God still had His way of leading, guiding and encouraging me. Right out of the blue people would be prompted to contact me with a strategic word of influence that spoke straight into my then situation. Deeply respected godly men and women took time to come and speak into my life. Over and over again God would meet critical financial needs in ways that could only have been God-inspired and directed. Through many years of extreme loneliness in the ministry, God sustained and carried me.

Ultimately, there was only one place to go with the cry of my heart, and that was into God, to examine my own heart with Him, and find the place where the peace of God reigns, for that is how the Scriptures tell us that He will guide us. I wrestled for days, weeks, months and years with all the issues, while God continued to do amazing things in and through the ministry. I had no doubts at all that God had clearly and definitely called me out of the business world, into my personal destiny. He had fully affirmed it with His presence, supernatural signs and His loving provision. This was where I was at home – and I knew that I could not leave the place where God's peace reigned in my heart. I could not turn back from where He was leading. And so I made my decision. It wasn't a decision I wanted to make and it was an extremely costly decision, which had consequences which would have to be worked through. But in the end, there was no other decision I could make and I simply had to trust God to walk with me, my wife and our children through the great sadness, the pain and the practical consequences of marital separation.

It was difficult enough in some Christian circles to be pioneering a ministry that included deliverance – for there were many who turned away from the work of Ellel Ministries because of that. But it was significantly more difficult when the word got out that my marriage had not weathered the storm and that I and my wife were living separately. And the storm intensified when many years later the reality of our separation was legalised in divorce.

How I thank God for His keeping power during this period and for the incredibly faithful and loyal team who stuck by the work, and by me, during the severe storms that were blowing around us.

And yet, it was during this season that we experienced some of the most amazing times in the history of the ministry. God had certainly not turned his back on the work, even though many things were being said against the work in church and media circles. But it was almost as though God's anointing on the ministry increased and, in time, the storms died down as God took the work across the country and around the world. And over thirty years later God is still taking the visionary seed that was sown at Ellel Grange and scattering it into one country after another as God moves by His Spirit to bring hope and healing to His people.

As I said earlier on in this chapter, if I were God, I would not have chosen me for this work. But maybe it is simply that God does not choose perfection, but rather loves to take an ordinary human life and if they are willing, available and obedient, He will turn their failure, their pain and their circumstances into His garden of fruitfulness. My story is not one of personal success, but one of God's overriding grace and faithfulness in the midst of human weakness and fallibility and I pray this will be an ongoing encouragement to many more to still trust Him, in spite of the things that may seem to be an obstacle to God's blessing on their lives.

Chapter 12

UNEXPECTED EXPLOSION

The Battle Belongs to the Lord!

Just as there are watershed moments in all our personal lives, there are watershed moments in the growth and development of organisations and ministries. The *Battle Belongs to the Lord* Conference, in February 1990 at the Brighton Centre in England, was one of those moments.

Looking back, it was a crazy decision to sign a contract and book such a huge auditorium as The Brighton Centre! This was an era, however, when Christians were attending conferences in their thousands and we were definitely being encouraged to share the good news of how God was radically healing people through both inner healing and deliverance ministry.

Much prayer went ahead of the event and as the day drew near, there was great excitement, as well as apprehension, in the team. Coaches and hotels had been arranged and every person's gifts and talents were used. And as the day approached a careful plan was put into action and the Ellel teams converged on the Brighton

Centre. The conference title, THE BATTLE BELONGS TO THE LORD, was displayed on the centre's premier advertising slot, on the promenade, for the whole world to see!

The day before the conference began, just as our teams were dismounting from the coaches, extraordinary gale force winds battered the Brighton Centre. Lighter members of the team had to be shielded by heavier ones as they crossed the pavement, to prevent them from being blown away! Once inside, our attention quickly turned to prayer, *"Oh Lord, please help us with the weather."* Intercessors and others alike were picking up that there was great anger spiritually at our declaration and the elements were reflecting this. By the next day, prayers had been answered and when the doors opened at 9am, the sun was shining and there wasn't even the faintest breeze blowing – and unseasonably calm and warm weather remained for the full four days of the Conference!

The declaration that the Sovereign Lord of Isaiah Chapter 61, who was also the Jesus of Luke 4, was still setting the captives free today, resounded loudly and clearly from the platform. And as it did, there was a great manifestation of Holy Spirit power setting people free both emotionally and spiritually. Ministry times followed all the teaching sessions and there was so much happening that the ministry teams never did get their tea or meal breaks! God was clearly at work and as the speakers gave their message, people were responding to the truth of God's Word all over the auditorium. One of the camera men, filming the event, fell to the floor and was unable to continue. He later gave testimony to his back having been completely healed!

Up to that point, Ellel Ministries was seen as a northern UK ministry of little consequence to the wider Body of Christ. But the *Battle Belongs to the Lord* changed so much that even now, more than twenty five years later, we are still hearing new stories of what God did at that conference, and of how people's lives and future destinies were transformed during those four extraordinary days.

The origins of the conference lay in our need for help with understanding deliverance ministry. Prior to the work beginning, the only training in deliverance that I had ever received was a workshop session at John Wimber's Healing Conference at Sheffield in 1985. Because of the way God has used Ellel Ministries to teach, train and minister healing through deliverance, it has often been wrongly assumed that deliverance was something I was already passionate about before the work started. In reality, it was only when the doors of Ellel Grange were opened, and we found ourselves up to the neck in deep personal ministries, many of which included the need for deliverance, that we realised how little we, and the wider church, knew about this primary aspect of the ministry of Jesus, as practiced in the Gospel accounts.

We were, therefore, desperate to know more, but we quickly discovered that, in those days, there was very little help available. And many of those we thought would be able to help us, were apprehensive about dipping their spiritual toes in such risky spiritual waters! There was no internet and no Google search facility, but the shelves of our local Christian bookshop did, amazingly, throw us a lifeline in the form of a little blue book by Bill Subritzky, a New Zealand author I'd never heard of before, from the other side of the world. His book, *Demons Defeated*, proved to be a life-saver at the time for, at the very least, it showed that we weren't completely 'off the wall'. There was someone else who had discovered that demons were real and it was comforting to know that there was at least one other person in the world who, in the twentieth century, was also seeing people dramatically healed through deliverance ministry.

Then in May 1987 I bumped into my old friend Chris Mungeam at the *Christian Resources Exhibition*. It was Chris who had arranged the publishing of *Mission England Praise* for me back in 1982. We hadn't seen each other for some time and it was great to catch up on what God had been doing in our respective lives. Chris told me how his decision to print 100,000 copies of *Mission England Praise* had probably cost him his job at Marshall Pickering. But that he was then able to use his severance money to start his own Christian Publishing House, *Sovereign World*, which he was now trying to get off the ground.

I responded by telling him what had been happening at Ellel Grange and pulled a copy of *Demons Defeated* out of my brief case and asked Chris if he knew who'd published it. His reply, *"I did,"* stunned me as I realised that the very first book that Chris's new company had published was the very one that was now helping us come to terms with the deliverance aspect of the ministry. I was discovering once more how the Kingdom of God is built through strategic friendships and relationships. Unbeknown to me at the time, the vision God gave me for *Mission England Praise* had now given birth to Chris's publishing company, *Sovereign World*, and Chris's first book was already being strategic in helping us with the ministry – how extraordinary is that! Chris was about to become a key player in both my and the Ellel Ministries story!

It wasn't very long before Chris arranged a first visit to the UK for his friend, Bill Subritzky, and Bill was able to visit Ellel Grange and share in our *Deliverance Ministry Training Course*. Chris encouraged us to think about inviting Bill and Pat Subritzky back to the UK to be one of the main speakers at a major conference sponsored by Ellel Ministries. Chris saw this as perhaps the best way of sharing what God was doing at Ellel Grange with the wider Christian community.

This was new territory for both me and the ministry, but the more we thought and prayed about the possibility it seemed that this was the direction God was leading us. A member of the team was inspired to suggest the *Battle Belongs to the Lord* as the name of the Conference and suddenly the bare bones of the plan were gaining flesh. The Brighton Centre was booked and destiny steps were being taken which would have far-reaching, and even world-wide, consequences and significance.

Looking back now, it seems as though the word God spoke to me about spending the rest of my life bringing healing to those in need and teaching others how to do it, was like an 'email' from God. But it wasn't just an email, it was an email with many different attachments, with each one being a strategic new development in the growth of the ministry. The *Battle Belongs to the Lord* Conference was definitely one of those attachments.

During those early years of the work there were many influential visitors to Ellel Grange, including a number of international figures who came to teach at special events such as John and Paula Sandford from the USA, Tom Marshall from Australia, Paul and Gretel Haglin from the USA and Bob Gordon from the UK. But it was the ministry of Bill Subritzky at Brighton that had the greatest impact – especially among those who were keen to find answers to unresolved problems in their own lives.

The popular success of the conference also attracted the unwelcome attention of the media, whose main interest seemed to be in sensationalising something they didn't understand, without any serious desire to examine either the Scriptures or the fruit of the ministry. Sadly, even though twenty five years have now passed since Brighton, there are still significant sectors and leaders of the church in the UK, who allow things they have heard from the past through the media to colour their opinions, instead of coming to find out for themselves and follow the scriptural encouragement to test a ministry by its fruit (Matthew 7:15-20). It has always been a huge disappointment that so many people have preferred to believe rumour and gossip and not wanted to discover the truth for themselves of how God has blessed the work.

It was just before Brighton that Chris Mungeam also introduced me and the work of Ellel Ministries to Derek Prince. Derek was very well known in the UK, but Bill was largely unknown. But Derek and Bill knew each other well and had mutual love and respect for each other and their ministries. So, at Chris's and Bill's encouragement, Derek was asked to lend his considerable theological and personal weight to supporting the publicity launch for the conference. By now Chris was not only keen to promote the work of Ellel Ministries because of our long-term friendship, but also because he had seen God bring wonderful healing to members of his own family! In subsequent years the friendship with Derek Prince was to be strategic in opening vital doors for the ministry with the Messianic community in Israel.

Booking the Brighton Centre had been a huge step of faith for what was then a small healing ministry in the North of England. But when the brochures went out all over the country, and adverts began to appear in various Christian magazines, the response was amazing and 3000 people crowded into the Brighton Centre for the event.

The conference title was taken from 2 Chronicles 20, when King Jehoshaphat proclaimed that *'The battle belongs to the Lord'* – words that have become almost synonymous with Ellel Ministries ever since, as subsequent conferences, with the same title, have taken place all over the world – indeed wherever the Lord opened doors for the ministry, a *Battle Belongs to the Lord* conference was often seen as the best way of launching the work in new territories, in places as far apart as Canada and Malaysia, Hong Kong and Australia, South Africa and Hungary. Through the conference God was giving an international platform to this still embryonic and largely unknown work.

From the very first song of the introductory time of worship, till the final farewells, the presence of God was heavy upon the Conference. After almost every session there were powerful times of ministry and it wasn't long before many remarkable testimonies began to emerge of what God had done in people's lives. Even today, members of Ellel teams regularly meet people whose lives were seriously impacted by the Lord at Brighton. The Conference lasted for four days, but the fruit of those four days will last for eternity.

One man who came to Brighton, from Hungary, was Zoltán Szöcs. Zoltán was both a Pastor and a Professor at the University of Budapest. But he had also struggled with a physical condition for fourteen years. He was healed at Brighton and as a result he became the bridge over which the work would cross and be established in Eastern Europe and Russia.

Jill Southern's life was dominated by fear. Despite her strong and colourful personality, fear was the core issue in her life. She had looked for answers all over the place, but when she saw in the publicity for the conference that Bill Subritzky would be teaching on *Freedom from Fear*, God got her attention. She knew nothing of deliverance at that point, but someone had told her it might help, so she booked in, not knowing where that single step of faith would take her!

After Bill's teaching session, hundreds of people stood, asking for help. Jill was prayed for by an elderly member of the ministry team from Ellel Grange. Both Jill and the counsellor were equally astonished by what God did to set her free and Jill returned home a different woman. The remarkable story of what happened next, in preparing Jill to become the first Director of the work of Ellel Ministries at Pierrepont, is now told in her own book, *The Miracles of Pierrepont*. Her personal story and that of Ellel Ministries, Pierrepont, are inextricably linked together.

Chris Leage, then the National Director of the *Lydia Fellowship*, one of the most influential prayer movements there has ever been in the UK, was also at Brighton. She and a team of Lydia intercessors provided continuous prayer cover throughout the conference. But Chris's friend was also unable to conceive a child until, that is, she was prayed for at the conference. Her doctors had told her that she would not be able to conceive, but shortly after the conference she did conceive a child and nine months later, Daniel was born!

At least ten years after the conference a man came running up to me at a meeting, put his arms round my neck and kissed me on both cheeks! *"Thank you,"* he said, *"for what God did for me and my family and my church through the Battle Belongs to the Lord. All have been dramatically changed"*. Down the years there have been hundreds of similar testimonies.

When that first *Battle Belongs to the Lord* Conference was over, a totally exhausted, but spiritually elated, team met together in our team room for a final time of thanksgiving as we shared communion and praised God for all that had happened. But just as the communion service was drawing to a close, Bill Subritzky stood up and spoke a prophetic word to the team, saying, *"I believe God is saying that Ellel Ministries is going to be strategic in Eastern Europe and Russia!"*

A stunned silence greeted his words! Just as we were preparing to retreat back to Ellel Grange to recover from running our first major conference, God had other ideas. He wanted us to know that Brighton wasn't the end of the road, but the beginning of the next stage of our journey. As the team bus travelled north on England's motorways, God was doing a new work of preparation in my heart.

Throughout my life overseas missions had been high on the agenda of the churches I had been part of, and my parents had been passionate about supporting overseas mission work – everything from the *Church's Mission to the Jews* to the *China Inland Mission* to being the main UK coordinators of support for the *Albarka Fellowship*, a remarkable medical mission to lepers in Central Nigeria. And now God seemed to be saying that Ellel Ministries was also going to become an overseas missionary organisation, taking the ministry of healing and deliverance to a very needy world.

I had absolutely no idea how such a word could possibly be fulfilled, but I was open for God to show me how it could happen. The beginnings of the answer came in a phone call just three weeks later, when I was asked to join an evangelism team into Romania, shortly after the fall of Ceausescu in the Romanian revolution of 1989. This was not an invitation that I could have turned down without being disobedient to the vision God had opened up through Bill's prophetic word to the team.

I had no idea at the time that within a year we would be conducting a *Battle Belongs to the Lord* conference in the Communist Party conference Hall in Budapest, simultaneously with the departure of the last Russian tanks! The world-wide need for discipleship and healing in the Body of Christ today, both at home and overseas, had become of central importance for the Ellel teams as they looked to the Lord for His direction in the years ahead. Ellel Grange was becoming the hub of an international ministry – it was no longer a teaching and ministry centre serving only the north-west of England. Our horizons had suddenly got much bigger.

One of the speakers at subsequent Ellel conferences at Brighton was Bishop Graham Dow. In the early days of the ministry when he was still a Vicar, we had conducted a weekend in Graham's church, Holy Trinity, Coventry. It was one of those memorable, milestone weekends, which cemented a friendship and relationship which has withstood all sorts of pressures across the years.

Graham's commitment to the healing and deliverance ministries led to his writing a short book on deliverance called *Those Tiresome Intruders*, which is still in print with Sovereign World as *Explaining Deliverance*. In spite of this venture into print, he was still appointed the Bishop of Willesden and, subsequently, the Diocesan Bishop of Carlisle. He is probably still the only Bishop in the UK to have written a book on deliverance and we will always be grateful for the way he publicly embraced the healing ministry and offered us his love, friendship and unswerving commitment to supporting the ministry. And there are many other leaders in the different churches who saw what God was doing, rejoiced and committed themselves to supporting the ministry also. They were all part of the strands that God was bringing together to provide a rope of safety for the many who were crying out to God for help.

Chapter 13

EXPANDING HORIZONS

Transplanting the Vision in a New Location

News of what God was doing at Ellel Grange soon spread far and wide. And within a few months of opening, people were travelling up and down the country to sample the *Training Courses* and *Healing Retreats*. It wasn't long before there was a steady stream of requests from people in the south of England for their own *'Ellel Centre'*. It seemed a logical next step for the ministry, but three obstacles stood in the way of this development of the vision – the need for people to lead it, a building to operate in and money to buy the building!

But if a vision really is from God, then obstacles are not a reason to hold back from moving forward! Faith, as the book of Hebrews says, is *"the assurance of things hoped for"*. The stories of the great missionary pioneers had thrilled my spirit since being a child – but nowhere in any of those stories did I read people saying that because there were obstacles, they were going to give up. Indeed, the very opposite had usually been the case! From the pioneering adventures of the Apostle Paul (read 2 Corinthians 11:16-29) to the extraordinary determination of those who even gave their lives for the translation of the Scriptures into English, to the great missionary pioneers of the eighteenth and nineteenth centuries such as William Carey (India), Hudson Taylor (China) and William Booth (Salvation Army) to the more recent exploits of Jackie Pullinger in Hong Kong – all had faced obstacles to their visionary obedience and pressed through. This was the bread and butter of Kingdom pioneers. So I didn't want a few minor obstacles on the road to stand in the way of responding to what I sensed was a true '*Macedonian call*' to establish an Ellel Centre in the South – so we began to pray into the vision, trusting God to show us the way forward.

It wasn't long before a prayer supporter told me about Glyndley Manor. This old Manor House was then being lived in by four Christian families who had joined their personal resources together to buy the building, as a direct result of a vision God had given to one of their number, Geoff Shearn. It was also being used at the time as offices for various Christian organisations.

In his original vision, Geoff had seen a large building, surrounded by many smaller buildings. People were arriving at the place with very sad faces and after a time inside were leaving with happy faces! He knew that God had done important things in their lives during their stay and was so impacted by the vision that he couldn't get it out of his mind. So he began to share his vision at various meetings around the South of England and, in faith, he also began to look for the building he had seen in the vision.

Eventually he found it! When he saw Glyndley Manor, and the 34 holiday bungalows that were in the grounds, he knew that this was the exact place God had shown him in the vision, and that he had to buy it for God's purposes. Unbeknown to Geoff at the time, this very building had first been registered as a place of worship by a group of dissenters over 300 years earlier! The dissenters were concerned that their fellowship should not be under the control of government through the established church and were equally concerned that it was God's Word, and God's Word alone, that should be the foundation for their faith and doctrine.

Alone, it was impossible for Geoff to purchase the property, but with the help of three friends and their wives, all of whom sold their houses so they could pool their resources, they managed to buy the property and move in. They were the first runners carrying the baton in a relay race of faith that would eventually lead to Ellel Ministries having a centre in the South of England. They had no idea how God was going to fulfil the vision, but all that God required of them was to take their step of obedience in buying the property.

A few years later I was introduced to Geoff and when he began to share his vision for Glyndley Manor, it became clear that this was the place God had chosen for Ellel Ministries, and that it had been purchased for the Lord by those four families, in anticipation of Ellel's future need. God had gone before in an extraordinary way and had prepared a people and a place, with the exact vision that God had given me in the first place for Ellel Grange! But the building then had to be bought from the four founding families.

We shared the vision for Glyndley Manor with everyone on our mailing list and many people gave sacrificially towards the deposit that would be needed to secure a mortgage from the bank to complete the purchase. Joe and Ruth Hawkey, two of our most experienced Associate Counsellors from Ellel Grange, responded to the call to move south and begin the work and Barry and Jan Jay poured their heart into helping with the foundations. So the three hurdles had been crossed – a building was found, the money was now available and the leaders were appointed. Glyndley Manor was on its way.

Twenty-five years have passed since then, with several different leaders taking the work forward in stages. Thousands of people have come up the Glyndley Manor drive with those saddened faces that

Geoff Shearn saw in his vision, and have left smiling, after all that God had done in their lives during their stay on a *Healing Retreat*, a *Training Course* or the longer *9-Week School*.

Not only was a new Centre being birthed at Glyndley Manor, but the first event at the new Centre was also going to be a first for Ellel Ministries. The work was growing rapidly and there was a steady stream of people coming from overseas for courses at Ellel Grange. They often commented that it was a very long way to come just for a weekend! By then we were teaching courses on many different aspects of healing and discipleship, and overseas visitors, especially, were wanting something longer that would justify the cost of the flights from across the globe.

As we prayed about the need, the Lord gave me a fresh vision for a 9-week residential training school to be called the *School of Evangelism, Healing and Discipleship*. It was another of those attachments to my original 'email from God' that was waiting to be opened. Running many different three-day courses was already a significant challenge for the leadership team. And the idea of running a training course which lasted for nine long weeks spoke to them of exhaustion and seemed an impossible target to aim at. And *"would anyone want to come?"* they asked!

By then I was used to facing opposition from without, but resistance from within was a new, but understandable, leadership problem! The difficulties were portrayed as giants, which could have a serious destabilising effect on what we were already doing. I was beginning to have some sympathy for Moses, when he sent in the spies to report on the 'promised land' and the people chose to listen to the fears of the ten, rather than grasp the opportunities described by the two! I needed to find a way forward that would have the support of the team.

Within a few weeks of the first *Battle Belongs to the Lord* conference at Brighton, stories of what God had done there were spreading like wildfire across the country and the world. People, who had missed the opportunity of attending, were looking for a second chance. So, in faith, we invited the same speakers to come again and, in faith, we re-booked the Brighton Centre for June 1991, at the same time as we were praying for the funds with which to buy Glyndley Manor.

As I prayed about the developing vision for a 9-week school, the Lord gave me His strategy for the way forward. The team were certain that no-one would want to come for a 9-week course, but I was certain that when God spoke to me about doing such a long school it was with the same encouragement that He had given me to look for a second centre. The second centre and the 9-week school were closely linked in my mind.

I would love to have produced a full brochure about the 9-week school and given it out at Brighton, but that would have been presumptuous on my part and too threatening for the team at that time. So, instead, I just mentioned from the platform of the conference that there might be a possibility of Ellel running a longer school for about nine weeks and that if anyone was interested, would they leave their names at the Conference reception desk. The announcement was so low key that if anyone responded, everyone would know that God was in it. By the end of the conference there were enough names on the form to fill every available bed in Glyndley Manor! The first *9-week School* was about to be born!

These longer schools have now been at the heart of the ministry ever since – and thousands of people have experienced God's powerful presence on them, as they have both learned together and been healed together. It's amazing how much God can do in such a short time of equipping the saints for the work of the Kingdom. In addition, these schools have provided important opportunities for training future leaders. And not a few marriages have resulted from what God has done on these dynamic training schools!

Eventually, Chris Mungeam's publishing house, Sovereign World Ltd, became part of Ellel Ministries, and its first Ellel Director met his Ukrainian wife on the 9-Week School at Glyndley Manor. Colin from Bermuda met Hedwig from Paraguay and both then went to East Africa as missionaries. It was there that Colin lost his life in the service of the King and became a martyr – a victim of the *Lord's Resistance Army*. His wife, Hedwig, with their daughter Shekinah, who was born after Colin died, is still serving the Lord in East Africa.

Pat Wakeham met and fell in love with the only man she ever wanted to marry as a young woman. But there were issues in her life which made it impossible to commit to marrying Denis Clark in her youth. So she trained as both a doctor and a medical missionary and spent the majority of her working life serving the Lord in India. Eventually, however, she was totally burned out and recognised her own need for deep healing – as well as for training in Christian healing to supplement her training in medicine. The Lord met Pat on that first nine week school in a very deep way – not only restoring her after the many years of service in India, but also healing the very issues that made it impossible for her to commit to Denis as a young woman. The icing on Pat's cake was that Denis was still waiting for her and their young love was still fresh in their hearts. Today, they are still serving the Lord in whatever way He leads, but as a very happily married couple! God is a God of miracles.

The stories of what God did in people's lives on the 9-week school at Glyndley Manor would fill a whole book. Two ladies arrived from Malaysia – both were deeply impacted by the healing that God brought to them personally during the school. One of them, a medical doctor, was struggling with a condition which limited her capacity to speak with a clear voice. God so healed her voice that she became a significant teacher on the healing ministry in her own country. The other is now the Director of a new Ellel Ministries centre in Kuala Lumpur, the capital city of Malaysia.

Having been delivered from fear at the first *Battle Belongs to the Lord* Conference, Jill and Ron Southern began to attend various courses at Glyndley Manor. On one occasion when they were there, God interrupted my teaching flow to share a word about how Elisha had burned his ploughing equipment so that there would be nothing to tempt him back into farming, from the prophetic call on his life. I knew that this was a word for someone in that meeting. Jill and Ron responded, and this proved to be the critical moment through which God confirmed the deepening call, on Jill's life especially, to the healing ministry. Jill followed this up by attending the second 9-week school and then became the Director of Ellel Pierrepont for its first twenty years.

God's guidance for the big things in life usually comes in small, manageable, faith-filled steps. It's as we respond to the leading of the Lord at each stage that little by little the Lord draws us into what is His best for our lives. If He showed us everything at the beginning of a pilgrimage of faith that He had for us along the way, most of us would probably never start the journey!

Each of the Ellel Centres makes its own unique contribution to the work of the wider Ellel family. The 9-week school is now known as *The Flagship School* and has moved from Glyndley Manor to Ellel Grange. In its place, today, Glyndley Manor runs a series of *Restoration Weeks* for those seeking deeper personal healing. Lives are being transformed at a very deep level. And some of the cottages in the grounds are now being used for the exact purpose which Geoff Shearn saw in his original vision. The precision with which God fulfils the visions that come from Him is astounding. What a faithful God we serve!

Some years ago I was struggling to understand why so many people were praying for a spiritual revival around the world, and yet so few had ever experienced what they were praying for. I remember as a child seeing very serious and sober people praying for revival but wondering what this thing was that was so often prayed for, but which never seemed to happen. I decided to take time out, not to pray for revival, but to ask God why, what so many perceived to be evidence of revival, was singularly absent from the church's experience. I was hungry for spiritual reality and desperate not to miss anything that God had for me or the ministry.

The answer to my question set me on a further journey of understanding. What I sensed God saying to me was that in praying for revival, people were praying for the wrong thing! *"How can that be, Lord? Aren't You interested in reviving Your Church? What should they be praying for?"*

The answer to my questions came in the form of three words, which the Lord shared with me over a period of a few days. The first word was *Vision*. I searched the Scriptures and followed up every reference or experience of vision that I could find. I discovered that vision was God's normal way of showing people what He wanted them to do. The next word was Faith. This was more obvious – for as the scripture so clearly says, *"Faith is the assurance of things hoped for"* (Hebrews 11:1). Faith is absolute trust in God's divine providence and that what He says, He will do.

But the final word was the deal-breaker – *Obedience*. Phrases from the Bible such as *"obedience is better than sacrifice"* and *"If you love me, you will obey me"* came flooding into my mind. And when I turned to my concordance, I discovered that there were more references in Scripture to obedience than both vision and faith put together. Without obedience all the visions in the world would remain just that – visions, but unfulfilled. Visions don't just get fulfilled as if by magic, they require human participation. And without faith, even the very best of visions will simply be an unfulfilled dream – because if you cannot trust God with what He has said, how can you ever walk with Him on an unknown pathway?

I then began to read about well-known revivals and discovered that they didn't just happen and land on unsuspecting believers, as it were, from outer space. At their core were people of vision who were exercising faith and walking in obedience to what God had already showed them. I saw that the journey from vision, through faith to obedience was a hallmark of those who were at the heart of the major moves of God's Spirit throughout history. I began to realise, sadly, that so many of those who were praying for revival were indeed praying for the wrong thing – they were praying for that bit of magic to happen, whereas they should have been praying for God to give them His vision for what He wanted them to be and to do. I was beginning to understand what God meant when He told me that so many people who pray for revival are praying for the wrong thing.

When Geoff Shearn had his vision for a place of healing, he didn't just sit back and wait for it to happen; he actively started looking for it. He was, in faith, exercising obedience. And in a similar way when we started looking for a place in the South we were exercising faith in obedience to what God had shown us was a Macedonian call (Acts 16:9) to the leaders of the work at Ellel Grange. The fruit has been twenty-five years of God bringing His revival, in His way, into the lives of hurting people at Glyndley Manor, and through the work there, to the world.

'The Battle Belongs to the Lord' Conference banner.

'The Battle Belongs to the Lord' Conference.

The Battle Belongs
to The Lord

Brighton Centre, England. 12th to 15th February 1990

'The Battle Belongs to the Lord' Handbook (1990).

The Brighton Centre.

The large crowd at Brighton.

Peter teaching at 'The Battle Belongs to the Lord'.

Bill Subritsky – Guest speaker from New Zealand.

Mezes Lozi ministering at Brighton.

Communion at Brighton.

Praying for people at Brighton.

Front of Glyndley Manor.

One of the 34 holiday cottages in the grounds of Glyndley Manor.

Joe and Ruth Hawkey, the first Directors of Glyndley Manor with the pioneering team (1991).

Launch conference of the new work at Glyndley Manor.

Spreading the word about Glyndley Manor.

Brochure for the first 9-Week School at Glyndley Manor.

Pioneering visit to Hungary (1990) – Joe Hawkey and
Otto Bixler at right.

Otto and Sharon Bixler –
pioneering leaders of the work in
Eastern Europe and Russia.

Szocs Zoltan sharing his
testimony of healing at Brighton.

'The Battle Belongs to the Lord',
Hungary (1991).

With the Hungarian Advisory Board.

Investing in Eastern Europe – launch brochures for the new Centre at Ur Retje.

Mike Carroll (2nd left) – the real estate agent who helped us buy Ur Retje.

Completing the deal – buying the land at Ur Retje.

The Hungarian Centre under construction.

The finished Hungarian Centre at Ur Retje (1998).

'The Battle Belongs to the Lord', Hungary (1992).

The Ellel team en route to Russia (1992).

'Battle Belongs to the Lord' in St.Petersburg, Russia.

St Petersburg Conference – man kneeling in prayer.

Presentation of brass Samovar to the team in St. Petersburg.

First conference in Ukraine.

Mezes Lozi teaching, with Alona translating, in Ukraine.

Otto & Sharon Bixler on the day of their retirement from leaving the work in Eastern Europe (2011).

'The Battle Belongs to the Lord', Orangeville, Canada (1997).

Ken Hepworth teaching at the conference.

Ellel Ontario at Derbyshire Downs.

Prairie Winds – the home of Ellel Calgary.

Aerial view of Ellel Ontario from Wolfe Lake.

Pierrepont Estate aerial view.

Ellel Pierrepont – the first brochure (1994).

Pierrepont Main House (Rear).

Ellel Pierrepont – the first brochure (back).

Jill Southern – first Director of Ellel Pierrepont – with her husband, Ron (1995).

Pierrepont Clock Tower (from Courtyard)

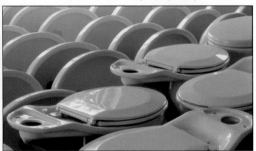

Toilets and wash basins – a gift from the Ministry of Defence!

Mountains of blue carpet tiles donated to Ellel Pierrepont by Shell UK.

Sun through the Great Hall window as it was in the beginning!

Jesus Heals Day, Pierrepont (Former sports hall)

Teaching NETS students in the Great Hall at Pierrepont.

The First NETS Brochure.

NETS Brochure.

NETS 2 students in the Great Hall at Ellel Pierrepont.

Opening Thanksgiving Celebration at Pierrepont (1995).

Pierrepont team with NETS 3 Students (Summer 1998).

Pierrepont Main House (front).

NETS Students at work on their Stage 3 Mission.

With Jill Southern, first Director of Ellel Pierrepont, at the 10th Birthday Thanksgiving.

NETS Stage 3: African open air mission meeting.

Dramatic skies above Gilbulla – the home of Ellel Australia.

Fiona with Lynda Hicks after she had been dramatically healed in 1996.

Ellel Australia – the Chapel in the grounds of Gilbulla.

Diane Watson, first Director of Ellel Australia with husband, Paul. Paul and Diane are now the Directors of Ellel Pierrepont.

Official opening of Ellel Australia at Gilbulla (1997).

David and Denise Cross with Aboriginal leader, Peter Walker, at the opening of Ellel Australia.

Blairmore House – home of Ellel Scotland.

Blairmore House, dining room

Blairmore House Conference Room.

Anna and Malcolm Wood – first Directors of Ellel Scotland.

Ellel Ministries International Leadership Team at Blairmore House 2005.

Fiona with Florence Wang & Lynda Tang training in the UK. Lynda became leader of the work in Kuala Lumpur.

With Kenneth and Ying Thien and their miracle daughter, conceived following prayer in Sabah.

Teaching on Healing and Discipleship in Malaysia (2005).

Titus and Esther Soo in China – leaders of the work in China and South-East Asia.

With Titus and Esther Soo at Ellel Singapore Training Day, 2017.

Fiona teaching at Wesley Methodist Kuala Lumpur.

Fiona signing her books at Ellel Singapore Training Day, 2017.

Ellel Singapore Team Training Day 2017.

Leaders Training School, Malaysia.

Michael and Linda Tang – leaders of the work of Ellel Malaysia at Klang Valley, KL.

June 2016 Official opening of the Klang Valley Centre.

June 2016 Official opening of the Klang Valley Centre.

Training Course for Chinese leaders in Hong Kong.

Ellel Sabah Team 2016.

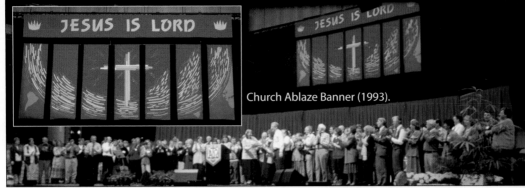

Church Ablaze Banner (1993).

The complete Ellel Team at 'Equipped for a Purpose' (1997).

Delegates at 'Into All the World', Blackpool (1995).

Worship at 'Into all the World' (1995).

Indian students sharing their testimonies (1995).

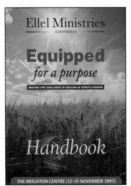

'Equipped for a Purpose' Conference (1997).

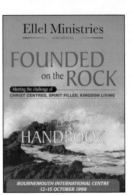

'Founded on the Rock' Conference (1998).

'Healing and Destiny' Conference (2006).

Jackie Pullinger-To teaching at 'Into All the World', Blackpool.

'Let the Oppressed Go Free' Conference (2001).

Chapter 14

HUNGARIAN ADVENTURES

Following God's Footsteps into Eastern Europe

When Bill Subritzky told us that he believed the ministry would be strategic in Eastern Europe and Russia, we were totally unprepared for such a word! But, we were totally ready and willing to follow in the Lord's footsteps, wherever it was He was leading.

One of those present at Brighton was Reza, a Swedish evangelist. Shortly after Brighton, Reza gave me a call and invited me and an Ellel team to join him in Romania for a mission. The Romanian dictator, Ceausescu, had recently been deposed and executed and this invitation to join a mission into the newly liberated Romania proved to be the door opener to the extensive work of Ellel Ministries that has developed in the region. In the circumstances it would have been sheer disobedience to the heavenly vision if I had refused!

But in God's extraordinary way of doing things it wasn't the Romanian mission, significant though that was, which was the reason God had me go with Reza. It was in order to meet up with Zoltan

Szocs in Hungary, who had also been at Brighton and experienced a significant personal healing. On our return journey from Romania, Joe Hawkey and I met up with Zoltán in Budapest's Aero Hotel. As I shared with him the developing vision for an Ellel Ministries Centre in the region, Zoltán shared a vision which he, too, had been nurturing for many years.

Zoltán's father had been a pastor in Hungary throughout the Russian communist occupation. All such pastors were under constant observation, harassment and pressure. At the same time as caring for their flocks, they had to try and earn a meagre living. The pressures on pastors' families were great. For years Zoltán's father had prayed that there could be a place in Hungary where pastors could go for personal respite, recovery and healing. He died still nurturing the vision, but the vision didn't die with him, Zoltán continued to believe for what his father had dreamed of.

As we talked together in the Aero Hotel, we were acutely aware of the Lord's presence. It was as if the two visions had become one, and what Zoltán's father had prayed for could now happen through Ellel Ministries. There would be much work to be done to bring the combined visions into reality, but in the heavenly realms it had already been fulfilled – it now needed to be brought down to Earth! The first step we agreed to at that first meeting was to bring the *Battle Belongs to the Lord* conference to Budapest the following year.

Otto and Sharon Bixler were Vineyard pastors from California and as referred to in Chapter 10, they visited England as part of John Wimber's ministry team in 1986 and stayed at Ellel Grange. The first names in our pristine Visitors Book were those of the Vineyard Team – and of these, Otto and Sharon Bixler were the only ones to add their home telephone number to their address! We were regularly in touch with them and eventually they offered to use their annual vacations to come over and help us – which they did, faithfully, on eight different occasions!

Finally, they came and joined the Ellel team in England for a year! But at the end of that first year's commitment, they asked the Lord, *'Is our time over?'*, and they sensed the Lord replied, *'I just told you to go, it was you that said a year!'* And so it was that Otto and Sharon went back to California, closed down their business, let out their house and shipped their left-hand drive Toyota across the Atlantic. They had burnt their bridges and were heading East!

They initially arrived in England in October 1990, just in time for Sharon to put all her Vineyard conference experience to good use as the coordinator for the second *Battle Belongs to the Lord* event in the UK, followed by the first one in Budapest in June 1991. That one conference in Budapest was to have extraordinary consequences in the lives of so many people. The Christian nationals of the region still refer to it to as *the 'spiritual bombshell that went off in Budapest and affected the whole region'*. They tell us how that event was a totally life-transforming experience! It certainly was for Otto and Sharon – for it was the place where God was to sow in them the seed of their life's calling and work in Eastern Europe and Russia.

Russian troops were still stationed in Hungary at the time of this first Budapest conference. Amazingly, Otto had been able to hire the Communist Party's own conference hall for the purpose! It proved to be an ideal venue, fully equipped with translation booths for delegates from many other nations. All those booths were put to good use as the teaching was simultaneously translated into six different languages so people could hear it in their own tongue.

Delegates came from thirteen of the former Soviet republics and satellite states and, almost symbolically, as the Isaiah 61:1 teaching about setting the captives free was being proclaimed in the Communist Party's own conference hall, the last Russian tank left the city on its way back to Moscow! What a way that was to mark the end of the communist dominated era in Hungary! The Hungarian captives were being set free in more ways than one.

There were many extraordinary happenings during the conference, especially during the session when delegates were invited to forgive their oppressors. A massive amount of deliverance, with subsequent spiritual, emotional and physical healing followed. It was an event which has subsequently impacted people from all the nations represented – such was the effect on their lives. It seemed like three quarters of the people present were receiving healing and afterwards those who had been bent over physically as a result of the constant oppression they'd been under, were then able to stand up and walk tall!

With the success of the *Battle Belongs to the Lord* Conference in Budapest, it became clear that Hungary was to be the place in Eastern Europe where God had put His foot down and Ellel Ministries was to be established. At the same time, it also became clear that the calling on Otto and Sharon was much wider than a supporting role for the ministry in England. So, once again they responded to the ongoing call of God on their lives, and in February 1992 they loaded up all their belongings into the left-hand drive Toyota and headed East across Europe, to establish the work in Hungary, in a car which was now much more at home in a left-hand drive world.

The early pioneering work of establishing the ministry in Hungary, took place in a tiny flat that Otto and Sharon managed to rent in Budapest. It was woefully inadequate for the task that lay ahead, so the search began in earnest to find an operating base for the ministry. There were no suitable buildings to be found. So the option of finding some land and building a centre was also considered.

A second *Battle Belongs to the Lord* Conference in Budapest, took place in May 1992. After the main event was over, we prayed together about the location of an Ellel Centre. As we pored over the map it was as if there was one particular district that God was highlighting, so the following day that's where I headed off to explore. I came across the high walls of the Hungarian Botanical

Gardens. Curious, I stopped the vehicle and had a walk round the beautiful grounds where I bumped into a man who turned out to be the curator of the gardens. He spoke a little bit of English and I tried to describe to him what we were looking for and why we wanted it!

That *accidental* meeting proved to be another of God's remarkable 'God-incidences'. The curator suggested I go to Orbottyan and speak to Péter Fekete, a Reformed Church Pastor who looked after an orphanage – perhaps he could help. The meeting with Péter Fekete and his wife Ilona did not, at first, promise well. Their English was of a similar standard to my own non-existent Hungarian!

It wasn't easy to use sign language to illustrate what we were looking for, but this was the man we had been directed to, so we persevered and, eventually, Ilona took a large map of the area out of a drawer and pointed to a piece of land, which seemed to be quite close to the orphanage. We all trooped out of the house to find the land she had pointed out on the map!

As soon as we walked on this piece of land, which was covered with glorious red poppies, surrounding a beautiful lake against a backdrop of trees, I sensed that this was already set apart for us and was holy ground. When, the following day, the rest of the Ellel team went out to look at the land, there was complete unity of spirit that this really was the place God had chosen to establish the work of Ellel Ministries in Eastern Europe. The team were literally running and dancing with Holy Spirit joy on the land in an unprecedented way. God was doing something special, but nobody at the time understood what.

If this was to be the place, then there were several, seemingly insurmountable, problems that would need to be overcome. Primarily, the land wasn't for sale; secondly, no-one on the team could speak the language; thirdly, following the many years of communist rule, everything was in cooperative ownership, making it almost impossible for property to be bought and sold in a way that we were familiar with in the west; and fourthly, of course, we had no money!

That night, as we were all having dinner in the roof-top restaurant of our Budapest hotel, we were excited about what God had shown us, but none of us knew what to do. But God always has a strategy mapped out in advance – and His way was, once again, full of surprises! We were learning yet again how God will place His agents in key places at the right time to do His work!

For there was another party having dinner in the hotel that night. The guests were all in fancy dress and were obviously having a thoroughly enjoyable time. I overheard one of them speaking English and, again curious, I asked him what was happening. *"Oh,"* he said, *"we're fun-runners and we're just letting our hair down after running a half marathon around Budapest."*

"And what do you do in Budapest?" I asked. The man replied, *"I work for a London Estate Agency and I'm probably the only English speaking person in Hungary right now, who is helping western organisations to buy land and property."* My knees began to quake and I could hardly believe what I was hearing, for here was the very man who could help us buy the land. So there and then I asked Mike Carroll for his help and gave him the job of enabling Ellel Ministries to buy the land, which the team had walked on that morning! Within eight hours of the team's visit to Orbottyan, God had introduced me to possibly the only man in a nation of 13 million people, who could help us with our otherwise impossible task! As I stood there in the open air, overlooking the River Danube, talking to a man in the most bizarre of fancy dress clothing, God had just worked an extraordinary miracle.

And so it was that Mike Carroll became God's special agent. He eventually had to negotiate with 46 different cooperative owners of the land which, we then discovered, was called Úr *Rétje*. In Hungarian, this simply means *The Lord God's Meadow.*' It truly was God's land.

After Mike had negotiated a deal for us, I called a long-term supporter of the work and explained the need to seal the purchase of the land. Within just a few minutes a private loan was agreed so that the work of Ellel Ministries in Hungary could proceed without delay. That man's instant willingness to help, and the loan (which has long since been repaid) was a critical hinge, on which the door to all that God has done in the region since has swung wide open. Eventually, in May 1993, Otto took two suitcases full of Hungarian Forints to the Mayor's Office in Orbottyan and there every single Forint was counted out and placed into the hands of the 46 different cooperative owners. Then the deeds of the property were handed over to Ellel Ministries.

We were then able to uncover the whole story behind Úr *Rétje* and why it was first called by this name. Back in 1928 the Professor of Divinity at Budapest University had been given a vision by the Lord to establish a place of restoration and healing for orphans and war widows. There were many in desperate need, following the First World War. He found this property at Orbottyan and negotiated to buy it from the owners, who gave him a deadline by which the deal had to be completed; otherwise it would be sold to another purchaser. But he had no money! Professor Kovács shared his vision locally, but no money was forthcoming. As the deadline approached, his vision seemed doomed, until news of the need reached the ears of Lord Rothermere, the owner of the London *Daily Mail*.

Lord Rothermere suddenly decided to take action, and sent Professor Kovács a telegram, telling him to collect all the money he needed from his bank in Budapest. Time was of the essence and by the time he had collected the cash, and his lawyer, and had travelled from Budapest to Orbottyan, the time was almost up. The deal was finally concluded with only minutes to spare and the land was set apart for its spiritual destiny as Úr *Rétje*, the *Lord God's Meadow*. Only a small part of the land was used at the time for a Children's Home – the very same home which was then being looked after by Péter and Ilona Fekete. It was indeed a remarkable God moment, when the Curator of the Botanical Gardens directed me to go and talk with Péter Fekete.

When Hungary fell into Communist hands, the rest of this beautiful tract of land that Professor Kovács had bought, was seized by the authorities, and put into cooperative communist ownership. The picture we have of Lord Rothermere, with the dignitaries of the Reformed Church, dedicating the land to God, had become a quaint bit of Hungarian history – but God does not forget vows that are made to Him. That land had been set apart for God's Kingdom purposes and in the heavenly realms it was still His! He was watching over it until that moment when I and the Ellel team walked on that very piece of land, and our spirits were responding to the presence and purposes of God for it as a place of healing and restoration.

Today, the vision of Professor Kovács , followed by the vision of Zoltán's father and finally the vision of Ellel Ministries, found their combined fulfilment in the extensive work that has now gone out from Úr *Rétje* right across the whole of the former Communist world. Those three visions were like a three-fold cord and, as Ecclesiastes 4:12 says, *"a cord of three strands is not easily broken."*

When Otto and Sharon were sent out to Hungary from Ellel Grange, at the *Prayer Support Group* in February 1992, the Scripture they were given was Isaiah 61:4-7, which tells how foreigners would be the vine-dressers or helpers, but the nationals would be called to be the priests of their own nations. The strategy that evolved from this Scripture, for the work across this vast region, was simply that we would work with the many different peoples in their own lands to bring them teaching on healing and discipleship (as the 'vine-dressers'), and then help them to establish ministry teams within their own churches (as the 'priests') to serve their own nations.

As a result, core teams of nationals have now risen up within the developing nations of the Ellel East region to administer and train people within their own language groups, and be resident in their own nations once they have been trained up by Ellel. This principle is well illustrated by the fact that the current Hungarian Directors of the work at Úr *Rétje* are Tamas and Angela Kovacs. Tamas's parents, Denes and Aneko Kovacs were two of the early Hungarian pioneers, without whose help the work would never have got off the ground.

Úr *Rétje* is now the hub of a crucial regional operation, developing new national teams within the Central and Eastern European Region, until enough nationals have been trained in each of these nations to continue the work from within their own countries. This process has already been established in Romania and Ukraine, where vibrant local teams are taking the work forward with vision and enthusiasm. The Romanian team has even started their own publishing house to produce the Sovereign World books in Romanian. And the Ukrainian team takes a video version of our Modular Training School the length and breadth of the land, even in the midst of the war-torn east of the country and across the border into Russia.

Úr *Rétje*, therefore, under God, has served to initiate, equip and coordinate multiple works across the region. Today, it is not only the Hungarian Centre for Ellel Ministries, but it is the Regional Centre for a work that has spread right across the former Communist world, with outreaches and teams operating in places as far apart as Romania, Ukraine, Siberia, Russia and Serbia. There are schools and courses in Baltic nations, Balkan nations, Central and Eastern Europe, Central Asia, and right across the Russian Federation. Much of the cost of this dynamic and developing work has been funded by supporters of the work in the UK, for whom 'Ellel East' as it was called for many years, is very close to their hearts. The financial needs are still great today, the costs significantly outstripping the support that can be raised locally.

At one of our pioneering conferences in Svitlovods'k, in Ukraine, an old man was heard to be constantly saying under his breath, *"It's worth it. It's worth it."* It was only at the end of the conference that anyone could find out what he meant, and then the story came out. As a pastor he was desperate for help, in bringing healing to the very hurting people in his congregation. He had heard about the conference and urgently wanted to be there, but he had no money to pay the train fare to get there. The only marketable asset they had was the family cow – but the daily milk was, of course, their sole means of income. He had a terrible decision to make. Should he sell the family cow and go to the conference or keep the cow and continue to have the means of providing for his family? Knowing that the conference could give him answers for his people he made the sacrificial decision to sell the cow and buy a ticket to the conference. And that is what he was saying at Svitlovods'k – *"it was worth it"* – the value of what he had received far outweighed the sacrifice of selling the cow in order to be able to go.

Not long after this I was teaching in Kiev. The meeting was over and I was aware that time was of the essence and I needed to be leaving for the airport, but the Pastor kept me there on the platform while I was getting more and more agitated about the possibility of missing the flight. Suddenly a young man came running into the auditorium and up on to the platform, and presented me with a gift in a large cardboard box. As I opened the box I pulled out the most beautiful piece of cut-glass I had ever seen, in the shape of a horn that was once used for carrying the oil of anointing.

The pastor then spoke into the whole work of Ellel Ministries when he said that he wanted me to take this thank you gift *"as a reminder of the fact that Ellel Ministries has been used by the Lord to pour out His anointing on the peoples of the region."* I was totally choked and speechless as I looked at the horn in my hands. All we had done was put our feet down one step at a time and watched as the Lord poured out the blessing and He did His work. It took me quite a while to dry the tears and even today, when I look at that cut-glass horn, I am taken back in the spirit to twenty years ago and can sense the extraordinary blessing God poured out in that precious season of the ministry, which today is bearing fruit across eight time zones and blessing many thousands of people.

The stories of what God has done in the lives of countless thousands of individuals right across these nations, are truly extraordinary – they would fill dozens of books. Only in eternity will the full record be available to see. Otto and Sharon had no idea what God would do as a result of their pioneering obedience in taking the vision for the work of Ellel Ministries into Hungary. God has, indeed, done marvellous things.

Today Otto and Sharon have retired from Eastern Europe and the reins of leading this vast work have been ably taken up by Roger and Chris Pook, who have now been working with Ellel Ministries in the region for over twenty years. Their extraordinary work embraces ministries in Hungary, Romania, Ukraine, Russia, Belarus, Latvia, Serbia, Croatia, Czech Republic, Poland, Slovakia, Slovenia, Armenia and Mongolia! Meanwhile Otto and Sharon are in a new season of their lives, serving as active supporters of the work by travelling to other Ellel Centres and teaching on Schools and Courses. There is no such thing as retirement for God's people from the affairs of His Kingdom!

And the work on the ground continues to be supported by many sacrificial, mission-minded individuals, who serve the ministry in these regions and join the teams for both the long haul and for shorter seasons. They are the backbone of the work as it continues to spread across Central and Eastern Europe Region. They are an amazing team whom God has used to be the vehicle of hope for a very hurting part of the world.

Chapter 15

THE GREAT REDEEMER

Building a Future out of the Ashes of the Past

There are many great themes that run through the Scriptures, but the one that is at the heart of the Gospel and which most accurately describes the work of Jesus on the cross is Redemption. God put His rescue plan for mankind into place right there in the third chapter of Genesis when He told Satan that one day, out of the woman, would come one who would crush his head (Genesis 3:15). This first Messianic prophecy speaks to the whole of man, for the whole of time, that God is a Redeemer from beginning to end and that it was His desire to make it possible to restore fallen mankind and give them a fresh start, both in the years of time that are allotted to us and in the timelessness of eternity.

How else can we interpret this great theme of Scripture when we see that God chose a murderer (Moses) to lead the Children of Israel out of Egypt; a man who would commit adultery (David) to be King; an apostle who betrayed Jesus three times to preach the first sermon at Pentecost (Simon Peter); a vicious anti-Christian campaigner to be the leading first century evangelist (Paul); and a notorious slave trader to write *Amazing Grace*, the most sung hymn of all time (John Newton)!

And in our experience, those who have suffered the most as a result of the very worst forms of abuse, persecution or have been terribly traumatised in accidents or suffered sicknesses, diseases or disabilities can, by the grace of God, be powerfully blessed and used to fulfil God's Kingdom purposes in their lives. Christian history is littered with the stories of those whose lives have been amazingly redeemed, in spite of the experiences they have gone through. Redemption from every possible situation is at the very core of the Christian message. Fanny Crosby, who wrote 8000 hymns, including two of the most popular and expressive hymns ever composed, *To God be the Glory* and *Blessed Assurance*, was blind from just after her birth. Her disability was gloriously redeemed.

I will conclude this chapter by sharing something of my own personal story of God's redemptive provision through marrying Fiona. But first I want to look at the way God redeemed the life of Sarah – a lady for whom the medical world had no answers and, but for God's intervention would probably not have survived very long in the prison of compulsory psychiatric care.

Some years ago I planned a special ten day Healing Retreat for people whose problems were such that the limitations of our usual three day Healing Retreat were too restrictive. Just before the retreat was about to start, I was contacted by Peter Lawrence (now with the Lord), a long term pioneer of healing in the Church of England and a personal friend. He explained how his Church Secretary had totally broken down, and was now in psychiatric care, that she had been put on a lifetime disability pension and there was little hope of her ever being able to live a normal life again. He said he would like to ask her psychiatrist's permission to bring her to Ellel Grange – would we help? How could we refuse his request?

The situation was critical and the only option we had was to offer her an extra place on the 10-day retreat. Peter Lawrence spoke with the psychiatrist and, amazingly, though not without caution, he was willing to release Sarah from his care in the hospital, in spite of knowing that she was a potential danger to herself. We later discovered that the psychiatrist had come to the end of what he could do to help her, other than to give her electric shock treatment, which Sarah definitely didn't want to have. Sarah was on the highest allowable dosages of psychiatric drugs.

So, with Peter Lawrence's wife, Carol, as her carer, Sarah, white faced and frightened, arrived at Ellel Grange for an experience that would not only change her life forever, but also take us to the end of ourselves on a journey of faith, and change many of the ways we would minister to others in the years to come. Sarah turned out to be one of those people who had not only been sent by the Lord for her own healing, but also as part of our training!

Because she was a late booking on the retreat, all the main ministry team members had already been allocated to other delegates and Fiona, therefore, was asked to step into the gap and be the leader of Sarah's ministry team. The full story of Sarah's journey to wholeness is now told in her own book, simply called *Sarah*.

Sarah had suffered the very worst of abuse in her home family situation and her only way of coping with all that had happened was to totally block out all memory of her experiences. Such was the damage that she had no memories whatsoever of what had happened to her before the age of eighteen. From then on she tried to build a normal life, with a good husband and a lovely family. But the inner devastation eventually took over and she was no longer able to control the outward symptoms caused by horrendous inner pressures and her life totally fell apart.

In the end, unpacking all that had happened to Sarah, and seeing God heal and rebuild her life step by step, took years rather than days and was a bit like the restoration of my *Alvis Speed 20*, that had been vandalised and so terribly damaged. There were many twists and turns along the journey of faith which eventually brought Sarah to complete wholeness. For Fiona, and all those who ministered to her, it was a costly but extremely rewarding period of discovering God's utter faithfulness in restoring a broken life.

Without Fiona's unswerving commitment to the call of God on her life, to bring His healing to the hurting and broken lambs that came through our doors, it is unlikely that Sarah would have made it to the end of her healing journey. Fiona tells the story in her own book (*Intercession and Healing*) of how, early in the ministry, God spoke to her through a deserted lamb that lay dying at the foot of a tree in a field. She climbed the fence, picked up the lamb and took it back to the farmer who lives by our gates.

He took the lamb in his hands and was then able to give it warmth and milk and nurse it back to life. Her joy was only tempered by the mud on her clothes and the tear in her coat from the barbed wire, as she had climbed over the fence. When she saw the damage, God spoke to her, asking if she would be willing to rescue His damaged and broken lambs, notwithstanding the hurt and the pain and the cost that this would entail. Her willingness to say *Yes* to the Lord's question is amply evidenced by Sarah's, and many others', walk from desperation to wholeness.

And such is the depth of healing that Sarah received, not only is she now completely healed, but the great Redeemer has totally restored her life in every other way as well. The very experiences she suffered in her childhood, and what God has done to restore her, are an incredibly powerful testimony to the healing and restoring power of God. Wherever Sarah speaks today, people are impacted not just by her amazing story, but also by the depth of knowledge and experience she has of the love and faithfulness of God. She has had to find God in places which, mercifully, most people have never had to experience and it shows in her character, personality and Christian maturity.

Instead of being a delegate on a Healing Retreat, she is now one of the most appreciated teachers on Ellel courses. She is a testimony to the truth that, no matter how awful are the things that have happened to us, when we are willing to humble ourselves and submit every area of our lives to God, whatever the cost, then there is no limit to what our redeeming God can do. Her years of psychiatric treatment and medication are all in the distant past. The psychiatrist signed her off long ago. Her lifetime disability pension is no longer needed and God is using her in an amazing way to bring hope and healing to others.

In addition to the intrinsic blessing of Sarah's healing, the lessons that Fiona and the team learned along the way, have given the whole ministry much greater understanding of the terrible damage that abuse can do, but also of how to minister into severe inner damage and brokenness. Sarah's life is now, therefore, being redeemed in the lives of hundreds of others, who are today experiencing God's healing in a way that would not have been possible, were it not for what she had suffered. Sarah is one of many who have played a key role in our journey of understanding of the underlying issues that can stand in the way of healing. Her pain has become the key to someone else's gain.

Certainly, Sarah herself could not have received the healing she did without the benefit of there being others who had gone before her in our pioneering years of crying out to God in intercession for keys to setting the captives free. She represents many who have entrusted their lives to God first, and then to the team of Ellel Ministries, and through their journey the Lord has imparted to us key principles of healing, which are an essential part of Ellel's training today. By ministering to the ones, God gave us the keys for the many. Looking back, my days in the garage, with the parts of my vandalised Alvis car spread around me, were when the Lord was imparting vision and faith for the most challenging of situations and the passion to see that God wants to restore every life however broken.

Through the doors of Ellel Grange came the disenfranchised, the unlovely, the unpopular, the weak, the sinful, the lame and the broken. We were like a spiritual hospital and soon learnt that God has no favourites! I witnessed time and again how merciful and patient God was. When my human patience had come to an end, God showed me, His had not! When Danny was down the pub yet again, after another lapse into alcohol, I learnt the lesson that God does not abandon us in our mess. As I held people in the depth of their confessions, I experienced God's heart as never before. Learning to separate out the difference between human suffering, human failure, human fallibility, human pain and that of wilful pre-meditated rebellion and pride was part of the walk. Experiencing God's grace and mercy in the coalface of so many lives taught me profound lessons

In a completely different arena, the message of hope that the redemption of Jesus brings, has been intensely relevant and important in my own life also. We have seen time and time again how Jesus our Redeemer is the healer of the broken-hearted. But following the heartbreak of my own marital breakdown I, too, was in deep need of His redemptive healing. How I thank God for those who ministered to me during those very difficult years.

I was, and am, deeply committed to both the sanctity of marriage and to walking in obedience to the Lord and there were many nights of agonising pain as I wrestled with what the consequences of divorce would be – both for me, the family and the ministry. I felt the pain of my parents, whose long and happy marriage I would love to have emulated. I felt the pain of my children who couldn't understand what was happening and who had their own unique struggles. I felt the pain of all those who were supporting the work and had their own struggles with its leader suffering marriage breakdown. And I felt my own loneliness and pain as for nearly eight years I lived alone in very confined circumstances in a single room at Ellel Grange, which doubled as a team meeting room and, sometimes, a ministry room as well.

At the same time these were the years in which God was forging steel into the backbone of the ministry and equipping it for the journey ahead. God was clearly moving in a supernatural way bringing divine appointments and provision. New centres were being birthed and doors were opening all over the world. I wrestled with the apparent impossibility of being called to head up such a ministry, which God was clearly blessing in extraordinary ways, at the same time as I was struggling privately with the consequences of my personal situation. God had clearly not left me, or the work, but how could God have chosen me for such a work of healing when I was struggling with my own situation and consequential healing needs?

My marriage had irretrievably broken down and the truth had to be faced. To walk in pretence, half-truth and false hope was no longer an option. It was time to be released to move on, each with our separate lives and I needed to trust God with the outcome. I learned that marriage break-down, divorce and re-marriage are not the unforgiveable sin and God is, indeed, the great Redeemer, even when we have failed to come up to the mark. I was still totally confident and secure in the love of God, however, and took great comfort from the many stories in the Scriptures of how God continued to use people in spite of their human fallibility and an unenviable track record in one or more areas of their lives. I found myself able to look to God again and trust Him for my personal future as well as for the future of my children and the ministry.

These were not easy days, but the team, family, friends and close advisors were remarkable in their encouragement and support and nevertheless remained totally loyal and committed to the vision God had birthed at Ellel Grange. I thank God for them all, for without each one of them holding fast to God's rope, I would not have survived the extreme pressures we were then under from many different directions.

Having lived alone for so long, the last thing I wanted to do was to enter into another marriage without being absolutely sure that this was God's provision both for me, and whoever I married. It also had to be a source of blessing to the work and had to be unequivocally of Him.

Fiona was one of the full-time team who had also gone through the pain of divorce, in her case through the unfaithfulness of her husband. As time went by it was becoming clear to us, and to the team who knew us well, that God was drawing us together in love to serve Him in the ministry.

Whilst we were gaining confidence in the possibility of our getting married, I still had to face and ask the question as to what effect our marriage would have on the work. Deep down, I knew that it was God who had brought us together, so it was safe to trust Him with the consequences. And we had many confirmations from many different directions, and from trusted Christian friends and advisors, that this was indeed the Lord's provision for us.

Our eventual engagement and subsequent marriage were times of great joy and thanksgiving, both for us personally and everyone we were working with in the ministry. Over two hundred people attended our wedding at Ellel Grange, with family and friends from down the years as well as those in the ministry with us. And for nearly twenty-five years now we have known the joy of marital love, harmony and companionship as we have sought to serve the Lord together, wherever He has taken us in the work – and what an adventure that has been!

At our 1994 team conference, just before our December wedding,

I was reviewing the way God was beginning to further expand and spread the work around the world, in ways that none of us could have imagined. In my teaching I used the illustration of a certain type of mushroom that grows to a very large size and multiplies by, literally, exploding, so that the spores are carried far and wide on the wind. I described how God was showing me that the wind of His Spirit was blowing though the ministry and in a similar way the work was going to explode and spread the 'spores of God's healing love' far and wide around the world.

Later that same afternoon, Fiona and I took time out to go and look at a house that was for sale that might be just right for us to live in. It was large enough to accommodate us and the two children who would be living with us, and there was enough space for all our four children and their families when, in due course, they came to visit us. It was also only ten minutes from Ellel Grange. What else we found at the house, however, was extraordinary and we returned to the conference in a state of divine surprise – maybe, even, shock!

The house was great and we still live in it today, but as we walked round the garden we came across two of the largest giant puff ball mushrooms I had ever seen – the exact ones I had been talking about not an hour earlier in my teaching. The teaching illustration had suddenly come to dramatic life. God was speaking to Fiona and me, as well as the leaders of the work, that our marriage and home would not be an obstacle to the work, but a means of blessing, which would contribute to spreading the spores of faith, that emanated from Ellel Ministries, around the world.

We can say without any hesitation that that is exactly what God has done. He has blessed our love and our families in ways that we could never have dreamed possible. We have never again seen such giant puff ball mushrooms in our garden, but God used that one-off production to remove any anxiety I might have had about our love and our marriage and to illustrate what were His future intentions. Together Fiona and I have been able to demonstrate that God is, indeed, the great Redeemer!

Out of the ashes of our past God has built a platform of joy for the future. But it has also been a platform which has given the work great security and been a strong steadying influence on the Ellel ship, strengthening what would have been a very fragile vessel in the many stormy seas we have experienced. And it is with that platform securely in place that we have been able to press on in the ministry and build together the work that God had planned.

I know that without Fiona alongside me it would not have been possible for the work to have grown to what it is today. She has been a huge personal inspiration, the impact of which few people, other than myself, will ever be in a position to fully appreciate or understand. As the founder and overall Director of the work, people tend to think of me alone as being the leader. But those who know us well, also know that we are a team.

There are countless times when the impact of Fiona's wisdom on decisions has been huge. Times when she has shared with me things that have come out of her own walk with the Lord, and which the Holy Spirit has then anointed for me to teach. Times when I've listened to her words of restraint, which have held me back from saying or doing things which, with the benefit of hindsight, would have been unwise and, even, dangerous for me or the ministry. Times when she has more accurately assessed character and motive of the heart and saved me from making unwise commitments. Times, when I have been hesitant, but she has been sure, and her confidence has given me the courage to press on. Times, when her sensitivity to other people and their needs, has kept me from riding roughshod over someone else's feelings. And times when she has helped me overcome the blindness of single-mindedness, to see myself as others see me and help me make important adjustments to my way of doing things.

She has been a constant encourager when times have been tough, when I have struggled with issues, and sometimes people, that have drained me to the limit. She has recognised those times when God was moving me forward with fresh vision and, often at considerable personal cost, endorsed what I believed God was saying and been alongside me in the journey. She has been patient when my own pre-occupation with today's journey has robbed us both of precious time that we would have liked to have spent together.

Many of the major breakthroughs in understanding the healing ministry have come through Fiona's discernment of the real, underlying issues – as well as discerning what was God's answer for some of the very profound questions that arose in ministry situations. This was none more so than in the ministry to Sarah, described in the earlier part of this chapter. Through ministry to Sarah and others, God opened Fiona's eyes to the blessings and healing that come through rediscovering our God-given creativity. Teaching on creativity is now a vital part of all our training courses and schools. There are so many ways in which the ministry could never have grown to what it is today without Fiona's input. In drawing us together in marriage, God has not only provided me with a wife, and Fiona with a husband, but He has bound us together with Him in a three-fold cord of love, through which, God being our helper, we will seek to serve Him for the rest of our days.

We are tremendously grateful to God, also, that in and through our marriage we have been able to enjoy loving and meaningful relationships with all our four children (and now nine grand-children!), all of whom follow the Lord and are involved in Christian activities, including two who are working in the ministry full time. I am extremely grateful to God as well that my former wife is also very happily re-married, and out of the pain has come God's redemption for her as well. It is not that anyone would plan or wish divorce, it is not how it is meant to be, and it is certainly not an easy option, but it is my experience that God does not desert or give up on those who have gone through the pain of marriage failure. He truly is the great Redeemer.

Chapter 16

THE OIL OF MONEY

Provision for the Work of the Kingdom

If the Holy Spirit is the spiritual oil which empowers the work of the Kingdom, then money is the practical oil which facilitates and pays for those Kingdom works to be established and funded. Without the Holy Spirit, we will be exhausting ourselves with dead works and without money we will not be able to do even those things which the Holy Spirit inspires us to do. For nothing can be paid for in the material world without money.

A striking definition of spiritual poverty is religion without power, but physical poverty is the powerlessness which is the consequence of a lack of money. The person with money can enter a shop and buy food. The person without money can only look at the food through the window. Just as it would be a sin for a person without money to steal food, it is just as much a sin for the person with money to even think that he can buy the power of the Holy Spirit (Acts 8:18-25)!

One of the names of God is Jehovah-Jireh (Genesis 22:14), the Lord our provider, but if He is our provider why is it that Paul had

211

to plead with the Corinthian Christians to share their wealth with those who had little or none (2 Corinthians 8:1-15)? And if God's Holy Spirit was the inspirer of great missionary endeavours such as the *China Inland Mission*, which He was, why is it that every issue of the mission's journal, *China's Millions,* carefully listed every single donation that had been received during the previous month as a reminder and encouragement to supporters to continue giving?

It is sometimes said that George Muller fed the hundreds of orphans, that God gave him care of, on *air and prayer*. That is not true – he gave them food. Virtually every page of his extensive journal is occupied with describing how this person and that person was moved to give to support the work, whether that was with the money with which food could be bought, goods that could be sold or, on rare occasions, with the direct gift of something like a cart-load of bread or, on even rarer occasions with resources which seemed to have no natural human origin. But there is no ministry in recorded Christian history that had its own private money supply, replenished only by angel power! And the only Scriptural record of supernatural supply becoming the norm is the daily provision of food for the Children of Israel as they made their way from Egypt to the Promised Land.

Yes, in both Scripture and the history of many ministries there are the moments when God's supply becomes supernatural. Times such as when the widow's oil keeps flowing , or when the loaves and fishes feed five thousand, or when Elijah, in his extremity, was fed by ravens, or, in our own story, when the leader of a group of Russian Christians, desperate to be part of the first *Battle Belongs to the Lord* in Budapest, kicked against something in the dark on the pavement, bent down and picked up a tightly rolled bundle of Hungarian forints, which proved to be just enough to pay all their expenses for the conference. These are the divine exceptions which inspire, thrill and challenge – but they are not the norm. They are not an encouragement to spend the rest of our lives staring at the pavement, looking for the next roll of banknotes to keep us going!

While I am sure there will have been occasions when the Apostle Paul knew God's supernatural miraculous supply, he was not generally a good advertisement for what is sometimes called the 'prosperity gospel'! In 2 Corinthians 11:27 he says, *"I have known hunger and thirst and have often gone without food; I have been cold and naked."* God did not stretch down his hand and feed and clothe him supernaturally. In the history of the work there have been rare occasions when God has made provision in ways that can only be described as miraculous, but much more often we have, like Paul, and every other believer down the history of time, cried out to God for provision, often in great extremity, and God's answer has normally come through the direct response of human beings, moved by the Spirit of God to be the agent of the Lord, our Jehovah-Jireh.

As described in an earlier chapter, the very first contribution to the work of The Christian Trust came through the miraculous via the agency of man, but every single pound that was necessary to purchase Ellel Grange, without which the whole work of Ellel Ministries would not exist, came through the agency of man, inspired through the Spirit of God. It was a massive spiritual battle which was only finally won with the very last donations, that came in on the last possible day, pushing the amount of money we had available over the finishing line of need.

What has constantly amazed me along this road of faith is that God has so often been preparing his solution to the problem, long before a crisis has driven us to our knees in desperate intercession. But it is only when we are in that place of divine dependence that the human solution God has been preparing comes into the light and prayers are answered.

There was a season in the history of the ministry in the mid-nineteen nineties when we were up against it financially in every possible way.

The pioneering work at Ellel Grange was not only having to support the cost of growth into the South of the UK at Glyndley Manor, and the huge developments that were taking place in Eastern Europe, but the international work was spreading through word of mouth to other nations and the longer term training that would be available at the 'teaching hospital' was waiting in the wings. In these extreme circumstances establishing the big new baby, Ellel Pierrepont, was a financial leap of faith out of all proportion to the resources available.

This represented a huge sacrifice for the already over-stretched Ellel Grange team in both the physical and the financial areas. This was, by far, the greatest financial test God had ever laid on me. And on top of all this it seemed as though the regular supply of funds had dried up! Some people at this point, understandably, felt that faith had gone beyond common sense and opted out. It was a very lonely walk and I found myself questioning the Lord about what I believed He had said, time and time again – but nothing changed in my spirit. I was still certain that this was the path God wanted us to travel.

Some people proposed that we should sell Glyndley Manor and amalgamate the work there with Pierrepont, but why would God have led us to Glyndley Manor in the first place, if that was what he was then saying? It seemed sensible advice, but it wasn't what God put in my heart. The Leaders at that time could do nothing else but focus their eyes on the Lord as the only possible source of an answer.

As the cost of this seemingly outrageous step of faith became a reality, there were large bills that hadn't been paid, the monthly staff allowances were overdue and the monthly bank loan repayments could not wait. We were totally desperate. On the Monday morning of what would prove to be a watershed week for the ministry, the wells had completely dried up and there were no obvious human answers.

We called the whole team to prayer and Otto Bixler shared what he felt the Lord was saying. He described a physical siege, where we were in a fortress being surrounded and attacked on every side. He urged us not to give in but to take our positions, hold our ground and fight with all that we had left. He said the Lord would break this siege.

The following day, Tuesday, the whole leadership team prayed all day. We were crying out to God and knocking, as hard as we knew how, on the gates of Heaven. We were more desperate on that day than at any previous time in the history of the ministry. We had absolutely nothing with which to meet any of the impending costs. We were constantly reminding the Lord of what Jesus had taught us to pray – and we were praying it: *"Give us this day our daily bread"* (Matthew 6:11). We need bread today, today Lord, today!

Very late on the Wednesday evening, I was prompted to ring David Cross at Glyndley Manor, not knowing that a serious crisis had been unfolding in the centre. David and Denise joined the team following a remarkable church weekend in Scotland – of which more in Chapter 21. At this stage of their Ellel journey they were key leaders at Glyndley Manor, living on the premises. But they were completely oblivious, in their second floor flat, to the fact that an armed robbery was taking place below! Four masked and armed men broke into the Manor and demanded to know the whereabouts of the safe. The spiritual siege across the ministry had now become a physical siege at Glyndley Manor! Mercifully, David was able to report that everything was now alright and God had protected us.

While the attempted robbery was going on, David and Denise were relaxing in their flat at the end of a busy day's ministry on a Healing Retreat. The rest of the team had decided to go out for the evening and the only person left in the reception area downstairs was a Polish girl, who had just arrived from Poland to join the young people's team and could hardly speak any English. And in the lounge was a member of the ministry team, who had stayed an extra night and was so rejoicing in all that God had done for the person she had prayed for on the retreat, that the robbers could not make any sense of what she was saying! She was probably praying in tongues!

The robbers got hold of the Polish girl, pushed her up against the wall and threatened her – but she had no idea what they were saying. She was, of course, praying desperately, fearing that her life was now in danger. But as she prayed, the Lord started to show her all the unfulfilled promises that He was going to do for her. Previously she thought she was going to die, but now she knew that God had plans for her life that He said He was going to fulfil, so there was no longer any need to be afraid and she was able to trust God with her future.

Suddenly one of the robbers found the safe in another room and their attention was then wholly given to trying to get inside it. All they succeeded in doing was move it to the middle of the room, but it defied their attempts to open it and they fled empty-handed. If they had got inside it they would, not surprisingly in the midst of our financial crisis, have found it completely empty!

As David told me the story over the phone, it seemed as though the enemy had thrown his last card on the table. Mercifully nobody was physically harmed and it was as if Satan had done his worst in both the spiritual and physical realms, but had failed to make any headway in both. In a strange way, even though it was a terrible ordeal for Glyndley to have endured, we recognised that the protecting hand of God had been on the team and, ultimately, the only damage done was a broken leg of the desk, under which the safe was kept!

The following morning our bursar, Philip Moore, opened an extraordinary envelope, but to fully understand its significance, you will need to come back with me several years in the Ellel journey!

THE OIL OF MONEY

Philip had taken early retirement from his job at Barclays Bank, where he had been an active member of the Barclays Bank Christian Union. After leaving Barclays, and joining the Ellel Grange team, he was keen that his Barclays friends should find out about the work of Ellel Ministries, so he invited the Christian Union to come to Ellel Grange for a weekend retreat, at which I would be given the opportunity to speak for a few minutes about the work.

It was a lovely weekend with a very nice group of people. But there was one lady in the group, not a wealthy person, who was one of the counter staff in a branch of Barclays. She was seriously touched by the vision for the work and in her mind she told the Lord, *"I would love to be able to give £100,000 to support the work of Ellel Ministries."* It was one of those prayers which she said from the heart and then shelved it in her spiritual memory bank. It was a promise that was unlikely ever to be called on by the Lord – how could she possibly ever have so much money to give away?

As a bank counter clerk she was well-liked by her regular customers, some of whom would wait for the place at her counter to be available so that they could be served by her. One day she realised that one of her regulars hadn't been in for a while, but thought nothing of it – people come and people go. But a few months later she received a personal letter from a solicitor to say that this man had died and as a mark of appreciation for all her kindness over the years as a counter clerk, he had left her the residual value of his estate after selling his house. When she heard that the value of the estate that was coming to her was £99,995, God reminded her of her prayer promise to Him.

Without hesitation, she confirmed her promise to the Lord and a few weeks later the first £50,000 instalment from the estate proceeds was in her bank. She immediately honoured her commitment to the Lord, arranged for a bankers draft for the same amount and mailed it to Philip Moore at Ellel Grange. And you've no doubt already guessed on which day that £50,000 bankers draft arrived – the morning after our day of intercession and the armed robbery at Glyndley Manor! Satan had done his worst, but now a banker's draft, which is equivalent to available cash, was sitting on Philip's desk and ready to be banked. A few weeks later the second cheque arrived, completing her prayer promise to the Lord. It remains one of the most significant gifts the ministry has ever received in the UK.

This side of eternity, I will never understand the spiritual dynamics of God's extraordinary provision in circumstances such as these. The wheels for the donation were put in motion when Philip invited the Barclays Bank Christian Union to Ellel Grange, and the timing of its delivery to Ellel Grange, several years later, was beyond extraordinary and almost beyond belief. It wasn't a creative miracle through which money was made out of nothing, but it was certainly a miraculous provision for the ministry at a critical moment in the story, through one of God's servants who was willing to be obedient to the vision from Heaven, that God had given her at Ellel Grange – and therein lies a key to the funding of Christian works, obedience to vision.

When Paul was giving his testimony before King Agrippa he said *"I was not disobedient to the vision from Heaven"* (Acts 26:19). Throughout Scripture obedience to vision is the key to spiritual success. Without Noah's obedience, the Ark would never have been built; without Moses's obedience the Children of Israel would never have left Egypt; without David's obedience, Goliath would have routed the armies of Israel; without Nehemiah's obedience the walls of Jerusalem would never have been rebuilt; and without Paul's obedience the spread of the Gospel would have been seriously hampered; without the willing support of my business friend the land in Hungary could not have been bought, and the massive work that has gone out from there across all the former Russian States would have been stifled at birth; and without the obedience of a Barclays bank clerk we may never have survived the financial crisis we were in and be still here today!

There are two types of donation money that are essential for the support of all pioneering ministries – the capital donations that are needed to establish a work and the regular income that is needed to facilitate and maintain the running of a work. In my experience people are more excited, and therefore more willing to be obedient, about getting in on the ground floor and helping something new to get established. People seem less excited about being obedient to a vision for paying the electricity bill and other routine overheads, without which everything would be closed down. It is vital that people should learn the protocol of the Kingdom, and look to God for His vision as to how to spend the resources He gives us, otherwise we could be in danger of being more persuaded by our emotions than by our obedience. And at the same time, those who are involved in the leadership of Christian ministries need to be alert to God speaking vision into their hearts, which will be a strategic means of releasing funding for God's work.

During my business days the Lord taught me many lessons about how to support the regular funding of my company overheads, through visionary projects that were initiated by Him. I learned on many occasions how God was just as interested in blessing His children by giving vision for a business opportunity as He was for more overt Christian ministry.

In Chapter four I told how the ideas for a set of technical volumes, called the *BRE Digests* and the vision for *The Sunday Times Book of Do-it-Yourself* were supernaturally given, but I then had to do the hard work and bring them into being. Those two productions paid all the overheads of running my company until the moment I sold it and, more than that, without those two productions as part of the publishing back-list of the company, I would never have been able to sell the company, and be free to move into what was my eventual calling to establish Ellel Ministries.

Vision is the normal way through which God leads and directs His people and I have come to the conclusion that vision is the normal way through which God intends to provide both establishment funding and the running costs of His work. Even before Ellel Grange had been purchased one of the small handful of prophetic words that God had given me directly, about how to run the ministry, ran something like this: *You must never charge for people to come for ministry or to take part in a Healing Retreat, but what you learn by ministering to people, to whom you give away the ministry, you can then put into training courses which people will pay for.*

It was exactly in this way that the running costs of the ministry began to be funded back in 1987. We launched the teaching programme with a one day course called *Getting Acquainted with the Healing Ministry*, followed by a three day course called *Moving on in the Healing Ministry*. On those courses we taught all that God had shown us so far. The illustrations were 'hot off the press', being the testimonies of what God had done for people we had prayed for. The courses may have been rather unsophisticated, but they were alive with up to the minute reality. Those courses were packed out time and time again. And it was the income from these and other courses, together with the donations people also gave, either at the time or through becoming regular givers as friends of the ministry, that kept the bills being paid and the work afloat. God is a very good businessman – even in the healing ministry!

This pattern is, of course, totally consistent with Scripture, for those who choose to live within the covenant promises of God. In Deuteronomy 28:1-15 God promises both blessing and protection and says *"All these blessings will come upon you if you obey the Lord your God . . . . The Lord will send a blessing on your barns and everything you put your hand to. The Lord your God will bless you in the land he is giving you* . . . . *The Lord will establish you* . . . " It seems, from this chapter, that the blessings for obedience are limitless, for obedience lifts us beyond our own self-imposed boundaries and puts us firmly in the place of God's limitless covenantal promises!

Everything would have been fine with the finances of the ministry, if the vision for Ellel Ministries had been restricted to running a work at Ellel Grange, and all the consequential income was only used for the funding of the original centre. The income coming in on a regular basis was more than enough to support the overheads of the Grange and to repay the loans that had helped us buy the property in the first place.

But God was rapidly expanding the work and within a short time we were stretching our resources to the limit and beyond. Our supporters gave very generously to help fund the purchase and development of Glyndley Manor, followed by the establishment of what proved to be a huge work that would spread out from our base in Hungary right across eight time zones to beyond Siberia! But the needs far outstripped the designated donation income that was coming in and the rest had to be found, out of the already stretched resources of Ellel Grange. And this was a process that was repeated extremely sacrificially, many times, by the Head Office team, as they put the needs of the newly developing centres ahead of their own. Ellel Grange became like a mother who would gladly sacrifice her own needs on behalf of her children's!

The work in Hungary was an increasingly precious operation, with remarkable stories coming out of Eastern Europe and Russia on an almost daily basis. But, there was virtually no money forthcoming from the believers in the devastated countries of the region, they had nothing. So, almost every single penny, for at least ten years, had to be sourced from our amazing body of supporters in the UK. How thankful we were for major donations that began to come in from overseas to support the work, as foreign nationals also became gripped by the vision and gave so very generously out of their income, their savings and, on one occasion, through an exceptional legacy a former delegate on the nine week school had received and chose to pass it on. And even today, the work there is still of a pioneering nature, as new territories are brought on stream, and cannot be totally funded locally.

The financial needs of running a ministry never go away. And, in today's world, things can happen so very suddenly, changing everything in a moment of time. Recent events in Crimea and Ukraine caused the Ukraine team to be suffering extreme hardship with dramatic rises in the cost of food as the value of the local currency fell through the floor.

Ellel Ministries has now become a major missionary society with significant outreaches in many of the poorest areas of the world and today we face fresh and increased challenges as we continue to trust God for His supply, in a world where opposition to the Gospel is rising fast at the same time as, especially in the West, the traditional churches are in rapid decline. But I take huge comfort from the fact that none of this is a surprise to God – and, just as the crisis we faced back in the mid nineteen-nineties was one that He anticipated and made provision for, we are trusting that He will raise up a new generation of 'bank clerks' who will want to be faithful to whatever vision God gives them. He still gives vision to His people to show them the way that He wants us to go.

God not only gave Nehemiah the vision to re-build the walls and gates of Jerusalem, He also gave Nehemiah the vision to ask Artaxerxes, the Emperor, who he worked for as a wine steward, to make available the necessary resources. For Nehemiah to have had a vision for the work, without also having a vision as to how the work was going to be resourced, would be inconsistent with the character of God.

As the work has grown and I have got older and many others

have carried the load of the ministry around the world, God has not lifted from me the burden of responsibility to hold the finances of the ministry before the Lord – almost on a daily basis. I'm constantly looking to Him for the new spiritual enterprises that will help support the work.

For example, one day, while the Executive Leadership of the ministry were praying together at Pierrepont about the finances of the ministry, I suddenly had a very clear vision of a major new development for the ministry. Not, on this occasion, for the establishment of a new work in a new place, but through the provision of a new means of reaching out to the world with all the foundational teaching that God had given into the work through the hundreds, no thousands, of personal healing ministries the whole team has been privileged to be involved in.

The world's needs are so vast that there is no way everyone who might want to learn about healing, and grow in their own personal walk with the Lord as a result, could ever get to an Ellel centre for either ministry or training or both. The new vision the Lord gave me as, we prayed, was to take the teaching to them via an internet training programme. While everyone else was praying, I scribbled down on my pad the simple words, *Ellel 365 – Personal Transformation – One Day at a Time*. In a moment of time I knew exactly what the vision meant and within minutes after the prayer time, I had written down the outline of a new Ellel website which would form the basis of a virtual centre to which anyone could go at any time. A centre that would provide daily training for people, in their own language, wherever in the world they were – provided they could hook up to the internet via a computer, which today includes most places in the world.

The following week I travelled to America to visit the team at Ellel USA, and as I walked into the base one of the team handed me a piece of paper on which was written a Scripture the Lord had given her for me. She had absolutely no idea that I had been thinking and writing about Ellel 365 on the flight over. The Scripture was from Habakkuk 2:2-3, *"Write down the revelation and make it plain on tablets so that a herald may run with it. For the revelation awaits an appointed time."* I read and re-read those words – for I had already started to write down the 'revelation' so that it could be made plain on tablets (everything from lap-tops to I-pads to mobile phones). Through the internet the revelation could literally run round the world in a fraction of a second. I am sure there could not possibly be a more relevant Scripture in the whole of the Bible than this one, confirming the vision God had given me. I was shaken and thrilled at the same time!

At one and the same time the Lord had given me the strategy for getting all our foundational teaching material out in a usable format, to anyone and everyone the world over. But because, also, Ellel 365 could be sold as a subscription service, it had the potential to be a major source of funding for the whole ministry. But God's vision for Ellel 365 was even bigger and while the original version did provide some significant income for the ministry, we are planning that the Mark 2 version of the website, under its new name *Journey to Freedom*, will be hugely simplified, with multi-language flexibility and we are then hoping to make it available free of charge to subscribers the world over. With as few as only ten languages available online, *Journey to Freedom* would have the potential to serve something like 70 – 80% of the world's population. In the years since the original website went live there have been hundreds of testimonies from people all over the world describing the healing fruit there has been in their lives as a result, and a printed version will also be available from Sovereign World.

I do not anticipate that managing the finances of what is now a large ministry will ever be easy, there will be constant needs as the work gets established in some of the smaller and financially less affluent nations, such as Rwanda and Papua New Guinea. But I have no doubt that the God who stirred the heart of a Barclays bank clerk can stir believers across the world to take up the baton as we run this relay race together.

But how I wish it wasn't such a huge struggle! There isn't one of the major pioneering works I've studied, that didn't regularly have to face financial mountains that they had difficulty in climbing. While the major, and even miraculous, financial breakthroughs, such as those described above, are a massive encouragement when they come, the day to day reality is more normally having to find today's money to pay today's bills, wrestling with banks and trying to help accountants walk through the fire which always fills the gap between pioneering faith and God's provision!

There can be constant tension, and consequential need for grace and yet more dependence on God, when God doesn't seem to appreciate the time frame of our human need! Or when He allows us to make mistakes, fail, learn another lesson and then get up and walk on yet again, testing our faith in one more crucible of experience, sometimes in the face of desperation, and to the point sometimes of people wanting to give up.

Worst of all can be the words of common sense, from well-meaning friends, that undermine faith accompanied, sometimes, by comments that imply 'you must be out of God's will if you're struggling so much.' Such words could easily have been spoken to the Apostle Paul when he was adrift for twenty four hours in the Mediterranean, wondering just what God was doing! But in reality he was exactly where God wanted him to be at that particular moment of his life. It's not easy trying to keep on moving forward in pioneering faith at the same time as fighting the elements of opposition to all that God is doing, and trying to sift out the difference between man's ways and God's ways!

I began this chapter by posing questions about why it should be that everyone involved in pioneering Christian work, from the Apostle Paul's times to the present day, has had to make some sort of ongoing appeal for funds to initiate new developments in their work and fund the existing ones? The reality is that we live in a fallen world and if the enemy of souls cannot stop you with direct temptations (such as the ones Satan tried on Jesus in His wilderness experience) then he will do everything he can to interrupt the supply lines that feed the ventures of faith that emanate from the heart of God.

It is not for nothing that Satan is referred to in the Scripture as a thief and a robber, or that Malachi indicates that withholding giving to God is in fact robbing Him of the resources that He needs for His people. And when direct opposition comes, it can have the effect of making people question whether or not they should give their hard earned money to this or that cause!

When the disciples were short of funds for paying their taxes, Jesus told Simon Peter to go fishing and he found a coin in the mouth of the first fish he caught! We rejoice in the miracle, which I believe Jesus did in order to show us that He is quite able to show us alternative means of funding His work. But no-one in Scripture, or in Christian history, has ever recommended that to send all the congregation out with fishing lines was the God-ordained way of funding God's work. You can't make a habit out of a miracle. That was a unique event for that unique moment. And whenever our financial circumstances have been hard-pressed, as that of the disciples clearly was, I am always on the look-out for today's equivalent of the coin in the fish's mouth!

For example, at the moment when we were finally sealing the purchase of Blairmore House for the work of the ministry, (see Chapter 23), I was in need of a significant six-figure sum in order to cover the cost of all the contents of the property, without which it was looking as though the whole deal would fall through and the work in Scotland would come to an end.

I was in the middle of an Ellel Conference at Lancaster University at the time, and we suddenly got news that my wife Fiona's mother had had a fall and was in urgent need of help. Fiona left immediately in our car. The next message was to say my help was also needed, but now I had no car. One of the delegates to the conference was nearby and offered to take me there. I gladly accepted the offer and jumped in his car. While we were on the way, this man started to ask me some penetrating questions – it must have been obvious I was under some form of pressure, and he wanted to know if there was anything he could do to help.

I am normally very confidential about sharing financial things and don't easily talk about the private walk of faith in circles beyond those who need to know, but in that car on that day, I suddenly felt complete release from the Lord, while driving to help Fiona's Mum, to tell him everything about the Scottish problem. I knew virtually nothing about the man at the time, but by the time we had completed that six mile journey, this generous man spontaneously offered to loan the full amount that was needed and, as a result, the future of the work in Scotland was secured. This was a classic example of a 'coin being found in the fish's mouth'!

A few years later Fiona and I were fishing for mackerel and pollock in deep water off the Outer Hebrides of Scotland. There were huge shoals of fish in the water and on virtually every cast we were pulling in three, four, even five fish on the lines which were 'baited' with feathered hooks. It was very exciting fishing. But there were so many fish that it was easy for the hooks to get tangled with each other and when that happened with Fiona's line, in order not to waste good fishing time untangling the lines, the boatman simply cut off the offending hook and threw it overboard.

Miraculously, the next fish that I caught on the other side of the boat had two hooks in its mouth – the one that it had been caught with and the loose hook that the boatman had thrown over the edge. We all laughed at the extraordinary coincidence and my mathematical mind was trying to work out the odds of that happening – they were off the scale! But then my line got tangled and the boatman did exactly the same for me, and threw my offending hook overboard. And even more miraculously, again, this second loose hook was also recovered, attached to the very next fish I caught! The mathematical odds of such a thing happening twice were now beyond imagination. This made Simon Peter's coin in the fish's mouth seem like a routine event!

As I meditated on what had just happened, I knew that God was speaking to me. If He could so orchestrate a single fish, twice, out of a shoal of many thousands, to return the very hook to me that had just been thrown over the edge as a loose un-baited hook, then cannot I trust Him to be the means of supply for the things He was asking us to do?!

And so we press on, usually without having enough in hand to do the works that faith has led us into. But at the same time knowing that if it is God that has led us, then we can trust Him to orchestrate the shoals of men and women to be the means of supply. Every difficult experience is a fresh opportunity, in all our human weaknesses, to learn to depend on Him and to come together as leaders, in humility, to own things where we 'got it wrong' and were as a result misguided, to yield afresh to His way, and continue to do our part in fulfilling the purposes God has laid out before us.

As Fiona and I have walked together in leading the work, the Lord has painfully had to teach us that there is no limitless supply, because we live in a fallen world and there are limitations. Together we have had to trust Him for our personal needs as well as the needs of the ministry. The tension between what we would like to do and what we can do will never go away. There will always be more money needed than we have available. Not being able to respond is sometimes painful. Allowing others we love, to walk the walk of faith and not have an answer for their immediate need is painful too, but nothing compares to experiencing God at work in and through these kind of trials, as He, in His covenantal love, forges a deep relationship of trust in the crucible of our human situation.

Learning that He is no man's debtor, and that He can turn every situation around for good (Romans 8:28), and has an eternal purpose being worked out in our midst, is eternally precious, whether it is in the experience of His miraculous supply or when He is teaching us how to live with lack. We would not want to exchange this walk of faith dependence for a pragmatic or common sense approach to finance. The gold of obedience is hard won on the sharp anvil of faith and I cannot pretend that the walk is easy. To this day we walk, along with the other leaders of Ellel Ministries, on the sharp, cutting edge of dependency on God for survival. Even as I write this book, there are critical situations for which we don't have an immediate answer and for which we are trusting God to show us His answer for every situation as He leads us forward in this precious work.

Chapter 17

GROUND UP MIRACLES

Reclaiming Ground from Enemy Control

The lady on the other end of the line sounded desperate. *"I've heard of all the good things God is doing at Ellel Grange and would like you to come and help our church."* She explained how numbers had been steadily declining, five of the men in the congregation had died in the past twelve months, their Pastor had left a year ago and his successor had now gone also, having only lasted six months. And, and, and . . . . . ! It was a dreadful tale of woe.

As I listened to her story my heart went out to her, but I had already concluded that this wasn't anything we could help with. I tried to explain that Ellel Ministries was a personal healing ministry and that if any of the members of the church wanted to come to Ellel Grange for help we would be glad to pray with them. But as I spoke I knew that my words were already turning to spiritual cardboard in my mouth – and I knew I was talking against what God was actually telling me to do! It was another of those God moments, through which He was opening up a new avenue of faith to walk down. Another one of those attachments to my original visionary 'email' from God was about to be opened.

I changed tack in the conversation and asked her what she had in mind. She explained how she was hoping I would come down with a team for a church weekend, spend time with the people, and see if God showed us anything about the church that needed healing. The healing of a church, as opposed to praying for individuals was new – at least it was to us during that first year of the ministry. I said we'd come and so it was that a couple of months later the Ellel team headed off down the motorway for a church weekend that would add a significant weapon to the spiritual armoury of the ministry.

Between that initial call and the weekend itself, I spent a significant amount of time scouring through the Bible looking for anything that would help us minister to a whole church! It reminded me of the days when I was looking for Jesus's teaching on the healing ministry in the Gospels and stumbled upon our foundational Scripture, Luke 9:11. And yes, I did stumble on another highly significant passage – this time in the Old Testament in 2 Chronicles 29, a passage which is headed in my Bible, *Hezekiah Purifies the Temple*. And that's exactly what we were being asked to do – to purify this local church temple. I was listening.

Hezekiah's father, King Ahaz, had been a very evil King. In his reign he had closed the temple doors, abandoned all worship of the living God and built altars, both in Jerusalem, and all over the land, on which to make sacrifices to all sorts of false gods. Hezekiah, however, had had a godly mother who had brought him up in the ways of his ancestor, King David, and he chose to do what was right in the eyes of the Lord. After his father died, the first thing he did when he came to the throne was to set to work to cleanse the temple and see it restored for the worship of the true and living God. I was excited to read the story – I was sensing that the keys to the forthcoming church visit would be found in this chapter and I read this, and the next two chapters, time and time again.

God showed me that Hezekiah had tackled the problem in two ways – first he spent time with the Levitical priests, and then he prepared them for the cleansing of the temple by first seeing that they themselves were cleansed and ready. He told them that before they could be allowed to start work on cleansing the temple building, they first had to deal with their own hearts and consecrate themselves to the Lord for the task that lay ahead. Many of the priests would have been spiritually compromised during the reign of Ahaz, and Hezekiah correctly saw that if the priests were not themselves spiritually clean, they wouldn't be able to bring spiritual cleansing to the buildings of the temple – they would be bringing their own spiritual uncleanness into the temple of the Lord.

Then Hezekiah told the priests to go and start work on dealing with all the uncleanness that remained in the temple buildings, following the apostasy and terrible sins of King Ahaz. And so *"they brought out into the courtyard everything unclean that they found in the temple of the Lord and carried it out to the Kidron valley."* The Kidron valley was the rubbish dump of Jerusalem where fires were continually burning up the rubbish that people left there. Those things that were made for ungodly purposes had to be removed and destroyed, and everything else had to be cleansed and restored.

The chapter concludes with the joyful statement that *"Hezekiah and all the people rejoiced at what God had brought about for his people, because it was done so quickly."* The next two chapters tell of all the blessings and prosperity that followed for the people of Jerusalem, as a result of Hezekiah's initiative in cleansing the temple and the priests' obedience in following the example of their king.

As I read, and re-read, these chapters, my spirit began to rise in anticipation of the forthcoming weekend, now knowing that there were clear principles in God's Word about what to do – first bring cleansing to the leaders, then to the buildings and consecrate both afresh to the Lord for His service, and trust God that He will then bless the place with His presence.

When we got to the church on a Friday afternoon, all six leaders welcomed us and poured out their hearts to us. It was a depressing account of the recent history of the church. Then I shared with them all I had learned from Hezekiah's story and explained that we would like to begin the weekend by spending time individually with each of the leaders, so we could help them prepare personally for the important spiritual tasks that lay ahead.

All except one were very happy to be open before the Lord in this away and apply the scriptural healing principles to their own lives, which we had already found to be so important and powerful on healing retreats. The one person who wasn't willing to go this road decided to resign from the church rather than travel this road. While this was sad, it was, nevertheless, an important step forward. Down the years we have met many people who were unwilling to be real about the things in their life which were out of line with God's order. They may have wanted God to heal them of their problem, but they didn't want God to have His way in the rest of their lives! We had some precious prayer times with all the other leaders who were completely determined that anything in their own lives, which could be standing in the way of God blessing and restoring their church, must be dealt with.

The first meeting of the weekend, on the Friday evening, was only attended by twenty to thirty people, including our team and it was spiritually hard work! It really felt as though we were worshipping through black treacle and battling against something unseen which was opposing what we were there to do. We began to understand why the church had been going through such difficulties.

Then on the Saturday we set about cleansing, and then re-consecrating, the land and the buildings. One of the ancient traditions of the Church of England was that once a year the leaders of the church and the people should *'beat the bounds'* of every parish in the land which meant, literally, walking the boundaries of the parish, exercising spiritual authority over everything ungodly that had been given access to the parish through sin or through the inroads of the enemy, and then rededicating everything to God. We adopted this principle and went round the perimeter of the church grounds, anointing every fence post with oil and taking authority, with the leaders, over every unclean spirit that had been given any rights over the land and buildings. Then we did the same with the buildings themselves and everything in the buildings.

It was during this process that we discovered a dedication plaque which had been placed there by the local Masonic lodge. None of the current leaders knew it was there or understood its significance, but it was clear from the plaque that there would be a spiritual hold over the property through freemasonry. When we explained how dangerous the spiritual foundations of freemasonry were, as an organisation in which the name of Jesus was banned from their meetings and any of their rituals, the church leaders were very glad to pray over these influences, repent of their demonic roots and to renounce all spiritual darkness which had come as result, which had affected the church and the congregation. The Lord was leading us once again on another steep learning curve.

By the time we reached the final service of the weekend the total atmosphere in the church had changed so much, that a family who had been away until the Sunday evening service looked around the building and wondered if it had been redecorated while they were away – such was the difference in the place. And that final service was indeed something different – the first service on the Friday evening had been a very turgid affair, but now the praise was lifting off, and there was such a depth to the worship and awareness of the presence of God that everyone knew God had done something very special over the weekend. And, to cap it all, God spoke to me personally through a lady who had never given a prophetic word before and had just been filled afresh with the Spirit!

Twelve months later I was back at a meeting in the same town and after the service a lady came running across the church hall to get my attention, and asked me to come over and meet their new pastor. She was the secretary of the church we had ministered at in the previous year. When I met the new pastor, he grasped hold of both my hands and thanked me and the Ellel team for what had happened over that special weekend. He explained that he had only been there for six months, they had done no organised evangelism in the district at all, but that there had been a steady stream of new people joining the church, most of whom were new believers who were being drawn to the church as a place where they could find God. And the congregation was growing steadily.

What the pastor reported seemed almost too good to be true, but seventeen years later we were sitting in the dining room of the House of Commons in London, with Dave Landrum, who was then a Senior Parliamentary Officer employed by the Bible Society to promote Scriptural truth to the Members of Parliament. I had met Dave earlier in the year and he asked if we would be willing to come to the place he worked – the Palace of Westminster, which included the House of Commons and the House of Lords, to see if we could offer him any help in praying over the buildings!

After touring all the main buildings we sat down to lunch with him among the flurry and buzz of parliamentarians and as part of the conversation Fiona asked Dave how he had become a Christian. He smiled as he said, *"Well, Ellel Ministries had something to do with that!"* This was news to us, but Dave went on to explain that neither he nor his wife came from any form of Christian background in their families. But while Dave had been working away his wife had been invited to church by a friend. And one

Sunday morning his wife crept out of bed to go somewhere and Dave decided to follow her to see where she was going and what she was doing!

To his utter amazement, he found himself following her down the road and entering a church building, so he followed her in and together they were so aware of the presence of God in the place that they came under conviction of sin, repented and before long they were born again. Dave had no previous Christian background whatsoever. His remarkable conversion experience was, indeed, truly miraculous – it was a wonderful story. But then Dave explained that the church they had gone to was the very church that we had been to a few weeks previously. What the pastor had told us about people being drawn to the building by the presence of God was now proven to be absolutely true. Here, seventeen years later, in the House of Commons dining room, we were hearing dramatic evidence of the fact, and that God had now placed Dave in a highly strategic and important spiritual role right at the heart of the nation. At that church meeting Dave encountered God, and everything changed. God took him as a Liverpudlian with no educational qualifications, to lecturing in politics with a PhD! Then to his work in parliament and today Dave is the Director of Advocacy for the Evangelical Alliance. It's always hugely encouraging to learn of the fruit of the ministry, especially where there has been such a long-term testimony as evidence of the reality of what God did.

There were many more such stories of how God used us to cleanse land and buildings, and before long we had worked through all the theology and teaching which underpinned this ministry from Scripture, and put it all together as a new course under the title *Claiming the Ground*. Fred Elgar, one of the pioneers of *Wholeness Through Christ*, another very significant healing ministry, was on that first course and sent a copy of the teaching tapes of *Claiming the Ground* to his *Wholeness Through Christ* friend and colleague in Canada, Alistair Petrie who, at that time, was the Rector of an Anglican parish on Vancouver Island.

For a number of years Alistair had been working through similar issues, and listening to the recordings of *Claiming the Ground* was a great encouragement to him at the time. It is always hugely encouraging to discover, when pioneering something new, that there are other people in God's Kingdom who have been going through a similar learning experience! Alistair, and his wife Marie, were soon to become close colleagues with us in the developing work of Ellel Ministries. Alistair, with his son Michael, also shared with us in that dramatic experience in the Houses of Parliament. In more recent years Alistair has been a regular speaker at our conferences and on specialist training courses at our Scottish Centre in the ministry. Alistair and Marie now head up *Partnership Ministries*, a world-wide teaching ministry that specialises in the cleansing and healing of the land.

When, in 1995, we acquired the Pierrepont estate in Surrey to become a major training centre for the ministry, we dedicated the land and buildings to God and asked Him to show us anything spiritual that needed to be done to further cleanse the place. Pierrepont had been a boys boarding school, but the Headmaster had recently died, the school had gone bankrupt and the auctioneers had sold off absolutely everything – but there was one item they had overlooked, or been unable to sell, a small weather station which the boys had used as part of their geography training.

Within a few weeks of acquiring the property a lady telephoned Pierrepont and asked if she could have the weather station for her son to use at home. We had no use for it and so she came to get the small structure which had been bolted to a slab of concrete. Once the weather station had gone the slab of concrete was a nuisance in the middle of a lawn and some of the team were asked to dig up the concrete and re-grass over the place. But under the concrete, they found a layer of gravel and amongst the gravel they found a bottle, in which were several sheets of paper on which were written out curses of death to the school and the Headmaster.

We were then able to pray over and break these curses in Jesus' name, and then, with anointing oil that had been prayed over, we were able deal with any residual cursing associated with the place where they had been found, and re-consecrate the land to the Lord. That was over twenty years ago. God clearly didn't want us to be labouring under the spiritual pressures that curses such as these would still be exercising over the land of Pierrepont. Within just a few weeks of our ownership God had shown us exactly where to go, and what to do, in order to free the ministry from having to operate under the influence of a curse of death and destruction!

God was teaching us some vital spiritual principles, which He has since used with amazing effect in every country we have ever ministered in. We have seen dramatic evidence of God fulfilling the promise He first made to His people, when He appeared to Solomon and said, *"If my people, who are called by my name, will humble themselves and pray and seek my face and turn from their wicked ways, then will I hear from Heaven and will forgive their sin **and will heal their land.**"* (2 Chronicles 7:14).

A minister was distressed because one after another of his congregation were falling into sexual sin. When the sexual sin of a previous minister of the church, that had been committed on the church premises, was exposed it was possible to deal with the problem. Firstly, the sin of the previous incumbent had to be confessed and then the whole building that had been used for the sin had to be cleansed and re-consecrated to the Lord. As a result, the whole spiritual atmosphere of the church changed.

John, a Baptist minister, came on our *Deliverance Ministry Training Course* and learnt about cleansing of land and buildings. He had laboured for ten years in his church, without seeing any real growth in his congregation. People had moved away and others had moved into the area to take their place. But as for dynamic new life, there wasn't any. After the course, he was prompted to research the history of his church and discovered that in years gone by there had been major divisions in the fellowship which had caused great acrimony between church members.

Psalm 133 talks about the blessings that God pours out on the brethren when they dwell together in unity. We have seen time and time again how the opposite of this is also true – when the brethren are in disunity, then the enemy has a right to bring cursing into the fellowship by bringing in darkness rather than attracting God's presence of life and light. The spiritual darkness then exercises a covert negative spiritual influence on the fellowship for as long as the sin of division remains unconfessed and uncleansed. Failure to deal with this can undermine the work of the Spirit of God to bring life, hope and healing to the people.

Having understood the root of their problem, John gathered his leaders together and they confessed that, in years gone by, other leaders of the church had opened the door to the enemy through division and hatred. They repented that the church had allowed this to happen and asked God to forgive the fellowship. They then covenanted together afresh to be in unity and took authority over every spiritual power that had been given rights through these sins. The effect of their cleansing the land of their church was astonishing. For ten years they had seen no growth in the fellowship, but as a result of what they did the church congregation doubled in size in the next twelve months, much of it from first time conversions.

None of these things were taught in the traditional evangelical churches of my upbringing. Neither was I taught to appreciate the sacramental nature of things like anointing with oil, even though the principles are clearly there in Scripture. For example, when Moses was preparing all the elements of the tabernacle in Exodus 40, God told him to *"take the anointing oil and anoint the tabernacle and everything in it; consecrate it and all its furnishings, and it will be holy"* (Exodus 40:9). It is through intercession and prayer that, little by little, the Lord taught us how to deal with the things that could carry with them spiritual power from the enemy and bring cursing into people's lives.

A minister friend had gone through a series of breakdowns and had been recently diagnosed with a form of mental illness. As I talked with him and his wife, we touched on their previous years of missionary service in West Africa. I asked if they had brought any artefacts back with them as souvenirs of their time overseas. His wife immediately ran upstairs and brought down an old suitcase from which she pulled out a black doll which had once been used in witchcraft. They had brought it back to show people the evils of witchcraft, but no-one had told them of the spiritual dangers attached to the doll! Another minister who had served many years overseas had a whole room full of such artefacts which he described as "trophies of grace". Sadly, they were the root cause of the deep depression which had settled over him. In both these cases strategic bonfires and prayers for deliverance were necessary. Another lady loved the supposedly ethnic ear-rings she often wore. But when she was delivered of what the enemy had put into her life through them, there were literally 'screams of deliverance' as she was set free.

In another large church overseas I addressed the issue of having ungodly things in our homes and what their spiritual effect could be on our walk with the Lord, our families, relationships and everything we do. The leaders were confident that this wouldn't be a problem for their people. But, just in case, they agreed that I could invite everyone to bring anything they owned, which might fall into the category of being a cursed object, the following morning, so that during the worship time we would take up what I call an 'occult offering' of things to be prayed over and destroyed. While the leaders didn't expect there to be anything significant, the following day they stood there with shaking heads, as dozens of their people brought everything from statues of Buddha to pornographic videos and filled fifteen huge black rubbish sacks with spiritual junk. Someone was sent out to buy some hammers and I will never forget watching the Pastors, using those hammers, to smash it all to pieces, as 2 Chronicles 29 was lived out before our very eyes!

I could fill a whole book with stories and testimonies of what God has done to bring life-transforming cleansing and wholeness through dealing with land, buildings and the things we accumulate in our houses which have the potential to be carriers of demonic power. The evidence of God's children being set free and lives transformed, is powerful witness to the saving, healing and delivering power of Jesus over all the works of darkness.

Chapter 18

ROLLER-COASTER!

The Ups and Downs of our
Canadian Experience

Simultaneously with doors for the ministry being opened in an easterly direction to Hungary and the whole of Eastern Europe, doors were also opening in a westerly direction across the North Atlantic or, as some people prefer to say, 'across the pond'!

Some Canadian leaders came to the second *Battle Belongs to the Lord* conference at Brighton and then joined with us as part of the ministry team for the first *Battle Belongs to the Lord* conference in Budapest. As a result, I was invited to bring an Ellel Ministries team to Canada and conduct several training courses on healing and deliverance.

The courses were all very well attended and very well received, the teaching being not just on deliverance, but on the whole scriptural foundations for the healing and deliverance ministries. Subsequently a number of Canadians began to come to the UK for schools, conferences and courses, including the inaugural nine-week school at the new centre in the South of England, Glyndley Manor, where Joe and Ruth Hawkey were the pioneering leaders.

Among those who came on that first school were some Board members of a Christian retreat centre. They saw how the Ellel vision closely fitted their ethos and Ellel Ministries was, subsequently, invited by the Board to use their premises for establishing a new Ellel Centre in Canada. Ellel Ministries was beginning to grow internationally at that time and our Executive leaders were glad to respond to this *'Macedonian Call'* and, very sacrificially, they asked Joe and Ruth Hawkey to leave their very successful pioneering work at Glyndley Manor, to go and fulfil a similar role for the emergent Ellel Canada.

The work took off right from the beginning and the Lord was blessing the ministry in Canada in an incredible way. But there was concern about the amount of investment, particularly of human and financial resources, that was being put into the development of the work there, when we were not able, as non-Canadians, to have a majority on the Board. We did not, therefore, have the operational legal authority, that we now know such a venture requires, in order to protect and guard the huge physical and spiritual investment that was being made in developing the ministry. The name of the work was formally changed to Ellel Ministries, but this didn't affect the structure of the Board in whom legal authority was vested.

In spite of the tenuous hold we had on the operation we trusted the people we were working with, believing that all would be well. Our most experienced UK leaders and team spent many years flying backwards and forwards, building the work into a very successful operation, with over 10,000 names from all over Canada on the database. Following Joe and Ruth Hawkey's initial leadership of the Canadian work, the baton was then passed to Ken and Jean Hepworth, experienced leaders who had worked with us at Ellel Grange since the beginning of the ministry. They, in turn, handed the leadership baton on to a Canadian to take the work forward and further develop the ministry.

During this season we were also taking legal advice as to how Ellel, as an international ministry, should be structured so as to protect the copyright and use of all our teaching materials and ensure that our spiritual authority could not be undermined in the places where God had opened the doors for the ministry. We were beginning to understand how a divided legal and, therefore, spiritual authority can provide fertile ground for the seeds of division to germinate and take root, bringing destruction from within, even to the heart of a work that was simultaneously being very blessed by God.

But we were completely unprepared for that happening to us in Canada. We were totally shocked when the four UK Board Members, who had just flown in from England for a regular Board Meeting were suddenly, and unceremoniously, voted off the Board, ordered out of the meeting and off the premises of the retreat centre, where we had pioneered and run the work for eight years! We can remember sitting at Tim Horton's coffee shop with nowhere to go, totally incredulous at the turn of events and seeking the Lord as never before!

Hindsight is a good teacher and looking back now, it is easy to see how those first steps in Canada towards establishing an international work, were done in faith, but also in naivety and with inadequate wisdom. We had agreed to work with an inherited board, for whom Ellel Ministries was not their personal calling, and on which we could not have a majority. We were left with no option but to legally withdraw the name of Ellel Ministries from the existing work in Canada, having been shut out from a decade of hard work and deep spiritual commitment to the Canadian people and, eventually, to start again.

This was an extremely painful episode and was one of the most salutary lessons we have ever experienced in the history of the work. I still grieve over being summarily cut off from the hundreds of people across Canada who had come to love and trust the work of Ellel Ministries and whose lives had been deeply impacted by the Lord through the ministry. If it hadn't actually happened, I would not have believed that such a course of events could have been possible. If it wasn't for the love and care of two close friends and supporters of the work, Gord and Jacqui Kerr, we would have, literally, been 'on the streets'.

The Ellel UK Leadership forgave those responsible for what they had done, and chose to trust God that the spiritual investment that had been sown into the lives of many Canadians, would still bring great fruit for the kingdom of God, in spite of the loss of the physical centre from which the ministry had operated. We knew that it was God, not man, who had called us to Canada, so we immediately resolved to keep moving forward. Ken and Jean Hepworth went back to begin the work of re-establishing Ellel Ministries and with the support of a number of key Pastors, especially Reg Lush and Josephine Kok, other local leaders and former members of the original ministry team, the work did not die!

And here is the good news! We saw so clearly in Chapter 15, that God truly is a great Redeemer and, as was magnificently demonstrated in the sufferings and redemption experienced by Joseph, *"God intended it for good to accomplish what is now being done, the saving of many lives"* (Genesis 50:20). Our Canadian experience meant that we were stung into a great sense of urgency to get our own house in order and ensure that nothing like that could ever happen again.

What transpired has proved to be one of our most surprising and ultimate blessings. There is now a structure in place which has led to unparalleled growth of the work internationally, with secure ministries now being well established in many different centres all over the world. Without the Canadian experience, we would never have understood how absolutely vital it is to ensure that both the legal and spiritual authorities of any ministry development are fully in line one with another right at the beginning of the work. And then, as Paul emphasised, the work of the ministry must be *"entrusted to reliable men who will also be qualified to teach others"* (2 Timothy 2:2).

Reaching that place of legal and spiritual safety was not an easy journey for the leaders to make. They wrestled for hours on end before the Lord as to how, as an international ministry, we should be organised and governed. But, in spite of, sometimes, heated discussions, we were desperate to stay in unity one with another. Were we to be an organisation which had many separate autonomous works loosely associated with the core, but each piece with its own decision making body separate from the whole? Or, alternatively, was I as overall Director to be given *carte blanche* authority to direct everything according to how I saw fit – as some kind of autocratic leader? The first alternative would have very quickly devolved into a dozen or so different ministries, each having different interpretations about how to do things, and probably pulling more against than with each other! And the latter raises the spectre of all that went wrong with the disastrous heavy shepherding movement of a generation earlier. Clearly neither of these alternatives were right for us.

The process by which we moved forward seemed painfully slow, but we had to be sure of what God was saying to us if we were going to have a structure that would facilitate the growth of centres, within secure parameters, which would remain faithful to the founding vision of the work. The fruit of all the battling is evidenced today by the great peace and unity that now prevails across the whole ministry through the structure, and using what *"seemed good to us and the Holy Spirit"* (Acts 15:28), as the Scriptural basis for all decision making. We resolved not to allow ourselves to part in conflict or go our separate ways, where there is an issue that could, otherwise, become a point of division.

A key part of our journey was when all the leaders took time out together at Blairmore House, our Scottish Centre, and sought the Lord as to what it really means to be living and working together in covenantal relationship with Him and with each other. The issue of covenantal relationships, as opposed to contractual (controlling) relationships, among the leaders was something the Lord highlighted to us as being very important.

We took three weeks in all to share the Scriptures and explore the meaning of covenant. As we did so, the Holy Spirit began to refine and join our hearts more closely together. In this process the very idea of making decisions in our meetings by either taking a vote on each issue, at one extreme, or letting the ministry be run by an autocratic dictator, at the other extreme, became anathema to us all. This led us to a structure which has remained strong and solid and brought peace, not just to the operational authority within the work, but to all who come through the doors for healing.

The covenantal principle, from the top down, of seeking the Lord for His way in the ministry, trusting each other's motives for the whole, preferring one another and only coming to corporate decisions following these principles, has brought true unity into the leadership and godly submission to the whole. In the rare event, however, of there being a situation where there were genuinely different directions that we could go, and there wasn't an overall unity, the leaders agreed (in full unity) that they would submit the issue to the Lord and entrust me to God to make the final decision, which everyone, whatever their previous thinking, would then be in corporate unity together about. I thank God that to this day I have never had to exercise that authority and make any decision other than the ones we have made in harmony and complete unity with all of the leaders. But the fact that being able to make such a decision, should it be necessary, ensures that there is no danger of a stalemate causing stagnation. There is always a way forward in unity.

Our mutual accountability has led to great blessing. This is not to say that there aren't times when this unity has been tested, but our mutual willingness to submit our individual stances to the Lord's direction through the whole, is a precious place of mutual accountability and peace. I am privileged and humbled to be a leader of a very fine leadership team, whose hearts have been first submitted to the Lord and then to each other in the Biblical principle of preferring and serving rather than claiming of rights. It is this principle of servant leadership which I believe the Lord has anointed in an unprecedented way, and provided the foundational security for the Lord to be able to work in power, bringing His hope and healing to people in all our centres, throughout the world. We are blessed that denominations and denominational teaching have never become a blockage or indeed a factor in any of our teams or with our delegates.

When all this happened in Canada, it felt like 'mutiny on the Bounty', but thank God He still had His plan for Ellel Ministries in Canada, tied in to the covenantal structure (legally and spiritually) which He had ordained for the whole ministry worldwide. But for our Canadian experience we would not have made this journey of understanding, learning how to lead a pioneering ministry in both spiritual security and under godly authority.

I have learnt over the years that God never leaves Himself without a witness and we will always be grateful that Gord and Jacqui Kerr remained faithful friends and offered their home to us – they had been equally incredulous at the turn of events. It was a traumatic time, but it left no room for complacency since the very essence and nature of the ministry was at stake. It was not so much about the retreat centre, but the fight (from our perspective) was to safeguard what the Lord had made Ellel Ministries to be. I knew that God had purposes for Ellel which were beyond my ability to express and which at that time would have been just words. Ken and Jean Hepworth held the rope tightly, faithfully conducting Modular Schools in local churches across the region and re-building the work from scratch waiting for the time when God would once again raise up local leaders to continue taking the ministry forward.

Out West Alan and Linda Fode had been using Ellel principles in the work of *Lifepath Ministries* in Calgary, Alberta on the West side of Canada, with full permission of the Ellel UK Board. Following discussions with them, Alan and Linda became the leaders of Ellel Ministries (Calgary). And then in Ontario, a young Canadian pastor, Kent Bandy, who had been hosting one of Ken and Jean's Modular Schools at his church, took up the cause. He and his wife Karen had been so personally impacted by the blessings they had received through the teaching and the ministry, that they began to sense God was calling them out of pastoral work into a wider teaching ministry, in support of a new Ellel work that now needed to be re-established in Ontario.

Today Kent and Karen are well established as the leaders of Ellel Ministries Ontario in a beautiful property on the shores of Wolfe Lake, near Kingston. It's interesting and significant that God led Ellel Ministries in Ontario to Derbyshire Downs through the inspirational encouragement of Gord and Jacqui Kerr, who had earlier been our rescuers and encouragers! We could not afford to buy it, but the owner of Derbyshire Downs caught the vision for what Ellel Ministries is all about, and having first agreed to sell the property to Ellel Ministries, he was then, generously, willing to wait for us to accumulate enough deposit money to acquire the property through a conventional mortgage.

The teaching and healing that had already gone to thousands of people through the ministry in Canada could never be taken away from them. On my first visit to Canada I had prayed with a lady who was deeply repentant over what she had done during her fourth pregnancy. She already had three children and she and her husband could not afford a fourth mouth to feed, so she started to pray that the baby would die – she literally wished it was dead in her womb. Mercifully God did not answer her prayer and the fourth child was born safely, a little girl. But forty years later, as she listened to me teaching on the need for forgiveness, she realised that what she had done was to invite a spirit of death into her life. She needed to ask God to forgive her and to forgive herself.

She had no idea what the spiritual effect of her actions had been, but she wanted to get right with God and came forward to confess her sin and ask for prayer for healing, according to James 5:16. I was able to speak the Scriptures about God's forgiveness into her life and she went through a very deep deliverance ministry.

When it was all over she returned to her seat, but as she was going I suddenly realised that the prayer ministry wasn't finished and called her back – I hadn't prayed for her daughter. I needed to pray that the Lord would also set her daughter free from the curse of death that her mother had wished upon her when she was in the womb. As I did so, the mother then went through another deep deliverance ministry – it was as if all the demonic power that had gone to the daughter through the mother, when she was in the womb, had now come back to the mother from her daughter. I didn't fully understand what was happening, but I knew for certain that God had done a very deep work in both their lives.

The following year I met the lady again. She came running towards me waving a photograph of a baby in her hand – obviously a very proud grandmother. She had to remind me of what I'd prayed the previous year, and then the story of what happened next came tumbling out. At the time her daughter had been married fourteen years and was, sadly, childless. But, within days of me praying to set her daughter free of the curse of death, she had fallen pregnant and here was Granny, thrusting a beautiful picture of her grandson, Alex, into my hands. That picture is a precious reminder of the fact that Jesus came to set the captives free – and of the fact that what God did during those early years in Canada can never be taken away.

It was God who had called us into Canada in the first place and God had made it very clear to us that He had not changed his mind and withdrawn the calling. And so it was that we continued with the work in Canada, with a renewed commitment to the calling of God on both my life, and upon Ellel Ministries, to bring the *welcome, teaching and healing* message of the Gospel to all peoples everywhere in an increasingly hurting and fragmented world.

Today the new centre at Wolfe Lake is a faithful expression of the vision that God birthed in the ministry all those years ago. And in Calgary, following their retirement, the pioneering work of Al and Linda Fode has been taken up by Alexander and Marion Morrison and, in the goodness of God they have been given a wonderful new facility called *Prairie Winds*, just outside Calgary where the permanent foundations of the work are being put down good and true, in accordance with God's plumb-line.

The work in Canada is being truly blessed and we are looking forward to all that God has in store for these precious centres that God has raised up for the Canadian people.

Chapter 19

MULTIPLYING
THE VISION

Training Leaders to Reach the World

When Ellel Grange was first established, back in 1986, it wasn't just a trickle of people who knocked on the doors asking for help – it was a flood! And when the first Healing Retreats began in early 1987, pastors began to send people to Ellel Grange from all over the country.

Often, their presenting symptoms proved to be totally different from the underlying cause of all their problems. Some had been prayed for many times, but in spite of all the praying, there had been little real change in their symptoms or condition. Often people had become disillusioned with God because of His apparent lack of interest in their situation. Some had despaired of ever finding an answer and were now on long-term medication to try and control their increasingly desperate symptoms.

Little by little the team gained understanding of the devastating consequences that can arise from all manner of negative life experiences. Abuse, trauma, involvement with occult practices, ancestral influences, relationship breakdown, rejection and betrayal are just some of the roots which can produce such bad fruit. There were many amazing testimonies of what God was doing in people's lives. But the result of the ministry wasn't always successful, for not everyone who came for help was willing to open up the inner depths of their lives to God and allow Him to bring restoration in His way. The cost and the pain of facing reality, not only of the things that had happened to them, but also of their responses, were sometimes too great. And the humility needed to own personal sins and issues was not always there.

But even with those who were ready and willing to go God's way, it wasn't easy to make progress, when the damage they had suffered was so great. They had been robbed of so much that it wasn't just a case of bringing God's healing to the damage, but of putting back in something of what had been stolen from them in their journey through life, living lives where love and provision had been replaced by cruelty and deprivation. At times it was exhausting work and the team were pushed to the limit of their endurance, as they sought to help people come to terms with the fact that their present-day physical, emotional and spiritual symptoms had their root in deliberate abuse.

One night, at the end of a particularly tough time of ministry, I collapsed into bed at 3.00am in the morning. I was exhausted, but also rejoicing at what God had done. At the same time, however, I was crying out to God with anguish in my heart. For how could we possibly sustain this sort of continued pressure and minister to the many other broken people who were waiting for help? The intensity of the work, and the size of the mountains we had to climb, seemed, at times, overwhelming. How could we share the burden of the work with others and multiply the fruit?

As I sank into exhausted sleep, the Lord spoke gently into my spirit with just two words, 'Teaching Hospital'. My brother, David, and my daughter, Anne, were both Doctors and so I knew exactly what a Teaching Hospital was – a place where the medical students would not only be taught the theory of medicine, but where they would also learn the practical side of medicine, 'on the job', alongside the medical consultants who carried the responsibility for the patients and the hospital.

As I slept that night, the whole vision for a new Ellel centre, which would be conducted in the style of a Teaching Hospital, formed in my mind. I saw how the work could be multiplied into the Body of Christ through students who would come from all over the world, stay for an extended period of time, and receive in-depth teaching and training. At this centre they would learn both from the teaching of their teachers and from the experience of seeing God at work in restoring people's lives.

By the time I woke up, the whole vision was in place – and the following morning there was both excitement and shock in the Ellel Grange leadership team, as I shared with them what I believed God had been showing me during the night. And so the search began for a place which would serve the purposes of this further expansion of the original vision for the ministry. Because people would be travelling to it from all over the world it would need to be close to a major international airport – which meant that it needed to be within an hour of one of London's main airports, Gatwick or Heathrow.

Once again, the Ellel Grange team were being stretched to believe for yet more of God's purposes and His provision for the rapidly developing work of Ellel Ministries! We looked at the details of properties that were on the market and even visited some of them, but nothing seemed to fit the vision. Perhaps God had a different way of directing our steps?!

It has constantly surprised me, in the history of Ellel Ministries, how many strategic events can be traced back to what God did at the *Battle Belongs to the Lord* Conference at Brighton in 1990. As mentioned in Chapter 13, Jill Southern had been crippled by debilitating fear. She had been trapped between floors in a malfunctioning lift (elevator) for over four hours. By the time the engineers managed to winch the lift up and get her out, she was a totally incoherent wreck. From that moment on fear controlled her life – so much so that no matter how tall the building, she always used the stairs. Lifts were a total no-go area as far as Jill was concerned!

So, when she went to that first Brighton Conference there was only one item on her personal agenda for God – she needed to be set free from fear. And that is exactly what God did in the ministry session that followed Bill Subritzky's teaching. She was delivered of a spirit of fear. This was a huge step forward for Jill in both her personal life and her theological understanding. It was her first encounter with deliverance. This was a new experience for her, but she couldn't deny the fruit of it in her life.

As a result she wanted to find out more about the ministry that had been so strategic in her life, so she took time off her work in sales to attend the second 9-Week *School of Evangelism, Healing and Deliverance* at Glyndley Manor. It was a life-changing nine weeks and as a result of all she'd learned on the school, she now wanted to bring those blessings to the local churches in the area of Frensham and Farnham, in Surrey, where she lived. So she set up a local area conference and invited me to come and speak and bring a team.

It was on the very Friday we arrived in Farnham, that the *Farnham Herald's* main headline told the sad story of the bankruptcy of Pierrepont, a large local school. Pierrepont was going to be sold. Jill had never been inside the grounds before and when she saw the local news, she wondered if it may be a suitable place for her church to acquire, so they could have their own premises. She knew nothing of my vision for a *'Teaching Hospital'*!

So, in view of my experience of establishing Christian ministries in old buildings, and the coincidental fact that I had just arrived in the area for the conference, she asked me if I would go and have a look at Pierrepont with her, and give her the benefit of my advice. This was late on a very wet and dreary Friday afternoon. It was already beginning to get dark. Otto Bixler was part of the team, so I took him with me and together with Jill and her husband, Ron, we walked up the Pierrepont drive for the first time.

It proved to be another one of those unforgettable, God-anointed, moments. As we walked up the drive, and the black and white exterior of the large mock-Tudor, half-timbered building came into view, the Lord clearly witnessed to me that this was the place I was searching for. I looked at Otto and just said two words *'Teaching Hospital'*. Almost immediately the Lord confirmed to Otto exactly the same thing, and by the time we reached the building, it was already clear in my mind that this was *'it'*.

The place was huge, and when Jill saw the scale of the Pierrepont estate, she realised this wasn't a building that could be used for a small local church, it was more like an English Village! The potential for the Kingdom of God, however, was enormous – but so were the potential problems!

Having made our initial walk round the buildings, we had to quickly return to Farnham for the conference. It was a great success, but the real highlight of the weekend wasn't the conference, it was the visit to Pierrepont! I couldn't get the place out of my mind, and so the following week I called Jill and asked if she and Ron could go around the Pierrepont estate again and take a lot of photographs, so that I could share the possibility of Pierrepont becoming the 'teaching hospital', with other members of the leadership and trustees of Ellel Ministries.

This time it was Jill's turn to experience a vision. While Ron was taking the pictures, God opened Jill's spiritual eyes to see a huge globe roll up the drive, covered with maps of all the countries of the world. The globe stopped outside the main house and a door opened on the map at India. Then a ladder appeared and she *saw* people from India stepping down the ladder and entering the building. After this, the globe turned to another country, and another, and another until people from all the countries of the world had climbed down the ladder into Pierrepont for a time of training.

Finally, they all left the Pierrepont buildings, climbed back into the globe and returned to their own countries. God was showing Jill in a very graphic way that Pierrepont was going to be used to train people from all the countries of the world. This was the first indication to Jill that she was going to have anything to do with the *'teaching hospital'* vision God had birthed in my spirit. But it is a well-established spiritual principle that the people whom God envisions, are usually the ones that He asks to be involved in its fulfilment! So, while it was a shock to Jill to be asked to pioneer the work at Pierrepont, it was clear that God had been preparing her for the job, with the support of her husband, over quite a number of years.

A video of Pierrepont was made, which was taken all over the country to show people something of the place, and tell them of the work God would do there. I showed this short video to a group of people in the North East of England. After the showing a man came forward who was totally stunned by what he had just seen. Back in the late nineteen-forties he had conducted Christian boys' camps in the grounds of Pierrepont. One day, as he had been praying at Pierrepont, God spoke to him something that he had never forgotten and had never before shared with anyone else – that a time would come when the whole Pierrepont estate would be used for Christian ministry!

As he watched the video, God reminded him of the vision from nearly fifty years ago and told him that this was now going to be fulfilled. Knowing that God had gone before in this extraordinary way was a huge encouragement as we wrestled with the practical realities of trying to fund the purchase of a two million pound property with nothing in the bank!

How Pierrepont was bought, equipped and has been used is a long and wonderful story. Negotiations were entered into with the vendors and the time came when the contract for the purchase of Pierrepont, for the *teaching hospital*, had to be signed and exchanged, with the handing over of a £333,000 non-returnable cash deposit the following day. That night all those who were praying for the work at Pierrepont gathered at Ron and Jill's house to pray. They were still £153,000 short and it was looking as though the vision for Pierrepont was about to die.

But during the meeting Jill received a phone call from a man who had just been prompted by the Lord to lend whatever the shortfall was. He asked how much it was and was not at all fazed by its size. It was too late to get a cheque issued and cleared through the banking system for the following day, so he calmly said that he would send the money by direct inter-bank transfer and it would be in the account by the time contracts had to be signed at 3.00pm! There was a mixture of stunned silence and great rejoicing at that particular prayer meeting. God had answered the prayers and once again, in a totally remarkable way, confirmed that the work that was being planned for Pierrepont really was His vision.

Subsequently, a mortgage for buying the property was offered by Barclays Bank. And in February 1995 Ellel Ministries took possession and began the work of turning a bankrupt school into a centre through which God would teach, train and minister to people from every country of the world. The *teaching hospital* was on its way!

When the school went bankrupt, every single item it had contained had been sold and we acquired a totally empty and semi-derelict estate. There was nothing, absolutely nothing, by way of furniture or equipment left. The full story of all that happened to turn this place into the dynamic training centre it is today has been told in Jill's own book, *The Miracles of Pierrepont,* but it's important to share enough here to understand that God was in every single step of the journey.

Jim Bluck, who had become a prayer supporter of Ellel Grange through our first House Wardens, Barry and Jan Jay, had, like Barry, been employed by the Ministry of Defence at Barrow-in-Furness. Jim was then moved by the Ministry of Defence to Tadley, near Aldermaston, not far from Pierrepont. Here he discovered that two recently refurbished accommodation blocks were being closed and were about to be demolished, along with all their nearly new furnishings and equipment. He immediately contacted Pierrepont and suggested they contact the Ministry of Defence and ask if they could get all the equipment out of the buildings before the bulldozers moved in!

On the second day of our ownership of Pierrepont, a Scripture had been given to Jill saying, *"Your gates will always stand open, they will never be shut, day or night, so that men may bring you the wealth of the nations"* (Isaiah 60:11). Completely unknown by the person who brought that Scripture was the fact that on that very same day, the huge wrought iron gates had been stolen – so now they could never be closed (they were no longer there!) and the wealth of the nation was about to be brought in through those gates, courtesy of the Ministry of Defence!

Jill applied to the Ministry of Defence for a Charity Licence to go and strip the buildings at Tadley of anything that would be useful to The Christian Trust, a Registered Charity. The permission was granted and a team of forty people worked night and day, using a seventeen-ton truck for transport, to strip every single usable item out of the buildings – even taking out the newly installed window frames from the building itself!

They took everything – every piece of furniture, every toilet, wash basin and bathroom fitting, all the kitchen and dining equipment, the security system, beds, sheets, bookshelves, cupboards, armchairs and a myriad of other valuable things. And it all came through those open gates – a gift from the nation to The Christian Trust for the work of Ellel Ministries at Pierrepont!

Through a prophetic word from one of the Ellel Grange team, God had also said that *"He would equip Pierrepont, down to every knife, fork and spoon"*. That prophecy was precisely fulfilled, for within all the Tadley equipment was enough cutlery to equip the kitchens and start the work. God had worked another extraordinary miracle.

Another supporter, who worked for the oil company, Shell UK, heard that two whole floors of their main building were to be let out. But the new tenant didn't like the colour of the recently laid blue carpet tiles. Again the seventeen-ton truck was hired and enough blue carpet tiles to cover two football fields were donated to the work by Shell UK. In this, and many other ways, God truly did equip the buildings and the grounds. The teaching hospital that would be used to train Christian leaders from all over the world, in the foundational principles of Christian discipleship, healing and deliverance, was being equipped for the purposes of God.

The foundational Scripture for Ellel Ministries is Luke 9:11. Andy Taylor, now the UK National Director of Ellel Ministries, was inspired to suggest that the new school at Pierrepont should be called the Luke Nine Eleven Training School, or NETS for short. The training at Ellel Pierrepont quickly became known as the NETS programme and it is still known as that today.

Originally there were only two terms in the NETS programme, but today there are four stages, providing a whole year's training and equipping for the delegates. Every one of the many buildings at Pierrepont has been brought into use and the whole centre is thriving. Jill travels extensively, sharing about the work of God at Pierrepont and taking the message of healing and deliverance to many different parts of the world – especially to Asia and Australia. As she gives people the vision, God plants a seed in their heart and today most Ellel Centres have some members of staff who have completed the NETS programme. It has become a place of equipping and calling for God's people as they re-evaluate their lives and God leads them into their future destiny.

One of the main objectives of a pioneer is to prepare the ground for their successor. After twenty years of dynamic pioneering Jill stepped down from her role as Director of the centre at the end of 2015 to concentrate on her wider teaching role, at Pierrepont and other Centres. And Paul and Diane Watson, the National Directors of the work in Australia stepped into her shoes and are now taking the work at Pierrepont forward into its next season. As you will discover in the next Chapter, Diane was the very first student to walk up the drive as a NETS student. It seems highly appropriate, therefore, that Paul and Diane should now be the Directors of Ellel Pierrepont.

As, every year, a new group of delegates come to Pierrepont for the two different intakes of the NETS programme (in April and October), Jill is ticking the nations off on her list. She is looking to God for fulfilment of the vision He gave her, to bring people from every nation of the world, to be trained and equipped for the work of bringing hope and healing to God's people.

Chapter 20

AUSTRALIAN MIRACLE

God's Strategy for the Work 'Down Under'

In his letter to the Romans Paul explained how it was that the Gentiles had come to faith in Christ and were willing to obey God – it was *"by the power of signs and miracles, through the power of the Spirit"* (Romans 15:19). There is absolutely no doubt that when people see God at work it has the potential to be a life-transforming experience, and even a nation-changing one.

The very first person to come up the drive of Ellel Pierrepont, to attend the first NETS school in 1997, was Diane Watson. Diane was the wife of an Anglican vicar in Sydney, Australia. Her very attendance at the school, entailing nearly six months away from home and family was, in itself, a miracle. In all their years of marriage Diane had never previously been away from Paul, by herself, for as much as a weekend!

Diane brought with her, in her Bible, a photograph of *Gilbulla* the Anglican retreat centre South West of Sydney, near Camden. Diane believed God had shown her that this would one day be the home of Ellel Ministries in Australia! Almost the first thing she did on reaching Pierrepont was to show me the picture and then, having faithfully delivered the message, she nurtured the vision in her heart for a considerable period of time.

It was not only a miracle that Diane had left her husband behind in Australia for six months, it was a very profound and real miracle that gave her the incentive to go to NETS. As a Pastor's wife, seeking after a deeper understanding of spiritual warfare, Diane attended a special Ellel Ministries conference for Christian medics and pastoral counsellors, held at Merroo, just outside Sydney, in September 1996. There is no doubt that when people experience the miraculous, it changes their understanding and challenges their future. For both Diane, and her husband Paul, that never-to-be-forgotten evening at Merroo changed the rest of their lives and has had a massive impact on the lives of thousands of other people, throughout the work of Ellel Ministries in Australia.

As Fiona and I watched God at work, we were totally stunned at the miracle that was unfolding before our eyes, as we ministered to Lynda together on the platform. What happened was the key that opened a huge door of opportunity. But before we look at the miracle God performed, we need to step back a little and trace the hand of God through a series of 'God-incidences', which illustrate once again how God can wonderfully direct the circumstances of life.

Greg Foote was a Sydney Doctor, on a visit to England with his wife. Being a member of *Health Care in Christ*, the Australian Christian medics organisation, Greg wanted to check out various healing ministries while he was in the country and Ellel Grange was one of his destinations. Greg and Merle stayed with us for a few days and were astonished at what they saw God doing on a Healing Retreat – so much so that after the retreat was over Greg asked for personal prayer for himself. We shared hearts for a while and identified some areas of need and I will never forget watching Greg's face as he realised that he, a doctor, was being set free from demons! Greg returned to Australia a different man and reported back to his colleagues in *Health Care in Christ.*

Another member of *Health Care in Christ* was Dr. John Ouw, a Chinese psychiatrist, practising psychiatric medicine in Melbourne, Victoria. As a Christian, John had experienced many things in his psychiatric consultancy which challenged both his spiritual understandings and his medical knowledge and experience. There were things he saw in his patients which clearly had a spiritual root, but which he had no facility to treat, other than with conventional psychiatric drugs. He was looking for answers beyond the parameters of his previous medical training. He was no longer content with simply offering medication for conditions that appeared not to be medical in their origin.

In his search for answers, John came across the first volume of my book *Healing Through Deliverance,* in which I set out the biblical basis for the healing and deliverance ministries as being a credible and normal part of Christian experience, a ministry which began, of course, with the ministry of Jesus himself. In Capernaum, Jesus delivered and healed a man with a spirit which made him shout out against who Jesus was, and what He was saying (Luke 4:31-37). And there are many other instances in the gospel accounts of Jesus setting the captives free in this way and bringing major healing into their lives. The stories of the woman with the spirit of infirmity, who had been bent double for 18 years (Luke 13:10-17), and the man from Gadara (Luke 8:26-39), whose condition today would be described by doctors using psychiatric diagnoses, exemplified this aspect of Jesus' ministry. Both were completely healed and restored by Jesus through the ministry of deliverance.

In the first years of Ellel Ministries the team gained much experience as they looked to God for answers to the issues and problems that underpinned many of the presenting symptoms in those who came for help. Little by little we saw how the healing ministry requires an understanding and practice of both the inner healing and deliverance Ministries. *Healing Through Deliverance*, quickly became established as a significant reference book on the subject. A second volume appeared subsequently on practical aspects of the ministry and today both volumes have been combined into one larger book covering the whole subject.

When John Ouw read that first volume, he immediately realised that the book contained answers for some of the patients he was seeking to help in his private practice. So, as a key member of *Health Care in Christ*, John proposed to Ken Curry, the Director of the organisation that the Ellel team should be invited to Australia to teach *Health Care in Christ* about their experiences in bringing healing through deliverance, strongly reinforcing the request from Greg Foote for something similar.

The result was a general conference in Melbourne called *Jesus Frees*. The videos from this conference went all over Australia and proved to be very powerful forerunners of the work that was to follow. After Melbourne, there was a special, private conference for *Health Care in Christ* members only, at the Merroo Centre, which was attended by Diane Watson, as a pastor's wife. There were many medical professionals listening to the teaching, ranging from surgeons, pain consultants, general practitioners, anaesthetists and psychiatrists, through all the different medical and nursing professions.

When Diane arrived at the conference she was allocated a room to share with a complete stranger, Lynda Hicks. Lynda had been a nurse, but for three years she had been out of the profession following a catastrophic accident, in which she had fallen off a cliff and broken her back in four places. At the time of the Merroo conference Lynda was suffering from chronic fatigue, was in constant pain, was unable to walk properly and was losing hope. She was registered as disabled by the Australian Government and had been placed on a lifetime disability pension, having been given no expectation by the medics that she would ever be able to walk properly and live a normal life again. As a result, she was now suicidal, having convinced herself that there's no point in living. There was no prospect of her ever being off pain killers and all hopes of marriage and children had disappeared out of the window of her rapidly disintegrating life.

Fiona and I met with Lynda over lunch and we tried to encourage her to believe that God could heal her. But when asked if she would like us to pray for her, she politely declined, saying she didn't want any more prayer – she didn't want to find out again that God didn't love her when she wasn't healed as a result. Her response was totally understandable, but to Fiona and I, who had seen God heal the consequences of accidents and traumas on several occasions, it was heart-breaking.

When ministering back in the UK, the Lord had shown us the principles of praying for people who were unhealed following accidents or traumas. I explained that the prophecy of Isaiah 61:1 said that Jesus would heal the broken-hearted and that when we have an accident it isn't just the body that gets broken, our heart – our spirit and our soul – can also be traumatised and broken as well. We explained how the medics are only able to do everything they can to heal the broken body, as they had done for Lynda, but healing the broken heart was outside the range of medical practice. And for the heart, only Jesus is the healer.

We patiently spent time explaining the healing principles to her, and told her stories of people who had been wonderfully healed from even long term consequences of accidents and traumas. She was especially impacted by the story of Jim, in Canada, whose arm had been severely damaged in a tractor accident seventeen years previously and who was both physically healed of the damage to his shoulder and also of the chronic asthma which he had suffered from since the age of six.

I was scheduled to teach on healing from the consequences of accident and trauma that night and at the end of our lunch together, Lynda very hesitantly and bravely volunteered to be prayed for in front of everyone present. What happened next was one of those seminal moments in the history of the ministry. For two hours, Fiona and I ministered into all the issues surrounding the accident, helping Lynda to forgive the person who had led her into a dangerous situation where the accident had happened, and delivering her from the fears and infirmities that had invaded her life as a result. God was bringing healing to the inner depths of Lynda's being and healing the condition of inner brokenness from which she was still suffering. If the inner being is broken and hurting, then the body becomes a reflector of that inner pain. But when God heals the broken heart, then the body can then be healed as well.

At the end of that time of inner healing and deliverance ministry, I anointed Lynda with oil, according to the Scriptures, and everyone watched as they saw God work a physical miracle before their very eyes. The Lord told us to stand back and watch what he did. No-one was touching her as her body was being stretched, as if by angels who came down and gave her divine physiotherapy! Her back was supernaturally moved backwards and forwards as it was being healed and restored. At the end of the evening, the pain had gone and she could walk normally. The following morning, she was no longer fatigued, but rose early to walk to a prayer room at the top of a hill and give thanks to God for her healing. Previously she had been unable to walk more than a few yards without having to stop to let the pain subside.

Later, Lynda went back to the government authorities, told them she was healed and today she is no longer disabled, no longer on a lifetime disability pension, and is married with three wonderful children. Lynda's full amazing story is now told in her own book, *'Lynda: From Accident and Trauma to Healing and Wholeness'*, also published by Sovereign World Ltd.

While what happened that night was, of course, dramatic for Lynda, God had a much wider agenda, for everyone was seriously impacted by having watched a miracle of healing take place. The effect was profound, not least on Diane Watson, who had been Lynda's roommate and had seen first-hand Lynda's incapacity. Lynda was now a very different person than the one Diane had first met a few days earlier. Diane's husband Paul had driven up to Merroo to take Diane home, and had stayed for the evening meeting. And so, in God's providence, he was also there to see what happened to Lynda. It was important that both of them together experienced what God did that night, for not only was God calling Diane into Ellel Ministries, but Paul was on God's agenda as well!

Having heard the teaching at the conference, and then seen what God had done, Diane started putting her new-found understandings into practice with her own family, with remarkable effect! But she also knew she needed a lot more training, so she told her husband, Paul, that she wanted to go to England for six months to join the first NETS School at Ellel Pierrepont! When Paul had recovered from the shock, they prayed together that if this was of God then He would provide the resources – for they had no spare funds to make it possible. Within six weeks their prayers had been answered. They had been given enough money by people who knew nothing of what Diane was contemplating, to cover her travel and the cost of the school. Diane was on her way to England on the back of her own personal financial miracle!

But Diane wasn't just travelling to England with a vision for her own life, God had touched her heart for her nation and so, into her Bible, she had slipped that picture of Gilbulla, believing that God had shown her that He wanted this beautiful place to be used in

Australia, in a similar way to that which Ellel Grange had been used to birth the ministry in the UK.

We made several more visits to Australia and conducted conferences in Sydney, Brisbane, Townsville, Melbourne, Perth and Adelaide. All the time, interest in the ministry was growing and it was becoming clear that Ellel needed its own home in the country. We looked at the possibility of buying a property in Melbourne, but that fell through, and then an important announcement was made by the Anglican Diocese of Sydney. They had decided that *Gilbulla* was now surplus to their requirements and that they intended to sell the property on the open market!

Diane's heart took a dramatic turn as she absorbed the news. Her faith moment had come. She had never lost sight of the vision God had given her for Gilbulla, in spite of the abortive attempt to set up an Ellel base in Melbourne. She remained faithful in intercession for the vision and God remained faithful to her. With Gilbulla on the market, prayer for the work in Australia intensified, and with the help of various donations, loans and a mortgage, Gilbulla was finally acquired and the work of Ellel Ministries in Australia could now be firmly established – in the very place God had put into Diane Watson's heart. And the first Centre Director of Ellel Gilbulla was, of course, Diane Watson!

It wasn't very long before her husband Paul joined her in the ministry and together they began to pray into the future development of the work throughout the Australia Pacific region. Today, Paul Watson is not only the Director of Ellel Pierrepont, but is the Regional Director overseeing the developing work in India, Australia and New Zealand, and Paul Ryan, a former Pastor from the north of Queensland is the Centre Director of Ellel Gilbulla.

And across the Tasman Sea to the East, Paul and Jillian Larsen-Robertson are leading the establishment of the ministry in Christchurch, New Zealand. Once doors have been opened through faith and obedience, there is no limit to what God can do in and through His people! There are now countless more stories of how God is transforming lives through the work in Australia and beyond – all because of the faith of a Sydney doctor and a Chinese psychiatrist and the miracle that God did at Merroo. And even as I write these words, God is opening up new works in Papua New Guinea and the Solomon Islands! All places that featured in that childhood stamp collection through which God gave me a world-wide vision!

Chapter 21

SCOTTISH ODYSSEY

The Zig-Zag Path of Faith's Straight LIne

Homer's Odyssey is an epic poem of ancient Greece, relating the ten-year wanderings of Odysseus, king of Ithaca, after the Trojan War. In modern English the word odyssey, therefore, has come to mean a long, adventurous journey. And that exactly describes our experiences in Scotland. God's straight line can sometimes look like a zig-zag, from our perspective. And there were some very sharp turns in the zig-zag road of our Scottish pilgrimage, through which God taught us some very profound and important lessons!

In the early days of the ministry, many people came from Scotland to attend healing retreats or training courses at Ellel Grange. Many of them wanted us to open a centre in Scotland. But we needed an invitation to start the ball rolling, and when it came, it was from a very unlikely source – a small church in the remote highland village of Kincraig, close to Scotland's ski-ing capital of Aviemore, where some of the members had an interest in the healing ministry.

I agreed to take a team for a weekend of teaching and ministry. The journey seemed to take forever and by the time we arrived at our destination, some of the team were wondering if I'd heard the Lord correctly in accepting an invitation from a church in such a remote location. But as I have discovered on so many occasions, God's ways of fulfilling His purposes are often very unusual and can take us by surprise. A young shepherd boy, for example, was not the obvious choice for Samuel when anointing the next King of Israel. And Nazareth, a remote northern village in Israel, was not the obvious place for the King of Kings to come from!

The weekend had begun well and just before lunch on the Saturday morning a youth suddenly got up from his seat and left the meeting quickly. A few minutes later, when the meeting was over, the pastor grabbed me by the arm and said, "*Come quickly and pray for James – he's lying unconscious in the doorway.*" I ran with him from the church hall, and on the way the pastor explained that James was a chronic epileptic, who had suffered epilepsy since birth. When I got to James, he was exactly as the pastor had described – in a state of post-fit unconsciousness.

If James had been an epileptic since he was a baby, then his epilepsy could not have been related to anything he had done or which had happened to him in his lifetime. The condition must, therefore, be a generational problem. I also knew that unconsciousness is only a function of the body and the soul. The spirit never goes unconscious and can still hear everything that's said. So, trusting that James, in his spirit, could hear everything I was saying, I led him phrase by phrase in a prayer of forgiveness, of everyone on his generation line who had done anything that had caused epilepsy to be an inherited condition in his life.

After each phrase of the prayer, even though I could not hear him physically, I trusted he was praying the prayer and left a space for him to be responding in his spirit. I then prayed that God would deliver him of every demonic power that had any hold on James's mind and body as a result. There was no obvious manifestation, but a minute or so later James opened his eyes, looked around him and the first words he said were, *"I'm healed!"*

Normally, after a fit, James told us that he would have to sit in a darkened room and had fearful headaches and flashing lights before his eyes for at least twenty-four hours. But even though he had had a serious fit, this time he had none of the related symptoms and was confident in his declaration. The next time James went to Aberdeen Hospital for a check-up the medics confirmed that there was no longer any evidence whatsoever of epilepsy. And the healing was so complete that they wrote across his medical records that the previous evidence of epilepsy must have been a case of misdiagnosis! James really was completely healed.

Just as would happen in Australia with Lynda's healing, through James's healing God got people's attention in Scotland. When God acts, people listen, including the husband of the leader of the Lydia Prayer Fellowship for Scotland.

Marguerite Connell had been praying for her husband throughout their marriage. He was locked into the deception of freemasonry and could never see his need of Jesus, but he agreed to keep her company on the sixty mile journey to Kincraig from their home in Huntly, near Aberdeen. God was moving powerfully by his Spirit in the meetings, touching the lives of many others, apart from James. And it was at Kincraig that he fully came to the Lord, his spiritual blindness was healed and he was delivered of his freemasonry.

Marguerite's prayers of a lifetime were wonderfully answered and she returned home rejoicing. But she also began to pray that Ellel Ministries would one day come to Huntly, the town where they lived. A spiritual prayer stake had been put in the ground for the work of Ellel Ministries in Scotland – but the pathway through which God would specifically answer her prayers would remain secret for a number of years. There were some serious purposes that God was to work out in me along the way.

Another couple who were an integral part of that weekend were David and Denise Cross. David was an engineer, and Denise a maths teacher who had found the Lord for herself in a dramatic 'Damascus Road' experience. The change in Denise was such that when they were in Hong Kong, David turned to the Lord for himself. In Hong Kong David had built bridges for the colonial government. Now they were running a ski centre and were really enjoying their self-sufficient highland life. But God had other ideas! From their experience in Hong Kong, they were very familiar with the Chinese people and 'God-incidentally', Whai Aun, a Chinese Singaporean member of our team was allotted to their home for accommodation.

After seeing what God had done over the weekend, David and Denise were full of questions and Whai Aun was happy to spend the whole night answering them. By 4.00am, experiencing both revelation and exhaustion, David and Denise were ready to start the journey of faith which would lead them first to Ellel Grange for training, then to give up their business and come and join the team. Kincraig was not the obvious place to look for key leaders of the ministry, but today David is the Deputy International Director of Ellel Ministries and for over twenty years both David and Denise have been pioneering leaders of the work!

The next stage of our Scottish odyssey was to be both exciting and salutary. We continued to be asked by people all over the country, whether or not we were going to open a centre in Scotland and several years had passed since James had been healed at Kincraig. Then, right out of the blue, I received a letter from a lady who had been on courses at Ellel Grange in the early days and was now the administrator of Kilravock Castle, near Inverness, the ancestral home of the Rose family.

Baroness Rose was a Christian and had put the castle into a

charitable trust to be used for God's purposes. The letter was an invitation to Ellel Ministries to use Kilravock Castle as our Scottish Centre, for which they would charge us a nominal rent of just £1 per year! The castle had a long Christian history and since 1631 an inscribed stone in the walls declared that *"Salvation is only to be found through Jesus Christ"* – and there was an excellent meeting hall in the grounds.

Fiona and I were on holiday at the time with our two Mums. Both our fathers had died and it was a blessing for both them and us to come and spend an annual holiday with us in the Isle of Harris at my brother's house. In their latter years they were our daily prayer supporters and we both have so much to thank God for in having had two praying Mums, Dorothy Bradshaw and Betty Horrobin. Dorothy had been a Lydia leader for many years. They both prayed daily for everything we did. The invitation to Kilravock Castle was so unusual that we didn't quite know how to respond, so we showed it to our Mums – our senior prayer team – and both of them sensed that this was of God and that we should respond positively, which we did.

Malcolm and Anna Wood, who by now were experienced leaders with us at Ellel Grange, were ready for a new challenge and agreed to take on responsibility for leading the new work and became Directors of Ellel Scotland. God gave us a clear vision for the work in the highlands, that in addition to it being the centre that would serve the people of Scotland, it would also be a place where we could invite people to the beautiful Highlands of Scotland from across the world for short-term international training schools. And this was the time, also, when God was developing strong links for the ministry with leaders in Israel and we became committed to praying with Messianic leaders in Israel for the people of God in the land.

The Scottish work was two years old. Malcolm and Anna had established the work well at Kilravock Castle, and people were coming from all over Scotland for courses, retreats and special prayer weeks. Suddenly, after a special prayer week for Israel, we hit a previously unknown brick wall. I was summoned to the castle to talk with Baroness Rose and her administrator and given an ultimatum which amounted to: *"stop teaching about Israel or leave. God has finished with Israel and we will not allow you to teach anything on Israel at Kilravock Castle."* There could be no discussion, that was it. Drop Israel or leave, just like that.

This was my first encounter with the solid brick wall of replacement theology – the teaching that says Israel rejected Jesus; all the promises in the Scripture in respect of Israel have now been inherited by the church; God has finished with Israel and the church has replaced it. I was totally and utterly shocked. God had been doing a deep work in my own life in respect of Israel and I was walking closely with key leaders in the land, as we saw the first evidences of God restoring his Body of believers in Israel itself. Our own position on Israel was also non-negotiable.

When Fiona and I stood on the deck of the Operation Exodus ship in December 1999, and sailed into Haifa with hundreds of Jews returning to Israel in fulfilment of Old Testament prophecy, our commitment to what God is doing in Israel in these extraordinary days became rock solid. But then, as I sat with Baroness Rose and her administrator it was as if the irresistible force of the end-time move of God's spirit had met the immovable object of replacement theology head on – and I was there to witness the crash. It was not pleasant. For the first time in my life I experienced first-hand the spiritual opposition that Israelis feel all over the world – especially from the nations that surround Israel today who would like to see the nation of Israel, and all its citizens, literally wiped off the map.

It was obvious we had a decision to make and I knew there was no middle ground or possibility of compromise – either we had to deny Scripture, and all that God had shown us in our years of pilgrimage with Ellel Ministries, and which had also been part of my foundational beliefs and understandings long before Ellel started, or we had to remain faithful to my convictions, lose everything we had invested in the work of Ellel Ministries in Scotland so far and walk away from Kilravock Castle. In reality there was no choice – we had to go. We gave them three months notice and prepared to leave at the end of 2002. But we had nowhere to go! And where else could we find a place where the rent was only £1 per year?!

The zig-zag journey of faith was about to take another unlikely change of direction. We were now in a crisis. Then I discovered that a neighbouring castle near Inverness was up for sale. We looked at it with great excitement and began to envisage how the work could fit into the fabric of Aldoorie Castle. I shared the crisis with a Christian business friend from overseas and he offered to help us out by buying the castle as an investment for us to use. But his maximum offer was topped by another offer and once again we were plunged into uncertainty. We had an advertised programme of courses to run in the New Year and we still had nowhere to go. We looked at another place, with our mothers this time on our way back from the isle of Harris, but it was totally unsuitable. But throughout all this part of the odyssey we were still at peace – the Lord had given Malcolm and Anna a Scripture which spoke right into the situation. *"My presence will go with you and I will give you rest."* (Exodus 33:14). We continued to look for God's place of rest.

I then telephoned a property agent in Edinburgh and explained our situation. Did he know of anywhere that might be suitable for our needs? His response was immediate and he pointed us to Blairmore House in Huntly, near Aberdeen – *"It's an original Scottish mansion which used to be the home of Blairmore School. It was then bought by a Swiss business man who wonderfully restored the mansion, but retained all the school buildings in the grounds in case someone else might have a use for them. It could be just what you need."*

Malcolm and Anna were sitting at Kilravock Castle waiting for news of what was going to happen to Ellel Scotland, when I gave them a call and asked them to drive over to Huntly and take a look at Blairmore House. Their post-inspection report was so positive that I booked a flight immediately. And as I flew north I looked back over the years of our Scottish pilgrimage.

Yes, God had clearly opened the door to Scotland. He had so clearly been in all that had happened at Kincraig. All the team were completely at peace that the road to Kilravock Castle had been opened up by the Lord. And everyone was equally clear that we could not stay there and countenance reneging on our support of Israel. God was saying a very clear NO to staying at Kilravock Castle. Then we thought God was providing a wonderful solution in Aldoorie Castle, but this turned out to be a false lead. But we did have the security of thinking that our overseas friend was willing to help us by buying a place for us to use. As I landed at Aberdeen Airport I had no idea whether or not this was just another leg in the zig-zag journey of faith or the end of our journey. But I was hoping and praying that we were coming home at last and asking God for some clear signs that He was in this latest stage of our Scottish odyssey.

Hans Baumann, the Swiss businessman, met my flight and Malcolm and Anna were already at Blairmore House. Just before we reached Blairmore we passed through Huntly. If I had known at the time that this was the place Marguerite lived, who had been praying since Kincraig that Ellel Ministries would come to her town, it would have been like a bright neon light in the sky of God's approval. But I didn't yet know that important piece of information – so I needed some other sign. And God didn't just give me one more sign, he gave me three!

Firstly, when we arrived at Blairmore House, Hans presented me with a copy of my own book, *The Complete Catalogue of British*

Cars, which had been published over twenty years previously, in 1978. He wanted to know if I was the same Peter Horrobin who had written his favourite book and, if so, he wanted me to sign his copy! For he had fallen in love with one of the cars I had pictured in the book – a 1949 2.5 litre Riley Sports. He liked the car so much that he went and found where that very car was and bought it. And there it was at Blairmore, on show in the old school dining room! I duly signed his copy of the book!

Secondly, years earlier I had loved a pair of French bronze statuettes which were owned by a friend. Every time I saw them in his house, I thought how much I would love to find a pair for my own home! One was a statuette of a young shipwrecked woman, crying out in distress. It was called *Au Secours*, the French for help. The other statuette showed the life boatman about to throw a lifeline to the young woman. This one was called *Le Sauveteur*, French for saviour, or rescuer. Together they spoke so clearly to me of Jesus our Saviour throwing out the lifeline of hope to a world in need. And there they were, on display, in Blairmore House! The coincidences were mounting up – God had certainly got my attention.

On Malcolm and Anna's first visit, Hans shared with them about the amount of time and effort that had gone into the restoration of the woodwork. He was touching the wood in the hallway and explaining how long it had taken for a team of men to strip off all the old chipped paintwork and bring it back to the bare wood, and then to smooth it down and patiently and painstakingly polish it with beeswax to bring it back to its original condition. It was at this point that Anna told Hans how that was so very similar to the ministry of Ellel and they shared how God was able to clean up and heal people from all the knocks and damage done to them in life and bring them back to the original condition of wholeness that He intended for them. God is able to restore people and that was our vision and purpose, as Ellel Ministries, for the use of Blairmore

House. God was speaking to Hans in a way that only God could have orchestrated.

And God was shrieking to us, loudly and clearly – *"this is the place"* – in much the same way as He had spoken to me on the day I was first shown around Ellel Grange. The rooms were beautiful the furnishings were amazing and the school buildings could be converted to make the whole place into a wonderful facility for teaching, training and for personal ministry.

Fiona and I, with all the Executive Leadership of Ellel Ministries, then visited Blairmore House again and Hans prepared a wonderful meal for us all in the dining room. Then, as Hans showed us round the wonderfully restored and furnished house – all evidence of 50 years of wear and tear from boisterous boys had gone – I pointed out two huge portraits on the staircase and asked Hans who they were. He had no idea. They were just two big paintings he'd bought from an antique dealer that he thought would look good on the walls.

I looked at those paintings carefully and found that the portraits were of Pastor and Mrs Irving. A quick search on the internet revealed that Pastor Irving had been a solicitor, practising in Edinburgh, who, seeing the distressful living conditions of the miner's families in Falkirk, resigned his legal practice, trained as a minister and asked to be appointed to one of the worst areas of Falkirk, where initially there was no church. He wanted to minister to the families who were struggling to live in appalling conditions, in homes without toilets and with the miners drinking much of their wages and robbing their wives and children of precious support. He and his wife were demonstrating in the nineteenth century exactly what Ellel Ministries was aiming to do in the twenty-first century.

There were tears in all our eyes – including Hans's, when we realised just who he had put on the walls of Blairmore House. The Lord had given us a third, very clear sign that this was the place he had been preparing for us. Later that evening, I sat down with

The courtyard at Shere House, home of Ellel South Africa.

Derek and Beryl Puffett – founding Directors of Ellel Africa (1998).

Shere House swimming pool.

Teaching hall at Shere House.

Welcome lunch for the Flagship School students at Shere House.

Rural Churches Leaders' course in the Transkei, South Africa.

First leaders conference in Rwanda.

Derek Puffett with the Bishop and clergy in Takoradi, Ghana after teaching a leaders' training weekend.

Leaders' training conference in Nairobi, Kenya.

With daughter, Anne, and Frida, whose family were all massacred in the 1994 genocide.

Rwanda thanksgiving – African style!

Two week USA training school in Colorado Springs.

English Acres Drive – the home address of Ellel USA.

The beautiful land at English Acres.

Peter and Fiona assessing the land with Renee Corzine, the sales agent for English Acres, USA (2005).

Temporary offices of Ellel USA.

Beatriz – leader of the first Ellel work in South America – in Ellel Colombia.

Ellel Leaders Israel tour and conference meeting up with David Davis and Peter Tsukahira (centre) at Carmel (2008).

Israel Leaders tour at the Western Wall, Jerusalem February 2011.

Eliyahu Ben Haim – one of the Israeli leaders who invited Ellel into the land.

Ellel Leaders tour of Israel at the Synaogue in Capernaum.

With David Cross and Peter Freeke, completing the purchase of
Huize Baak for Ellel Netherlands (2007).

Ellel Netherlands – Huize Baak with moat.

Guests enjoying the beautiful
environment at Huize Baak.

Marc and Margaret Schuthof came
from Australia to be the new leaders of
the work in the Netherlands.

Some of the early pioneers who helped establish the work of Ellel Ministries

Sister Aine at Peter's 50th Birthday - member of the first Advisory Board.

Don and Maddy Binsted – pioneering Trustee and adviser.

Bobby and Grace Cooper – members of the founding Prayer Support Group.

Rev Chris Woods – early Adviser and friend of the ministry.

Malcolm Colmer, with his wife Ann, lifelong friend and first Chairman of the Trustees.

Bishop Graham Dow – long-term friend and Adviser to the ministry.

Joe and Ruth Hawkey – first directors of Glyndley Manor.

Barry and Jan Jay – first House Team leaders of Ellel Grange.

Chris Mungeam – founder of Sovereign World – and lifelong friend and encourager – with his wife Jan.

Signing the papers with Chris & Jan Mungeam as Sovereign World joins Ellel Ministries (2006).

Jim and Muriel Russell – developers of the first Modular School.

Rev. Fred and Barbara Elgar – Pierrepont pioneer team.

Paul and Gretel Haglin – two of the many visiting teachers from around the world who contributed hugely to the developing work of Ellel Ministries.

Tom Marshall, hugely influential and encouraging author and teacher from Australia.

Paul and Liz Griffin – key members of the Ellel Grange team for over 25 years.

The Ellel Teaching Team in 1998.

Key events in the Ellel Story – as told through some of the Newsletters

The first newsletter.

Ellel Ministries

News Letter

May 1992

Centres for Training & Ministry in Christian Healing & Counselling
Ellel Grange, Lancaster, LA2 0HN. Tel. 0524-751651 (FAX 751738)
Glyndley Manor, Stone Cross, Nr.Eastbourne, E.Sussex, BN24 5BS
Tel. 0323-440440 (Fax 440877)

FEED MY SHEEP

A Team Member Reflects - Ellel Grange, Lunch Hour, 13 March 1992

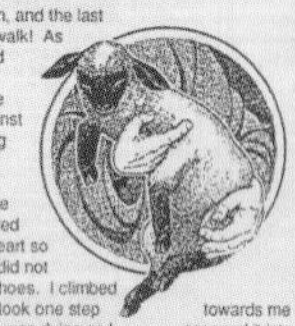

The wind was howling, the rain lashing down, and the last thing I wanted to do was take the dog for a walk! As I struggled down the lane, my eyes focussed on a tiny bedraggled lamb, hardly able to stand on its legs and unable to move. There were no other sheep around and it was against a tree totally alone, sopping wet and freezing cold.

Immediately my heart went out to this vulnerable, weak little lamb. I ran back to the house, grabbed a towel, left the dog and raced back to the spot where the lamb was. My heart so much wanted to rescue the little lamb that I did not stop to think of my best coat, trousers and shoes. I climbed over the fence and into the mud. The lamb took one step towards me with what seemed its last strength. I knew it was dying as I scooped it into my arms, wrapping the towel around it. Back over the fence the lamb was taken to the Christian farmer whose land adjoins ours. I knew that there it would be looked after. Once the lamb was in safety, I then looked and saw my muddy clothes.

The Lord spoke directly into my heart *"Don't you see that this is what I have called you to do. I have called you to rescue my lambs, those who have been abandoned, without shelter or food, and who are bleeding and dying with no-one to help. Many have been neglected. I have called you to bring my lambs to safety, to bring healing to them and to bring them to those shepherds who will care and tend for my flock. It will not be easy and you may get muddy and hurt but the joy I will give will be everlasting".*

Many people who come through our doors are deeply in need of God's love, healing and spiritual food in order to live and grow. Many too need gently leading to shepherds who will watch and care for them. The Lord spoke so deeply into my heart at a time when I needed it most. I was overwhelmed by His love, and renewed my commitment to His call upon my life to feed His lambs - whatever the cost!

"To Jesus Christ be the glory and power for ever and ever!" Rev. 1:6

Students at our 1st School of Evangelism, Healing & Deliverance: Rev Aggrey Anyembe, Rural Dean from Kenya; Rev Reuben Ciupe, Pentecostal Pastor from Romania; Rev Lorraine Burrows, Pastor of Crossroads Christian Centre, Palmerston, Ontario; Nannette Thorburn, Scripture Union worker in Scotland; Edmund Kivuye, from the Africa Revival Ministry of Burundi.

It only takes a spark!

School of Evangelism, Healing and Deliverance

45 delegates attended our first nine-week training school at Glyndley Manor. Ten came from Canada, two from Romania, others from Switzerland, Eastern Germany, Kenya, Ghana, Burundi and all parts of Britain from St. Austell to Aberdeen!

The first four weeks were of intensive teaching by Peter Horrobin and Graham Powell from Canada. During the half-term assimilation week specific study projects were designed to help them apply the teaching received to their own situation.

For the second half some of the delegates transferred to Ellel Grange. Three Healing Retreats were held at each Centre, providing valuable practical experience in ministering alongside our Associate Counsellors.

"Thank you all for every-thing. My life has changed. The School was one of my greatest experiences"
Rev. Lorraine Burrows, Pastor from Ontario, Canada

The delegates from Africa and Eastern Europe were sponsored by churches and individuals throughout the country. Most have met up with their sponsoring churches. Reuben Ciupe, a Romanian Pastor spent the half-term week with the small congregation of only 15, who had contributed £1000 for his travel and accommodation costs! Rev Aggrey Anyembe, a Rural Dean from Kenya, preached at three local churches, one of which in Eastbourne has made him a gift to help him get round his large Rural Deanery in Kenya and will be shipping out a motor bike for him! He also returned loaded with books and a supply of clerical collars and studs for his Deanery Pastors, all donated by the churches he visited.

Through this school a spark has been lit in many people from different nations. We believe the fires that result will change many lives. We praise God for all He has done.

Ellel Ministries

News Letter

November 1992

The word Ellel means 'All Hail Jesus: King of Kings and Lord of Lords'

Centres for Training & Ministry in Christian Healing & Counselling
Ellel Grange, Lancaster, LA2 0HN. Tel. 0524-751651 (FAX 751738)
Glyndley Manor, Stone Cross, Nr.Eastbourne, E.Sussex, BN24 5BS
Tel. 0323-440440 (Fax 440877)

The Lord God's Meadow!! (Ur Retje)

In the last Newsletter we focussed on the commission we have to care for the sheep. This time we focus on the meadow in which some of the sheep will be cared for! In an extraordinary way, last June, the Lord led Peter, with other members of the team, to a piece of land in Hungary, that wasn't for sale, but on which there was such a presence of God that they believed this was the place God was leading them to for building our Eastern European Centre.

They had looked at many buildings for a new centre, but all were in such bad condition that the cost of restoration would be prohibitive. Then they were led by the Holy Spirit, in a remarkable chain of 'God-incidences', to this ideally placed piece of land, just 23 kilometres north-east of Budapest, in a delightful rural area.

A Land Prepared

In 1928 a group of Christians in the Reformed Church believed for the provision of a centre to care for First World War widows. They found a property with lots of land at Orbottyan. They agreed a price with the vendors and started to pray for the money. But nothing happened. The vendors lost patience and said the property would be sold to someone else at 3.00pm on the 21st March 1928 if the sale was not completed by then. At 9.00am on the 21st they still had no money, but at 10.00am a cheque arrived at the bank in Budapest - a donation from the English peer, Lord Rothermere. Dr. Kovats, professor of Divinity in Budapest, hastened to Orbottyan, arriving at five past two, just in time to complete the purchase only minutes before the 3.00pm deadline! As a testimony to the Lord's amazing provision the group of Christians renamed the land Ur Retje, Hungarian for "The Lord God's Meadow"! **It was this very land that the team sensed was already anointed of God without knowing anything of its history!**

Orphans were cared for at Orbottyan during the war, but when the Russians occupied Hungary in 1945 the healthy orphans were removed to communist "education centres", leaving behind the unwanted mentally handicapped and disabled children. So began a major work in Hungary by the Reformed Church caring for the children the communists rejected.

Redeeming the Land

In the post-communist era much land has already returned to private ownership and the present owners of Ur Retje have agreed to sell it to The Christian Trust for building our Eastern European Centre, which we know is part of God's plan for this work. Whilst building costs in Hungary are much lower than here, the land itself is probably more expensive. The cost of the 40 acres is expected to be about £200 - 250,000 - money which we will probably need by the end of this year. It seems like the story of Ellel Grange all over again! It's an exciting prospect, believing God for the money to redeem (buy back) *The Lord God's Meadow* for the original purposes God intended by caring for 'wounded sheep' and also for teaching the shepherds how to tend their own wounded flocks.

Peter praying the land

Please see the special Eastern European Supplement for more details of all that God is doing here through Ellel Ministries. ***The full account of The Story So Far about Ur Retje is a remarkable document detailing the precise way in which God's hand has been on the team as they have sought His will for this extension of the work. For a copy please send a large stamped addressed envelope asking for the story of Ur Retje.***

Steve & Chris Hepden Join the Team

For the past 15 years Steve and Chris Hepden have been in leadership with Bristol Christian Fellowship (BCF). With them they have had a dynamic and strategic ministry which in recent years has extended their sphere of influence to national and international horizons. They have worked with Ellel Ministries on numerous occasions, especially in teaching some very successful training courses and holiday schools. This summer Steve led the team into Lithuania following the Budapest Conference. Their vision for ministry closely parallels the one God gave to Ellel Ministries. Their presence will add considerable strength to the overall Ellel Ministries leadership and teaching teams. We welcome them and look forward to all that God has in store for the work through their involvement. We are grateful to BCF for so generously releasing them into this new phase of life and ministry. Steve and Chris have two children, Zoe and Joanna. Joanna is studying music at Cardiff University. Zoe is currently taking a year out of education in Germany and then hopes to study politics at London University.

"I will look for those that are lost, bring back those that wander off, bandage those that are hurt, and heal those that are sick" (Ezekiel 34.16).

We give real praise and thanks to God, for His love and faithfulness, for our work in Eastern Europe. Thank you, each and every one who by prayer support or giving, have undergirded the work in these countries. We are rich and they are poor, and yet, they have taught us so much.

Ellel Ministries

News Letter

May 1993

The word Ellel means 'All Hail Jesus: King of Kings and Lord of Lords'

Centres for Training & Ministry in Christian Healing & Counselling
Ellel Grange, Lancaster, LA2 0HN. Tel. 0524-751651 (Fax 751738)
Glyndley Manor, Stone Cross, Nr.Eastbourne, E.Sussex, BN24 5BS.
Tel. 0323-440440 (Fax 440877)

Jesus said, "I will build my church and the gates of hell shall not prevail against it." Matthew 16:18

THE CHURCH ABLAZE

The impact of our previous conferences at The Brighton Centre went far beyond all our expectations! Through *The Battle Belongs to the Lord,* in 1990 and 1991, the lives of hundreds of people were changed, a large number were healed, and many churches have moved forward in dynamic new ways.

In spite of many requests we did not believe the time was right for another event in 1992. But we have been praying and seeking the Lord for the way ahead. A follow-on event, to be called ***The Church Ablaze***, is the result.

INTERNATIONAL TEACHING CONFERENCE October 26-29 1993 at the Brighton Conference Centre Main Speakers: Peter Horrobin, Tom Marshall and Graham Powell

Many individuals in the Body of Christ are sick - not just in body, but in spirit and soul - and so the church also has become weak, sick and in places it is dying. Just as God longs to heal individuals and has raised up people all over the world with a burden to pray for the sick, we believe God's desire also is to bring restoration and healing to His Church.

Wherever we go, we are finding people who are catching the vision for a Church that truly reflects the heart of God for his people.

"God is on the move, stirring His church from complacency into action."

We live in momentous days, days where God is speaking prophetically to his people bringing conviction, warning, direction and healing. In the midst of the darkness, God is on the move, stirring his church from complacency into action. Faith is on the increase. We are called not to be ignorant of Satan's devices. The church must not be found slumbering, but alert, trained and on the offensive.

We are *expecting* a mighty outpouring of the power of God as we move forward to teach all He has laid on our hearts. Full details of the programme are on the conference brochure.

The Church Ablaze with the Father's glory is the objective of the conference and we believe God is going to speak to His church prophetically and radically at this conference.

Jesus is coming back and He wants His church prepared and ready. We hope you will come to the conference, meet many friends and experience a time of great personal challenge and blessing.

Please order extra brochures and copies of the poster (see illustration) from the office at Ellel Grange

Eastern European Explosion!

Otto and Sharon write from Budapest. . .

Our report is nearly the same that Jesus sent to John the Baptist: the blind see, the lame walk, the mute speak and those formerly dead to God are now alive!

Serving the people at one of our Conferences

As of February this year, the Eastern European work will have been running for two years. We have had two international conferences with an attendance of approximately 1000 people each and four training courses presented in two separate cities - that's 4600 people who have come for a minimum of three days instruction and ministry into their lives, many of them being pastors and leaders! Increasingly, the Ellel vision is being picked up by those touched by our activities, and many come to work and visit us daily. Among many others these include Borbala (from Hungary) who trained for a year on the Young People's Service Team in England, Jozsef and Krisztina who have been to England with us for orientation, Feri who came to us through our training courses and an American missionary from the 'International Team' organisation.

Continued overleaf

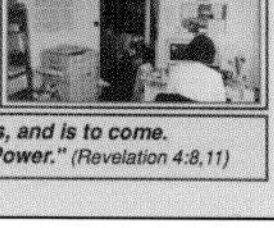

At work in the Budapest Base

"Holy, Holy, Holy, is the Lord God Almighty, Who was and is, and is to come. Our Lord and God! You are worthy to receive Glory, Honour and Power." (Revelation 4:8,11)

The Church Ablaze
Brighton Centre
October 26-29

Autumn 1993

Ellel Ministries NewsLetter

Centres for Training & Ministry in Christian Healing & Counselling
Ellel Grange, Lancaster, LA2 0HN. Tel. 0524-751651 (Fax 751738)
Glyndley Manor, Stone Cross, Nr.Eastbourne, E.Sussex, BN24 5BS.
Tel. 0323-440440 (Fax 440877)

And Now

Ellel Canada!

Now we know why God has given us such strong links with Canada! With over 30 Canadians having already attended our International School, and our Ministry Teams having been on a series of trips to different venues on the West Coast and in Central Canada, we might have known that it was on God's heart for Canada to be the home of an Ellel Ministries Centre!

In an amazing way God has opened the hearts of the Trustees of Singing Waters, a Christian Conference Centre at Orangeville, just North of Toronto, to change the name of their Trust to Ellel Ministries (Canada) and make the Centre permanently available for the work. It is an incredible and very special seal on the ministry which God has called into being.

Part of Ellel Canada with (insets) Ruth & Joe Hawkey

Whilst we will be giving spiritual direction, some teaching input and management advice to the work, Ellel Canada will be largely supported by Canadian Christians. The ministry in Canada will be launched at *"The Battle Belongs to the Lord"* in Toronto in September. Joe and Ruth Hawkey will be going out to Canada as Pioneer Directors of the Canadian Centre, whilst retaining their Headship of the work at Glyndley Manor. They will be supported by Ruth Dahl, also from Glyndley, as they develop Healing Retreats and Training Courses and build a ministry team. Please pray for them in their demanding new role. *See also "Peter Writes" overleaf.*

The Church Ablaze

Numbers coming to *The Church Ablaze* are rising fast. There is an increasing sense of expectation as the team and delegates are preparing themselves for this major conference.

Already there are more booked in at this stage (1530 with ten weeks to go at the time of writing) than there were just six weeks before *The Battle Belongs to the Lord!* So, it looks as though it could be a full house.

If you are thinking of coming please complete your booking form as soon as possible - early booking will help enormously with the huge amount of administration a large conference like this entails. If you can't come yourself, please pass on the enclosed copy of the booking form to someone else who might be interested.

"The harvest is large, but there are few workers to gather it in. Pray to the owner of the harvest that he will send out workers to gather in the harvest." Matt. 9:37

Headlines

Hungary
Land Acquired

See Page 3

Russia
St Petersburg Conference Exceeds All Expectations

See Pages 2 & 5

England
The Church Ablaze Numbers Rising Fast

Canada
Ellel Canada Opening Soon

See Pages 1 & 2

Malaysia
Doors Open for the Ellel Team

See Page 7

Key events in the Ellel Story
– as told through some of the Newsletters

July '98

Ellel Ministries
INTERNATIONAL

Summer '98 Edition

newsletter

Ellel Grange
Glyndley Manor
Ellel Pierrepont
Ellel Canada
Ellel Eastern Europe

CENTRES FOR TRAINING AND MINISTRY IN CHRISTIAN HEALING AND COUNSELLING

God's Creativity in You!

Pioneer Healing Course at Ellel Grange

Behind the scenes at Ellel Grange, many hours have been spent ministering to deeply broken individuals. During these times, when the heart of God was bringing significant healing and restoration, the vision for a new weekend's Healing Course was born.

It has been very moving to see the Lord release creative giftings that have been deeply locked away and watch as people express them in a variety of different ways. Immense healing has come as a result, not just from prayer ministry and counselling, vital though these are, but also from the release of God's creativity within the individual, bringing healing at very deep levels.

So our pioneer *"God's Creativity in You!"* weekend was not just about: woodcarving, dancing, drama, music, marbling, vegetable printing, hand-made card making, bottle painting, making decorative boxes, printing, painting, creative walking, creative writing, shell painting, dry stone walling, sewing, collage and banner making but ... entering into an experience of the Father heart of God and the healing power of His love.

John Allen brought his own unique contribution on woodcraft and spoke about hearing the Lord's voice through creativity. **Edward Barnes** brought deeply meaningful insights from the

Continued Overleaf

Power Installed
at Ur Retje

Otto Bixler by the New Pylon at Ur Retje

The beginning of June was a tremendously exciting milestone in the development of our Hungarian centre! Our own electricity pylon was installed, enabling us to draw power from the national supply. Little by little we are occupying the land and seeing the building equipped for service. ***(Cont. page 3)***

Hope and Healing
by Peter Horrobin

Our understanding of hope depends on our situation. We may hope it is going to be a fine day tomorrow - with little expectation that it will be so. But we may also hope that if we travel on the motorway, in the direction indicated for London, that we will eventually reach the capital city. This time our hope is much more certain to be realised - provided, that is, we stay on the motorway and don't break down on the journey!

In terms of our Christian destiny, hope is much more like the journey on the motorway - if we stay on the right road and don't break down we are certain to reach our eternal destination.

But Jesus not only gave us a certain hope for eternity. He also focused attention on bringing hope to people in their present circumstances. He came as the Good Shepherd who would both care for the sheep and lay down his life for them. Both aspects of the ministry of Jesus are vital.

Continued on page 2

FOUNDED ON THE ROCK
UPDATE

Bournemouth '98 will be one of the most strategic events that Ellel Ministries has ever sponsored. For this reason we have prepared a free cassette explaining the vision for the conference and why we believe it to be such a significant milestone ***(copies available free of charge from Ellel Grange).***

Founded on the Rock will provide major keys to understanding the integral part healing has to play in true discipleship and equip you with a knowledge of foundational truth and Godly discernment.

It is in times when God is moving in great power, that we most need to know truth and exercise discernment. For we are living at a time when worldly ways and beliefs can seem attractive and basis Christian truths are too easily put on one side in favour of moral compromise and deceptive spiritualities.

Continued Overleaf

12-15 October
Bournemouth International Centre

God's Creativity • South Africa Diary • Australian Reflections • Student Sponsorship • "Standing Up"

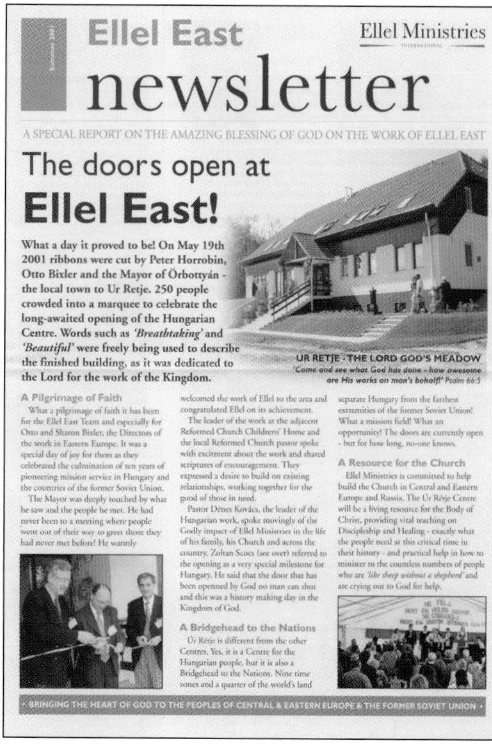

Summer 2001

Ellel East newsletter

Ellel Ministries
INTERNATIONAL

A SPECIAL REPORT ON THE AMAZING BLESSING OF GOD ON THE WORK OF ELLEL EAST

The doors open at Ellel East!

What a day it proved to be! On May 19th 2001 ribbons were cut by Peter Horrobin, Otto Bixler and the Mayor of Örbottyán - the local town to Ur Retje. 250 people crowded into a marquee to celebrate the long-awaited opening of the Hungarian Centre. Words such as *'Breathtaking'* and *'Beautiful'* were freely being used to describe the finished building, as it was dedicated to the Lord for the work of the Kingdom.

UR RETJE - THE LORD GOD'S MEADOW
'Come and see what God has done - how awesome are His works on man's behalf!' *Psalm 66:5*

A Pilgrimage of Faith

What a pilgrimage of faith it has been for the Ellel East Team and especially for Otto and Sharon Bixler, the Directors of the work in Eastern Europe. It was a special day of joy for them as they celebrated the culmination of ten years of pioneering mission service in Hungary and the countries of the former Soviet Union.

The Mayor was deeply touched by what he saw and the people he met. He had never been to a meeting where people went out of their way to greet those they had never met before! He warmly welcomed the work of Ellel to the area and congratulated Ellel on its achievement.

The leader of the work at the adjacent Reformed Church Childrens' Home and the local Reformed Church pastor spoke with excitment about the work and shared scriptures of encouragement. They expressed a desire to build on existing relationships, working together for the good of those in need.

Pastor Dénes Kovács, the leader of the Hungarian work, spoke movingly of the Godly impact of Ellel Ministries in the life of his family, his Church and across the country. Zoltan Scocs (see over) referred to the opening as a very special milestone for Hungary. He said that the door that has been openned by God no man can shut and this was a history making day in the Kingdom of God.

A Bridgehead to the Nations

Úr Rétje is different from the other Centres. Yes, it is a Centre for the Hungarian people, but it is also a Bridgehead to the Nations. Nine time zones and a quarter of the world's land separate Hungary from the farthest extremities of the former Soviet Union! What a mission field! What an opportunity! The doors are currently open - but for how long, no-one knows.

A Resource for the Church

Ellel Ministries is committed to help build the Church in Central and Eastern Europe and Russia. The Úr Rétje Centre will be a living resource for the Body of Christ, providing vital teaching on Discipleship and Healing - exactly what the people need at this critical time in their history - and practical help in how to minister to the countless numbers of people who are *'like sheep without a shepherd'* and are crying out to God for help.

• BRINGING THE HEART OF GOD TO THE PEOPLES OF CENTRAL & EASTERN EUROPE & THE FORMER SOVIET UNION •

Winter 2001

Ellel Ministries
INTERNATIONAL

www.ellelministries.org

newsletter

Ellel Grange
Glyndley Manor
Ellel Pierrepont
Kilravock Castle
Ellel Canada
Ellel East
Ellel Australia

CENTRES FOR TRAINING AND MINISTRY IN CHRISTIAN HEALING AND DISCIPLESHIP

inside ...

New Centres!

In a miraculous way God has opened the door for two new Ellel Centres - one in Scotland and the other in Australia.
Read the amazing story of God's provision inside ...

Kilravock Castle, Scotland

Green Gables, Australia

New CDs!

Ellel Music has produced two new worship albums: ***'The Joy of Healing'*** & ***'Jesus, Healer of the Nations'***.
For more information and to order your CDs see the back cover of this newsletter ...

The Joy of Healing

New Hope!

Peter writes on the extraordinary providence of God

Ellel Ministries International Conference
13th - 16th February 2001
LET THE oppressed go free!
The Brighton Centre, England

Proclaiming a relevant Gospel to a needy world

Peter HORROBIN
Derek PRINCE
Johannes FACIUS
Peter WALKER
Eliyahu BEN HAIM
Kimberly DANIELS

All around we see the devastation and personal suffering caused by oppression. Both individuals and whole people groups carry the scars of man's inhumanity to man and their only hope of restoration lies in the Gospel that Jesus came to proclaim. *'Let the Oppressed go free!'* declares this wonderful truth and seeks to share God's heart for the oppressed in a way that both points to freedom and provokes action.

We are thrilled that **Derek Prince** has chosen to join with us at this conference to share from the scriptures what he believes to be one of the most important challenges facing the Church today. *His presence at Brighton will, however, be subject to his health and we would ask you to pray very specially that he will have the strength to speak out what God has laid on his heart.*

At the beginning of the work of Ellel Ministries God brought to us many people in desperate need. Through ministering to them God taught us deep and profound lessons about many aspects of healing, deliverance and living discipleship.

In recent years, however, God has shown us how some people cannot receive healing until the yoke of oppression has been lifted off them. We first saw this profound truth being expressed in Eastern Europe as people forgave their communist oppressors and experienced major healing as a result. Then, in Australia, we saw how the Aboriginal peoples have been suffering for generations through the oppression of white settlers. When forgiveness flowed we saw people enter into deep healing and experience great restoration and liberty. It was wonderful to see people being released into a life of fulfilment and purpose that was not previously possible. ***This is the cry of God's heart for a broken world - a message of hope for this generation.***

One of the most important challenges facing the Church today ... the cry of God 's heart for a broken world

In addition to Derek Prince an out-standing teaching team will be proclaiming the truths of the Kingdom and will share how God can bring His healing to the oppressed and the hurting.

Johannes Facius will speak from his own profound experience of being healed from the terrible curse of crippling depression.

Continued overleaf

• BRINGING THE HEART OF GOD TO THE HEART OF MAN •

bringing the heart of God to the heart of man

Ellel Ministries
INTERNATIONAL

news

July 2006

What's Inside...

- Powerhouse of Prayer
- Indian Explosion
- Africa, Oh Africa
- Miracle in Rwanda
- Kingdom Businesses
- Reaching Europe
- New Canadian Centres
- Ellel USA gets ready!
- New Ellel Diploma
- Quiver youth programme
- Money Matters

As Long as it is Day...

... Peter Horrobin writes

Over twenty years ago I heard a prophetic word at a camp meeting. It deeply impacted me then – and still has the power to do so today. It referred to the fact that darkness was coming over the earth, but urged us not to fear the darkness, for as the darkness gets darker so the light becomes brighter! Just as, at night, the stars are more visible, when spiritual darkness is over the earth those who look to Jesus will see Jesus as the Light of the World with ever greater clarity.

In my relatively short lifetime the world has changed radically. Increasing darkness has spread over the face of the earth. Traditional understandings of morality, good and evil are no longer respected and in many cases are seen as not being politically correct!

Every morning we face a world which is sliding ever faster into moral decadence, spiritual decline, disrespect of authority and the random use of violence for political and even religious motives. This is a world which frequently refers to what is good as if it is bad and what is bad is portrayed as being good - a world where truth is the victim and is dying on the streets.

No wonder Jesus encouraged his disciples to action with the words, ***"As long as it is day, we must do the work of him who sent me. Night is coming, when no one can work."*** (John 9:4).

In March 2006 the whole Ellel Team – including all the leaders and many team members from around the world - gathered at Pierrepont for a special Team Conference, to give thanks for the first twenty years of Ellel Ministries. Afterwards all the leaders met for a private conference of prayer and planning. It was here that God spoke to us so very clearly about the work He had called us to do.

As leader after leader shared their recent experiences, we were all deeply impacted by the news of good fruit from around the world - news of devastated lives being transformed by the power of God, people finding Jesus on Healing Retreats, victims of terrible trauma being radically healed and restored, Pastors and leaders, broken in the battle, being restored and strengthened in their calling.

In spite of these wonderful encouragements, when you are stretched to the very limit responding to the cries and needs for help from so many of God's people around the world, it is sometimes tempting to look the other way, or put up your hands and say, No More! It sometimes feels like being part of the Red Cross in a war zone! But there is an urgency on the heart of God and the Spirit of God continually stirs God's people to action with renewed energy.

The work of healing and deliverance is about undoing the yoke of oppression and injustice (Is. 58 v6-11) and setting the oppressed free. Bringing strength and restoration to the church is a vital factor in bringing the heart of God to the heart of man. Frida's testimony in this Newsletter amazingly illustrates the power of God to heal and transform lives, as she shares something of the terrible trauma

Healing & Destiny
AT
THE FORUM, BATH
31ST OCT - 3RD NOV 2006
WITH
PETER HORROBIN
AND THE ELLEL TEAM
AND
GUEST SPEAKERS
WAYNE HILSDEN
JIM GRAHAM
GEORGE VERWER
ALISTAIR PETRIE
SEE ENCLOSED BROCHURE FOR FULL DETAILS
DON'T MISS IT!
BOOK NOW

The Ellel Ministries Handbooks – 2001-2016

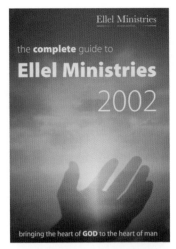

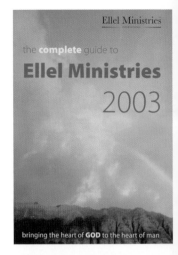

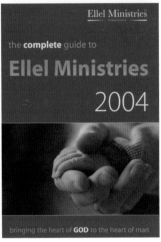

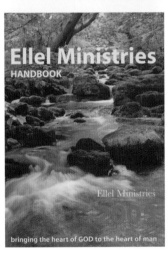

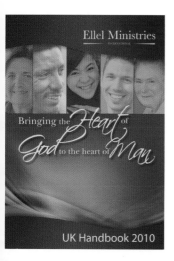

Ellel Ministries
OVERNATIONAL

Bringing the *Heart* of *God* to the heart of *Man*

UK Handbook 2010

Ellel Ministries
International

25

years of

bringing the heart of God to the heart of man

UK Handbook 2011

www.ellelministries.org

Ellel Ministries
International

Handbook 2012

www.ellelministries.org

BRINGING THE HEART OF GOD TO THE HEART OF MAN

Ellel Ministries
International

Handbook 2013 UK & Ireland

www.ellelministries.org

BRINGING THE HEART OF GOD TO THE HEART OF MAN

Ellel Ministries
International

Handbook 2014 UK & Ireland

www.ellelministries.org

BRINGING THE HEART OF GOD TO THE HEART OF MAN

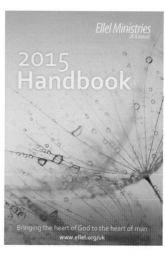

Ellel Ministries
UK & Ireland

2015 Handbook

Bringing the heart of God to the heart of man
www.ellel.org/uk

LUKE 9:11 Ellel Ministries
UK & Ireland

JANUARY-APRIL 2016
ISSUE 04

2016 COURSE CALENDARS | ARTICLES | ELLEL NEWS | CENTRE INFORMATION

BRINGING THE HEART OF GOD TO THE HEART OF MAN

Andy Taylor (UK & Ireland Director) shares about the significance of this phrase and its connection to the Great Commission that we are all called to.

JESUS, ISRAEL AND THE KINGDOM OF GOD

Murray Dixon leads us into a series of courses to be held in 2016 at all 5 UK Ellel centres.

BRINGING THE HEART OF GOD TO THE HEART OF MAN

www.ellel.org/uk

LUKE 9:11 Ellel Ministries
UK & Ireland

MAY-AUGUST 2016
ISSUE 05

2016 Course Calendars | Articles | Ellel News | Centre Information

HEALING THROUGH CREATIVITY

Fiona Hartshaw explores the reasons why we are creative and how God uses creativity to bring healing to His children. Page 20

RESTORATION THROUGH JESUS CHRIST

Lacy Symecko asks the question: 'What comes to mind when you hear the word restoration?' Page 06

BRINGING THE HEART OF GOD TO THE HEART OF MAN

www.ellel.org/uk

LUKE 9:11 Ellel Ministries
UK & Ireland

JAN-APRIL 2017
ISSUE 06

2017 Course Calendars | Articles | Ellel News | Centre Information

· 1986 · 30 Years · 2016 ·
ANNIVERSARY

BRINGING THE HEART OF GOD TO THE HEART OF MAN

www.ellel.org/uk

The Ellel Ministries
International World Map – 2017

01 CANADA
Ellel Canada West
Ellel Canada Ontario

02 Ellel USA Florida

03 Ellel Colombia

04 UK & IRELAND
Ellel Grange
Ellel Glyndley Manor
Ellel Pierrepont
Ellel Scotland
Ellel Ireland

05 Ellel France

06 Ellel Switzerland

07 Ellel Netherlands

08 Ellel Germany

09 Ellel Norway

10 Ellel Sweden

11 Ellel Finland

12 HUNGARY
Ellel Hungary
Ellel Central & Eastern Europe
Ellel Central & Eastern Europe Development

13 Ellel Romania

14 Ellel Russian Language

15 Ellel China

16 Ellel Middle East

17 AFRICA
Ellel South Africa
Ellel Kwa Zulu Natal
Ellel Rwanda
Ellel Kenya

18 Ellel India

19 MALAYSIA
Ellel Sabah
Ellel Kuala Lumpur

20 Ellel Singapore

21 Ellel Papua New Guinea

22 AUSTRALIA
Ellel Western Australia
Ellel Australia (Sydney)
Ellel Victoria

23 Ellel New Zealand

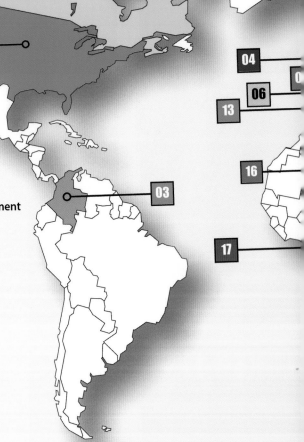

Jesus welcomed the peop
Kingdom of God and
Luk

Ellel Ministries
International

...aught them about the
...aled those in need.

Ellel Ministries International Leaders – November 2016.

Peter and Fiona Horrobin,
International Directors.

Andy and Cath Taylor,
UK National Directors.

Hans in the dining room and we talked money. I was able to tell him of my friend who had offered to buy a place for us to use and, confident that the money was available, we shook hands on a deal for the house and all its contents and furnishings. With everything still in place, Malcolm and Anna would be able to continue their Scottish programme of Ellel events almost seamlessly. We planned to complete the last event on the 2002 Ellel programme at Kilravock Castle and then begin the 2003 programme at Blairmore House in February 2003.

After putting these details in place, we left Blairmore House rejoicing. God had gone before us. We had reached the end of our zig-zag road. The work in Scotland had a new home. Or so we thought! Then, suddenly, out of the blue, BOMBSHELL. I received an email from my friend overseas who said he'd been praying about Blairmore House and did not feel God was telling him to buy this property. I read and re-read the email several times. There was no mistaking what it said. Tears and pain welled up from within, followed by a deep sense of disappointment and then devastation. I showed the email to Fiona and we stood there in silent shock as we tried to give the situation to the Lord and look to Him for what we should do. My heart was already going out to Malcolm and Anna, who were starting to pack up everything at Kilravock Castle. I had hit the biggest single brick wall I'd ever come across, but I knew I couldn't lie at the foot of the wall in pieces, I had to get up and carry on.

Amazingly, I knew that, at a deeper level still, I had a certain sense of knowing that whatever happens, God was still in charge. I saw a minute glimmer of hope at the end of a very long tunnel, but had no idea where it was coming from. We had absolutely no cash resources within the ministry and I knew that the bank would not be able to support any new work in Scotland for at least two years. We did not have a long enough operational track record in the region to raise a commercial mortgage. We were between a very big rock and a very hard place.

The last thing I wanted to do was let Hans down – he had already been let down by two previous potential buyers – and I had promised him that we had the money and would not be a third. It was already nearly ten o'clock at night, but I knew I had to tell Hans right away. Very reluctantly, I picked up the phone and dialled his number.

He was obviously pleased to hear my voice at first, but then I had to break the news. *"Hans,"* I said, *"the man who I was depending on for the money has just emailed me to say that he is unable to help. We are going to have to pull out of the deal. I am so, so sorry."* There was a prolonged silence on the other end of the line, and then Hans, in his profoundly marked Swiss-German accent said. *"Peter, there is more than one way of skinning the cat. I believe God wants you to have this house. I need to talk with my wife. I'll call you back."*

The next twenty minutes were, perhaps, the longest twenty minutes of my life. I don't think I even tasted the cup of tea I had in my hand, but suddenly it was gone and I didn't remember drinking it! I was shaking as I picked up the phone when it finally rang. Hans, and his wife Monique, were very clear in their decision. *"Peter,"* he said, *"we believe you should have Blairmore House for Ellel Ministries, so why don't you just move in and start your work there and pay us when you can."*

My jaw hit the floor. This was the most surprising business deal I'd ever heard of. Had I really heard properly what Hans had just said? I repeated back to him what I thought he'd said. And it was true. God had spoken to Hans more deeply than any of us had realised. He was gripped by the vision and wanted us to have the property. And so it was that we took over Blairmore House in February 2003 and Hans trusted that one day he would get his money.

It was a remarkable, even miraculous arrangement that was put into the words of a legal document by our solicitors in Edinburgh. Even though Hans was responding to God's desire for us to use the place for His purposes, it was still a huge risk for both Hans and the ministry to take. Andy Taylor and I sat in our solicitor's offices and reviewed all the documents that had to be signed. Then the solicitor left the office for a few minutes, leaving us alone. Andy remembers how we looked at each other, in his absence, thinking what a crazy thing it was that we were about to do (financially at least), but then being totally overwhelmed by the presence of God in that solicitor's office and both of us knew that there was absolutely no way we couldn't sign those papers! It was an unforgettable moment. And the agreement worked!

Two years later we were able to arrange a mortgage on the property, and in the extraordinary circumstances that I have already described in Chapter 18 another supporter of the work loaned us the money to buy all the furnishings and contents, and we were able to honour our commitment to Hans and Monique. Every time I think about the Blairmore Story, I marvel at God's incredible faithfulness and attention to detail! The work there has been powerfully used by the Lord ever since, despite ongoing battles to pay the mortgage. Yet, we remain in faith for God's timing on these things too.

Then there was yet another amazing confirmation of the vision for Blairmore House. Malcolm and Anna sold the house they owned in Lancaster and chose a wonderful old house in Huntly. It was only some time after they had bought it that they discovered that this was the very house in which Marguerite Connell had led the Lydia Fellowship and Faith Mission prayer meetings for over 30 years – the very house in which she had prayed that Ellel Ministries would come to Huntly! You can imagine our joy when Marguerite turned up at one of our prayer meetings at Blairmore House and told us this story. She added, also, that the Lydia prayer meetings had previously been held at Kilravock Castle too and it was during one of those times they saw a vision of flames in the room as God was showing them that revival would come again to the Highlands of Scotland.

Huntly, also, turned out to be a town with a remarkable Christian history. It was little surprise that this was the place God had brought us to. We discovered that Huntly had played a major part in Scotland's nineteenth century Revivals. The Duchess of Gordon, whose home was *Huntly Lodge* was a devout Christian woman. In 1837, her frustration at the state of the Church was clearly evident as she wrote in her diary these striking words, "*We must pray very, very hard for more labourers in the Lord's vineyard, and that He may send us pastors after His own heart. I do not see where they are to come from at all, and therefore I think I can pray with the more entire faith, and feel sure that the Lord will give them in His own time and way.*"

In 1859 there was a new move of the Spirit of God called the Aberdeenshire Revival. Duncan Matheson, who was born in Huntly in 1824, had been a Scripture reader with the British Army in the Crimean war. Wherever he preached, great multitudes gathered and in 1860, the town of Cullen was moved "*as by an earthquake*". In Huntly, Duncan Matheson preached to over 10,000 people in the Castle Park, Huntly, with the kind permission of the Duchess of Gordon, who must have rejoiced to see her prayers being answered. Special trains brought in the people from the surrounding areas. These were the largest Christian gatherings ever recorded in Scotland at that time. The converts were many and there is evidence today of this spiritual heritage in many of the local towns and villages with Scriptures engraved in the town squares, on plaques and harbour walls. And this was the place God's zig-zag had brought us to.

Today, Blairmore House, apart from having been the ancestral home of David Cameron, the former British Prime Minister, whose father was born there before it became a school, now has an international ministry that is touching the world. I cannot go to Blairmore House without being deeply touched in my Spirit by the lengths that God took to get us there. What a privilege it is to be playing a small part in the answers to the Duchess of Gordon's prayers. One day the whole of this wonderful story will be published and be an inspiration and encouragement to all who read it.

It is impossible to include in this book even a sample of the numerous stories of lives which have been touched and transformed at Blairmore House. In many ways, Blairmore House is a secret place, hidden away in the Highlands, where people can come apart for a while and meet with God in strategic ways. Although it is used for Healing Retreats it is also used specifically for Leaders Retreats and for times of inspiration and strategy.

The journey from Kincraig to Blairmore House was one of the most spiritually challenging possible, but it was also an even steeper learning curve for me in trusting God yet more – knowing that, even when it seems like His purposes are being thwarted, God is in reality working out His purposes. We need not fear even if, on occasions, we have to walk away from the place of God's previous provision to avoid the compromise of denying the Word of God.

And one of the most remarkable aspects of the work at Blairmore House is that it is now the home of the annual *Intercessors for Israel* prayer conference – complimenting the parallel event that meets every year in Jerusalem. That could never have happened at Kilravock Castle!

Chapter 22

AFRICAN DAWN

Taking the Message Home

E ven though I was born and brought up in England, my South African, Huguenot heritage has always been an important part of who I am. I will always be grateful to those pioneering French Huguenots, for whom trust in God and faithfulness to His Word was everything. Hundreds of thousands of them lost their lives for their faith and thousands more fled France, with little more than the clothes on their backs, to start a new life in other parts of the world. Wherever they went, their faith went with them and in South Africa the Huguenot families put a straight edge of spiritual steel into the developing nation for which I have deep personal reasons to be thankful. There are many times when I have been acutely aware of that godly heritage, especially when it was necessary to push through against spiritual opposition, and ever since the work of Ellel Ministries began to flourish it was my dream that, one day, I would be privileged to take back to my maternal ancestral 'home' the fruit of my own generational background.

1986 was a vintage year for the birthing of new and potentially significant Ministries. It was a season of new beginnings. In the UK, for example, not only Ellel Ministries, but also UCB (United Christian Broadcasters) and Sovereign World Ltd (Christian Publishers) were founded in 1986. And in South Africa *Telefriend* was first introduced to the South African public by Derek and Beryl Puffett as a new Christian telephone helpline. Down the years I have come across many Christian organisations, especially those concerned with some aspect of the healing and counselling ministries, who date their origin to that particular period of the twentieth century.

Derek Puffett had been a businessman, living and working at Windhoek in Namibia (formerly South West Africa) for a motoring supplies company. Even though he and Beryl were not yet believers, their compassion for people in need led them to establish *Lifeline*, a telephone counselling service for people who were struggling with personal problems. But Derek was soon out of his depth and late one night, while trying to help someone, he realised that what he was doing was really God's work and he needed to know God for himself! So he began his own search for answers to the key questions about life and about God. He went from church to church, asking minister after minister to tell him how to get closer to God. To his utter amazement, none of them could answer his question!

But he knew that there must be answers out there – somewhere, and even though he didn't yet know the Lord, he began to formulate the structure of an organisation he'd like to set up, which would provide the answers to his own, and many other, questions! If the ministers couldn't give him the answers, he determined that once having found them for himself, he'd find a way of providing those answers for other people as well!

His company then moved him to Pretoria, in South Africa, where, mercifully, he did find a church where the minister could answer his questions and he, together with his wife Beryl, came to personal faith in Jesus through the ministry of Pastor Ed Roebert at Hatfield Christian Church. His son Michael had been invited to a youth camp with Hatfield and was the first member of the family to really meet the Lord. On his return all the family saw the difference in him. Beryl's personal transformation took place at a morning ladies meeting and a couple of months later Beryl invited the area pastor of Hatfield for tea. Derek was like fruit 'ripe for the picking' and it only took the pastor a few minutes to lead Derek to the Lord. Then, with his own natural evangelistic gifting, Derek was able to lead their daughter, Janine, to the Lord. 1982 was the turning point in the Puffett household.

It wasn't long afterwards that Derek honoured the promise he'd made to himself (and, unknowingly at the time, to the Lord) that once having got the answers, he'd help provide them for others also. And so the ministry of *Telefriend* was born in 1986 at almost exactly the same time as God was birthing Ellel Ministries in the UK! The aim of *Telefriend* was to give telephone callers in need the answers to their problems from God's Word, and to pray with them over the phone.

Telefriend took off – and before very long there were *Telefriend* Centres all over the country, answering thousands of calls from desperate people in need. Derek eventually resigned his day-job and responded to a full-time call to become part of the leadership of Hatfield Christian Church. He was ordained as Pastor by Pastor Ed Roebert and given responsibility for a mixed race congregation in the City Centre of Pretoria.

Almost exactly fifty years earlier my own mother, Betty Lane, a South African by birth, was married to Fred Horrobin – also in the centre of Pretoria, at the Methodist Church. For obvious reasons, therefore, I regularly dreamt, envisioned and prayed about the possibility of seeing a work of Ellel Ministries established in South Africa. When I was nineteen I visited the country on my first long vacation from University. I was powerfully envisioned by both my family's history, and also by working for a while with a small South African General Mission team in Swaziland while I was there.

During the early years of Ellel Ministries, several Christian leaders from South Africa visited Ellel Grange and experienced something of what God was doing. They all urged Ellel Ministries to consider opening a Centre in the country, because the deep needs of their hurting country were so huge. But it's not easy to do that without having strong connections with people on the ground, who could and would carry the vision forward – people who are committed to persevere in establishing the work. The right relationships had to be made and built.

Chris Mungeam, who had already had a significant influence on the growth of Ellel Ministries through *Sovereign World Ltd* and the *Battle Belongs to the Lord* conference, had strong links to key people in South Africa through his publishing connections – including with Ed Roebert and the remarkable work that was going on through Ed at Hatfield Church. Ed had written a book for Chris in the Sovereign World *Explaining Series*. At that time Hatfield was becoming famous across the world as a Church where the Spirit of God was moving powerfully. So Chris and Jan invited Fiona and me to accompany them to South Africa on an exploratory visit, to see what doors God might open up for Ellel along the way.

And so it was that we also got to know Ed and Pal Roebert, and Ed introduced us to some of the other leaders at Hatfield with an interest in counselling. Derek Puffett was one of those who were present at the meeting and his heart was touched by what I shared about establishing centres for bringing hope and healing to hurting people. It was exactly what God had put in his own heart for *Telefriend*. The wind of God was blowing and the Maker of all things was nurturing the seeds that were being sown (Ecclesiastes 11:5-6). He was putting embryonic relationships in place, through which He would build His Kingdom. But while it was a good visit to South Africa, which we enjoyed immensely and some important connections and relationships were made, nothing immediately transpired.

But God has a way of using even the smallest of contacts to be the bridge to His eventual purposes being fulfilled. *Telefriend,* was growing rapidly and the needs of the people who called in on the telephone lines were now overwhelming. Derek knew that he needed to extend the work into a face-to-face prayer and counselling ministry, but he had no experience at all of how to do it. He needed help to find a way forward.

One day, while Derek was on a mission in Lesotho, he got a call from Ed Roebert asking if he and Beryl would like to go to the UK to attend the Alpha Conference at Holy Trinity Brompton, with the intention of bringing the Alpha ministry back to Hatfield. Derek jumped at the opportunity. It only later dawned on him that he could perhaps make contact with Ellel at the same time, not even knowing where Ellel Grange was in the UK!

A friend, however, had gently cautioned them about going to Ellel Grange *"because they did deliverance"*, but that actually delighted Derek and Beryl. They already knew that deliverance needed to be an essential part of a Christian healing ministry – especially in Africa! In those days many leaders in the UK considered the work of Ellel to be very much on or beyond the fringe of mainline church activity, even though many of their people were coming to Ellel for the personal help and training that wasn't available in their local church. But as far as Derek was concerned, we had seemed to be decent enough people when they met us in South Africa, so he took the risk of giving Ellel Grange a call and asking if he and Beryl could come and visit.

The answer was an immediate '*Yes*' and when we all met and began to talk, we all knew that, somehow or other, this almost casual meeting at Ellel Grange, was the link that Derek needed. Here he found that the training in face-to-face counselling for his *Telehelpers* was available and at the same time God was introducing us to the very people who would eventually establish the work of Ellel Ministries in South Africa. God was working out His purposes in His own unique way! (Job 42:2 and Romans 8:28). Fiona and I also knew that Derek and Beryl would become good friends. We were immediately at one with them in heart and purpose.

Also staying at Ellel Grange at that time was another healing ministries pioneer, Harold Dewberry, from the USA. At breakfast, the next morning, Derek and Beryl were introduced to Harold, who gave them an autographed copy of his book, *'Feed my Sheep, Feed my Lambs'*. Gratefully they accepted this gift, little knowing how that title, in the following hour, was to play such a huge part in confirming their calling from the Lord.

What Derek and Beryl experienced at Ellel Grange was exactly in line with their own vision – except for the magnitude of it all! It was far bigger than anything they had ever dreamt of. They had a lot to think and pray about and went back to their room bewildered. Their minds were spinning, almost out of control. *"God, what are you saying to us?"* they asked.

Beryl lay on the bed and Derek sat on a chair under the window and as they were praying, *"Lord, please speak to us"*, Derek had Harold Dewberry's book on his lap, *'Feed my Sheep, Feed my Lambs'*. The title was screaming at them! Then the most amazing event took place. Suddenly, there was a huge commotion outside their window, which overlooked the surrounding fields. It was the sound of sheep bleating. The bleating became so loud and distressed, that both Derek and Beryl got up to see what was wrong. There at the boundary fence of the adjacent farm were about seventy sheep, all of them bleating loudly, and all of them looking straight up at their window!

At that moment the presence of the Lord came down upon them and they burst into tears as they realized that God was speaking to them personally and saying, *"Feed my sheep, feed my lambs."* There was nothing more they could say or do. And at that moment there was nothing else they wanted to say or do, but to savour the moment, hoping it would never go away. God was speaking loud and clear, *"I want you to go back to South Africa and to feed my sheep and feed my lambs."* It was one of the most powerful God moments in their whole life.

They sat in silence during their return train journey to London's Heathrow Airport. The presence of the Lord was still so tangible that talking would have ruined the moment. They'd never heard before of God speaking to anyone through a flock of sheep and the title of a book! Their call to be part of Ellel Ministries was solidly confirmed. Ellel had the training courses that Derek was looking for and in Derek and Beryl, God had leaders who knew the need and had a strong reason to take the vision forward. Plans were immediately drawn up for another visit to South Africa and a series of *Telefriend* Healing Conferences took place in Johannesburg, Durban and Cape Town. These conferences proved to be the foundation of the work of Ellel Ministries in South Africa.

Derek and Beryl both knew that they had a lot to learn in order to take the work forward, so, after much prayer, fasting and counsel from different spiritual leaders in the community, they resigned their job as Pastors at Hatfield and entered into, perhaps for the very first time in their lives, a real walk of faith. Even at the time of their calling to be Pastors, they were both aware that they were entering a season of training for the unknown work that God was preparing them for.

They went to Pierrepont to start their training on NETS in June 2000. They spent fourteen months there, followed by four months *'on the ground'* training with the team at Ellel Grange. At the end of that time Derek and Beryl returned to South Africa to await God's leading as to the way forward for both *Telefriend* and Ellel Ministries, with a sensing from the Lord that initially they were not to contact anyone, but trust God for Him to show the way.

But on their return, one person after another contacted them to offer their help, and before long they had an emerging team of supporters who were looking to Derek and Beryl to lead them in both the development of *Telefriend* and the establishment of Ellel Ministries in South Africa. At that time Derek and Beryl were working out of their own home. From here they pioneered a ten day Ellel Training School in Muldersdrift, near Johannesburg, and various other events, all of which served to create a hunger and a need for a physical Centre. They saw much healing taking place, including the physical healing of a young woman with a deformed neck in much the same way as God had healed Lynda in Australia. God was getting people's attention.

The work needed a base from which to operate – it had already outgrown Derek and Beryl's home – and so Fiona and I travelled to South Africa for a few days to look at a place that Derek and Beryl were considering as an office and base for the work. But it was obviously far too small for the size of the work that would be necessary to service the needs of this large and very hurting nation. As soon as we walked into the place the Lord told me this was an *'Ishmael'* and we had to look for the *'Isaac'*! We had to gently lift Derek and Beryl's eyes to a larger horizon and encourage them to look for a much bigger place! After teaching at various events, we only had one day left to look for *'the Isaac'*, so I asked Derek to find a property agent who would drive us around a few larger properties, within what they thought would be a sensible price band and distance from the centre of Pretoria.

The agent took us way out into the countryside to see some pretty, but very remote buildings, but they were all set in land that would be very difficult to manage and maintain or keep secure. Nothing available seemed suitable and everyone was getting frustrated. The day was passing and in a very short time we would need to be heading back to the airport for our flight home. Time was of the essence. So I asked the agent to forget the price band Derek was thinking of, and show us anything that would be much more suitable for the work we wanted to do.

He immediately headed back towards Pretoria and we entered an area where there were a number of large, well-fenced and secure properties. One of them was for sale, and as we drove through the gates of Shere House, and into the secure environment of a very unusual and beautiful property, peace descended and we all knew that Ellel had *'come home'* – this was it!

The owner of the property was contacted and within twenty minutes the future destiny of Shere House was settled. Notwithstanding the fact that at that time Ellel South Africa had absolutely zero funds available, a price was agreed and we headed off for the airport, leaving a totally stunned Derek and Beryl holding the biggest baby imaginable and with the seemingly insurmountable problem of finding the money to pay for it all! But God really was in charge.

When we shared the vision for the work in South Africa, some significant donations came into the ministry from supporters in the UK. And these, together with donations from South Africa, and a serviceable mortgage, ensured that the agreement to buy the property was fully honoured on time. Shere House not only became the headquarters for the work of Ellel Ministries in South Africa, but eventually Derek was invited to join the Executive Leadership of the ministry and he became the Regional Director of the work throughout Africa (South of the Sahara), and Beryl became the Centre Director of Ellel South Africa.

A few years ago Fiona visited South Africa to lead the first *Healing Through Creativity* course at Shere House. It was an amazing time when God broke through the barriers of people's hearts in extraordinary ways. During one of the workshop times, an artist friend of the ministry came to Shere House, unannounced, loaded with painting materials she wanted to donate to the ministry. She brought with her a friend, and, completely unknown to this friend, they were on the way to the very house she and her husband had built many years previously. As they walked round Shere House, seeing what God was doing through the Creativity course, her friend couldn't fight back the tears. She was openly crying.

When she was asked what was happening to her, she told of how she and her husband had built the first house on this piece of land. Then they had to leave because of her husband's business interests and the property was sold to the people from whom Ellel eventually bought it. She then explained that she had really loved the place and didn't want to leave, but before she did so she prayed right round the property, giving it into the Lord's hands and praying that one day it would be used for the healing of God's people!

In just the same way as had happened in Hungary, God had led us to a property that had already been prayed over and set aside in God for the very work that Ellel was now doing in that very place! Once again we were experiencing how the extraordinary hand of God will go ahead of us, preparing the way for what He wants us to do. What the lady saw on that day was an exact fulfilment of what she had been led by the Lord to pray for. No wonder she was crying – she was walking in the destiny that had been facilitated by her own prayers.

It was no surprise, therefore, that even though Shere House was vastly bigger than anything Derek and Beryl had dreamt of, when we first stepped on the land, we were all immediately at peace that this was the place God had chosen! God's people had gone before and prepared the way for a work that now has significant influence across the whole continent.

Today, Shere House is bulging with people of all races coming on courses, *Healing Retreats* and *Training Schools*. The property is positioned half way between the City of Pretoria and the huge African Township of Mamelodi. The walls of separation are coming down as black and white learn and grow together. Teams go out from Shere House to places as far afield as Rwanda, Kenya, Ghana, Zimbabwe, Botswana and Mozambique, with remarkable fruit. God has so blessed the work that urgent plans are now being put in place to significantly expand the accommodation available.

A businessman travelled to Shere House from Namibia. Having seen what God was doing there, he was convinced that if the employees of his company were saved, and healed of their past hurts, his staff would be more dedicated and efficient. So, after learning what Ellel was all about, he sent twelve of his staff to the next ten-day course. They weren't all Christians when they came, but they all were when they went back! The effect on their company's atmosphere, efficiency and profitability has been huge! The Gospel is going into the market-place and changing lives.

Now Derek is taking the foundational discipleship training into local churches, with a whole year's programme called '*Growing Seeds Discipleship Course for Cell Groups*', using my *Living the Life* and *Truth and Freedom* DVDs. The testimonies coming back are profound – including from the local prisons where the DVDs are having a major impact and prisoners themselves are then becoming pastors to other inmates, using the Ellel materials to teach and minister. The work is growing beyond all expectation, because the need is so great. God has heard the cries of the hurting and the broken in Africa, and is answering their prayers.

So often, we have seen how one step of obedience leads to hidden fruit in years to come as new strands of destiny are established in the lives of others. God used that very first Ellel/Telefriend conference at Durban, in what is now KwaZulu Natal, to impact many people's lives, including Ken and Joy Rowat, who are now the Directors of Ellel South Africa's second centre in Durban, and a young man who came as a member of the young people's team at Pierrepont and is now our son-in-law! Who knows what stories the succeeding generations will have to tell?!

When Shere House became not only the headquarters of Ellel Ministries in South Africa, but the regional base for the work of Ellel Ministries across the whole of Africa south of the Sahara, God challenged Derek to look at the map of Africa and ask Him where He wanted Ellel Ministries to go first. Derek's attention was grabbed by the smallest nation on the map, Rwanda, famous as the source of the River Nile but infamous as the place where a million people lost their lives in the Hutu-Tutsi inter-tribal genocide that took place in the early nineteen-nineties. Rwanda was one of the most spiritually devastated places in the world and in desperate need.

Our first contact with Rwanda was through Frida, a Rwandan Tutsi who had been buried alive with fifteen dead members of her family. Someone sat on the shallow grave, into which all the massacred bodies had been thrown, and heard a noise from below. They quickly dug up the grave and found 13 year-old Frida, still alive. It was a remarkable escape. She fled the land and eventually, in Gabon, found the Lord. By then the genocide was over and having read in the Bible that Jesus wanted us to forgive those who had hurt us, she went to the gaol, where the man who had murdered her own family was now in prison, to forgive him.

Eventually Frida came to the UK to train in healing and counselling so she could help her own people. But thirteen years after the event she was still suffering the constant headaches and nightly traumas associated with what happened when her killers thought she was dead and threw her in the grave. On a 9-week school at Ellel Grange, God totally healed her through the teaching and ministry on accident and trauma. The following morning she reported having had the first nightmare-free sleep since the event and the constant headache, in the place where she had been hit on the back of her head, had gone!

Not only was God drawing Derek's attention to this tiny but very hurting nation, but the Archbishop of Rwanda, Emmanuel Kolini, was also desperate to find answers for his people and when visiting the UK for the Lambeth Conference of Bishops and Achbishops, he sought me out at Ellel Pierrepont and we spent a day together sharing hearts, healing principles and vision for his nation. He totally understood the need for teaching and ministry on healing and deliverance and invited us to go to Rwanda and begin a work in his country.

That first visit to Rwanda, with a combined English and South African team, will never be erased from my memory. As a Hutu man translated Frida's Tutsi testimony, the Spirit of God came down on the place where we were meeting and also, I believe, on the nation. It was an extraordinary time of teaching and ministry as one person after another came and nailed the names of those they wanted to forgive to a large wooden cross. God's presence was tangible and the foundations of a major work were being established.

God then called Lambert Bariho to head up the work in Rwanda under the covering and leadership of Ellel South Africa. Lambert, with his American fiancée Catherine, spent a year at Shere House in training and today they are heading up a remarkable and very dynamic work that is touching the nation at every level, including government leaders who are seeing that only God has answers for the devastation of their nation.

Rwanda is just one of the many African nations that God is now touching through the work of Ellel South Africa. When God told Derek and Beryl to *"feed my sheep, feed my lambs"* they had no idea how big a flock God wanted them to have care of. Now a new generation of leaders has grown up and taken on the responsibilities for both the centre in Pretoria and the work across the African continent. No-one could have envisaged what would be the eventual fruit of Derek's obedience in starting *Telefriend* back in 1986!

What about *Telefriend* now? Well, it's still taking in the calls from people all over the country, people who are looking for God's help in their lives. But *Telefriend* and Ellel Ministries have now joined forces and are two arms of one ministry, building God's Kingdom truths into the lives of His people across the nation.

There are many chapters yet to be written of the developing work across the continent of Africa. For me it is a huge encouragement to see that Ellel Ministries is returning blessings to the land for which I, personally, am so grateful. What an amazing God we serve!

Chapter 23

BEYOND MY WILDEST DREAMS

Hope and Healing for the Chinese Peoples

O ne of my main objectives in writing this book has been to illustrate the amazing providence of God in preparing things in advance in order to fulfil His purposes. These strands of destiny that can be traced down the generation lines are a constant reminder that the ways of the Lord are, indeed, not our ways and that it is only in retrospect that we can see the extraordinary care with which God prepares people and circumstances for what is His will and purpose.

One of my favourite pictures is a painting called *'Simeon's Moment'* which beautifully illustrates that moment when the aged prophet recognises the baby he has spent all his life waiting for, and makes that Holy Spirit inspired declaration to a waiting world that *"my eyes have seen your salvation, which you have prepared in the sight of all people, a light for revelation to the Gentiles and for glory to your people Israel."* (Luke 2:30-32). Simeon had been prepared by the Lord over a lifetime for that startling moment when he walked on the stage of history to declare to Gentiles and Jews alike that God's salvation had come.

This principle, of God's providence in advance, is wonderfully expressed by Paul in the early chapters of his letter to the Ephesians when he said, *"For we are God's workmanship, created in Christ Jesus to do good works, which God prepared in advance for us to do"* (Ephesians 2:10). This principle is, perhaps, most strongly illustrated in my own experience through the work of Ellel Ministries that is now growing rapidly throughout the Chinese peoples of East Asia and, most remarkably, within mainland China itself.

On the 18th July 1993 I stood before a congregation of Chinese people crowded into a small church in Rawang, a small town about an hour East of Kuala Lumpur in Malaysia. The tears were pouring down my face as I looked at this wall of Chinese faces who were listening intently to every word I was saying. I had no idea why I was crying – for it didn't seem as though they were my own tears – and I didn't really know whether these were tears of pain or tears of joy, so intense were the feelings I was going through. While I was speaking to the people with conscious endeavour, I was, at the same time, speaking with God and asking Him what was happening.

God's answer was spoken right into my spirit as He told me, *"You are part of the answer to the prayers of your Uncle Will."* For a moment those tears became uncontrollable as a deep knowing descended on me and I understood, probably for the first time, that when we enter the eternal dimension through intercessory prayer, and pray the will of God, those prayers remain in place in the timelessness of eternity, enabling the release of God's power from eternity into time. At that moment I was experiencing both the release of God's power and the immediacy of His presence as the reality of Uncle Will's ninety-nine year old prayers was empowering me to speak out truths which would, in time, impact a whole nation. It's little wonder that for a moment those tears were uncontrollable.

The story goes back to 1894 when Uncle Will, as a young man, was being impacted by news reports from China about the work of Hudson Taylor and the China Inland Mission (CIM). Copies of *China's Millions*, the monthly journal of the mission, were circulating in the Churches, providing precious information from a very far off land as an encouragement to both prayer and giving. Uncle Will's local church, St Peter's, Halliwell, Bolton, was a seriously mission-minded congregation and there was only encouragement when the young Will suggested that they should start a prayer meeting for the CIM. That simple act established a prayer meeting that was to meet, under Uncle Will's leadership, every single month until Uncle Will died in 1960.

There were three people that I know of, present at that first meeting: Will (my great uncle), his brother Fred (my grandfather), and William Grundy, who became known in the family as Uncle Grundy. Uncle Grundy was to become the first of several people from that meeting who would offer as missionaries to serve with CIM in China. Years later, when sorting through some second-hand books in my shop, I came across bound copies of *China's Millions* which contained mention of William Grundy's service in China. The headquarters records of the CIM describe how William Grundy had been influenced by the preaching of William T Horrobin – Uncle Will! William Grundy sailed for China from Liverpool, with a group of other new missionaries, on 26 September 1895 on board the SS *Valetta*, which was the first ever passenger vessel to have electric lighting! The CIM party of nine new recruits and three returning missionaries, arrived in Shanghai on 11 November 1895.

Uncle Will and my grandfather were at Liverpool docks to watch the *Valetta* set sail and here it was that they gave Uncle Grundy a gold ring, inscribed with all their initials, which was, in effect, a prayer covenant ring, as Will and Fred committed to pray for him throughout his years of service for the Lord. When William

Grundy finally retired he sent the ring back to my Grandfather in thanksgiving for all the prayers that had released God's hand of protection upon him. He even survived imprisonment in the Boxer rebellion, during which 127 CIM missionaries lost their lives. The ring had been hung round his neck in prison, beneath his shirt, and was never discovered by the Boxers, who had stolen every single other thing that the missionaries possessed.

Many years later, long after my experience at Rawang, as I was teaching on the history of Christian missions to NETS students at Ellel Pierrepont, I suddenly came under conviction of the Holy Spirit that I was to find that ring, which I knew was somewhere among my father's personal possessions, and wear it as a constant reminder of the call of God upon my life, and upon Ellel Ministries as a result, and I still wear it to this day – a daily reminder to pray for the work in China.

Our journey of providence, from Ellel Grange to Rawang, came through the agency of Wong Kim Kong. Kim Kong was the Director of *Malaysia Care*, a Malaysian Christian Charity in Kuala Lumpur, the capital of Malaysia. He had read an account of the developing work of Ellel Ministries and was keen to invite me and the team to come to Malaysia to teach on deliverance. But he first took the trouble to come to Ellel Grange and see for himself what God was doing. Kim Kong was influential among the evangelical Christian leaders of Malaysia, and felt he would have considerable support in the country for a deliverance ministry course, which he would organise at his home church in Rawang.

In the Asian environment there is a much greater awareness of the demonic, the powers of darkness and the need for deliverance than there was at that time in the West. So, a few months later, an Ellel team headed east, for their first venture into Asia, to conduct a special course on *Healing and Deliverance*. Such was the interest in the course that people came from all over the country, including a number of key and influential church and business leaders. It was on the first day of this course, that I found myself trying to fight back the tears. For all the reasons explained above, standing in front of all those Chinese faces was a very emotional and deeply spiritual moment.

Many lives were impacted by the Lord at Rawang. There was much healing and deliverance and such was the blessing that God poured out on the people that there were many invitations to members of the team to teach in different areas of Malaysia and East Asia. Conferences and schools have taken place many times in Kuala Lumpur, Penang, Singapore and Sabah in West Malaysia. Vincent and Orwan Lau joined forces with Linda Tang and established Rapha Ministries in Kuala Lumpur, largely using Ellel's teaching and ministry principles. Today, Linda is the Director of the new Ellel Centre in Kuala Lumpur. Florence Wang, a medical professor in Kuala Lumpur, with her brother Paul in Sabah and his wife Cathy, strongly supported the ministry.

With Paul and Cathy's encouragement the work in Sabah began to flourish and had a significant impact among the Churches, not least of which was All Saints Anglican Cathedral. Succeeding Bishops have seen the work of Ellel Ministries as a significant and beneficial influence in the diocese. The most recent Bishop, Albert Vun, first experienced the ministry when a team visited his congregation on the East of Sabah (the old North Borneo) at St.Patrick's Church, Tauwau. Bishop Vun instituted Ellel training courses for all the clergy in his diocese! Sadly, Bishop Vun died in 2014, but he has left behind a remarkable legacy of commitment to the ministry of healing and deliverance across his large diocese.

Sabah stands at the northern tip of the island of Borneo. Over the years there have been major revivals in the island among the indigenous peoples and some of the most exciting stories of God at work, in the power of the Spirit, emanate from here. Some of these indigenous leaders were present at a very special 10-day school, held at the *Beringgis Hotel*, just south of Kota Kinabalu and financially sponsored by one of the businessmen who had been present at Rawang. All the local churches were well represented.

There was a young Anglican priest on the school called Kenneth Thien. He and his wife Ying had been married seven years and were unable to conceive a child. They had been given no medical hope of ever being able to have a baby of their own. But during the Beringgis school they were prayed for, for healing and deliverance. Four years later I was back in Kota Kinabalu at a Pastors and leaders meeting. Unexpectedly, there was a young child present at this leaders meeting. Kenneth and Ying had brought their miraculous daughter, Zachariah who, in spite of the medical impossibility, had been conceived and safely delivered less than a year after the Beringgis school. They brought Zachariah to the meeting to express their thanksgivings to the Lord for his goodness. Today Kenenth Thien is still a priest within the Diocese of Sabah, but he was also the first National Director of the work of Ellel Ministries across Malaysia.

Many other people were deeply touched by what God did at the school and today there is a significant work right across Sabah as a result. The work in Sabah is now under the leadership of Kenneth's brother, Thomas. Prayer Support Groups in both East and West Malaysia have supported the work there for many years and have faithfully met month on month, undergirding both the local and the international work.

On a visit to Singapore I spoke at a special healing service in St Andrew's Cathedral. Present was a young married couple who already had a heart for the healing ministry. Titus was then an Ordained Deacon in the Diocese of Singapore and his wife, Esther, was working on the pastoral staff of the Cathedral. God lit a flame in their hearts for the work of Ellel Ministries, which has become a forest fire sweeping through the lives of Chinese people all over East Asia.

Prior to joining the Cathedral staff, Titus was on his Sabbatical leave from his previous church, and decided to go to the UK for the NETS training school at Ellel Pierrepont. Later having served at the Cathedral the Lord led Esther to prepare for the new season. She resigned from the Cathedral and became the founder of Ellel Singapore and with her dynamic, unstoppable faith she set about establishing the ministry on Singapore Island.

The work quickly grew and as part of her vision for training many Chinese people, Esther pioneered a new form of one or two-week schools for hundreds of people at a time. To each of these schools Jill Southern took a team of teachers from the UK. To date these schools have taken place in Singapore, Malaysia, Thailand and Hong Kong. The work in Singapore now has a considerable infrastructure, running a continuous series of Healing Retreats and Training Courses, but Esther's eyes have been lifted to the more distant horizon of mainland China!

Here, the house church has grown to be a huge spiritual force within the nation, but they are also a suffering and persecuted church. The era of Hudson Taylor and the CIM put down remarkable and solid foundations in the hearts of Chinese leaders all over the nation. That generation paid a heavy price for the fruit of blessing. Hundreds paid the ultimate price as they lost their lives for the sake of the Kingdom of God. The blood of the martyrs was thick upon the land.

Then came the rise of Chinese communism, which brought with it total hatred of believers and the elimination of all evidences of Christianity across the nation. CIM, and other missionaries were expelled from the nation in 1949, and driven out of the land across the borders. One of those who had gone out to China as a result of Uncle Will's prayer meeting was shot dead as she was making her escape across the border into Thailand.

But the Gospel cannot be eliminated by any governmental edict.

You may be able to drive missionaries out of the land, but you cannot drive Christ out of the hearts of those who know Him. The church went underground and in the pressurised circumstances of opposition and persecution, instead of disappearing forever, the people found and knew their God in a deeper way than ever before. There are hundreds of horrific stories of what believers suffered, but nevertheless the hidden church grew and today, seventy years after the Communist government attempted to eliminate God and his followers from their land, there are more believers than ever before. In December 2011 over 600 leaders from underground churches and official churches all over China, made their way across the recently opened border with Hong Kong and gathered in the Hong Kong YMCA for the most intensive period of training Ellel Ministries has ever conducted.

The delegates were only able to enter Hong Kong for seven nights and they wanted to learn every single thing they could while they were there. Teaching and ministry sessions began at 8.00am in the morning and didn't finish until 10.00pm. By the time that week was over we were totally exhausted. But a massive deposit of truth had been left in the hearts of all those people, which they could then use to minister to their own people across all the provinces of China.

While the tears had poured down my cheeks at Rawang, when I first spoke to a Chinese congregation, the school in Hong Kong was of a dimension that could never have been thought of or anticipated. It was no longer tears that were flowing, but the beating of God's heart for His people in China was thumping in my spirit. The blood of the martyrs had been on the land, but now the power of the blood of the Lord Jesus was washing people clean and through healing and deliverance their lives were being transformed and they were being equipped to bring hope and healing to the suffering church in China. As I looked at the ring on my finger and thought back to that day in 1895 when William Grundy had sailed for Shanghai, I marvelled once again at the ways of the Lord and gave thanks for raising up Esther and Titus as truth and light bearers into the great land of China.

Today there is a greater open-ness once again to the Gospel in the land and Esther's vision is for an Ellel Centre in every one of the 23 provinces of China, Hong Kong (Special Administrative Region) as well as in Taiwan, the former offshore Chinese province. In July 2014, Titus was released by the Bishop of the Anglican Church in Singapore, and was seconded to Ellel Singapore as the full-time Centre Director, thus releasing Esther into her wider vision for the Chinese peoples in every country in the region and, especially, in China itself.

There already is an Ellel Ministries presence in three of those provinces and preparations are now in place to establish the first Training and Retreat Centre (City Of Refuge) in the country.

Fiona and I had visited Hong Kong on several occasions, usually en route to events in Australia. There were some very memorable moments, especially when teaching and ministering with Jackie Pullinger-To at Hang Fook Camp. On one occasion, Jackie asked if we would pray with a friend of hers, a lady Baptist minister from the USA, who was chronically fatigued, unable to function properly and had to be constantly drinking water.

As Fi prayed with Becky, God showed how, as a baby, she had been severely neglected and traumatised. In the core of her being, she was still suffering the deprivation of an exhausted and thirsty little baby. She had managed to override the symptoms for most of her life, but for the past seven years symptoms of exhaustion and fatigue had overwhelmed her. As Fi and the team ministered to Becky, God healed the hidden trauma of her childhood. The transformation in her symptoms was instant. She went from being totally exhausted to being full of energy and the next day went with us on a seventeen hour prayer trip, walking across the border into mainland China!

In 1996 Jackie Pullinger was the main speaker at the Blackpool Ellel Conference, *Into All the World*. Her uncompromising message, calling complacent Christians to the reality of missionary service still stirs the heart of those who were there to hear her speak or have listened to the recordings.

In Taiwan, the work of Ellel Ministries has been well established in and through some large local Churches. The Senior Pastor of the *Truth Lutheran Church*, Peter Yang, has supported many students in their training on the NETS School at Pierrepont. Through their agency, all the notes for the school are now available in Mandarin and there have been special Chinese Nets schools at Pierrepont, when all the teaching is translated simultaneously for non-English speakers. Such has been the fruit of the ministry in Taiwan, that all the two thousand strong members of the church are now encouraged to go through an Ellel style Healing Retreat, as part of their journey of Christian discipleship.

An Anglican leader in Bangkok, Thailand, had been sceptical of Jill's teaching on deliverance and was reluctant to let her teach it but, after examining the notes, agreed to let it go ahead. Not long afterwards, this same priest experienced problems with one of his own people, who was having severe, out-of-control, demonic manifestations and he didn't know what to do. His Bishop requested Titus and Esther to go and help, which they did. In a very short time the root of the problem was identified, deliverance took place and the woman was restored and in her right mind. Subsequently, she was baptised and together with her church leaders they went to her village to destroy her tribal dance headgear and other occult objects. The evidence of God's healing love is not only life-transforming, it is also opening the eyes of leaders to the dynamic reality of the presence and power of God.

Today, God is raising up a major work through Ellel Ministries among the Chinese peoples of the world. The Singapore team are running the race hard as they redeem the time and seek to serve their own people across the whole region with the dynamic message of the Gospel, bringing hope and healing to a people, many of whom have suffered greatly for their faith.

Chapter 24

ISRAEL

Into the Land Where Jesus Walked

Before the work started, opening the mail was always an exciting experience as we waited on God for the funds to buy Ellel Grange. You never knew what would be in the next envelope. One of the greatest surprises and blessings came in a letter from Christ Church in Jerusalem, with a £3000 donation from the Rector of the only Anglican Church within the walls of the Old City. It was an extraordinary donation from a remarkable source which I have never forgotten. Even before Ellel Grange had been purchased God was speaking to me that one day the work that He was establishing would have a presence in Israel, the land where Jesus walked, though it would be many years before this generous piece of 'bread', that had been cast upon the waters would return to the Land (Ecclesiastes 11:1).

Paul's words in Romans 1:16, that the gospel is the *'power of God for the salvation of everyone who believes: first for the Jew and then for the Gentile'* had always been an important foundation stone of my theology. The Gospel came to the Jews first – and even though the majority of Jews have, to date, rejected their Messiah, the time would come when Ezekiel's prophecy would be fulfilled and God would gather his people from all the countries to which they had been scattered and, in the land, give them *"a new heart and a new spirit"* (see Ezekiel 36:24-38).

In 1948 there was a miraculous move of God at the United Nations in New York, as Israel was once again established as a sovereign, independent nation in the land of promise. And, ever since, Jews from all over the world have continued to 'make aliyah', returning to their own land from the countries to which they had been scattered, to make their homes once again in Israel. The terrible holocaust of the Second World War and the continuing rise of anti-Semitism, in the twentieth and twenty first centuries, has hastened the flow of returning Jews to the land of Israel.

But in parallel with this extraordinary twentieth and twenty-first century migration, something else has been happening in the land of Israel – exactly as Ezekiel said it would. Jews are coming to know Jesus (Yeshua) in the land in increasing numbers as they finally discover that the Messiah of the Christians was indeed their Messiah first! Today, there are well over a hundred Messianic Congregations in the land with upwards of fifteen thousand Jewish believers experiencing what Paul described as *"life from the dead"* (Romans 11:15). And alongside these are many born again Arab believers also. Biblical prophecy is being fulfilled among all the different communities in Israel.

But I'm running ahead of myself! I need to go back to another letter I received from a Swiss business man, Gustav Scheller, back in the early nineties. Gustav was an extraordinary man. He and his wife Elsa not only knew the Scriptures about what God would do in the latter days to restore His people to the land of Israel, but they had also read that the Gentiles would be involved in helping the Jews to return to the land. Gustav was one of those who was prompted by the Lord to be an initiator of the process. So he started to put in motion a strategy for helping the Jews from the *land of the north* to make their way home (Jeremiah 31:8). He established the *Ebenezer Emergency Fund* to enable many thousands of Jews who were residing in the lands directly north of Israel (mainly from the former Soviet Union) to return home by ship and to re-settle in Israel, the Israeli Government making this possible to all who had proof of their Jewish origins. The work became known as *Operation Exodus*.

In founding what grew into an amazing work of God, in fulfilment of Scriptural prophecy, Gustav knew that he was about to start what he called 'a holy work' and he wanted to prepare himself spiritually for what lay ahead. Hence his letter, in which he explained that he wanted to spend time with me, praying through every area of his life and asking God for cleansing and healing. This was to be the first stage of his personal preparation for the holy work that lay ahead of him. My admiration for Gustav went sky high and I was convicted by the Lord as to how vital it is for those of us who are leaders to humble ourselves and receive preparation in a similar way, for whatever God has called us to do. For if God who is holy, has called us to do it, then it is, by definition, a holy work.

Many years later, I was privileged to be praying with Gustav again. This time he lay critically ill in hospital with terminal cancer. By then *Operation Exodus* had completed almost one hundred sailings from Odessa in Ukraine, to Haifa in Israel, with most sailings crowded to the limit with Jews leaving their Russian or Ukrainian homes and making aliyah to Israel. For Gustav, his earthly work was nearly over, but the fire of his vision was still burning as brightly as ever and his every thought was still concerned with the details of his pioneering work. In conversation I told him about our son Paul, a very talented photographer and film maker, and even though Gustav was seriously ill, he wanted Paul to visit him in hospital so Gustav could recruit Paul to go to the former Russian states and make films of the work! As a result, Paul spent seven precious years making films and serving the ministry in various capacities.

With the 100th sailing from Odessa to Haifa being imminent, Gustav invited Fiona and me to travel on the ship on this special sailing and get first-hand experience of what it was like for the Jewish people to make aliyah to Israel. What an extraordinary privilege it was to be on board that particular voyage. We were in the middle of the mandatory lifeboat drill when a Ukrainian Jewish lady looked up at Fiona and said, *"Why do I see love in your eyes? We are Jews and no-one loves us."* Fiona was able to reply, saying, *"We Christians worship the same God as the Jews and He has given us a love for you."* There were hundreds of returning Jews on the ship and I was able to make a personal video for Gustav of that very special 100th sailing. I just managed to get the video edited in time for Gustav to see it before he made his own aliyah to the place of his eternal destiny.

There must have been enormous joy in Heaven as Gustav was welcomed home, after spending the latter part of his life as one of those who enabled the fulfilment of Jeremiah's prophecy, *"'So then, the days are coming,' declares the Lord, when people will no longer say, 'As surely as the Lord lives, who brought the Israelites up out of Egypt,' but they will say, 'As surely as the Lord lives, who brought the descendants of Israel up out of the land of the north and out of all the countries where he had banished them.' Then they will live in their own land"* (Jeremiah 23:7-8).

It had been a deeply spiritual and emotional experience for Fiona and me, standing on deck, as the ship made its dawn landfall in Israel, with some of those who were about to start a new life, living in their own land, having come from 'the land of the north'. We were all welcomed to Israel with a dramatic sunrise over the mountains of Carmel, bathing the scene in liquid gold. As we walked down the gangway and put our feet down on Israeli soil, we both sensed it was something of a homecoming for us too. We were about to touch, for the first time physically, the Jewish roots of our faith.

That trip proved to be highly strategic for Ellel Ministries. God had used Gustav, right at the end of his life, to get us in the right place at the right time to hear the voice of God for a new season in the work of Ellel Ministries, serving the growing Body of Messiah in the land of Israel itself. Through the experiences and relationships made on that unforgettable trip, we became personal friends with many key leaders in the land or associated with the work of Operation Exodus, such as Eliyahu Ben Haim (*Intercessors for Israel*), Wayne Hilsden (Pastor of *King of Kings,* Jerusalem), Johannes Facius, Derek Prince and Murray Dixon (the then Rector of Christ Church, Jerusalem, and later a member of our Ellel team at Pierrepont until his retirement in 2016). All of these, and many others, became key supporters and influencers in the development of the work of Ellel Ministries in Israel. At a later date, Peter Tsukahira, Tony Sperandeo and Eitan Shishkov would become key advisers to our developing work. We have relied heavily on our local advisers to help us establish the ministry in fellowship and relationship with the local Body of Messiah.

These relationships deepened even further after Gustav died when I heard that Gustav had asked that I be invited to join the board of the *Ebenezer Emergency Fund*. God builds His Kingdom and fulfils His Kingdom purposes through relationships and I knew that God was using all these relationships to draw me and the work of Ellel into the land of Israel. But it had to be in God's way and in His timing and we were watching and waiting for what He was going to do next.

Let the Oppressed Go Free was the last international conference we held at the Brighton Centre, in 2001. Derek Prince had been instrumental in encouraging people to attend the *Battle Belongs to the Lord* with Bill Subritzky at the Brighton Centre over a decade previously and now we were privileged to have Derek Prince and Johannes Facius as two of our principal keynote speakers at another Brighton Conference. This also proved to be the last major conference at which Derek was able to be a speaker. Subsequent to that he generously wrote the *Foreword* to the revised edition of my book *Healing Through Deliverance*. But his health was beginning to fail and when he returned home to Israel, his adopted nation, it would be to a final season of his life which was devoted only to writing.

At the end of the conference Derek spoke to me privately about Israel, explaining that the Jewish people were the most rejected and hurting people in the world, surrounded by nations who want to obliterate them and a world in which anti-Semitic persecution was rising. *"Then,"* he said, *"the Messianic Jews who have recognised Yeshua (Jesus) as their Messiah are doubly rejected and hurting, because they have not only been rejected for being Jews, but are facing huge opposition from their own people also. They are desperately in need of healing."* Our conversation ended with Derek, who had lived in Israel for many years, asking us to bring the healing work of Ellel Ministries into the land of Israel itself. As we hugged each other and said farewell at the end of the conference, I knew what we had to do.

From this point on the doors began to open. First, in 2007, Eliyahu and Hanna Ben Haim, who had been constantly asking us to bring Ellel MInistries to Israel, conducted a private, eye-opening tour of Israel for six of the Ellel leaders, to help us understand the history and the present realities of Israeli life. Hanna is a gifted, fully qualified, and registered, professional tour guide who gave of her services free of charge to support and help establish the ministry in the Land.

During that tour there was a divine appointment with Peter

Tsukahira and Eitan Shishkov in Haifa. Eitan and Peter were long-serving leaders of Messianic congregations. As they heard about the call of God on the work of Ellel Ministries, I will never forget Eitan holding out his hands towards us, saying, *"Come over and help us"*. It was this additional Macedonian call that was the confirmation we needed from God, that we were actually being invited in and not pushing ourselves upon an already burdened Body of believers. Our calling has always been to serve the Body wherever it is that God leads us and we are invited by local leaders.

Fiona and I also had the joy of meeting with David and Karen Davis who, along with Peter and his wife, have an extraordinary story of how the Lord led them from America to Israel and set their feet down on Mount Carmel, to establish what is today a thriving Messianic fellowship. David and Karen had come from David Wilkerson's ministry in New York. Karen is an amazing musician and Peter's wife has pioneered and established a shelter primarily for women and children fleeing war torn Africa.

We were humbled to get to know David and Peter as founding pastors of Carmel Congregation and count them and their wives as dear friends. The work on Mount Carmel is a shining light and testimony to God's grace and faithfulness. I will never forget David's injunction to me, while standing on the walls overlooking Haifa Harbour. He had been talking about the former UN Mandate, that Britain had been given in 1917 to establish a Jewish homeland, but which had never been delivered by the British government.

What David saw spiritually was that, while the period of that original physical mandate may have ended in 1948, there still remained a spiritual mandate from the Lord, that believers from the UK have a responsibility to fulfill. It was from the Haifa Harbour, which was spread out below us, that the final British legal and military presence left Israel in May 1948, when the last Governor sailed out of the harbour. It may not have been coincidence that

Fiona and I, as British citizens, sailed into Israel and disembarked in the self-same spot from which the Governor had left, and that our first national Conference in Israel took place in Haifa. There may yet be more of that original mandate left to be fulfilled!

An introductory conference was planned for both Haifa and Christ Church, Jerusalem, in 2008, which was attended by representatives of the Messianic Body and Arab Churches from all over the land. It was another breakthrough event and people began to speculate as to when was the last time it was that healing and deliverance had been taught and ministered inside the walls of the old city. It was as if a gap of history, spanning almost two thousand years, had miraculously disappeared and the days of Scripture were being relived in the land as we ministered freedom to those who were captive and healing to the broken-hearted.

I was very much aware during the Jerusalem Conference of that original significant donation from Jerusalem to Ellel Grange. The bread which had been cast upon the waters had come home! Murray Dixon, the Rector of Christ Church, remembers how the response to the conference there absolutely amazed them. One of their staff, a Russian immigrant, had been travelling to work one morning when her bus was attacked by a suicide bomber. The bus was blown to pieces, with blood and body parts everywhere. People around her were dead, but she, miraculously, was preserved with no physical wounding. She remained, however, severely traumatised by the experience. She was ministered to at the conference and beautifully set free.

On our first visit to Jerusalem, following the 100th Operation Exodus sailing we had looked out of the windows of our Jerusalem hotel at a land that was parched by drought. On the ship Eliyahu Ben Haim had pleaded with us all to spend time when we were in the land praying, with them, for rain. It was a time of national crisis. Without fresh water a nation dies and the Sea of Galilee was several metres below its required level. We were joining in the prayers of thousands as we brought the needs of the land before the Lord. The drought broke the next day and the end of the video I was making, shows the streets of Jerusalem turned into rivers and the most dramatic of rainbows descending from the clouds to find its resting place in the waters of Galilee. The drought had broken and the prayers of a nation had been answered.

But as, then, I saw the physical rain falling and the roads become rivers, I saw in my spirit how over recent years God had begun the work of bringing a different form of drought to an end. The waters of His Spirit were rising over the land and it wouldn't be long before these trickles of new life would become rivers of joy for God's people as they rediscovered their Messiah.

Murray Dixon was one of those who, with his wife, had attended the nine-week school at Glyndley Manor. During that school he had been given a prophetic word and Scripture that God wanted him to bring Ellel Ministries into Israel. At that time a former Ellel Grange staff member was also working on the Christ Church team and was able to help, and Murray's prophetic word was finally fulfilled in 2008, during the last two weeks of his season as Rector of Christ Church!

As that first Ellel conference in Jerusalem was coming to an end, I realised that, through ways that were totally beyond the capacity for man to have planned, we were somehow or other involved in the process of bringing new life to the people of God in Israel. What a privilege it was to be adding a stream to that river, whose waters were beginning to spiritually nourish the land. A double rainbow, right over the place where the Haifa conference had taken place, served as a huge encouragement from the Lord that what was happening was truly of Him.

So often we have seen how, when God brings people together for a purpose, those strands of destiny are woven together by Him to create a rope of opportunity and a tapestry of grace. We recognised that nothing could develop for Ellel Ministries in Israel itself, without us having our own leader on the ground. And this was no easy hurdle to overcome. Without a leader a work goes nowhere!

Steve, a former secondary school music teacher, who later gained some legal and business experience within the ministry, went on the NETS 4 training programme at Ellel Pierrepont. Unsure of what was his next step after NETS, during a time of worship he had offered himself to serve the Lord in Israel, if that was His calling. After completing the school, he returned to serve in the ministry as a member of the team and proved himself to be very loyal and committed in all he did, but there was an area of his life which was not being satisfied through the various roles he fulfilled.

During post-graduate studies at Cambridge University, as a young man, Steve discovered that his ancestry was Jewish and, through miraculous financial provision, he was able to visit Israel for the first time a few months later. Deeply inspired by what God had done in restoring His people to the Land, he regularly attended prayer meetings for Israel and went to Jerusalem to study at the only Messianic Bible College in the land, *Israel College of the Bible*.

During this time the first intifada began, when Israel was under heightened and constant threat of terrorist attack. It is God's sovereign protection that Steve escaped being killed or injured from two car bombs attacks. Having been deeply saddened by seeing some of the wounds of believers in the Land, he asked the Lord to bring a healing ministry like Ellel Ministries to Israel. He had no idea then that he would be part of the answer to that prayer!

Some while later, it became clear to us that there was a definite call on Steve's life to work in Israel and at the same time I was wanting to talk to him about his future in the ministry. We sat together in the lounge at Glyndley Manor and talked through the possibilities. Then, in Jerusalem, following our conference at Christ Church, I felt led to ask him if he might be interested in returning to live in Israel and be the pioneer who oversaw the introduction of Ellel Ministries into the Land. Both his heart and his eyes were immediately alight with expectation as another piece of the Ellel jigsaw slotted into place. It was a deeply moving time for him, as Fiona and I prayed for him as he was about to step into his God given destiny in Israel

Local leaders in Israel facilitated the ministry going forward. Their local congregations sent their people, musicians, translators and servants to help establish the healing and training courses. It was truly a partnership with a growing and profound trust and unity between Arabs and Jews. Ellel teachers and prayer ministers were able to share their stories, teach the keys of healing and deliverance and pray for those in need. There has been some wonderful fruit and some amazing testimonies have begun to emerge from participants and many congregations have been touched by what God is doing. Some past students on the modular schools are now ministering regularly in their local congregations in Israel.

There is a lot of misunderstanding, particularly in the western church, about Israel. Some of this is due to a lack of knowledge of the Scriptures about Israel but the worst has residual anti-Semitism at its root, fuelled by a distinctly unsympathetic media, and we wanted to do our part to help dispel the confusion. So we started inviting leaders to join with us on special leaders' tours. And so the work grew. In the grace of God we have been enabled to work in close relationship with many parts of the Body in Israel, who have welcomed us, allowed us to use and rent their facilities and to build Kingdom bridges across the land.

It's been my privilege to teach the foundations of faith which underpin the ministry of healing and deliverance in many different parts of the world. But nowhere have I been more impacted than when I taught this vital material on the Modular School in Haifa to a congregation made up of believing Jews and Arabs, together with some Gentiles from overseas. In Ephesians Chapter 2, Paul talks about Jews and Gentiles alike becoming One New Man in Messiah – united in their belief in Yeshua, their Messiah, their Saviour. As we worshipped together in this mixed congregation and came to our Saviour for healing, we were united as brothers and sisters in our need of Him. The Spirit and presence of God was almost tangible as the joy of the Lord descended bringing hope and healing to each in their respective situations and need.

During the Deliverance Ministry module, we experienced the most sudden and violent thunderstorm I had ever witnessed. It literally shook the very foundations of the building we were in! Whether one interprets this as a direct hit from the enemy, who hated the teaching we were giving, or the approval of God who was also blessing the land with desperately needed rain, doesn't really matter. Whichever it was, everyone witnessed that the subject we were teaching seemed to be getting a measure of supernatural authentication!

This was the same place in which Steve had been anointed, at the beginning of his call to leadership of the work in Israel, by two Messianic Jews and two Arab Christian leaders alongside the Gentile leaders of Ellel Ministries. It was an extraordinary statement of the 'One New Man' that God was intending to be evidenced in the Land through the work.

As the lightning flashed and the thunder roared I remembered Derek Prince's words and wept, as I realised his prayer for healing the people in the land was being answered before our very eyes. Watching Arabs pray for Jews and Jews pray for Arabs breaks every wall of prejudice you could ever have erected. Many members of the teams, who have ministered with us in Israel, have found it a deeply spiritual and emotional experience. This work in Israel has been regularly hall-marked by the hand of God on different aspects of the ministry. For example, one lady who wanted to minister with us at the school found that a sum of money mysteriously appeared in her bank account, from a totally unknown source, which was enough to cover the costs of her trip!

And so the work has continued week by week, month by month and year by year. Who knows where it will lead, but what is abundantly clear is that God is restoring His ministry of healing and deliverance to His people, in the land where Jesus first fulfilled the amazing promises about him that were spoken by the prophet Isaiah and recorded in Isaiah 61:1: *"The spirit of the Sovereign Lord is on me, because the Lord has anointed me to preach good news to the poor. He has sent me to bind up the broken-hearted, to proclaim freedom for the captives and release from darkness for the prisoners."* And once again that is exactly what Jesus is doing in the land through His people today. He is healing the broken-hearted and setting the captives free and it is indeed marvellous in our eyes!

Chapter 25

AMERICAN PILGRIMAGE

An Old Message for the New World

One hundred and two Puritan believers, later known as *The Pilgrim Fathers*, boarded the good ship *Mayflower* on the 6 September 1620 and set sail from Plymouth, England, bound for the New World. England was rapidly losing its Christian character and the Puritans believed that a new start in the New World was their only chance of living life, as they believed it should be lived, in a scripturally faithful way. The believers who survived the journey, disease and their first severe winter went on to provide a solid Christian foundation for the new colony. And their influence on American history led to the inclusion of godly principles in the *Declaration of Independence* at the foundation of the United States of America on the 4th July 1776.

While the USA was never able to maintain the spiritual ideals of *The Pilgrim Fathers*, there has, nevertheless, been a resulting, strong Christian influence across the whole of the nation, even to this day. There are many people around the world who have reason to be thankful to God for this. For example, more missionaries have gone out from the USA, to carry the Gospel around the world, than from any other nation. And, as I mentioned in an earlier chapter, were it not for the meetings held in Dublin and London in the nineteenth century by one of the greatest of American evangelists, D.L.Moody, my parents would never have met and I, my brother, and all our children and grand-children would never have been born! And who knows how many people across the world would not have found faith in Jesus, were it not for the ministry of Billy Graham? The world owes a huge debt of gratitude to these, and many other Americans, who have proclaimed the uncompromising Gospel of Jesus Christ to a spiritually needy and hungry world.

In the political and military history of the twentieth century, were it not for his American mother, Winston Churchill would not have been the greatest Englishman of the twentieth century, saving the nation from certain defeat. And were it not for the eventual involvement of the USA, in both the First and the Second World Wars, the world as we know it would have been gone forever, swept away by a German war machine of terrifying intent. Today, the USA is a vast nation of over 300 million very diverse people, living in the 50 States that now make up the Union.

I first visited the States in 1974 on a business trip for my publishing company. My next venture stateside was in 1991 as one of the speakers at a Spiritual Warfare Conference. The first volume of my book *Healing Through Deliverance* had just been published and the work of Ellel Ministries was beginning to be known. The teaching was very well received and many people received prayer for healing. I loved the open-ness of the American people and we are still in touch today with some of the people whose lives were changed as a result.

But this conference was also my first real encounter with charismatic excess when one of the speakers, who called himself a prophet, offered wonderfully encouraging prophecies to those who would put large gifts in the offering, starting with $1000 dollar donations. In the end he wouldn't give any prophecies to those who gave less than a $100! I'm told that this man is still giving 'prophecies' for money, but now as a new age 'seer' who has turned his back on the church. It was a salutary lesson and I was deeply, deeply shocked at this perversion of the use of a gift of the Spirit.

I was not only shocked at what this so-called prophet did, in giving prophecies in exchange for money, but that the people and the organisers didn't rise up and put a stop to what was happening. I clearly had a lot to learn about the lack of discernment that can operate in the charismatic Christian world and, more worryingly, about the spiritual blindness that prevents people, who ought to have known a great deal better, from seeing that there's anything wrong, especially when there are so many warnings in Scripture about the dangers of false prophecy (see, for example Deuteronomy 13, Ezekiel 13 and Jeremiah 23).

In subsequent years I received many invitations to teach in various parts of the USA and these, together with the increasing influence of the work in Canada, prompted many people across America to ask when we were going to open a centre in the States. There was a genuine hunger for more teaching on healing and deliverance. The publication of my books in the USA by Chosen Books, was having a significant influence on this process, as were the visits to our Centres in the UK by various well-known American leaders.

To further 'test the waters' of a call to establish the work in America we ran two highly successful two-week schools – one in Colorado Springs and the other at Rancho Capistrano in California. In every place we went we were looking for that 'footprint in the sand' – the sign that would indicate that here was the place where God wanted us to put our feet down in a permanent way.

America is a very big place and we were beginning to feel that the zig-zag journey we had been on to our eventual home in Scotland, was very short and simple compared with the giant zig-zag paths, carved out by our travels across the States! But, in spite of all the places we went to, there was nowhere Fiona and I felt God was saying was the place where Ellel should make its US home until, that is, we were invited to Florida.

Robin Harper, a pastor's wife, had travelled with her friend to Rancho Capistrano. The report she brought back to her husband, Len Harper, was not only that their church needed what was being taught at our Californian school, but that her own testimony of what God had done spoke for itself. So Len invited us to come and lead a healing conference in his church. Fiona and I went and stayed with them and for a few days the windows of Heaven were open, as God poured His Spirit upon South Brandon Worship Centre.

We were made welcome by both the people and the Lord and as the time went on we sensed that this tiny (compared with other events we had been involved in and compared with the size of the USA) welcome mat that God's people had put down, was to be the place of entrance for Ellel Ministries into North America. Here was a door that was open and where we saw the Lord's 'footprint in the sand.'

With Tampa International airport lying less than an hour to the West, and the Orlando hub of Disneyland USA, being only an hour away to the East, there were many direct flights a day to and from the area from all over America, and many direct flights every day from Europe as well. It was a very convenient location for teams to fly in and out of from the UK. And with Florida being a warm and welcoming climate throughout the winter months, we recognised that this would be an attractive place for people to come to for training throughout the year – even during the long, harsh winters that were the annual experience of the northern states. It was also a place with a strong Hispanic population and was a good location for

Spanish speaking people from the southern States and from South America to come to.

South Brandon may have been a tiny pin-prick on the map of the USA but, as Zechariah said, *"Who dares despise the day of small beginnings? Men will rejoice when they see the plumb line in the hand of Zerubbabel"* (Zechariah 4:10). When a plumb line is held up a building can be constructed that is straight and true – and we sensed that the day would come when men and women would begin to rejoice that a plumb line of truth about healing and deliverance was being held up at this place in the USA.

My next teaching trip to the USA allowed for a few days rest between a conference in Colorado Springs and another near the East Coast. I decided to fill the gap between the two events with a few days writing, in a hotel. But as I settled down to write I felt increasingly uncomfortable and wondered why. As I prayed, I had one of those Elijah moments when God was asking me *"What are you doing here?"* (1 Kings 19:9). I sensed the Lord was urging me to use that time to go down to Florida and look for the Lord's next footprints in the Floridian sand! I thought back to those days in Hungary when the Lord directed me to a particular area outside of Budapest, and we found the land on which the Ellel building now stands. I wondered what God was going to do next!

Len and Robin kindly put me up and Richard Mull, a member of their church who was heading up his own ministry in the area, acted as driver as we went from one place to another, looking for a suitable building in which to establish the work of Ellel Ministries, USA. There were no large old buildings that could be adapted and my thoughts began to turn to the possibility of finding a piece of land on which we could build. I was, almost casually, flicking through a magazine advertising hundreds of available properties when one of the advertisements seemed to jump out of the page – **140 acres of beautiful land, farm it or develop it**. It got my attention. 140 acres is a lot of land (56 hectares), but nothing else caught my eye, so we called the agent and arranged to meet Rene Corzine at the entrance road to the site.

Rene invited us to climb into the back of her vehicle so she could give us a tour of the land. But before we headed off, I wanted to explain to her why we were looking at the land. Not knowing that she was a Christian, I spoke in very general terms about the sort of usage the land would be put to. She turned round to look at us and with a huge unforgettable smile on her face, explained that she was a Christian also, that her husband was a pastor and that this piece of land was actually owned by members of their church, with whom they had just been praying for its sale and future usage! They wanted it to be used for the Lord's purposes! This piece of land was definitely hallmarked with a Christian heritage. It certainly seemed that God was leading us! Then I looked out of the van and my eyes rested on the name of the driveway, where we were parked, that led from the main road to the land – it was called *English Acres!*

We drove down the driveway between overhanging trees and suddenly it opened out into an incredibly beautiful, completely secluded area of land. It was totally crazy, but this huge area of very private land, surrounded by woodland on all sides, with a lake at its centre, felt like home, albeit a very big one! The price was just over two million dollars – an impossible amount of money for the ministry to fund, but if God was in it, He would find a way. I was at peace in my spirit, but at the same time my mind was working overtime, envisioning the potential of this amazing piece of land, as the hub for the work of Ellel Ministries in the USA.

While I was thrilled with what I sensed God was doing, it was a huge step of faith for the Executive Leadership, and I was probably more surprised by their united agreement than I was by the discovery of the land itself! It was with a trembling hand of faith that I signed the offer document with the sales agent! In years to come many different people would walk on that land and know in their spirit, that this was holy ground, set apart for God's purposes.

There were many different confirmations that 'God was in it'. And we were deeply grateful for the confirmatory offer of a loan, to enable us to complete the purchase, from the same business friend who had originally offered to help us with the purchase of a property in Scotland. And so *English Acres* became the first home of Ellel Ministries, USA. We had a place on which to start putting down our feet.

Otto and Sharon Bixler, the former Californian Vineyard Pastors, who had pioneered the development of the work in Eastern Europe, came to help for a season. Different team members flew over from the UK to teach and minister. Two double-wide mobile home properties that came with the land were adapted to become the offices of the ministry and, eventually, our first teaching hall. The embryonic ministry was beginning to put down its feet on solid American ground. For a time we wondered if Richard Mull would join the team and lead the work on a permanent basis, but the Lord had other ideas and Richard continued serving the vision God had given him in the local area. So, the big question remained, *"Who is going to lead and build the ministry in America?"*

To answer this critical question we need to wind the clock back to the early days of the work in England. Cath Sharp, a qualified secretary, was serving on the Young People's Team at Ellel Grange. Her year was nearly up and she was preparing to leave to join another ministry. Just prior to her departure, we had been invited to teach a Church Weekend in Wales and Cath came as part of the team. It was one of those amazing weekends when the power of God was so clearly at work, bringing people to faith and healing. The whole team were deeply impacted, for there really is nothing like being on the sharp end of applied faith, being involved with God at work. During one significant ministry I asked Cath to use her short-hand skills to take down a few notes.

On the way back to Ellel Grange we stopped at McDonalds for a break, and as we consumed our burgers, Cath voiced the thrill of her own experience and voted with her feet by saying, *"Do you think I could stay on another year?"* And so it was that instead of leaving, Cath stepped into a gap in the office and later became my secretary. It was a God-anointed decision.

Almost simultaneously, God had his hand on Andy Taylor, a young man fresh from having a completed a marketing degree at Plymouth University, the place from which the Pilgrim Fathers had set sail three hundred and seventy years previously. Andy had served a year's placement at Ellel Grange as part of his degree course, but now he was joining the team permanently. Having seen God at work in people's lives during his placement year, he knew that Ellel Grange was the only place he wanted to put his newly acquired skills into practice, and for many years Andy master-minded all our publicity.

But Andy was to have a much more important and largely hidden role within the ministry. These were some of the most difficult years for me personally and I needed help. In the Scriptures, Timothy was described as a young disciple of Paul who travelled extensively with the Apostle and was part of his pioneering team that went with him into Europe. Andy became that for me and I will never cease to be grateful to the Lord for the blessing that Andy has been to me as a 'Timothy', in the extended journey of faith that Ellel Ministries has become. Few people will ever know the depth of his commitment and service.

But God was not only master-minding the critical help I needed at that time, he was also master-minding something else – Andy and Cath fell in love and became 'an item', as they say, and it wasn't long before they had the joy of being married at Ellel Grange by Andy's former Pastor, Jim Graham, who wrote the Foreword to this book.

Together they served the Lord and the ministry in many different capacities and became well-seasoned and experienced in the work, as the Lord was equipping them to be future leaders.

Two sons later, we asked them to go and support Diane Watson for a season in the establishment of *Gilbulla*, as the operating base for the work of Ellel Ministries in Australia. Their two years of support and influence was critical in helping Diane to put the foundations down 'good and true'. They also returned home with Isaac, an Aussie-born brother for Jake and Ben!

Andy and Cath had only just settled back into their work in the UK, with Andy now serving on the Executive Leadership of the whole ministry, when the doors began to open for the work in the USA. With all the experience, and understanding of the ministry that was already under their belt, Andy and Cath were ideal candidates to establish and lead the ministry forward. We were expecting that the stage would now be set for the steady growth and development of Ellel Ministries in the USA.

But instead of the growth being rapid, it proved to be a tough challenge. Some had predicted that people across America would soon donate the funds to repay the land loan and build the centre. Some amazing plans were drawn up and everything looked set to roll. Instead, God began to send people on the courses and on healing retreats from all over the States, but in relatively small numbers. Nevertheless, through Andy and Cath's determined and faith-filled walk with the Lord, very solid foundations were being put down and there was outstanding fruit in the transformed lives of many.

By now we had also acquired some excellent American advisers such as George Otis (Sentinel Group and the inspiration behind all the *Transformations* videos), Stuart MacAlpine (Pastor of Christ the Shepherd in the capital city, Washington DC), Lee Grady (former Editor of Charisma Magazine), Alistair Petrie (Director of Partnership Ministries), Steve Fry (Founder of the Messenger

Fellowship), David Kyle Foster (Founder of Pure Passion Ministries) and Henry Wright (President of Be in Health, Global), all of whom were supporting and encouraging the work.

After eight years of faithful sowing into the USA, it was then becoming clear that Andy and Cath were needed again back home in the UK. While the whole family loved living in the USA, it had, in many ways, been a seriously tough season for them, struggling with some of the seeming impossibilities they had to face at regular intervals. Andy describes their time in the states as *"the most challenging and blessed time of their lives"* But it was also a season when God forged steel into their spiritual backbone, as they experienced the faithfulness of God on numerous occasions, to be their provider, both personally and also for the ministry.

On one occasion they were especially desperate and crying out to God for an answer. The ministry had been wrongly classified by the county in respect of Property Taxes, and had therefore missed out on the non-profit organisation exemption that should have been applied. They had to battle this legally and were eventually reclassified and awarded the appropriate exemption. But nothing could be done about the previous bills – they still had to be paid. With the finances as they were, the $40,000 hurdle was an impossible one for them to jump. Under American law when the final deadline for payment of property taxes has passed, the land can be sequestrated by the government and sold to a new owner! They were in danger of seeing the ministry losing everything!

Simultaneously, however, God was speaking to a couple in Perth, Western Australia, who were doing the Modular School at the Perth centre. They knew nothing about what was happening in America, and without any human prompting they sensed God was asking them to donate one hundred thousand Australian dollars for the work of Ellel Ministries USA. The gift was sent in two parts and the first part arrived just in time, and after currency conversion, was also the exact amount of money needed in US dollars to settle all the property taxes! By the time all the banking processes were completed on that never to be forgotten deadline-day, Andy managed to get the funds into the local Government office less than five minutes before the draconian deadline. I have absolutely no doubt that the God who could orchestrate such a donation from the other side of the world, from people we didn't personally know, has the destiny purposes of Ellel Ministries USA very much on His heart!

The time had come for Fiona and I to enter a new season of our own life and ministry. I needed to lay down executive responsibility for the management of the UK Centres and both of us were ready to begin a season of writing. Andy and Cath were the natural and obvious choices to step into the breach as the UK National Directors. Andy was now the same age as I had been when the work started back in 1986. This was the right next place for them both, notwithstanding the rather important fact that we didn't yet have a new leader for the work in the USA! But if God knew what He was doing, then He would also know where the answer to our prayer for a new leader would come from. And it was at what seemed to be the very last minute that Matt and Becky Moore stepped forward into the forthcoming breach.

Matt had been a very successful corporate lawyer before entering the Pastoral ministry at the church which Andy and Cath attended. When Matt began to face some of his own issues he approached Andy for help, and as a result both Matt and Becky now have a very real and life-transforming personal testimony of the healing and deliverance that God brought to them through Andy and Cath's ministry. They started referring members of the church, who were also in need, to Ellel and little by little there was built up a body of people whose lives had been significantly impacted through the ministry. Matt also travelled to the UK and took part in our national conference at Blackpool.

By now, Andy and Cath had been walking with Matt and Becky for some long time, and as long as six years previously the Lord had picked Matt out to Andy and said that he would be the next leader of Ellel USA! But Andy didn't tell Matt that, until after he'd agreed to take on the role. God was, however, already at work in Matt and Becky's hearts as they processed together the developing call on their lives to take up the reins of leadership of the work in the States and be the first Americans to carry the Ellel flag in the USA.

Before finally accepting the role, Matt came over to the UK again – this time to share his heart with me about the love God had given him for the Jewish people. He wanted to know that his desire to be ministering to the Jewish people would be compatible with the ministry. I was able to share with him something of my own pilgrimage in that respect, and tell him of what happened in Scotland when we lost the castle because of our unwillingness to compromise on scriptural teaching about Israel. He went home at peace and told Andy and Cath that he and Becky were going to take on the responsibilities of directing the work of Ellel Ministries USA.

The timing of their final decision was such that there was an almost seamless transition between Andy and Cath leaving and Matt and Becky taking over. God had not only put another foot print down, but he had also provided the leaders whose feet would stand in the footprint, for the next stage of the Ellel USA journey.

There is still a massive amount of work to do before we can see the work in America at English Acres reaching its potential. Serious funding is needed to repay loans and build the centre, but the step by step evidence of God's faithfulness is clearly there and we can look forward with expectation to seeing how God's plan unfolds. The needs in America are huge. The Centre is still a work in progress, but God is in the midst of it.

Fiona and I have taught on many schools, courses and conferences at English Acres and the presence of the Lord is always heavy upon the land. There are many who have experienced significant healing in their lives during Andy and Cath's time leading the work. And now, under Matt and Becky's leadership, many more will go out rejoicing after God has transformed their lives. The American Pilgrimage is very much alive! The message that God birthed in the heart of Ellel Ministries so many years ago is both old and ever new – and both the 'old world' and the 'new world' desperately need to know that God is still changing hearts and restoring lives.

Chapter 26

DUTCH MIRACLE

Many Strands – One Purpose

Of all the stories that lie behind the different Ellel Centres around the world, the way God brought about the establishment of Huize Baak, as Ellel's centre in the east of the Netherlands, is almost beyond belief. If it hadn't happened exactly as the story unfolds in this chapter, one would have been tempted to say it was made up! There are so many different strands to this extraordinary story of God's faithfulnesss, in responding to the prayers of God's people in the Netherlands, that it's hard to know which strand to pick up first!

I could begin with the healing of Lynda Hicks at Merroo which led to the establishment of the Australian Centre at Gilbulla. I could begin with a Dutch American business man who married an Aussie girl. Or I could begin with Peter Freeke and his vision for an Ellel Centre in the Netherlands. But let's begin with a young Dutchman called Marc Schuthof.

Marc did not have an easy childhood and early on he determined to make his own independent way through life. His parents divorced. He was educated in France for two years before completing his school education in Holland. He did Dutch military service and in 1984, at the age of 21 he was wondering what to do with his life. His mother was now living in Sydney, so a holiday in Australia with his Mum and his sisters was the obvious first stop off. But it proved to be a very long stop-off, for he fell in love with Australia and decided to stay.

At exactly the same time as I was pioneering the purchase of Ellel Grange for the establishment of what became Ellel Ministries, Marc was beginning his search for answers to life. But on the back of an atheistic upbringing, he joined a new age meditation group where he met Margaret, a catholic girl, the sixth child of eleven, who was also looking for answers. Marc describes how he experienced what felt like the hand of an angel physically directing him to this girl to become his wife! God was undoubtedly at work in their lives. They were married in an Anglican Church on the 28th November 1987.

Their first two children were baptised by the local Vicar, without any questions being asked. But now, living in a different area, the Vicar who agreed to baptise number three would only do so after preparing the parents for what it means to be a Christian through a six week *Christianity Explained* course. It was towards the end of that course that both Marc and Margaret said the sinner's prayer and began their own Christian pilgrimage.

Some while later they were asked if they would host an Alpha follow-up course, called 'A Life Worth Living', in their home and after that was finished the group continued to meet for fellowship, one of whom was Cate, a single lady who became close friends with Margaret. It was she who recommended that Marc and Margaret go for a Healing Retreat at Ellel Ministries. That visit to Gilbulla, where they listened to Paul Ryan explaining the Christian faith, was a life-changing experience for them both. And so it was that both

Margaret and Marc faced the realities of their own lives and began to discover God's healing for themselves. This was quickly followed by them signing up for the monthly Modular School and, in time, Margaret was also volunteering in the ministry office, where she first heard about Huize Baak.

In the world of work, Marc had first established a motor-cycle courier business in Sydney and after selling this business, established Cornerstone IT Solutions and he loaned his expertise to Ellel in looking after the IT needs of the base. At this point in the story Marc and Margaret were well-established in Australia, with a successful business and participating regularly in the work of Ellel Ministries.

Meanwhile, Cate, who was part of the Board of an Australian company, got to know and eventually married Sid, the Board Member who flew into Sydney from the States for Board Meetings. While Sid was born an American, he began life the son of a Dutchman who had emigrated to the USA – and so it was that Cate joined her friend Margaret in having a Dutch connection. Cate left Australia and settled in the USA.

In the meantime, back in the Netherlands, a young man called Peter Freeke had caught the vision for the work of Ellel Ministries. He first became aware of Ellel while serving with *Youth With A Mission* in South Africa. Later he attended Ellel courses at various centres and did a nine-week school at Ellel Canada. Such was his commitment to the ministry and awareness of the need in his native Holland, that he began to share with me his own vision for establishing a Dutch Ellel centre. A new work in a new country can only be established if there is a pioneering visionary to see the work brought to fruition. Here was the visionary and he had a vision, so with the encouragement of the international leadership Peter Freeke returned to the Netherlands and began to search for a place where the work could be established.

In his own praying about the vision, and sharing with his friend

Johann Evenblij, he believed God had shown him which part of the country the centre would be located, but he did not share this with anyone else until after an Estate Agent told him of Huize Baak, a property that was shortly to be coming on the market and which was in exactly the same area that God had already revealed to him.

Huize Baak was originally built as a castle in 1294. It was rebuilt around 1730 as a large manor house, and is still surrounded by a moat. After centuries of private ownership, it was acquired by a Catholic Order of Nuns. Then, in 2007, they needed a larger place and decided to move and put Huize Baak on the market. The original castle had been extended to include a manor house with two coach houses and a farm house. Over time, the two coach houses were converted into a dining hall and an accommodation building. The farmhouse had been converted into a conference hall. In 2007 property prices were rapidly escalating and the negotiated price of 3.2 million euros was, at the time, thought to be a very good deal.

The vision for the work was shared with the Christian people of the Netherlands and supporters in the UK and enough donations came in for there to be a big enough parallel deposit to secure a 3.2 million Euro mortgage loan, with the healthy prospect of the ongoing earned income from training courses and subsequent donations being adequate to make the regular quarterly loan repayments to the bank.

Peter Freeke proved to be a visionary pioneer who, with the regular support of team members from the UK, worked incredibly hard to equip and develop the whole facility in an amazing way. It's always tough getting a new work off the ground, but things got measurably more difficult with the great recessionary financial collapse, affecting the whole of Western Europe, that took place in 2008. Property prices plummeted, donation giving almost dried up and the numbers coming on the courses were not adequate to meet the bank loan payments. We faced a huge financial crisis. The ministry in the UK was going through similar recessionary problems and could only help in a very limited way.

There came a day when we had failed to meet our obligations to the bank and unless we were able to find £98,000 by the end of the week, the bank were intent on repossessing the property, and we would lose everything that had been invested in the work so far. I was daily in touch with the bank and the burden of the financial responsibility weighed heavily on my shoulders as I drove into Ellel Grange for the final evening of a special two-week training course.

As I stood at the front of the meeting room during a time of worship, next to David Cross, I was suddenly taken aback by an overwhelming sense that I had to share the Dutch problem with the 60 or so people who were at the Grange that night, even though none of the people on the course had anything to do with the work in the Netherlands! I'd never done anything like that before and tugged the sleeve of David's coat and whispered in his ear what I was sensing God was asking me to do, thinking that he would veto the idea. But, conversely, he gave me the thumbs up to share the situation with these people.

So, after the worship time I stood up and told them the story of Huize Baak and asked them to pray. Then, in a time of corporate intercession I found myself being forced to my knees by the Spirit of God and I entered into a visionary experience of seeing Hannah kneeling at the altar and crying out to God for a son (1 Samuel 1:9-20) and then, at the end of the story, Eli the Priest saying to her, "Go in peace, and the God of Israel will grant your petition". At that moment I knew that God had answered the prayer and that the God of Israel would answer my petition for the funds to save Huize Baak for the work of the ministry. But I had no idea how!

Immediately after the meeting, a couple who were present on that course asked to see me privately. That very week they had received a benefit of £50,000 and they had been asking the Lord what He wanted them to do with it. As I shared about the need at Huize Baak, the Lord had spoken to both of them independently, saying they should give it all. I was totally stunned – over half the immediate need had already been supplied and within a few days the whole of the £98,000 had been given by that small group of people who caught the vision for what God was doing in the Netherlands.

The bank were impressed, and from that moment on, even though we were unable to pay any more instalments on the bank loan, they chose not to close the ministry down and auction the property to the highest bidder. And I now knew, without a shadow of doubt, that God's hand was on the ministry in the Netherlands and that He was in charge of the destiny of Huize Baak, even though humanly speaking the future looked impossible. The pressures on the Dutch team were very great, so great in fact that Peter Freeke felt unable to continue and the centre was left without a leader, without any money and on the edge of closure. It is a well-known Christian saying that *'Man's extremity is God's opportunity'* and that's exactly what proved to be the case.

There was one more training course on the Huize Baak programme at the end of August 2012, for which a number of people were booked in. Paul and Liz Griffin were scheduled to fly over to Holland to teach the course and to tell people that this would be the last course at Huize Baak, as we had no staff and no funds to continue! We had to face reality, even though faith was looking at the impossible and saying, *"What next, Lord?"*. There was one person on the course who had not been on any previous course at Huize Baak. His name? Marc Schuthof.

Returning now to Marc and Margaret's story. The years passed until, at the beginning of 2012, Marc was certain that God had told him to sell his business and move on, even though he had no idea what God had in store for him next. So, in agreement with his business partner, the business was put up for sale and within three months the business was sold and Marc was a free agent. Marc and Margaret's son Matthew had by now announced his engagement to the girl of his dreams and Marc had a deep desire to enjoy some personal time with his son before he got married. So they booked a visit to Europe for the end of August 2012, ending with two days together in Holland before Matthew left for home and Marc stayed on in his home country for a week, hoping to touch base with some old friends.

It was then he saw that there was a course on that weekend at Huize Baak and decided to go and see how Ellel Netherlands did it. He enjoyed the course, but was completely oblivious to all that was happening at Huize Baak behind the scenes until, on the Saturday night of the course, Paul made his announcement about this being the last course that Ellel would be able to put on at the centre.

At that moment, a spiritual explosion went off in Marc's mind and at the end of the course he spoke to Paul and said, *"Is there anything I can do to help?"* The extraordinary God-incidences of Marc being present on the very day when Paul gave out the news and of how, earlier in the year, Marc had sold his business, so that he was free to help, had all the hallmarks of *'God at work!'*

Suddenly, the pilgrimage of faith, which had led to Marc and Margaret's long-term involvement in the work of Ellel Ministries in Australia, all began to make sense. As a Dutchman he knew the language and the culture. And they well understood the work of Ellel Ministries. Within three weeks Marc and Margaret had taken a massive leap of faith and were installed as the new Directors of Ellel Netherlands, commissioned with the task of building the work up again from scratch, with a volunteer team and a massive unresolved mortgage! Margaret returned to Australia to pack up their house and Marc returned briefly to Australia for the wedding of Matthew and Zoe, but they were soon both back at Huize Baak getting on with the work.

But Marc and Margaret still had to face the biggest and most severe test of their lives, and no-one would have questioned their decision, if in February 2013 they had decided to give up the vision and return to Australia. I will never forget receiving the phone call from Marc, very late in the night, with the tragic news that only two months into their marriage, their only son Matthew had been killed in a road traffic accident. No words are adequate to describe the deep, deep trauma and shock that any parent would experience on the receipt of such news. Once again they were in the air on their way to Australia, having so recently flown out for the wedding, but now they were *en route* to their son's funeral.

We have often said that the theology of suffering and the theology of healing need to be equally understood. For we live in a fallen world, where Christians are not exempt from the tragedies that can happen. It is in moments like these that we plumb the depths of our faith and determine to press on, hand in hand with the one whom Paul described as *"the God of all comfort"* (2 Corinthians 1:3). There are no easy answers when things like this happen, but it is pressing on with the things that you know, which helps us to face and walk through the things that we don't know, or don't understand. And press on they did.

Back at Huize Baak it was becoming obvious that the work had turned a corner. The spark of faith had not gone out and people began to believe again for the impossible. Eventually, however, the bank could not wait any more for us to settle their debt and they exercised their right to put the property on the market via a national property agent. The property market had not recovered and the value of the property was now about two million Euros and the bank would have been reluctantly happy to settle for this and write off the rest of our 3.2 million Euros debt.

The bank understood that we did not want to leave Huize Baak, but they could not allow the debt to remain un-serviced indefinitely.

In spite of Marc's calm faith that God had the matter in hand, it seemed as though the end of the road was very close. Marc and Margaret, with the small but faithful team supporting them, persevered in putting on Healing Retreats and Training Courses and maintaining the property and, in time, over twenty different potential buyers came to look at the property! But not one of these twenty potential purchasers came forward to make an offer! Two, even, made donations to the ministry thinking that it would be best if the work we were doing could carry on at Huize Baak! What was God doing?

Meanwhile, in the USA, Cate kept in touch with her friend Margaret, now working with Ellel Ministries in Holland. Sid had never been to an Ellel event, so Sid and Cate flew down to Florida to attend a conference that Fiona and I were teaching. Sid must have appreciated what he heard and enjoyed the experience, for before very long they flew over to Holland to spend some time with Marc and Margaret and see Huize Baak for themselves. And when they saw the potential of the work in the Netherlands, God touched their hearts and Sid and Cate determined to try and help his own ancestral country via a Charitable Trust that they were involved with in the USA.

Initially the Trust offered a million US Dollars to buy out the property from the bank but, not surprisingly, the bank, having set an asking price of about two million Euros declined the offer. But, the property still did not sell and one of Sid's business friends in Holland went to see the bank on his behalf and eventually a deal was struck, whereby the American Trust was able to provide 1.5 million Euros and Huize Baak was free from the control of the bank. All outstanding debts from Ellel Netherlands to the bank had been written off – thanks mainly to the devaluation caused by the property recession. It was a totally extraordinary miracle of God's grace.

Today, the work in the Netherlands is growing steadily. Peter Freeke's vision for the work to be established at Huize Baak has been fulfilled and we are seeing this wonderful property being not only a place that will serve the people of Holland, but we believe it will be a future hub for the work of Ellel Ministries across the whole of Western Europe.

How God took the strands of Ellel Australia, Marc and Margaret's lives, Peter Freeke's visionary obedience and Sid and Cate's commitment to the work, and wove all these factors into the tapestry of Ellel Ministries Holland is beyond human understanding. But it's true. God did it and the vision he gave to Peter Freeke and the word He so clearly spoke to me as I knelt on the floor of Ellel Grange have indeed been fulfilled – God granted our request!

It is now abundantly clear that God was in Peter Freeke's original vision for the work in the Netherlands at Huize Baak. God has redeemed the property for His kingdom purposes and we must be prepared to enter in to all that God has planned and purposed for the future work across the whole of Europe.

Chapter 27

SOVEREIGN WORLD

Publishing the Sinner's Friend

I don't exactly know when the deep inner desire to write and to publish was birthed in me, but it must have been when I was very young. I still have the first hand-written, 66 page 'book' I wrote, at the age of 10, about cars and bicycles, and I started a weekly newspaper, when aged thirteen. This ran to 101 hand-typed weekly issues, published by the so-called *Horrobin News Agency*! Each issue recorded all the family events of the week and was mailed every Monday morning to the Lancashire and South African branches of the family!

To produce the newspaper, I saved up my weekly spending money and paid my father's secretary seven shillings and sixpence for her old *Imperial*, inked ribbon typewriter. I produced five copies of each issue using carbon paper and heavy fingered typing – long before the days of photocopiers, computers and printers! My fingers still type with a heavy thump, as if they are trying to produce five carbon copies at once, and I am constantly wearing out the keyboards on my computers as a result!

I mention the above for a very specific reason – to illustrate yet again how God can lead us in our youth to enjoy doing the things that He wants to train us in, so as to fulfil the future destiny calling that He has for each one of us. It took a great deal of determination as a child to hand-type multiple copies of 101 issues of a weekly publication over a two-year period – I still have a copy of all but the very first issue! Not only was God teaching me about writing, typing and publishing, he was sowing those essential qualities of determination and perseverance into my character, without my knowing that I was in a unique school of learning! For me it was fun.

I was always fascinated by hymns and whenever the sermon at church didn't grab my attention, I took to reading the hymnbook and learned to enjoy reading hymns as poetry, and not just as something you had to sing at regular intervals throughout a church service! I must have been a late teenager, when I discovered Charles Wesley's great pioneering hymn, *"Give me the faith which can remove, And sink the mountain to a plain."*

The words of the third verse were exactly what I felt in my heart – they echoed the call of God on my life, even from a very young age, to share the Gospel with those who did not know the Saviour:

I would the precious time redeem,
And longer live for this alone,
To spend, and to be spent for them,
Who have not yet my Saviour known.

I knew that Jesus did not come to call the righteous – but sinners to repentance (Matthew 5:32) and it was the last two lines of the fourth verse that totally captivated me:

My talents, gifts, and graces, Lord,
Into Thy blessed hands receive;
And let me live to preach Thy Word,
And let me to Thy glory live;

My every sacred moment spend
In publishing the sinner's friend.

The idea of publishing the good news of the Gospel – spreading the knowledge of the Son of God – became a major motivating force in my life. And this rhyming couplet became the backbone of a regular prayer of personal commitment to the cause of Jesus Christ, to spend my days *in publishing the sinner's friend.*

Then I linked these words with two very memorable lines from the last verse of Kipling's *If,*

If you can fill the unforgiving minute,
With sixty seconds worth of distance run

Together these two snatches of poetry, from two very different writers, became a potent, energising combination. They both carry the same message of the urgency of passing time. A minute passed can never be relived, time is unforgiving. And, to the believer, every moment of life is a sacred moment – a moment of opportunity that can never be lived again. Somehow or other, by the grace of God, this urgency of the Gospel was planted in my heart at an early age and couplets such as these served to remind me that every moment should be made to count for the Kingdom of God.

I have no doubt that God was drawing on the inspiration of those early and primitive publishing ventures, when I left the security of the academic world for the unknown realm of running a real life publishing business. And my early love of hymns and choruses provided the foundation for a moment of clear God-given vision, which birthed the idea for *Mission England Praise* in my spirit and led me to be back in touch with Chris Mungeam, my old friend from teenage days, who arranged for its publication by Marshall Pickering.

But, even though *Mission England Praise* would become a very successful, best-selling product for the company, as was mentioned in Chapter 12, Chris was forced to leave the company with a year's severance pay and, completely unknown to me he, and his wife, Jan, were sitting on a small pot of severance money and they were wondering what to do with it. Chris was already known in the book trade as an enterprising, charismatic personality and his wife, Jan, was a Director of the Bible Society and totally committed to the publishing of the Word, in every possible language under the sun. They were a truly dynamic duo, embodying in their own marriage a commitment to the Word and a commitment to the Spirit.

Suddenly it became obvious what God wanted them to do – launch their own publishing company, which would seek to heal the divisions, that were creeping in to the Church at that time between the Spirit-focussed charismatics and the Word-focussed evangelicals. Both are right in declaring the need for the Spirit and the need for the Word – but not separated from each other. Both together are essential for spiritual health and strength. And so it was that *Sovereign World Ltd* was birthed – a brand new publishing company, with the specific objective of publishing books that were committed to bringing together the truth about both Word and Spirit.

The story of what happened next reads like a series of stories from the Acts of the Apostles, as God led Chris from one Christian leader to the next, picking up books for the growing Sovereign World list. The Lord brought authors and books to them in an amazing way. *"But,"* as Chris says, *"Who, in their right minds, would start a new publishing company with two books on Deliverance by two unknown authors, who believed they had something important to say?!"* At that time both Bill Subritzky and Graham Powell, who wrote those first two Sovereign books, were virtually unknown as authors, but they had a message to bring as part of God's strategic plan in restoring healing through deliverance to a church under transition, as the charismatic renewal continued to blossom in the last quarter of the twentieth century. And in due course Sovereign World became the publisher of my own books on *Healing Through Deliverance*, publishing them in the UK and co-publishing them in the USA with Chosen Books.

God was leading Sovereign World and Ellel Ministries along parallel pathways. It was Bill Subritzky's book that encouraged us with our own exploratory journey into understanding deliverance, when we were in need of help. And in due course Chris introduced us to other Sovereign World authors, such as Tom Marshall, another "down-under spiritual giant", author of *Healing from the Inside Out* and other important books. Tom became a regular, much-loved speaker at Ellel Grange and was a huge encouragement to me, when I was walking through some very dark and difficult days.

Bob Gordon was another who endeared himself to the Ellel team. On one occasion, he taught an unforgettable course on *Men of a Different Spirit*, based on the character of Joshua and Caleb, the two spies who were not afraid of the giants in the land, if it was God who was telling them to go in their direction. Bob happened to be with us at the Grange when I was facing the most difficult season of my own personal pilgrimage.

I shared my heart with Bob, sparing him none of the details of the difficulties I was facing. I don't know whether God used Bob in this way regularly or not, but it was suddenly quite apparent that the Holy Spirit was speaking through Bob prophetically, when he said directly to me, *"Even though the path you are on is heading straight for the edge of a steep cliff, you must keep on walking in that direction, trusting God for every step of the way. It will look as though you are about to walk off the edge of the cliff and face total disaster, but you must keep going. For it is only when you get to the very edge, that you will see the steps that are cut in the cliff face, and you will be able to walk down these and on with your journey in perfect safety."* This prophetic word was a massive encouragement to me at the time and it proved to be an absolutely true word. What a loss it was to the Body of Christ on Earth, when Bob passed away so prematurely.

And then there was another close link between Sovereign World and Ellel Ministries. In my teenage years I had known Chris's father, who went to school in China where Chris's grandfather was serving God as a missionary, with Hudson Taylor's *China Inland Mission*. It is almost certain that Chris's Grandfather and my 'Uncle Grundy' will have met each other while on missionary service. This deposit of China in Chris was quickly made manifest in Sovereign World and, in time, Sovereign was responsible for placing over a million books in Chinese into the hands of the Chinese underground church by working together with another agency!

Jan's major contribution to the mission work that emanated from Sovereign World, was the founding of the Sovereign World Trust, a UK registered Charity whose specific objective was to give away huge quantities of books around the world to Pastors and Leaders who were working in third world situations and had no other way of obtaining good Christian literature. It is an amazing work that is still serving the Body of Christ across the newly developing world.

More than 500 overseas editions, of about 50 different Sovereign World titles, were made available in foreign languages, especially for believers living in poorer countries. As the walls of communism fell and Eastern Europe opened up to the Gospel, Sovereign World was one of the first organisations to get books onto lorries and enable translations of vital books into Russian and other Eastern European languages. Believers smiled, along with everyone else, when they were given toiletries, clothes, chocolate etc, but they started crying with joy when they received Christian books.

When the time came for Chris and Jan to be retiring from business life, and God was asking them to lay the company down and move into their own new season, they were actively looking for a new home for Sovereign World which would love, honour and respect the objectives and history of the company. At the same time, I was acutely aware of the growing amount of material that was being birthed within the ministry, and which would need to be published. And so it was that in 2006, God brought the two operations together, in harmony of vision, and Sovereign World became part of Ellel Ministries International, with the operational hub of the company moving to Ellel Grange.

At that time, our son Paul Stanier, who had served seven years with Operation Exodus in Eastern Europe, and had met his wife on the nine-week school at Glyndley Manor, was looking for the next stage of his life and career. He accepted our invitation to grow and develop Sovereign World as the publishing arm of Ellel Ministries International and for another seven years continued to build on the foundation that Chris had laid for the company.

In more recent years, however, Sovereign World, like all other Christian publishing companies in the UK, was severely shaken by massive and turbulent changes in the world-wide Christian publishing industry. The collapse of the largest distributor of Christian books in Europe and the growth of internet companies like Amazon, which have so undercut prices that a large percentage of Christian bookshops the world over, have not been able to survive the resulting financial storm, has changed the face of publishing forever.

Paul now operates Zaccmedia, his own book packaging and self-publishing service for Christian authors. As such he is still able to produce books for Sovereign World and, unlike many Christian publishing houses, Sovereign World has managed to survive the perfect storm that shook the publishing world, through being absorbed into the Head Office functions of Ellel Ministries. So, the precious work of Sovereign World has been preserved as the publishing arm of Ellel Ministries International, and is now finding its feet in a slimmed down format, operating on lower overheads.

The storms may rage in the world-wide distribution market-place, but the written word will always be the vehicle through which information is communicated – be it via traditional books, online, viewed on mobile phones or downloaded via whatever electronic marvel is dreamt up next! And I have a sense that Sovereign World is about to enter the most important and influential stage of its history! There is so much precious material that is waiting to be written by different leaders within the ministry who hold important keys to the understanding of many different topics.

The *Truth and Freedom Series* of books is designed to do just that, prepare people to receive the truth so that they can enter into the freedom that only God can give – not just on many more traditional teaching topics, but on subjects such as Fiona's *Healing Through Creativity,* which gets right to the heart of many people's healing needs. In discovering their creativity and letting our Creator God into the depths of their inner pain, people have experienced amazing healing. Getting these, and many other books, into print, so that people the world over can share in the journey, is now a prime objective of my life. For me, personally, it feels as though I've come full circle and that once again writing and publishing has become my major occupation.

God has raised up the next generation of leaders who are carrying the load and taking the work forward in all the Ellel centres across the world. And I'm finding truth in the old saying that, *what goes around comes around* and realising afresh that there is nothing wasted in God – the experience in one stage of our lives, He uses, often in ways far beyond the reach of our imagination, in succeeding stages of our journey with Him. All those years of writing and publishing experience at the beginning of my adult career that preceded Ellel Ministries, are being redeemed for the sake of the Kingdom, as the wheel of life has continued to turn.

By their very nature, publishers are always on the look-out for new books and shortly before this book was published I received an email from Jim Graham, who wrote the Foreword to this book. Jim was formerly the Pastor of Gold Hill Baptist Church and has been one of my closest friends over the past twenty-five years. Jim has taught at different Ellel Centres and Conferences on many occasions and His fatherly input, encouragement, correction and direction have always been immensely valued.

I knew Jim wasn't well at the beginning of 2016 as he had cancelled some teaching appointments, because of what he thought must be flu. But Jim's email of the 19th March 2016 contained the detailed diagnosis of his condition by his medical consultants. In this he said: *"In reality, Peter, it looks like I am heading to the finishing line. I am content and completely free of anxiety. Please pray that I will finish well! Looks like, too, Peter that my teaching days are over."*

My eyes filled with tears as I dwelt on those many years of rich fellowship and the prospect of Jim no longer being part of God's family on earth. I will never forget the few hours we were privileged to spend together on the 6th April, mainly talking about the Lord, and the precious days Jim was now living through, with his family around him, awaiting his call home.

It was not until the 25th April 2016, however, that I heard of the existence of Jim's personal *'translations'* of Paul's Epistles. I wrote to him immediately, urging him to consider allowing them to be published. Very graciously, he arranged for a copy of all the letters he had completed to be sent to me, together with a Preface he had just written, should the material ever be published. He called the book *The God-Life.*

In my commercial publishing days, prior to the establishment of Ellel Ministries, I had, on occasion, been fortunate enough to discover and publish significant books and have the privilege of bringing them to the market as best-sellers. Moments like those are never forgotten. But when I started to read *The God-Life*, I realized I was holding in my hand something far more precious and valuable than anything I had ever discovered in the secular world. This was a 'publishing moment' to exceed all others. For when I read the text of *The God-Life*, I realized I was not only reading a manuscript of outstanding significance and quality, but it was as if I was standing on holy ground!

From time to time I had heard Jim illustrate his teaching with profoundly impacting readings, but I had no idea that they were extracts from his personalized translations of most of Paul's Epistles. In his email Jim had said *"my teaching days are over"*. But what I was reading was so profound that I sensed the very opposite would be the case – Jim's wider teaching ministry to the whole Body of Christ was only just beginning!

Paul wrote many of his letters in prison to teach and encourage the saints in the developing new churches. He had no idea that his writings would form part of the New Testament and be available to teach and encourage the saints for the rest of time. And in a similar way, when Jim wrote these personalized translations of Paul's letters he was doing it in obedience to a personal Word from the Lord, but largely, as he thought, for his own benefit. But now the whole Church, until Jesus comes again can benefit from Jim Graham's profound, Holy Spirit inspired, understanding of Paul's amazing letters. It was an incredible privilege to prepare *The God-Life* for publication, knowing that this book would enable Jim Graham's extraordinary teaching gift to be an inspirational blessing to countless other people, as they journey through life to their own finishing line.

As I write these words I am also preparing a major new series of training modules to help people discover who they are in God – what an encouragement it is to know that Sovereign World is there to continue waving the banner of Word and Spirit, in a world that is less and less cognizant of the love of God that was made manifest in the world through Jesus. There is still a lot of work to be done and I doubt if we will ever cease asking for God's grace and help as we continue to spend our days *in publishing the sinner's friend!*

Chapter 28

INTO ALL THE WORLD

Healing for the Church – One Life at a Time

" *I* look upon all the world as my parish; thus far I mean, that in whatever part of it I am, I judge it meet, right and my bounden duty to declare unto all that are willing to hear, the glad tidings of salvation. This is the work I know God has called me to; and sure I am that his blessing attends it." John Wesley's Journal, June 11th 1739.

I personally have many reasons to thank God for John Wesley. Ever since I realised that I was studying at the same college that he had attended, two centuries previously, and I started to read some of his writings, he has been a personal inspiration to me. The determined perseverance of his life has been a constant challenge. A few years ago a lady from America heard me teaching about John Wesley in a session on the history of Christian missions. Later she sent me a beautiful leather model of *'John Wesley's horse'*, to be a constant reminder to me, and the work of Ellel Ministries, that just as God used John Wesley to proclaim the truth of salvation to an eighteenth century world, that was hell-bent on running away from God, God had called Ellel Ministries in this century to take the message of salvation and healing to an equally desperate world, especially the very hurting and broken who are suffering the consequences of 'man's inhumanity to man'.

John Wesley referred to the world as his parish. And as I added stamps to my childhood collection, and studied intently the catalogues of all the world's issues, my imagination was constantly being stirred by images of distant lands – lands I could only dream about, and capture a flavour of, from the pictures on the stamps. But God used those childhood dreams to give me a world-wide vision. There is nowhere in the world where the full message of salvation, through Jesus the Saviour, the Healer and Deliverer isn't needed.

There was a night when Fiona and I had been ministering to a very hurting lady at Ellel Grange. She had suffered greatly in her past and we had seen the miraculous take place before our eyes, as she had taken a huge step forward in allowing God to bring order into her life and experience His healing. At the end of the evening, as we were walking across the landing towards the staircase, we were both, suddenly, overwhelmed by the presence of God and were driven to our knees right there, on the landing.

Instinctively we both knew that this was one of those God-moments, when words were inadequate to express the depth of God's love that we were feeling for His children, suffering without a knowledge of Him, in a broken world and those who had a knowledge of Him, but did not know that He was their healer as well as their Saviour. Without needing to say anything we both knew that this was a moment when God's call on our lives and the work of Ellel Ministries was going deeper than it had ever done before. I couldn't fight back the tears and we both knew the meaning of the words of Jesus when He said, *"Lift up your eyes and look on the fields, they are white and ready for harvest"* (John 4:35) and *"The harvest is plentiful but the labourers are few"* (Matthew 9:37). The work we were doing seemed so terribly inadequate and so pitifully small when faced with the reality of a world that was determined to reject God and His answers for man's condition.

The lessons God had taught the ministry through those early years of pioneering are applicable to every human being of whatever age and from whatever country and we knew that, small as we were, there could be no restriction on our willingness to respond to His leading when He shows us where next to put our foot down for Him. The shamed Aboriginals of Australia, the oppressed peoples of Eastern Europe, the genocide survivors of Rwanda, the veterans of war all over the world, the victims of child and sexual abuse; they all have the same fundamental need – to be loved back to life by those who both serve the God of love and take seriously His instructions. The work of the church is not just to tell people that when they die they can go to Heaven, but to seek out the hurting and the lost, and to bring healing to those who are described by Ezekiel (in Chapter 34) as sheep who have been scattered, without a shepherd to care for them.

I believe there is a significant reason why God is once again raising up the healing ministry right across the world, in our generation. God wants people to both know and experience the depth of His love for them. Without healing, the disciples of Jesus will be controlled by their limitations and be victims of their past, struggling to survive and live normal lives in an increasingly abnormal and ungodly world. The world is becoming a very hostile place for believers. God's people need to be strong – both for their own sakes, and for the sake of the countless millions who, in their hearts, are looking to God for His answers. Many are wondering if anyone will come and provide the answers they are looking for. Who will become the vehicles of God's life-changing truth to them? Who will go for Him? The question God put to Isaiah is still being asked of God's people today (Isaiah 6:7).

In October 1995, we were blessed and privileged to have Jackie Pullinger-To as the main speaker at our *Into All the World* Conference at Blackpool. We had seen Jackie's work first hand at Hang Fook Camp in Hong Kong and wanted to give people in the UK a rare opportunity to hear her speak her heart into what was and is a very complacent church.

Few who were there will have forgotten the explicit message there was in her teaching. The air was electric with spiritual challenge. At the end of her teaching she asked people if they would like prayer for an anointing – there was an overwhelming response as hundreds stood in silence and waited for her prayer. But then came the shock, she followed up her question about wanting to be prayed for, by saying she would like to pray that they would receive an anointing to die!

You could see the shock waves rippling across the audience as they began to take in the implications of what she was saying, echoing what Jesus had said to His disciples in Matthew 16:24-26, "*Whoever wants to be my disciple must deny themselves and take up their cross and follow me. For whoever wants to save their life will lose it, but whoever loses their life for me will find it. What good will it be for someone to gain the whole world, yet forfeit their soul? Or what can anyone give in exchange for their soul?*"

We can all be guilty, on occasions, of teaching something from Scripture that has patently not yet become our own reality. At times like that, the teaching may be true to the Word of God, but it can lack the cutting edge of reality, the consequence of personal, first-hand experience. But that wasn't so in Jackie's case. She had gone to Hong Kong as a young woman and lost herself, her reputation, her past and her present, and sacrificed her future, in the confines of the Walled City, now demolished. But then it was a place where few westerners dared to put their foot down. And in going there, she found herself and her destiny and gained everything. She was in the place where God had put His foot down for her, in her own personal journey of faith. This was where the presence of God was – with those who were suffering and in desperate need. As a result, she had earned the authority to place such a challenge before God's people who were there at the conference.

The story of how God took the sacrifice of her laid-down life and, through her obedience to her calling, transformed the lives of thousands in the violent, drug controlled environment of Hong Kong and the Walled City, has become the stuff of modern-day legend. But, I can assure you, in her case, it isn't legend. It's reality. You could have heard a pin drop in that Blackpool auditorium as Jackie prepared to pray for people. What Jackie had taken into the Walled City was spiritual high explosive – unconditional love and uncompromising truth. And the people at Blackpool suddenly had to start asking themselves if that was what they really wanted to experience in their own life – the high explosive of God's unconditional love and uncompromising truth reverberating round the confines of the 'walled city of their heart'. The fact is, we only truly discover ourselves when we let Him into that secret place, lay down our own agendas and take up His.

I used to say to the people who came on Healing Retreats that the symptoms of the problems they had come with were their agenda for God, but God had an agenda for them which was more important than their agenda for Him! For many people, the reason why they have never seemed able to move forward into their healing and their destiny, is because their inner being, with all its hurts, pain, sins, bad choices, rejection, bitterness, unforgiveness, betrayal, disloyalty, traumas, fears and shattered dreams, has become like an inner walled city, which they do not want to touch, and is dangerous for anyone else to dare to try to enter. For some, those defences are so well constructed that they have no idea what lies on the other side of their own walls!

They are oblivious to the fact that what's inside the walls of their heart outworks in every area of their lives, and can be the source, for example, of many types of relationship problems, personality issues, psychosomatic conditions, illness, sickness or disease. They struggle with their external symptoms without realising that it's what lies behind their inner walls that puts a limit on their capacity to be whole. They feel that if they can carry on life, with an external show of normal humanity, then that is infinitely preferable to walking the path of humility and wholeness that King David chose to walk when he prayed, *"Search me, O God, and know my heart; test me and know my anxious thoughts. See if there be any offensive way in me and lead me in the way everlasting"* (Psalm 139:23-4). It takes a certain amount of courage and a lot of humility to invite the Lord to show us the truth about ourselves, yet so often that is the fundamental key which needs to be inserted in the lock of life which is protecting our own private walled city!

The older we have got, the more aware we have become that if Ellel Ministries has any message for the world-wide church in the twenty-first century, it is simply that the practical humility of owning truth, about both God and man, and then resolving the issues that the truth of God's Word exposes, is the only way in which the authority of the church will be restored and the power of the Holy Spirit will become the life-giving, transforming agency, that the world so desperately needs. This is a message that the church needs to hear and live out 'on its knees', if it is to rise from its knees and fulfil the purposes of God.

Sadly, this isn't a popular message! It doesn't tickle the ears or entertain large congregations, but it does change lives. Prior to John Wesley's Holy Spirit experience with the Moravians at 28 Aldersgate Street, London, in 1738, he had gone to America as a missionary. It was here that he came face to face with himself and the disaster of preaching a Gospel of which he was personally ignorant! He wrote in his diary, "*I went to America, to convert the Indians; but oh! Who shall convert me? Who, what is He that will deliver me from this evil heart of mischief? I have a fair summer religion.*" (*Journal, January 24th, 1738*).

A 'fair summer religion' is one that is comfortable and entertaining when things are going well, but valueless in every other circumstance of life. John Wesley had witnessed, and was jealous of, the living faith of the Moravians on board ship, when it looked as though the ship was sinking. And after returning from America with 'failure' stamped on his spiritual passport, it was with the Moravians that he found the answer he so desperately needed.

On Wednesday 24th May, 1738, John Wesley records in his journal: "*In the evening I went, very unwillingly, to a society in Aldersgate Street, where one was reading Luther's preface to the Epistle to the Romans. About a quarter before nine, while he was describing the change which God works in the heart through faith in Christ, I felt my heart strangely warmed. I felt I did trust in Christ, Christ alone, for salvation. And an assurance was given me that he had taken away my sins, even mine, and saved me from the law of sin and death . . . Being again in St Paul's in the afternoon, I could taste the good word of God in the anthem which began "My song shall be always the loving-kindness of the Lord: with my mouth will I ever be showing forth thy truth from one generation to another." This I know, I now have peace with God.*" Truth had impacted John Wesley's heart and it transformed every single day of the rest of his life.

And in respect of the need we all have for God's healing, truth not only needs to be discovered, it needs to be applied! When Jesus said to the disciples "*the truth will set you free*" (John 8:32) they were not words that He used in isolation from our responsibility to be proactive in taking steps towards our own healing! "*To the Jews who had believed in him, Jesus said, 'If you hold to my teaching, you are really my disciples. Then you will know the truth, and the truth will set you free'"* (John 8:31-32). The existence of truth did not change anyone, but it was the application of truth by those who would be His disciples, which was life changing and through which freedom was a consequence.

Jesus longs to penetrate the defences we build about the events and circumstances of life which we find hard to handle and, often, don't want to face. When we ministered to Jackie's Pastor friend in Hong Kong, the childhood suffering that lay behind the walls of her heart was brought to the light and forgiven (see Chapter 23) and seven years of suffering came to an end. Jesus penetrated the walls protecting Lynda's inner torment, following her fall from a cliff which had broken her back in four places. She was physically healed and ceased to be a disabled and dysfunctional ex-nurse (see Chapter 20). The walls surrounding Sarah's great pain were very thick, but she came to the point of being able to trust the Lord with ALL of her heart and today she is no longer a psychiatric patient with no hope and no future (see Chapter 15).

Paul and Gretel Haglin, two of our close American friends, who have also ministered with us on many occasions in the UK have, as the strap-line for their ministry, *Evangelising the Heart of the Believer.* What an incredibly apt description that is of the need which resides in the hearts of so many people – even those who profess to be believers, but for whom their view of salvation is more akin to something that they believe is awaiting them when they die, than a reality that God wants us to experience and enjoy here and now. Jesus didn't just come to give us a place in Heaven, He also taught us to pray that Heaven would come down to earth! (Matthew 6:10).

John's Gospel begins with a remarkable account of what happened when Jesus, the very Word of God, came into this fallen and broken world. John described it as a light shining in the darkness – but He was a Light which the darkness did not understand (John 1:5)! He was described as *"the true light that gives light to every man."* (John

1:9). And then John describes the incarnation in one explosive, all-embracing sentence, *"The Word became flesh and made his dwelling among us. We have seen his glory, the glory of the One and Only, who came from the Father, full of grace and truth."* (John 1:14). Without the grace and truth of Jesus there is no hope for a very hurting world. But with Him and in Him we have everything!

John summarised this extraordinary message, which is the heart of the Gospel, in John 1:12-13, when He said, *"to all who received him, to those who believed in his name, he gave the right to become children of God – children born not of natural descent, nor of human decision or a husband's will, but born of God."* There is a natural birth and there is a spiritual birth, but in today's hardened, secularised world, the words 'born again', describing the spiritual birth, have become words of ridicule, but in the Scriptures they are the key to Life. The god of this world will always prompt people to ridicule that which undermines his authority. You can be sure that if the enemy of souls is ridiculing something, then that which is being ridiculed deserves more than a second look!

It is a fact that on virtually every single one of the thousands of Healing Retreats that have been conducted in Ellel Ministries centres around the world, there were people who came to personal faith in Jesus and were born again. They found resurrection life. For many this was the fundamental first step on their personal journey to wholeness and healing. We cannot separate evangelism from healing and neither can we separate healing from discipleship. These are all at the heart of the same Gospel message and wherever in the world the Lord may open up the doors for Ellel Ministries, it will be the same message of hope that our teams will minister to those who walk through them. The commission Jesus gave to the church through the disciples was *"go and make disciples of all nations" (Matthew 28:19).* Neither the commission nor the message has changed!

At no time have I sat down with the leaders of the work to strategise the growth of an international ministry, with an expansionist policy – mercifully, we have never had the funds to even think of such a thing! If we had we would definitely have 'got it wrong' and been tempted to build an empire, instead of walk an often lonely path of obedience. We have simply sought to go where the Lord has gone before to find and feed His lost and broken lambs.

More often than not, this has been at times when we have already been stretched to the limit and been crying out to God for help with our existing commitments! It is in those places where the doors opened, that we looked for His footprints on the sands of time. Sometimes the footprint we found was a clue to where the next footprint in the sand might be – at other times the footprint was a clear indication, that this was the place where permanent roots must be put down. We had to know that we were in a place where God had gone before.

There are several occasions when Ellel teams in different seasons of the ministry have been impacted by the words from Exodus 33:14-15: *"The LORD replied, 'My Presence will go with you, and I will give you rest.' Then Moses said to him, 'If your Presence does not go with us, do not send us up from here.'"* The message of these verses is so very simple – if God moves, we move. But if God stays put, so do we! We have no interest in being in any place where people will not be impacted on their journey to healing by the presence of God.

Space does not permit in this book to tell the stories of how God opened up the work in so many more places. Behind each country there has been a walk of faith with local leaders grasping opportunities with both hands as they have been inspired and challenged by the Luke 9:11 message of welcome, teach and heal.

Norway, Sweden, Germany, France, many countries of the former Soviet Union, Rwanda, Colombia, India, New Zealand are some of the other places where God has now established the work, sometimes in totally amazing ways. I honour and thank God for all the teams and their leaders who are constantly ministering God's love and healing in these very scattered places. The work of Ellel Ministries has become a world-wide mission! This is His work and at times we have had to stand back, almost speechless, and watch God at work providing answers that are hope and healing for His people in so many different parts of the world.

At the beginning of his ministry, Jesus called Simon Peter to be one of His disciples with the simple words, *"Follow me"* (Matthew 4:19). Simon Peter had no idea what that would mean, but he was willing to trust Jesus and start following. At the end of His life and ministry Jesus again called Simon Peter, with the same words, *"Follow me"* (John 21:19). But there was a significant difference between the two calls. The second time God had pulled together the strands of destiny in his life and Simon Peter knew what it was all about! He knew exactly what Jesus had done and he was now being called to do the same, to lay down his life in proclaiming the Kingdom, healing the sick and casting out demons. Today, God is looking for 'Simon Peters' all over the world who will allow Him to pull together the strands of destiny in their own life and respond to that never-ending call of the Master to walk in His footsteps and do His work of healing the broken-hearted and setting the captives free.

"Then Jesus came to them and said, 'All authority in heaven and on earth is given to me. Therefore, go and make disciples of all nations, baptizing them in the name of the Father and of the Son and of the Holy Spirit, and teaching them to obey everything I have commanded you. And surely I am with always, to the very end of the age'" (Matthew 28:18-20).

EPILOGUE

View From a Distant Hill

Each season of life provides us with new opportunities and a different perspective. As a youth I climbed the mountains of Kerry in the Republic of Ireland, known as Macgillycuddy's Reeks, the highest point in the whole of Ireland at 1038 metres (3400 ft). As we climbed through the low cloud cover and came out on the knife-edge ridge, which takes you to the summit, the view was suddenly crystal clear and the County of Kerry lay before our eyes – magnificently spread out like a table of delights for the eyes to feast on. We were seeing things from a very different perspective than the one which had challenged our bodies at the beginning of the climb.

Life is a bit like that – the perspective changes as we get older. Things that seemed important when we were young can seem irrelevant when we are older – and vice-versa. Right now I am standing on what used to be a distant hill, but are now the foothills of eternity, seeing life from a perspective which I could only imagine as a youth, when all of life had yet to be lived. Those who fired my imagination and dreams with the challenges of youthful opportunity are no longer with us and I am left, still standing by the grace of God, with the percentage of my time on earth still to be lived getting smaller by the day! It is true, relatively speaking, that time goes faster as you get older – just one year for me now might be five, ten, twenty or more per cent of the road yet to be travelled, who knows? But, as a teenager, a year was just a blip in the seemingly endless life which stretched ahead, with ever-widening opportunities and almost limitless potential. But life does not go on forever.

My brother David, a distinguished medical scientist of uniquely creative genius, died at the still tender age of sixty-three, with myriad uncompleted dreams of things he longed to do, dying with him. Very recently, I stood at his graveside on the Isle of Harris, in the remote Outer Hebrides of Scotland, and gave thanks for an elder brother who, from the days of my childhood, had challenged and inspired me and whose sacrificially generous donation had been instrumental in kick-starting my own journey of faith with Ellel Ministries.

As I sat with David and gave him communion, during the last days of his life on earth, he described his time of waiting to die as being like standing on a station platform, knowing that a special train was on its way to stop and pick him up. As I started to write the Epilogue to this book, I was reminded of this graphic picture. One day a special train will come for each one of us and will stop at the platform of our life, taking us into eternity where our perspective will, suddenly, be transformed out of the limitations of time, space and a fallen race into the truly limitless horizons of eternal life.

To use another illustration, there is a bridge which spans the gap between time and timelessness, between the realms of physical time and space and eternal spiritual reality. It is a bridge that one day we will all have to cross – no exceptions! Whatever image we may wish to use to describe the process of leaving this world behind and entering the next, it is our responsibility to be in a state of readiness for when that moment comes. No-one else can pack our bags and get ready on our behalf! Jesus may have said He was going to prepare a place for us, but it is our choice whether or not we wish to put our name down on a piece of heavenly real estate and have a place in eternity with Him!

One Christmas, I stood by the grave of my parents and wept tears of thanksgiving for a Mum and a Dad who gave everything they had in our childhood years, to ensure that their children could grasp opportunities of life that they had never had. I will never cease to thank them for all they did for me and, as much-loved grandparents, for my children. But, as I stood there, above all I thanked God for the day when I knelt at my bedside with my father and welcomed Jesus into my life. I saw in Mum and Dad the love of God and wanted with all my heart to know the God they served. So when my own time came to decide to follow Jesus, even though there was an enemy of souls who opposed my choice, Jesus was the only name on my voting card for eternity! Choosing to follow and serve Him was the best decision I ever made.

I often look at the photos of those who contributed a great deal to my life when I was young. Most of them were completely unaware of the depth of influence they were having on me, or my future life, at such a tender age. I am so grateful to the Lord for each one of them. As, now, I look back from these foothills, down the road of life my feet have travelled, I marvel at the extraordinary grace of God, whose hand has been on my life all those years in spite of the difficult times, mistakes and failures there have been along the way. I see those strands of destiny coming down the generation lines being spread across the sands of time and then woven into a tapestry, whose image can only become clear when viewed from the distance of succeeding years.

My Dad was not an academic, by any stretch of the imagination, even though his professional life was spent in building education. His early years were as a labourer apprentice on northern building sites, learning to be a carpenter – a very appropriate craft for a follower of Jesus! His most well-used book, apart from his Bible, was *Daily Readings from C.H.Spurgeon* which was never far away from his bedside. He loved the sermons of G.Campbell Morgan, F.B.Meyer and other great preachers from the past. He read Dickens' *A Christmas Carol* every year at Christmastime and would regularly dip into another of his favourite books, John Bunyan's *Pilgrim's Progress*. Classic books on cricket and fishing featured in his book collection, as well as stories of missionary endeavour which thrilled his soul. And occasionally he would read poetry!

He had no time for esoteric poems which had no relevance to his calling and mission in life. But there were certain poems that I came close to knowing off by heart, because of the number of times he would quote from them and build them into his many sermons! Without question, his favourite poem was by Alfred, Lord Tennyson, Queen Victoria's Poet Laureate for over forty years. Tennyson's rectory upbringing, by a minister father who taught his children carefully, left its mark on much of his work, including Dad's favourite poem, *Crossing the Bar*:

> Sunset and evening star,
> And one clear call for me!
> And may there be no moaning at the bar,
> When I put out to sea,
>
> But such a tide as moving seems asleep,
> Too full for sound and foam,
> When that which drew from out the boundless deep
> Turns again home.

Twilight and evening bell,
And after that the dark!
And may there be no sadness of farewell,
When I embark;

For tho' from out our bourne of Time and Place
The flood may bear me far,
I hope to see my Pilot face to face
When I have crost the bar.

> *Alfred, Lord Tennyson*
> *(note: Bar refers to the sandbar that often builds up*
> *outside a harbour*
> *And Bourne is an old word for Limits)*

In this poem Tennyson saw the end of life being like the voyage of a sailing ship, leaving a known and secure harbour and heading out to sea, then crossing the sand bar on a full tide for an unknown destination. Dad often used this powerful image in his sermons. But for Dad there was no veiled agnosticism about what might happen when he crossed the bar, for he had already met his *"Pilot face to face"* at the age of ten and known and trusted Him all his days. The greatest desire of his life was that others may come to know the Saviour who was so firmly in control of the vessel of his life.

Many images have been used to describe our journey out of this life, be it my brother's train, my bridge or Tennyson's crossing of the bar – they are all delicate euphemisms for the process of dying. But even though I may, yes, be standing on one of those distant hills, that I surveyed from afar in my youth, death is not my pre-occupation – it's life! For, like my Dad, having met my *"Pilot face to face"* I'm still wanting Him to keep piloting the vessel of my life, to every place and destination that is on the course He has charted for me before, one day, *we cross the bar together*. But right now there is still *'distance to run'* and I want to fill *'each unforgiving minute'* with that which pleases Him in all the years I am still privileged to be living on Earth.

I described the moment when God spoke to me about how I was to spend the rest of my life in Chapter 5. Those words have inspired my personal journey of faith ever since. They were like receiving a personal email from God – an email which came with many unopened attachments. The second half of this book describes what happened when, one by one, many of those attachments were opened. I don't know how many more attachments there are yet to open, but I still view each day with the excitement of wondering what God has in store and I'm looking forward with anticipation to more surprises from Him!

This book began with the wreck of an old car and God saying to me at 4.00am in the morning, *"You could restore this broken car, but I can restore broken lives."* And then asking me that very simple question, *"Which is more important – a broken car or a broken life?"* I would love to say that the car has been fully restored – but broken lives are more valuable, more precious and more important than a broken car. However, around the world there are thousands of formerly broken lives which have been restored by the grace of God, who now know that Jesus is not only their **Saviour** but that He is also the **Healer** of those who come to Him, the **Deliverer** from all the powers of darkness, and the divine **Restorer**. I rejoice in what He has done. He truly is a miracle–working God.

But there is still a lot of work to do. We have only scratched the surface of need in a world which is progressively and rapidly marginalising the truth about Jesus, and assigning it to a basketful of contrasting and contrary beliefs that secular and humanistic governments relegate to the trash can of insignificance. The godly inheritance, on which most of the western nations was founded, is now fossilised in the annals of history and a spiritual vacuum has become the covering of the nations, creating an *'anything goes'* society.

Hosea spoke right into this very situation, describing what happens to a nation when the people break God's covenant and rebel against God's law (Hosea 8). When God's Word and God's law are no longer considered appropriate as an educational foundation for our children, you can be sure that those children will grow up without any moral compass and without any moral boundaries. And the protection that would otherwise have been afforded to a nation, under God, has been replaced by a spiritual covering provided by the enemy of souls! Or, as Hosea so graphically expressed the consequences of spiritual rebellion, *"they have sown the wind and reaped the whirlwind"* (Hosea 8:7).

The last chapter (14) of Hosea's otherwise heart-rending prophecy, however, brings a message of hope – and it's a message of healing. This whole chapter is about what happens next when people choose to come back to God in repentance for their sins and turn from their covenant-breaking behaviour. God says, *"I will heal their waywardness and love them freely"* (v 4) . . . and people *"will dwell again in His shade (protection)"* (v 7). And that, ultimately, is what I believe God has raised up Ellel Ministries for, to remind His people of the unchanging, age-old message of His salvation, His forgiveness, His healing and His restoration – even in the midst of a generation that has renounced His ways. There is a desperate need for leaders across the world to rise up into their calling as Shepherds who will *"strengthen the weak, heal the sick, bind up the injured and seek the lost"* (from Ezekiel 34:1-10) and our heart is to teach and to train the Shepherds while there is still time and it is yet day.

Hosea ends his prophecy with the simple statement, *"The ways of the Lord are right, the righteous walk in them, but the rebellious stumble in them"* (v 9). We have seen on countless occasions how, when people choose to start living their lives in accord with the ways of God then the blessings of God follow them – and that blessing includes everything that flows from the heart of God to the heart of man, bringing His message of hope into a world that desperately needs Him. My prayer is that all those strands of destiny will be woven into a covering of hope which God's people everywhere can run into and be safe. What a message! Hallelujah! What a Saviour!

And so it is with excitement in my spirit and still with a spring in my step that I turn to keep walking up the foothills of eternity towards the summit of my own personal mountain range. The mountain top is still shrouded in clouds, which occasionally part to show the way ahead.

In Bunyan's *Pilgrim's Progress*, when Christian and Hopeful entered the Delectable Mountains they were welcomed by four shepherds whom the Lord of the land had placed there to guide pilgrims on their way. The Shepherds were called Knowledge, Experience, Watchful and Sincere. *"Then said the Shepherds one to another, Let us here show to the Pilgrims the gates of the Celestial City, if they have skill to look through our perspective glass. The Pilgrims then lovingly accepted the motion; so they had them to the top of a high hill, called Clear, and gave them their glass to look. Then they essayed to look, but the remembrance of that last thing that the Shepherds had shown them, made their hands shake; by means of which impediment, they could not look steadily through the glass; yet they thought they saw something like the gate, and also some of the glory of the place. . . . When they were about to depart, one of the Shepherds gave them a note of the way. Another of them bid them beware of the Flatterer. The third bid them take heed that they sleep not upon the Enchanted Ground. And the fourth bid them God-speed."*

From the *Delectable Mountains* Christian and Hopeful were able, from the top of the high hill called *Clear*, to catch a glimpse of the Celestial City through the Shepherd's perspective glass. From where they were, they could both look back on the way they had come and with the aid of the Shepherd's perspective glass they could see where they were going. But they still had a distance to go, there were dangers ahead and they needed help to know the way. The Shepherds warned them of two things – look out for the Flatterer and don't go to sleep on the Enchanted Ground. The enemy of souls will always be at hand to try and take us off the way, the flatterer will always try and make us take glory to ourselves for what God has done and in the season of our lives when we should be the most fruitful for the Kingdom of God, the god of this world will try to charm us into sleepy inactivity and ineffectiveness!

In telling his personal story in 2 Corinthians 10 and 11, Paul, also, was aware of the dangers of boasting and commending himself (10:17-18) and falling into the traps laid by the flatterer. Yet he was compelled to tell the story as it was, so that his readers would know the extraordinary reality of what God had done, in spite of himself, and give God the honour due. He was willing to boast in his own weaknesses (11.30) to show that all God had done through him was but a demonstration of the extraordinary grace of God.

In telling my own story of the journey so far, I have not tried to hide mistakes and weaknesses, but have sought to live in the reality of truth. I am totally and utterly amazed at what, in spite of being myself, God has done and am trusting God to help me stay awake across whatever enchanted ground I may still have to traverse, before the gates of the Celestial City come into sharper focus and a *perspective glass* is no longer needed to catch a glimpse of them. To God be all the glory, great things He has done – this is His story – not mine!

ABOUT THE
AUTHOR

Peter Horrobin was the Founder of Ellel Ministries International in 1986. Though originally established as a ministry of healing for the north-west of England, the work has now been established in over thirty different countries.

Peter was born in 1943 in Bolton, Lancashire. His parents gave him a firm Christian foundation for life with a strong evangelical emphasis. After graduating from Oxford University with a degree in Chemistry, he spent a number of years in College and University lecturing, before leaving the academic environment for the world of business as a publisher.

In his twenties he started to restore a vintage sports car (*an Alvis Speed 20*), but discovered that its chassis was bent. As he looked at the broken vehicle, wondering if it could ever be repaired, he sensed God asking him a question, *"You could restore this broken car, but I can restore broken lives. Which is more important?"* It was obvious that broken lives were more important than broken cars and so the beginnings of the vision that inspired Ellel Ministries was birthed in his heart.

Sixteen years were to pass before the work began at Ellel Grange, a country house just outside the City of Lancaster. A hallmark of Peter's ministry has always been his willingness to step out in faith and see God move to fulfil His promises, often in remarkable ways.

Outside of Ellel Ministries, Peter was the originator and one of the compilers of the amazingly successful and popular Mission Praise, now in its 30th Anniversary Edition.

He is also an enthusiast for fishing and classic cars. His Complete Catalogue of British Cars has long been a standard reference work on the history and technical specification of every model of every make of British car manufactured between 1895 and 1975!

Peter wrote the teaching contained within the online training programme *Ellel 365*. This is about to be relaunched, both on-line and in book form, as *Journey to Freedom*. This 365-part programme provides daily input to those seeking healing, training and an understanding of what it means to be a follower and disciple of Jesus. Many have testified to the life-transforming blessing it has brought to their lives.

Further Books by Peter Horrobin

Forgiveness – God's Master Key

Forgiveness is key to the restoration of our relationship with God and to healing from the consequences of hurtful, damaging human relationships. From the cross, Jesus prayed these dramatic words to God, "Father, forgive them, for they do not know what they are doing." Learning to forgive others is the beginning of a lifetime's adventure with God – it really is the most powerful prayer on earth!

Paperback 110 pages, £6.99, ISBN 978-1-852405-02-1

Healing Through Deliverance

The Foundation and Practice of Deliverance Ministry. In this ground-breaking book, Peter Horrobin draws on his thirty years of experience of ministry to lay out the biblical basis for healing through deliverance.
He provides safe guidelines for ministry, helps the reader identify demonic entry points and teaches how we can be delivered and healed from the effects of demonic power. His prayer for the reader is that their commitment to Christ will be deepened and that they will respond afresh to God's call to heal the brokenhearted and set the captives free.

Hardback 630 pages, £24.99, ISBN 978-1-852404-98-7

Healing from the consequences of Accident, Shock and Trauma

Traumatic events leave a scar on broken lives. Unhealed trauma is one of the primary reasons why some people do not easily heal from the consequences of accidents or sudden shocks. This ground-breaking book is the culmination of thirty years of experience praying for such people. Peter carefully explains what trauma can do to people and how to pray for healing. This foundational teaching has been instrumental in bringing permanent healing to people all over the world. An essential manual for those who regularly pray for people – a life-transforming handbook for those who are struggling themselves with unresolved and unhealed issues – including the consequences of shock and injuries sustained in the military.

Paperback 176 pages, £9.99, ISBN 9781852407438

Living Life God's Way

'Living Life God's Way' is an immensely readable and practical book. In this revised and updated edition of 'Living the Life – Practical Christianity for the Real World', Peter Horrobin draws on his thirty-five years of Christian leadership to present the reader with a practical guidebook for living the Christian life.

Peter uses real life testimonies, parables and illustrations to unlock some of the most difficult of life's issues, that often make us stumble through our Christian walk. What never seemed to make sense is suddenly crystal clear – even for the most experienced Christian, helping all of us to discover how to Live Life God's Way!

This book was written to help new Christians get established in their faith and to provide older Christians with the kind of realistic help that is needed to keep their lives on track with God.

Paperback 222 pages, £10.99, ISBN 978-1-85240-758-2

Other books by Peter and Fiona Horrobin which are available from Ellel Centre Bookshops or direct from Sovereign World at www.sovereignworld.com

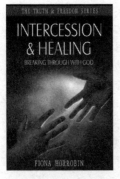

Intercession & Healing – Breaking Through with God *by Fiona Horrobin*

Intercession & Healing is for ordinary people in their walk with an extraordinary God. It is about breaking through with God in the most difficult of life's issues.

God has called His Church to be an intercessory bridge, bringing people to the heart of God and into the blessing of His truth – truth that will release them from the deep pains that hold them back in life. The Father yearns for His children to know Him in the core of their being and enjoy His protection, safety and peace.

This, in essence, is true healing.

Through persevering intercession we find the heart of God truly responds to our desire for the healing of others. Fiona conveys her passion for the healing ministry and explains in down-to-earth, practical terms about: Godly order, anointing, strongholds, discernment, the human spirit, dangers of soul power, faith and healing, covenant, angels & demons and much, much more.
Paperback 176 pages, £7.99, ISBN 978-1-85240-500-7

The Truth Stick

A Parable for Adults and Children

This is a truly enchanting story of Ratty, Mole and Badger and the adventures they have discovering the amazing secrets that lie hidden in Wild Winters Wood! Ratty's question "What is truth?" reveals the answers every child needs to know. Whether young or old, you will be delighted with this refreshing tale.
Hardback 128 pages, £9.99, ISBN 0-9546380-1-8

The Parables of Harris

Lessons from the Real-Life Adventures of a Black Labrador
From the founders of Ellel Ministries International comes this amusing and entertaining book about Harris, their black Labrador. *"From the day Harris came home our lives were changed for ever! From the moment he put his first huge paws over our threshold, and took control of the home, we knew we were in for an adventure!"* And his adventurous exploits have become modern-day parables of life.
Paperback 128 pages, £6.99, ISBN 0-9546380-0-X

For details of many more books published by Sovereign World Ltd, please visit our online shop to browse our range of titles.

www.sovereignworld.com

or write to the company at the headquarters address:

Sovereign World Ltd.
P.O.Box 784
Ellel
Lancaster
LA1 9DA
United Kingdom

Or email us at:
info@sovereignworld.com

Most books are also available in e-book format and can be purchased online.

About Ellel Ministries International

Ellel Ministries
International

Our Vision
Ellel Ministries is a non-denominational Christian Mission Organization with a vision to resource and equip the Church by welcoming people, teaching them about the Kingdom of God and healing those in need (Luke 9:11).

Our Mission
Our mission is to fulfil the above vision throughout the world, as God opens the doors, in accordance with the Great Commission of Jesus and the calling of the Church to proclaim the Kingdom of God by preaching the good news, healing the broken-hearted and setting the captives free. We are, therefore, committed to evangelism, healing, deliverance, discipleship and training. The particular scriptures on which our mission is founded are Isaiah 61:1–7; Matthew 28:18–20; Luke 9:1–2; 9:11; Ephesians 4:12; 2 Timothy 2:2.

Our Basis of Faith
God is a Trinity. God the Father loves all people. God the Son, Jesus Christ, is Saviour and Healer, Lord and King. God the Holy Spirit indwells Christians and imparts the dynamic power by which they are enabled to continue Christ's ministry. The Bible is the divinely inspired authority in matters of faith, doctrine and conduct, and is the basis for teaching.

For full details about the world-wide work of Ellel Ministries International, please visit our website at:

www.ellel.org
or write to:
Ellel Ministries International
Ellel Grange
Ellel
Lancaster, LA2 0HN
United Kingdom

390